# Witness to Power

# Witness to Power

## The Life of Fleet Admiral William D. Leahy

### BY HENRY H. ADAMS

Naval Institute Press
Annapolis, Maryland

Copyright © 1985
by the United States Naval Institute
Annapolis, Maryland

Library of Congress Cataloging in Publication Data
Adams, Henry Hitch, 1917-
  Witness to power.

  Bibliography: p.
  1. Leahy, William D.  2. United States.  Navy—Biography.  3. Admirals—United States—Biography.  I. Title.
V63.L39A74  1985      359'.0092'4 [B]      84-27187
ISBN 0-87021-338-5

Printed in the United States of America

To all who have served in peace and war,
that this nation might survive to work
toward the ideals for which she stands.

# Contents

# Preface

The United States Naval Academy has provided many graduates who have gone on to serve their country in positions of high leadership, considerable power, and awesome responsibility.

Fleet Admiral William Daniel Leahy, United States Navy, after forty-two years of active service, retired as so many others had done. But then he went on to new jobs undreamed of by him, and which made him a part of the inner circle that won World War II for the United States and its allies.

This book is the story of that man. It is not a history of the navy nor a history of the first half of the twentieth century. Where the events of the time affected Leahy, they of necessity are told, but their telling is not the essence of this book. Other works will deal with the Battle of Santiago in the Spanish–American War, with the administration of the navy during the years between the two world wars, with the government of Puerto Rico, with Vichy France, with the Teheran and Yalta and Potsdam conferences. Leahy had something to do with all of them, but he is the focus of attention, not the conferences, the administrations, the wars.

Bill Leahy, throughout his naval career, had a full understanding of the importance of history, and he was determined that his part in the history of his time should be properly recorded. Like many others, he kept a journal of his day-to-day activities, but few have shown such self-discipline and perseverence. He wrote from the time of his graduation from the Naval Academy until he was forced by illness to abandon the journal three years before his death. With only a few exceptions, notably a term of duty teaching at the Naval Academy, he made entries almost daily for fifty-nine years, resulting in an overwhelming mass of data about his daily activities. At first he wrote his journal for his own amusement and for the benefit of his family. Later, when he had risen to high command, he realized that his journals would someday be read by historians, and he made arrangements for their preservation in duplicate copies in the Navy Department and in Wisconsin, from where he had received his appointment to the academy, and to where he returned more and more in his later years.

Unfortunately, the journal is of less use than it might seem from its great bulk, for conventions of the time and the personality of the admiral conspired to keep it from being the revealing document it might have been. The late Victorian and early Edwardian years, which were the formative ones for Bill Leahy, taught young men principles of responsibility, patriotism, honor, duty, and bravery; they also taught them not to wear their hearts on their sleeves. In keeping with these principles, we find entries in the journal praising brave actions of others and extolling the virtues of other leaders, such as Captain Clark of the *Oregon* in the Battle of Santiago. We find moral indignation over the assassination of President McKinley, but we look in vain for the personal touch. He hid his feelings of disappointment or elation. Realizing that his journal might be for the use of historians and no longer a personal record for his family, he became reticent. Historians had the right to know what he had done; those things were a part of the public record. But he did not intend to let those same historians into his heart.

Part of the difficulty is his inability to express his sentiments with the decorum which he felt the journal required. When his son was seriously ill as a plebe at the Naval Academy, the father recorded the symptoms, his dissatisfaction with the treatment Young Bill was receiving, and his admiration for a nurse who did more for him than any of the doctors, but there is little expression of a father's worries, and none at all of what Louise, the mother, was doing or feeling. It was stiff upper lip all the way.

Thus it has been extraordinarily difficult to bring out something of the man who rose to the top of his profession as chief of naval operations, only to go on to perform his most important services after he had retired from the navy's highest office.

Far less known than other leaders of World War II, Leahy was content to perform his services for his country and for the two presidents he served so closely, Franklin D. Roosevelt and Harry S. Truman. In his final job, the one he held longer than any other in his career, chief of staff to the commander in chief, he was the president's man. He spoke for the president, he represented the president, he advised the president, and he disagreed with the president when he believed he was wrong. But he did not make waves outside. He seldom gave interviews. When he made his occasional speeches, he talked on mundane subjects such as patriotism or what a proper naval education and naval career entailed. He kept silent—in public—on politics, on international affairs, on controversial issues. He made his opinions known where they mattered.

In testifying before congressional committees during the tours when he was chief of BuOrd and BuNav and as CNO, he made his reports factual, unimpassioned, clear, businesslike. He knew the congressional system. He got to know the right people, and he made friends. Most powerful of all was, of course, Congressman Carl Vinson of Georgia, the navy's greatest friend on the Hill.

Yet there is no evidence in the journal that Leahy and Vinson were anything more than friends in the office. There is no statement that the Leahys ever entertained Vinson in their home or went to his. Leahy does record visits to the homes of friends in the service but nothing of any social affairs with others in the Washington power establishment.

Strictly a black-shoe sailor, Leahy did learn to value naval air and later the importance of air power. As he matured, he learned how the services complemented each other, and he was able to make balanced judgments which he could recommend to the president. In the opinion of George Elsey, one-time assistant naval aide to President Truman, Leahy's greatest contribution was keeping the Joint Chiefs of Staff in line.

Always dependable, loyal, shrewd, and intelligent, Bill Leahy was next beside the president in the turbulent years of World War II and in the first few years of the rebuilding, offering counsel and advice. Only Harry Hopkins was closer to Roosevelt, and no one on the military side was closer to Truman. George Marshall undertook more jobs for Harry Truman, but Bill Leahy was the one who was in the White House every day until his health demanded that he step down.

To most laymen and to many naval officers, he is a forgotten name from the past, one of those shadowy figures whose name is given to buildings and ships, whose picture appearing in books of history is passed over as the eyes fall upon the face of the more prominent man he is with.

The reason for his lack of prominence is simple. He did his greatest work in the shadow of two dynamic presidents. He led no fleets during World War II, fought no battles, commanded no theaters of operation. In fact, he fought in only one battle in his entire career, the Battle of Santiago in the Spanish–American War, from a gun turret aboard the battleship *Oregon*, after her famous cruise around South America.

Leahy was a superb example of the highly competent naval officer who provides the instrument others will use in the fight. After a long, distinguished career as a professional officer, during which he commanded nearly every kind of surface ship and held top naval posts in the tangled world of peacetime Washington, including assignments as chief of the most important bureaus, Ordnance and Navigation, he reached the top of his profession with his appointment in 1937 as chief of naval operations. During this tour, working with and sometimes against Roosevelt and with the important aid of Representative Carl Vinson of Georgia, he started the buildup of the navy that became the most powerful sea force the world has ever known.

But the story did not end with his retirement from the Navy in 1939. His appointment as governor of Puerto Rico that same year is widely credited with bringing stability and strong government to the island. His tenure in that job coincided with the strengthening of U.S. defenses in the Caribbean, as America prepared to defend herself.

A year before the attack on Pearl Harbor, Leahy was called from Puerto Rico to assume the post of ambassador to France. Three-fifths of her land lay under German occupation, and the government was forced to set up temporary headquarters at Vichy. Leahy managed to keep the despairing French leaders from throwing in their lot with the Nazis. For his pains, he was derided in the American press as a Francophile and an admirer of the aging Marshal Pétain, who was excoriated by the same journalists for being pro-Nazi. Those who knew what Leahy was accomplishing in Vichy paid no attention to such criticism, and when Leahy returned home, following French surrender to Nazi demands, he came to a position of even greater responsibility.

He at first did not want that new job; his wife had died in France, and he wanted nothing better than to withdraw from the world. But his great friend, Franklin Roosevelt, brought him out of himself by appointing him chief of staff to the commander in chief. In that capacity, Leahy was *ex officio* chairman of the Joint Chiefs of Staff. In his White House job, he was one of three men who constituted the very spearhead of war direction, the other two being, of course, President Roosevelt and Harry Hopkins. Neither Hopkins nor Leahy had any power other than that given them by the president; neither of them had any personal ambition, any place in the succession, any constitutional function, but they were the *only* two, under the president, who knew literally everything that was going on. They knew production, strategy, diplomacy, the daily course of the war, and where the bottlenecks were. Hopkins concentrated more on production and on relations with Churchill and Stalin, and Leahy dealt with strategy and plans, but it was more a matter of emphasis not of division of responsibility. Every message that came to the White House from Churchill, from Stalin, from Chiang Kai-shek, from de Gaulle, from Mackenzie King, from anybody of significance, was read by one or both of them. At least one of them attended every conference between Roosevelt and Churchill. Leahy was at all of the Big Three Conferences, Teheran, Yalta, and Potsdam.

One of Leahy's greatest contributions was his indoctrination of President

Truman at the time of Roosevelt's death. FDR had kept his vice president entirely in the dark on all matters pertaining to the war, and Truman had to learn, and learn fast, what was going on. No one could do this task as well or as thoroughly as could Leahy. Hopkins had been ill and out of touch for weeks, and Leahy took the job very seriously. The result was that with Leahy's help and with his own native ability to work and remember what he had learned, President Truman was able to take over the leadership of the war with a minimum of disruption.

When the war ended, Leahy remained at his post, serving as arbiter between the army and the navy in all of the political maneuverings and infighting leading to the establishment of the Department of Defense in the so-called unification of the armed forces. He stepped down from his post only after he had achieved, with the cooperation of Secretary of the Navy James V. Forrestal, a plan of unification he felt was, if not reasonable and strategically sound, then the best that could be achieved. He refused to be seduced by the politically popular program of strategic bombing as the way to wage war on the cheap. He knew war was never waged on the cheap, and he knew that the next war, if it came, might be the last.

Never one to shirk a fight, he counseled blockade of Japan in cooperation with the British after Japanese planes had sunk the United States gunboat *Panay* in the Yangtze River in December 1937. He believed that firm action then might have averted war with Japan. Similarly, when the Russians blocked access to Berlin in 1948, he stood with those who refused to yield; he supported the Berlin Air Lift, even at the cost of exhaustion of the supply of military aircraft of the United States. He believed that the Soviets would not go to war over Berlin, and he was right.

One of the first "hard-liners," he favored firmness with the Russians as early as the months between the Teheran Conference and that at Yalta. When idealists dreamed of close cooperation with the Russians, he hoped they were right, but believed they were wrong. In any case, he was a strong proponent of keeping our powder dry.

He hated the atomic bomb, and he believed that the United States would have to answer at the bar of history for first use of the weapon. He felt that warriors did not make war on women and children and that there were few left who were, as he put it in his journal, *sans peur et sans reproche*. But he tried to uphold those standards throughout his long career.

No book such as this can be the work of a single person. The author can only acknowledge the help of those who so generously give of their time and efforts to help bring to the public the record of one of our greatest military officers. To all of them, I give my thanks.

Rear Admiral William H. Leahy, USN, Retired, has read the entire manuscript and has made himself available to me for interviews and queries by mail. His reminiscences have added dimension to the character his father kept private.

Dorothy Ringquist, the admiral's personal secretary, friend, and confidante from early 1943 until his death in 1959, has graciously submitted to long interviews and has read and commented on the entire manuscript. Her help has been invaluable, both in remembering items of interest and in pointing out where I had misinterpreted some action of the admiral. She was devoted to Admiral Leahy, but she has too good a sense of history to try to make him seem better than he was. But she wanted me to have a clear understanding of "her" admiral.

My former colleague and long-time friend, Professor Emeritus E. B. Potter, of the United States Naval Academy, has read and evaluated the entire manuscript. His perceptive comments caused me to make extensive revisions, to the improvement of the book.

Mr. George Elsey, president of the American Red Cross, but during the war a watch officer in the White House Map Room, and later holding various positions of trust in the White House of Harry Truman, has read and commented on the parts of the story he was familiar with, from the time of Leahy's return from France until his death in 1959.

Vice Admiral John V. Smith, USN, Retired, who was an aide to Leahy during the time of the Yalta Conference, has read that chapter to my profit.

Others who have granted me interviews or answered questions by mail or telephone include Rear Admiral Frank Pinney, one of Leahy's aides, Captain Robert V. Adrian, USN, Retired, another aide, former chiefs of naval operations, Admirals Robert Carney and Arleigh Burke. The former ambassador to the Soviet Union, Averell Harriman, consented to a lengthy interview.

The staffs of the Franklin D. Roosevelt Library at Hyde Park and of the Harry S. Truman Library at Independence have been most helpful, and Dr. Dean Allard, director of the Operational Archives Branch of the Naval Historical Center in Washington gave generously of his time and knowledge to help me with materials and information. Similarly the staffs of the National Archives and the Manuscript Division of the Library of Congress were unfailingly helpful. So also was the staff of the Nimitz Library at the U.S. Naval Academy.

Most important is the contribution of my wife, who has done all the important things which enabled me to complete the book.

St. Petersburg, Florida
July 1984

# Witness to Power

PART ONE

The Navy

# CHAPTER 1

# Called to Duty

It was a cold night in Vichy. A black limousine turned into the Avenue Thermale and drew up in front of the American embassy. Out stepped the new American ambassador to France, Admiral William D. Leahy, former chief of naval operations and recently governor of Puerto Rico. With him were his wife, Louise, and members of his staff.

Vichy was a sad place in those days. A conquered France lay at the mercy of the Germans who had shown none in their humiliation of France. The Wehrmacht had defeated the "finest army in Europe" in a matter of weeks. The Germans had then put the capstone to their triumph by forcing the beaten French to sign the armistice documents in the same railroad car in which the humbled Germans had signed another armistice on 11 November 1918.

Now, as Admiral Leahy prepared to undertake his new duties in that cold January of 1941, the French endured the misery of occupation and the bitter knowledge that their semblance of independence could be snatched away at any time by their conquerers.

Three-fifths of France lay under German occupation. Hobnail jackboots tramped along the Champs Élysées in the shadow of the Eiffel Tower. From that proud monument, high over the city of light, the Swastika flew in mockery. French citizens in the capital lived in desperate want, hungry in their ill-heated homes, and in constant fear of a brutal nighttime knock which would signal the arrival of Gestapo agents.

Admiral Leahy warmed his hands before the fire while he reflected on the events which had brought him to that place at that time. The journey from Washington had been difficult and miserable, but they had at last arrived. Outside the house on the Avenue Thermale lay a foot of snow, but inside it was warm and comfortable. With relish he and Louise thanked the staff as they sat down to enjoy the excellent supper ordered for them by the first secretary of the embassy, H. Freeman Matthews, known to all as "Doc." It was just a few minutes after midnight on the morning of 6 January 1941. The Leahys had been traveling for nearly eight weeks, and they were dead tired. All the jobs that the admiral had held up to that date were but preparation for the vast difficulties that lay ahead for the American ambassador to France, whose temporary capital was Vichy.

His job was to see to it that the French remained as free as possible and that they gave no more to the Germans than was demanded by the armistice. If he could not make France an ally of the Anglo-Saxon powers, he at least had a reasonable hope of keeping her from joining the Axis.

When France had succumbed to the Germans the previous June, Admiral Leahy had been retired as chief of naval operations for nearly a year, and he had served as governor of Puerto Rico for less than twelve months. At sixty-five, he was in perfect physical condition for his age and had boundless energy. He was recognized by those in power as having a shrewd ability to get things done.

Just eight weeks earlier, on 15 November, Governor and Mrs. Leahy had been enjoying a leisurely breakfast in the small guest house on the grounds of the Fortaleza, the official residence of the governor. Built in the sixteenth century, the palace was undergoing repairs required by years of neglect. The governor and his lady resided in the guest house as the saws and hammers of the workmen prepared the ancient building as a suitable home. Leahy had good reason to relax. His even-handed support of the principles of democracy, his firm protection of voters at the polling places, and his refusal to be drawn into the camp of any faction had led to the fairest election in four decades in islands where bloodshed had been a way of electioneering.

An aide approached, bearing a wireless message from President Roosevelt, who had recently been elected to an unprecedented third term. He was cruising in the Caribbean aboard the presidental yacht *Potomac*.

Leahy had been expecting a summons from the president, but the one that came was a complete surprise. When he had stepped down as chief of naval operations on 1 August 1939, Leahy had been told by FDR that if war came, his place would be in Washington at some unspecified job at the right hand of the president. Therefore, he felt some astonishment as he read the message he had just been handed.

We are confronting an increasingly serious situation in France because of the possibility that one element of the present French government may persuade

Marshal Petain to enter into arrangements with Germany which will facilitate the efforts of the Axis powers against Great Britain. There is even the possibility that France may actually engage in the war against Great Britain and in particular that the French fleet may be utilized under the control of Germany.

We need in France at this time an ambassador who can gain the confidence of Marshal Petain who at the present moment is the one powerful element in the French Govt. who is standing firm against selling out to Germany. I feel that you are the best man available for this mission. You can talk to Marshal Petain in language which he would understand and the position which you have held in our own navy would undoubtedly give you great influence with the higher officers of the French navy who are now openly hostile to Great Britain. I hope therefore that you will accept the mission to France and be prepared to leave at the earliest possible date.

What would you think of Admiral Reeves as your successor in Puerto Rico?

Please send me your reply via navy radio as I am on the USS Potomac. Signed Franklin D Roosevelt.[1]

With no hesitation, Leahy scribbled on the back of the message, "I can leave Puerto Rico in a week."

"Send that," he said, handing the message back to his aide.

And so another duty was ending, and another was beginning. There had been many changes of duty over the years, years spanning America's change from a rural, unsophisticated society to a world power. That change had been felt in America's navy and by the men who served in it.

Hampton, Iowa, is far from the sea. It lies some ninety miles north of Des Moines, and, as the last quarter of the nineteenth century began, it was a sleepy little town in no way remarkable from any other midwestern country village. Its economic life depended on the farmers who came to town Saturday mornings to sell their produce and to buy the clothes, sugar, tools, and other necessities of agricultural America.

Here, on 6 May 1875, the first child, William Daniel, was born to Michael Arthur and Rose Hamilton Leahy, a prominent attorney and his wife. The father was a veteran of the Civil War and proud of it. He had served as a captain in the 35th Regiment of the Wisconsin Infantry, and for the rest of his life he attended regular meetings of veterans' organizations and led Fourth of July parades, proudly wearing his uniform. This military heritage, if it might be called that, he passed down to two of his children, William and Arthur, who were to enter the naval service.

Young William vividly remembered his grandmother, Mary Egan Leahy, as "a very gentle and a very old lady," who "entertained a bitterness toward the British very like that felt for 'Yankees' by irreconcilable old lady rebels of our southern states."[2] This grandmother told him of the family history, of how the Leahys had migrated to the United States in the early part of the nineteenth century. The name, she told him, derived from the Gaelic phrase *Laod Haigh*, but if she told him its meaning, he did not remember it.

The family came from Galway and, according to family tradition, had been chiefs for many centuries until displaced by the British. An ancestor who had served Charles II as an officer in the Battle of Boyne (1 July 1680) had, after the Glorious Revolution in 1688, fought to try to restore his brother, James II. For his pains he was exiled or executed—the record is not clear. Troops on the other side were led by John Churchill, the first Duke of Marlborough. Their remote descendants would join hands in the fight against tyranny twenty-five decades later.

Mary Egan Leahy, who had been born in 1810, accompanied her husband Daniel to the United States in 1836. They settled in West Brookfield, Massachusetts, and there, two years later, on 30 October, was born their first child, Michael Arthur, who was to be the father of the future fleet admiral.

Daniel soon moved his family to Great Falls, New Hampshire, where a second son, John Egan, was born in 1841. Two other sons, Stephen and Bartholomew, had come along by 1845, four years before the family once again uprooted itself and moved to Wisconsin, settling in Dodge County in the village of Portland. There the four boys went to school. Stephen died in 1853, but the others prospered, Michael and John both serving with distinction in the 35th Wisconsin Infantry Regiment.

Following the war, Uncle John moved to Wausau, Wisconsin; here he opened a lumberyard and became active in local politics. Michael studied law in Ann Arbor, Michigan, obtaining his degree in 1868. Settling in Hampton, Iowa, he hung out his shingle as an attorney and married Rose Hamilton, a Wisconsin girl. He, too, entered politics, serving briefly in the Iowa legislature, but a few years after the birth of his first child, decided to join John in Wausau. In quick succession, William was followed by John, Earl, Michael, Arthur, Stephen, and Robert, as well as by a daughter, Margaret. The children received the typical education of the time, expressed in the old song:

Readin' and Ritin' and 'Rithmetic,
Taught to the tune of a hickory stick!

There was also a solid grounding in the virtues of middle America: thrift, truthfulness, honesty, patriotism, and love of God. At the same time there was no lack of the usual boisterous behavior of healthy children in a large family.

Years later, in confiding his journals to his family, he was to write:

[P]ride of ancestry has been and is of value to us in that it makes repugnant any deviation from traditional ideals and gives strength with which to resist temptation to drift into a lower order of human society. . . .

The present changing social order stimulates appreciation of the fact that circumstances, customs, fortunes, families, and everything in history, except people, change; and that those individuals who succeed are the ones who take advantage of the environment in which they find themselves.[3]

Many years later, on revisiting Wausau, he found the city "full of memories and ghosts of departed years." Where his Uncle John's house had stood was now the "Opera House," and all traces of the lumber mill had completely disappeared, "and the mill yards, once filled with sawdust and lumber, are heavily overgrown with bushes and grass, so that a present generation of children can have no idea that great busy lumber mills and great rivers full of logs were once there."[4]

After Bill had completed his lower-grade studies at Wausau, the family moved some 175 miles northwest to Ashland, Wisconsin, on the southern shore of Lake Superior. The next few years in high school instilled in him a love of the city and the state which he never lost. In his later years he made many trips to Ashland to see friends and classmates. He helped celebrate the centennial of the city, and throughout his life he maintained his contacts with its people. On one occasion he entertained aboard his ship in Long Beach all the former residents of Ashland he could find. A good number of them were high school classmates.

As high school graduation approached in 1892, Bill had to resist the pressures of his father, who wanted him to go to the University of Wisconsin and, eventually, into law practice with him. Perhaps his father was right, for later, after Bill had reached the rank of rear admiral, a reporter at a high school class reunion in Ashland remarked that young Leahy had done very well in the navy. "He would have done much better in law!" snorted one of his former teachers.[5]

At any rate, Leahy was not destined for the law. Stories of his father's military career, brief as it had been, appealed to him, and he sought out his congressman for an appointment to the United States Military Academy at West Point. The congressman had no more appointments to the Military Academy, but did have one for the following year to the U.S. Naval Academy at Annapolis.

Young Leahy had never given a moment's thought to a naval career, but the prospect was too bright to pass up. Thus it was that in the summer of 1893, William Daniel Leahy became Naval Cadet Leahy of the class of 1897, having spent the previous year cramming for the entrance examinations. The year's delay in entering the Naval Academy was perhaps just as well, for the superintendent, Captain Robert L. Phythian, had recently added algebra as an entrance requirement. The mathematics taught in the average high school in those days was by no means sufficient for the rigors of the naval service as decreed by Annapolis officials.

A middle-western, inland background was by no means unusual for an aspiring naval officer. Then, as now, the students at Annapolis represented all the states, and one who had never seen saltwater had just as good a chance of rising to high rank as those nursed on a marlin spike. What mattered was aptitude and devotion to duty.*

In 1893 the Naval Academy, standing on the shore of the Severn River near Chesapeake Bay, was a small institution with only 263 naval cadets in the four-year program. Originally it had been an army installation, Fort Severn, but in 1845, Secretary of the Navy George Bancroft arranged for its transfer to the navy for use in training future naval officers. Bancroft would be remembered by the huge dormitory that bears his name.

But Cadet Leahy would never live in Bancroft Hall. At the time he was a naval cadet—the term *midshipman* would not be used for students at the Naval Academy until the class of 1905—prospective officers lived in buildings in a style unchanged since the Civil War. In summer they sweltered in the heat and humidity, and in the winter they froze.

Today midshipmen entering the Naval Academy report early in July for indoctrination and orientation in a program known as "Plebe Summer." In Leahy's time, part of them at least, reported early and went to sea to learn seamanship. A third of the class of 1897, Leahy included, arrived in late May, and on 3 June 1893 reported aboard the old wooden frigate *Constellation*, veteran of the Quasi-War with France and the War of 1812. Under command of Commander Colby Mitchell Chester, the venerable square-rigger had a complement of officers including Lieutenant William F. Halsey, father of the future dynamic admiral of World War II. Originally built in 1797, the *Constellation* afforded few comforts, especially for the lowest of the low, plebe naval cadets. It was intended to make the new cadets aware of the old naval tradition of "wooden ships and iron men." Leahy and his classmates were so indoctrinated with a vengeance. As they wrote in the *Lucky Bag* for 1894, the first issue of a yearbook for the Academy, "Pell mell, slipping, sliding on the slanting deck, our faces distorted with the keenest anguish, we hurried to [the rail] to give our tribute to old Ocean, and then to lie down and feel that death and dry land were the two finest things in the world."

Bill Leahy served as a foretopgallant-yard man, which meant that he had his full share of handling sail with the ever-needful warning of "one hand for the ship and one for yourself!" The food differed little from that which had been served aboard the *Constellation* when Captain Thomas Truxtun had commanded her nearly a century earlier. It consisted of salt beef, salt pork, salted

---

*Many examples come to mind of those who were born far from the sea and who reached high command in the navy. Of Leahy's six predecessors as chief of naval operations, only one, Admiral Charles F. Hughes, of Bath, Maine, was brought up within smell of the ocean. Three contemporaries of Leahy are obvious: his classmate, Thomas Hart, from Michigan; Ernest J. King, from Ohio; and Chester W. Nimitz, from Texas.

The USS *Constellation*

codfish, and as anti-scorbutics, sauerkraut, and, the only modern touch, canned pears.

The cruise was intended to take them to Europe, but in the mid-Atlantic they encountered a heavy gale that forced them to take refuge in Fayal in the Azores and then to make repairs while anchored off Funchal, Madiera. By the time the ship was again seaworthy, she had to return her passengers to Annapolis for the academic year.

Instruction at the Naval Academy in those days was highly formalized. Each student took the same curriculum, including steam engineering, physics, chemistry, history, international law, mathematics—including trigonometry, geometry, and calculus—navigation, English, and seamanship. His only choice was which foreign language he would study. Leahy, along with most others of the time, studied French.

Classes were small, about eight to ten cadets making up a section in one of the required subjects. Each cadet "recited" in each subject each day, for he had to receive grades every day. The most common method was for the instructor to prepare questions covering the day's lesson on slips of paper, one for each cadet. After the section had been presented by the section leader—"Sir, Section Three reporting, one man absent"—came the command, "Seats."

The instructor would place a slip under the closed textbook of each student, then command, "Gentlemen, man the boards." Each cadet took the slip and went to the blackboard, where he wrote the solution to a problem or the answer to a question on the board. Only then did he receive any criticism or help. If he was unable to work out the equation or parse the sentence, he would be corrected and assisted so he might do better the next time, but he would be "unsat" in that subject for the day. If he was "unsat" for the week, he was said to be "on the tree," and assigned compulsory extra instruction until his average rose above the minimum passing grade, the magic 2.5.

In those days the Naval Academy followed the navy practice in assigning grades. Perfect performance rated a 4.0. An overall standing of 3.6 in all subjects allowed a cadet to "star," that is, wear a star on his uniform to indicate his academic excellence. If his average in a subject fell below 2.8, he was "on the bush," and therefore suspect.

The system fostered self-reliance and discipline but did nothing to encourage imagination and independent thinking. Still, somehow, the graduates emerged a closely-knit group who kept up their loyalty to their class and their institution far longer than is customary in a civilian institution. So it was with Leahy's class of 1897. In 1947, of the thirty-seven surviving members, seventeen, including Leahy, turned up for their fiftieth anniversary dinner at the Army and Navy Club in Washington.

Certain faculty members were remembered with affection and admiration. In 1937, Leahy recorded the death of Professor of Mathematics Paul J. Dashiell at the age of sixty-nine.★ "Dashiell was a young instructor in chemistry at the Naval Academy forty-four years ago. At that time and for many years after he was a nationally known authority on college athletics, and his personal friends include every officer of the Navy who graduated within the past forty-five years."[6]

The athletic program had recently been upgraded, and during his years as a cadet, Leahy played tackle in the B squad, while others sought the glory of intercollegiate football. In the summer of 1894, from 15 May to 5 September, he and the others cruised along the Atlantic coast of North America in the USS *Monongahela*, a gunboat veteran of the Vicksburg campaign in the Civil War. Ironically, the ship carried no guns except for a saluting battery.

Later, after he had seen the great importance of being able to write and speak good English, he had a few caustic words to say on the lack of instruction at the academy in such skills. He wrote that the only tutelage he had in English was in spelling and in memorizing a few poems that he had completely forgotten.

---

★The Naval Academy was and is unique among the service academies in having permanent civilian professors. In Leahy's day the official title of a civilian professor there was "professor of Mathematics," regardless of subject taught. Thus Dashiell was professor of Mathematics even though he taught chemistry.

The class was duly graduated on 4 June 1897, Leahy standing fourteenth among the forty-seven graduates. An additional thirty had dropped out along the way. Years later, his classmate and lifelong friend, Admiral Thomas C. Hart told of Leahy's academy career:

> Bill Leahy . . . was a queer combination. As a student at the Academy he was not good, a little lazy. But when his classmates had a problem, a dispute about it, someone would say, "Let's go and ask Bill Leahy. He's got better sense than all the rest of us put together." That was always true for his common sense, his wisdom, was profound all through his life.[7]

The Class of 1897 was in many ways remarkable. It furnished the highest percentage of flag officers of any class to graduate from the Naval Academy. In addition to Leahy, who was to become a fleet admiral, there were four admirals and five rear admirals, some of whom had attained higher rank before reverting to permanent grade on the retired list. In addition, there was a rear admiral in the Supply Corps and a major general in the Marine Corps. Thus over a quarter of the class attained flag rank.

Graduation day brought no commissions. In those days, graduates had to serve a two-year period with the fleet as naval cadets (or passed midshipmen) before they were promoted to commissioned rank. And that promotion was by no means sure. A formidable set of examinations had to be faced.

Young Leahy and five of his classmates were assigned to the battleship *Oregon*, which was on the West Coast. This was a prize assignment, for the *Oregon* was one of the three newest battleships in the fleet. Like her sisters, *Massachusetts* and *Indiana*, she displaced over 10,000 tons, and with a 16-knot top speed, she could bring her four 13-inch, eight 8-inch, four 6-inch, and twenty 6-pound guns into play against nearly any ship in the world with little fear of defeat.

After chasing their ship all across the Pacific northwest, the graduates finally caught up with her in Victoria, British Columbia, where she had gone to participate in celebrations in honor of Queen Victoria's Diamond Jubilee. The six cadets found themselves considered rather more as nuisances than as useful members of the ship's company. Captain Albert S. Barker was something of a sundowner—a disciplinarian—and "his very superior ideas of what officers should do, especially junior officers, sometimes made it inconvenient for us, but his ability as a seaman and his courage were generally conceded by everybody in the ship."

Most of the summer was spent operating between Tacoma and San Francisco. The young Leahy was not at all impressed by the city by the Golden Gate, finding "irregular, miserably paved" streets lined by wooden sheds that looked as "though they were about to fall to pieces." He soon, however, began to like San Francisco better as he and his officer shipmates were invited to such illustrious places as the Bohemian Club.

The USS *Oregon* as she appeared immediately after the Battle of Santiago

During the winter, operations were routine, and there was the usual change of officers. After a two-month regime under Captain Alexander H. McCormick, the *Oregon* received as her commanding officer, an 1864 graduate of the Naval Academy, Captain Charles E. Clark. This remarkable man had a profound influence on everyone aboard, and Leahy considered him very close to his ideal of a naval officer.

Captain Clark took command at a good time, for the *Oregon* was about to steam her way into naval history and naval legend. For some time rumors of possible war with Spain had been circulating on the West Coast, and the battleship had received orders to prepare for a long cruise. As the six naval cadets joined other junior officers in speculating over their possible destination, their days were taken up with the inevitable chores of supplying, loading ammunition, and coaling, the last of these exercises a hideous operation requiring all hands to turn to filling the bunkers, while the coal dust settled everywhere and on everything. At length all was done and the ship steamed out of the Golden Gate on 19 March 1898, bound for Callao, Peru, where further orders would be waiting for them.

One of the great myths of the history of the U.S. Navy is that on receiving news of the sinking of the battleship *Maine* in Havana harbor on 15 February 1898, the *Oregon* set forth at once on a high-speed run around Cape Horn and, without a pause, entered the Battle of Santiago off Cuba, guns blazing as soon as she came in range.

The truth is considerably different, but it does not in any way diminish the *Oregon's* remarkable feat. The voyage she made was unprecedented, considering its length and the need for several stops to take on provisions and to receive orders. In those days, of course, no radio existed to keep them up to date on the course of the war.

Yet no one felt any sense of haste, at least in the early stages of the voyage. "We steamed slowly southward," Leahy wrote, "through beautiful quiet seas at a speed of about eleven knots, the voyage seeming more like a yachting trip than anything else."

They even had leisure to observe the time-honored ceremony of Crossing the Line as the *Oregon* reached the equator. Leahy devoted several pages of his journal to the festivities, describing at length how on 31 March, King Neptune came on board over the bow, accompanied by "Queen Amphitrite" and numerous courtiers. Neptune's beard looked suspiciously like unraveled rope.

Enlisted members of the crew suffered from the unrelieved attentions of the "Royal Barber," the "Royal Surgeon," and the piratical members of the court, enduring soap pills, shaving with lather made of oil, molasses, flour, and saltwater, before being dunked in a tank. Officers, including the cadets, were afforded a less honorable but more comfortable way out, purchasing immunity by "paying a large ransom in beer." So many officers bought their way out in this manner that King Neptune was completely unable to deliver his farewell speech. Instead he stood up on the forecastle, swaying back and forth, and repeating "I am satisfied," until members of the court led him and his queen back the way they had come. A few minutes later, several petty officers were seen coming from the direction of the bosun's locker, still swaying from overindulgence in beer, and one murmuring to himself, "I am satisfied."

Everyone, in fact, seemed to be well satisfied, and four days after the ceremonies, the ship reached Callao to find coal lighters waiting for them. Although coaling demanded all hands, Leahy, by working continuously for twenty-four hours, did manage to get away to visit Lima. This was typical of him. He never missed an opportunity of seeing the places he visited, and his journal is full of sensitive and perceptive descriptions. He seldom got carried away, though. In Lima's cathedral he refused to spend money to see the remains of Pizzaro, stating that "bones are bones."

On 6 April, her bunkers gorged, and with 200 tons in sacks on the decks, the *Oregon* set out for Rio de Janeiro, over 5,500 miles away. By now, everyone on board was convinced war was coming and their ship would be needed as soon as possible. Gone were the yachting days as the ship drove south at best cruising speed. Gradually the weather turned colder as the Antarctic autumn reached up to meet them.

On 15 April, they reached the Pacific end of the Strait of Magellan and at once encountered a freezing southerly gale. "Under the onslaught of these gigantic seas," wrote an awed Bill Leahy, "the ship dove, trembled, shook them off, and dove again, while her great engines . . . drove ten thousand tons of steel forward at a uniform speed. We said she smelled the Spanish fleet."

Two weeks later, on the 30th, the ship reached Rio de Janeiro to be informed by the harbor master that the United States had been at war with Spain since 21 April.

"It was a sight," Leahy recorded, "to see the sailors show their approval of this news. The band broke into popular music, the ship's quartette sang 'America,' the 'Star Spangled Banner,' and 'The Oregon,' while everybody showed their joy in the noisiest way they could think of."

As soon as they had sailed from Rio, Captain Clark mustered the crew on the fantail and filled them in on the war situation. There was Commodore George Dewey's masterly victory at Manila Bay. Although the *Oregon* had been ordered to try to avoid the Spanish fleet steaming across the Atlantic, the *Oregon's* skipper hoped to meet up with it and "impair its fighting efficiency."

Instead, on 14 May, the *Oregon* encountered quite a different vessel. It proved to be the tiny sloop *Spray*, which was on the last leg of a round-the-world solo voyage under Joshua Slocum. Captain Clark signaled to Slocum, "Are there any men-of-war about?" "No," replied the astonished Slocum, but then he had the last word, "Let us proceed together for mutual protection." Captain Clark could not see how the *Spray* would be able to be of much assistance to the *Oregon*, and having better things to do, he refused Slocum's offer. Soon the little sloop was a speck in the distance astern.

For the final leg of the voyage, Captain Clark pushed on at 13 knots, ready for action, the ship darkened at night. The *Oregon* arrived without incident at Bridgetown, Barbados, on 17 May. A week later, on 24 May, the ship anchored off Jupiter Inlet, near Palm Beach. "Our first sight of the home country after leaving San Francisco was not very attractive, as the only things visible were a bright white light, and the long, low Florida coast vanishing in the darkness on either bow."

An officer was sent ashore to search for a telegraph office in order to report arrival and request orders. He trudged miles through mangrove swamps before finding one, and then had to wait hours for a reply from the Navy Department. When orders finally came, they were an anticlimax. After her sixty-four-day voyage, the *Oregon* was ordered tamely enough to proceed to Key West, which she reached on 26 May.

After coaling, the *Oregon*, in company with the *New York* and other vessels, departed Key West and arrived on 30 May off Santiago de Cuba, where the Spanish fleet under Admiral Pascual Cervera y Topete had taken refuge.

The dash around South America was over. Now came the waiting.

Rear Admiral William T. Sampson commanded the American fleet off Santiago. It comprised six ships in his own squadron and five more in Commodore Winfield Scott Schley's "Flying Squadron." Matters were at an impasse off Santiago, for the six Spanish ships in the harbor dared not try to break out in view of the eleven opposing them. The American ships could not storm the harbor because of mines and the powerful forts guarding the channel. The force of marines aboard Sampson's ships was too weak to seize the forts, which were protected by a combined Cuban-Spanish army ashore.

Once the *Oregon* engaged in shore bombardment at some of the batteries, but to no effect. In the middle of June there arrived an odd-looking ship called *Vesuvius*, bearing a strange battery of guns fired by air pressure, which hurled 500-pound shells. Unimpressed, Leahy noted, "The report of the gun, a strange, long, hoarse cough, was followed by a shrieking. . . . These shells must have a moral effect on the enemy, but as it is said to be impossible to point the guns with any degree of accuracy, I do not believe that they actually do much damage."

Help was on the way in the form of an army unit under command of Major General William R. Shafter. Arriving on 20 June from Tampa, Shafter and his troops were supposed to take the harbor forts from the land side so that Sampson's ships could enter the harbor and destroy Cervera's fleet.

Shafter had little use for such a tame role for himself and his men. After demanding everything the navy could supply to help land his men, and insisting that the principal task of the navy was to keep him supplied, he ignored his orders and, to Sampson's fury, began a campaign against the city of Santiago rather than against the forts.

While his classmate Tommy Hart was slaving away in the boats supplying Shafter's army, Leahy was fortunate enough to be in Guantanamo Bay while the *Oregon* coaled. He and classmate Harry Yarnell visited a hospital ship and were presented to Clara Barton, founder of the Red Cross. "If Clara Barton," wrote an awed Leahy, "does not get an elevated position in our celestial hereafter, the other place will be terribly crowded."

Back on station off Santiago, the *Oregon* joined the other blockading ships. The six big ones, the *Oregon* herself and her sisters *Massachusetts* and *Indiana*, supported by Sampson's flagship *New York*, the *Texas*, and the *Iowa*, occupied the center of the line, while the flanks were guarded by the lighter *New Orleans* and Schley's flagship *Brooklyn*.

A few days later, on 1 July, Leahy managed the incredible feat of sleeping through a bombardment which began about six o'clock that morning. Lying on a transom in one of the staterooms, only a few feet from an 8-inch turret, he continued to slumber as the guns roared. Just as it was ending, he woke up complaining of the noise.

July 3 dawned bright and fair. It was a Sunday, and as the ships resumed their day stations some five miles from the Morro, church pennants began to flutter from their mastheads. Admiral Sampson took the *New York* to the eastward for a conference with General Shafter. That left Commodore Schley in the *Brooklyn* in command on the scene.

Below decks in the steerage, Leahy and other junior officers were struggling into their white uniforms, preparing for the weekly inspection. Suddenly the battle alarm gongs rang out. Cursing idiots who held battle-station drills on Sunday mornings, Leahy ran to the forward 13-inch turret as an officer shouted, "We have them for sure! The fleet is coming out!"

From his station in the turret, Bill Leahy found he could see very well what was happening. The *Oregon*, he was proud to note, fired the first shot of the battle as Cervera's blackhulled *Infanta Maria Teresa* emerged past the Morro and turned westward, paralleling the southern shoreline of Cuba. In the view of the young naval cadet experiencing his first action, the American ships were badly organized and, "without any order or formation," started to close the enemy.

The *Oregon*, as one of the newest and fastest ships, drew ahead in the pursuit and soon her shells were falling on the hapless *Maria Teresa*, which grounded about five miles from the Morro, "her flag flying and flames bursting from every opening." Other ships dealt with the slower Spanish vessels, while the *Oregon* and the *Brooklyn* rushed on at top speed in pursuit of the escaping *Colon*, whose pounding engines were carrying her swiftly toward safety. It seemed that she might get away altogether.

Sometime after 12:30, Commodore Schley signaled to Captain Clark: "Try one of your railroad trains"—meaning the *Oregon* was to fire one of her 13-inch shells, the largest in the navy arsenal at that time.

Since the *Oregon* was directly astern of the *Colon*, it fell to Leahy's mount to fire its "railroad trains," until "our big 13-inch projectiles began to strike ahead and on all sides, and seeing that further resistance would be useless, her Captain ran his ship aground and hauled down his flag."

Leahy's journal reports the battle in a splendidly detached way, with no hint of his own excitement. It was very properly professional and cool. But a messmate gives quite another picture of him standing by his turret, jumping up and down, slapping his leg with his cap, and yelling his head off.

Leahy himself recorded that when the last enemy ship had hauled down its flag, the men of the *Oregon* cheered themselves hoarse, and when they could cheer no more, they got band instruments and "made the day hideous" with their noises, but everyone was too happy to care.

Captain Clark, who might have taken issue with the loud and unseamanlike cheering of the crew, said nothing about it. Instead of singling any one out for special mention, he submitted the roster of officers as an annex to his battle report and declared that everyone had rendered meritorious service.

In a way, the action was the high point of Leahy's career. He never participated in another naval battle.

CHAPTER 2

# Steaming at
# Various Courses and Speeds

Leahy's euphoria after the Battle of Santiago was short lived. He helped supervise the transfer of wounded soldiers to ships that were to take them back to the United States. Sobered by their suffering, he wrote sententiously, "There is glory enough for those of us who return safely or who are killed in the discharge of hazardous duty, but to the wreck of a man lying in a hospital tent, and to his mother, there is little glory in war."

About a month after the battle, Captain Clark, much to the distress of all the officers, was involuntarily retired for medical reasons. As he left the *Oregon* for the last time, he was rowed ashore by officers who had drawn lots for the honor of pulling an oar in his gig. Leahy had been one of the lucky ones. "Captain Clark," he wrote, "was respected, admired, and loved by his officers and crew, and there was a lump in the throat of each one of his gig's crew as we silently rowed back to the *Oregon*."

The *Oregon* soon entered Brooklyn Navy Yard for overhaul, and most of the naval cadets were transferred, Leahy going to the battleship *Texas*, which was staying idly in New York. Thoroughly bored, he managed to get a transfer to the 1,000-ton gunboat *Castine* and set out for Manila in her. He only got as far as Columbo, Ceylon, where he received orders to return at once to the Naval Academy and present himself for examinations for promotion to ensign.

He had to take commercial passage home and reached Annapolis long after his classmates had completed their own examinations. He had no difficulty with his exams and was duly commissioned ensign.

After a brief tour aboard the *Philadelphia*, he was reassigned to the cruiser *Newark*, Captain Bowman Hendry McCalla commanding. McCalla was a strict disciplinarian, and the executive officer had the reputation of being "the most disagreeable officer in the navy." With these gloomy thoughts in mind, Leahy unhappily set out for a cruise to the Philippines. The voyage was grim, the wardroom made up of "the most disagreeable collection of officers that I have ever seen. At the table there is no conversation, no officer speaks to another, except officially, and the place is as full of gloom as a funeral feast."

Things looked up when the *Newark* finally arrived at Cavite on 25 November after stops at Hawaii and Guam. There riding at anchor was his beloved *Oregon*. As soon as he could, he went on board and managed to wangle a transfer back. But under her new commanding officer, the *Oregon* was no longer the ship she had been. "She is probably efficient," he wrote unhappily, "but she is no longer smart."

At any rate, he had little time with the ship he had once loved, for in about three weeks he was again transferred, this time to the *Castine*, the ship he had last seen departing from Columbo harbor nearly a year earlier. Except for a naval cadet, there was no one on board who had made the long voyage from the United States to Ceylon with him. To make matters worse, her skipper, Commander Samuel W. Very, was generally said to be the most disagreeable person on the worst ship on the station. On the happier side, however, he struck up a friendship with a shipmate, Lieutenant Albert P. Niblack, seventeen years his senior, who was to become his lifelong friend and his brother-in-law to boot.

Scuttlebutt had it that Captain Very would be relieved as soon as the *Castine* returned from her next trip to Hong Kong and Nagasaki, and it was with considerable anticipation that her crew took the little vessel out of Cavite in mid-January 1900 for the voyage. The ship reached Hong Kong, but on departure from the Crown Colony, her engines began to labor. She took refuge in Shanghai, just in time to help out in the protection of the International Settlement during the Boxer Rebellion while her engines were being repaired. On the way back to Manila, the little ship was ordered to stop in at Amoy to investigate reports that the Japanase had seized the island.

During the Shanghai stay, Commander Charles C. Bowman relieved Commander Very as skipper of the *Castine*, and everyone on board went about his duties more cheerfully.

On 28 August, the Boxers having been crushed, the *Castine* sailed for Amoy. The Navy Department reminded Commander Bowman that the United States insisted on its right to land troops to protect American lives and property in the event that the local authorities could not or would not do so.[1]

This reminder presented Commander Bowman with something of a problem. The *Castine's* meager crew could not hope to fight its way ashore against any respectable force. Accordingly, Bowman set out for Amoy with many misgivings.

The *Castine* arrived at Amoy on 31 August to find that a large Japanese force on the island had no intention of leaving. The presence, however, of the American vessel gave the American consul his opportunity. The British, who were nearby, agreed to land forces so they could be recalled. Then the Americans "demanded" that both sides, the Japanese and the British, withdraw their forces. All this was backed up by the might of the tiny *Castine*.

The scheme worked. The Japanese backed down. Leahy was given a valuable lesson in the use of sea power—if the little gunboat can be so dignified—in forcing settlements in international disputes. By the time the *Castine* resumed her voyage to Manila, six other naval ships of four nations had arrived. But the *Castine* had been there when it counted.

She was far less effective in coping with the Philippine insurrection, which was still causing misery in the interior of the new American possession. To this dreary war the *Castine* was assigned, doing nasty little jobs that were both dangerous and discouraging. They seemed to lead nowhere. One such task was to make a survey for a possible naval yard on the island of Iloilo. By day the Americans would put out survey markers and signal towers, and by night the insurrectionists would tear them down. "Having made a fairly good start by the beginning of the twentieth century," Leahy observed wryly, "we hope to finish it before it ends."

The survey party had to keep sharp eyes alert for insurrectionists. Leahy and his men had not been bothered in the early weeks, but they knew this was too good to last. Especially they knew it would be a bad time to be taken prisoner, for a native priest, known as the "Padre of Molo," had died because of mistreatment when captured by the American army. The story of the "Padre of Molo" made a profound impression on the young ensign, and he agonized over it in his journal. The entry reveals an old-fashioned concept of the code of the warrior as accepted by a twenty-five-year-old naval officer.

> Such things make one doubt that this is the beginning of the twentieth century. . . .
>
> I have been taught from childhood that it is the duty of every soldier to forget his own troubles in those of his comrades, to fight with courage while the fight is on, and when it is finished, to make less bitter the defeat of the vanquished. . . .
>
> My father was that kind of a soldier, but in this war there are few sans peur and fewer sans reproche. . . .
>
> One doubts if there ever were more than a few good ones outside the story books.

Naive, perhaps, but such a sense of honor would be a part of Bill Leahy all his life.

Relief from this frustrating duty came when he was selected to command the gunboat *Mariveles*, his first opportunity for independent service. To be sure, she was not much of a command. Only 250 tons, the little ship was schooner-rigged, with a stack for her two reciprocating engines between the two masts. Her battery consisted of a brace of three-pounder guns, a pair of one-pounders, two machine guns, and a Colt automatic for each of the two officers aboard. As a crew, Leahy had Naval Cadet Loveman Noa, three years his junior at the academy, and twenty-three enlisted men. Commissioned with full ceremonies at the Cavite Navy Yard on 1 May 1901, the ship was not, in the naval phrase, "in all respects ready for sea" for some time.

On 18 May the *Mariveles* finally got under way for Cebu and Iloilo. Off Cebu she ran aground but floated free on the next high tide. That was a bad beginning, but worse was to come. On 2 June, "the port engine suddenly tried to jump overboard." Examination revealed that the screw and most of the shaft on that side had disappeared. The *Mariveles* returned ignominiously to Cavite in tow, where she was declared fit for nothing but scrapping. His first command at an end, Leahy cooled his heels waiting for the arrival of the supply ship *Glacier*, which reached port on 15 July.

For over a year, Leahy served aboard the *Glacier*, making repeated trips to Australia to bring back beef for the soldiers in the Philippines. It was dull duty, but he did learn a great deal about inshore navigation by watching the Aussie pilots take the ship along and through the Great Barrier Reef, the 2000-mile chain of islets and coral reefs off the east coast of Australia.

On the first voyage to Sydney, the crew of the ship was enraged to learn of the assassination of President McKinley by anarchist Leon Czolgosz. Indignantly Leahy wrote, "Czolgosz, the cowardly assassin, should have been turned over to the crowd to save time in the administration of the punishment which he will undoubtedly get." In those days capital punishment was taken for granted as the proper way to deal with murderers, and in a very short time, Czolgosz was executed to the general satisfaction of everyone.

Leahy liked the people of Australia, although, conservative and authoritarian as he was, he believed that the labor unions had too much power. The government he criticized as being too paternalistic, "unsuited to a sovereign democracy such as we have."

When the *Glacier* returned to Cavite in August 1902, after Leahy's fourth trip Down Under, he had high hopes for orders home. But there were only orders to take the examination for promotion to the rank of lieutenant (junior grade). Incident to the examination, which he passed easily, he had access to his previous fitness reports and was considerably and agreeably surprised to find that even Captain McCalla and Captain Very, neither of whom had ever missed an opportunity of pointing out to junior officers their very considerable shortcomings, had given him outstanding ratings.

The new lieutenant (jg) attended a reception on 29 September in honor of Governor William Howard Taft, who, in his two years in the Philippines had won the hearts of the people in a way that no other American was to do until General Douglas MacArthur became their hero. While Leahy, along with 99 percent of his fellows, contemptuously referred to the "natives," Taft called them his "little brown brothers." He welcomed them not only officially but as friends. Leahy, on the other hand, quoted without comment in his journal a soldier who jostled a Filipino official from the sidewalk, snarling, "You may be a brother of William H. Taft, but you ain't no brother of mine!"

Leahy approved of the 340-pound governor, who seemed to him "fat and good natured," as he welcomed each visitor "with a pleasant word and looked as though he didn't have a trouble in the world." Still, Leahy didn't think much of Taft's methods. "The natives are proud, ambitious, and sensitive, and our people will not actually admit to social equality any large number of an alien race."

His long-awaited orders arrived on 24 October 1902. He sailed for home via Hong Kong, Nagasaki, Kobe, Yokohama, and Honolulu, arriving at San Francisco on 2 December. After leave to visit his father and friends in Wisconsin, he reported at the end of January 1903, aboard the receiving ship *Pensacola* in San Francisco. "I could not," he wrote with satisfaction, "have chosen a more pleasing assignment to duty." Since most of the actual instruction of recruits was done by petty officers, Leahy found the duties not at all arduous. This gave him plenty of time to get better acquainted with the beautiful city by the bay.

One of the places he began to frequent was a house on the corner of California and Buchanan streets, where Louise Tennent Harrington lived with her mother. Her sister Mary was the wife of Lieutenant Commander Albert Niblack, formerly Leahy's shipmate in the *Castine*.

During the pleasant assignment to the *Pensacola*, Bill Leahy courted Louise with the usual methods of the early part of the twentieth century: rides, concerts, walks, picnics, calls, teas. They enjoyed horseback riding in the Golden Gate Park. Soon the couple became engaged, and the wedding was set for the following February, a suitably long engagment for persons of their social station.

In January 1904, he was detached from the *Pensacola* in order to study for examinations for promotion, which he passed with his usual distinction. On 30 January, Lieutenant Leahy helped to commission the USS *Tacoma*.

His mind, however, was on other things during the commissioning. On 3 February, he and Louise Harrington were married in her mother's home in San Francisco. It was a quiet wedding, for her father had recently died, but the tragedy was not permitted to cast a shadow on the ceremony. Two weeks leave followed for the honeymoon in Santa Barbara, where "everything is beautiful."[2]

Six months later, when the *Tacoma* received orders to proceed to the East Coast, Leahy, with Louise pregnant, exchanged assignments with an officer on the *Boston*. He reported aboard on 30 June to find a goodly number of former shipmates.

The ship was in overhaul at Mare Island Navy Yard, so there was ample time for exploration and leave. Obtaining a three-day pass in August, Bill took Louise and her brother Tennant to Colusa in the Sacramento Valley of California, the birthplace of his wife and the site of the family homestead. There the Harringtons ran the town bank for the little community of two-thousand, which was situated at the upper limit of barge navigation on the Sacramento River. Colusa handled grain by barge, by wagon, and by the narrow gauge Colusa and Lake Railroad, which connected with the Southern Pacific at Colusa Junction. Leahy immediately felt at home in Colusa, for it was similar to Wausau, with fine houses and friendly people.

After the *Boston* left the yard, she went to San Francisco to await the pleasure of Rear Admiral Casper F. Goodrich, who would take her and the rest of her squadron to Magdalena Bay on the west coast of Baja California. When the ships reached Man o' War's Cove in the bay in late September, Leahy found the country barren and desolate, "not a single tree or blade of grass being visible from the ship." The only point of interest was a small village of ten huts or so, which was off limits to the sailors.

The drudgery of target practice and other exercises occasioned considerable grousing in the ship, the wardroom agreeing that "while all admirals are more or less of a nuisance, this one is worse than average." The complaints increased when Admiral Goodrich announced his intention of setting out on a long, leisurely cruise down the west coast of South America, which Leahy grumbled would "burn about $27,000 of coal" and would be pointless "unless there is some political reason unknown to us for sending the fleet to South America."

This attitude perhaps can be excused as the anxiety of a father-to-be far away from his wife when her time was due, but the anxiety was eased when the ship arrived at Acapulco on 4 November, and he received a wire that William Harrington Leahy had been born on 28 October and that both mother and son were doing well.

Arriving in Panama on 14 November, Leahy, as he rushed ashore to send a telegram to Louise, looked around him and was not impressed by the newly created state of Panama. He soon met a son of the president of "this ridiculous Republic" and learned that the "general commanding their comic opera army" had recently tried a *coup d'état*.

Since American engineers were at that time getting ready to begin the serious work of digging the Panama Canal, any instability was unacceptable, and no one was very surprised that Admiral Goodrich's squadron received orders to remain in Panama indefinitely. Making the best of a bad situation, Leahy kept his mind busy by exploring the countryside, being especially interested in the old forts and old cities which had been razed by the pirate Henry Morgan. "Panama was rich in Morgan's time," he wrote, "a potentially rich and productive country, and the resources of this particular part of America will begin to develop when it comes completely under the control of the United States."

Continuing in the attitude of manifest destiny, he added, "The gigantic task of building a canal is now just beginning under the direction of active young men from the north, whose energy must be a surprising revelation to the indolent natives."

The young officer certainly failed to realize that native indolence might be the result of dietary deficiencies or of diseases such as hookworm or malaria or the dreaded yellow fever. In time, he learned of the danger of tropical disease. In fact he himself nearly died of Yellow Jack. Several men aboard the *Boston* came down with the disease. Dr. William Gorgas boarded the ship and correctly diagnosed yellow fever. The invalids were carefully nursed, but in spite of everything, the ship's doctor and an enlisted man died.

> The others of us slowly gained strength on a diet of beef tea, barley, and hard-boiled egg, administered in teaspoons full each two hours night and day, until on February 3, we were strong enough to be moved ashore to the hospital at Ancon. . . . Jolting through the rocky streets of Panama in an army ambulance gave me a shaking that caused violent and persistent pains in my stomach which the doctor in charge of our ward finally eased with an injection of morphine. When I woke, the pain had gone, and it has not since returned, but for a few hours I thought I was going to follow [the doctor].[3]

After a few weeks in the hospital, during which time the *Boston* sailed for home, Leahy was discharged and sent across the isthmus to take a steamer to New York, which he reached in early March.

After a thirty-day convalescent leave with his family, Leahy rejoined his ship on 11 April 1905, just in time for a six-week cruise to the Hawaiian Islands. By this time he had developed into a mature officer. A believer in hard, sound training, he laid the recent defeat of the Russian navy at the hands of the Japanese in the Battle of Tsushima squarely to their lack of training and discipline. "An untrained man on board a ship in action is of much less value than the space he occupies."

He intended to take no nonsense from the men under his authority. "Be men!" he would exhort them, whether he was dealing with their manning of the guns or their conduct on liberty. "If a man knows how to fight his gun, I can make him do it better whether he wants to or not, but if he does not know, personal bravery will be of no value except perhaps to get him into an exposed place where the chances of getting rid of him are better."

That fall, after a summer in the Pacific Northwest, the *Boston* was ordered to return to Panama. En route the ship made a stop at Mare Island, and the Leahys took the opportunity to have young Bill baptized into the Episcopal church. The father wryly noted that, while the young man took loud and vigorous objection to the rite, it probably served its religious purpose.

Earlier Leahy had taken the step of converting to the Anglican faith. The family had been Roman Catholic from time immemorial, but during his academy days and during his early career, he had never had any strong religious feelings. So he was willing to go along with Louise, who had been brought up in the Episcopal church. He was not, however, confirmed for many years, and then took that step at the same time his son did. From that time forward, however, he became much more serious about matters of religion.

The trip to Panama was mercifully short this time, and by mid April the *Boston* was back in the San Francisco area following a routine spring of exercises and a few days in Coronado. On the night of 17 April 1906, the Leahys went to bed as usual in the California Street house of Louise's mother. The social life of the city was in full swing. Parties livened the St. Francis and Mark Hopkins hotels, and the great tenor Enrico Caruso performed *La Traviata* at the Opera House. The Leahys, however, preferred to get some rest after his vigorous days at sea.

"I was awakened from dreams of a train wreck," Leahy wrote later, "by a desk toppling over onto the floor, . . . the house shaking, windows rattling, and chimneys tumbling into the street outside."

The great San Francisco earthquake had begun.

The imperturbable Leahy, who had slept through gunnery practice aboard the *Oregon*, was preparing to resume his slumbers after the shaking had subsided, when he heard shouting and screaming in the streets. Leaping to the window, he could see smoke, dust, and fire rising from the ruins of the city. Fearing that the firemen would exhaust the water supplies, he had the family fill all bath tubs and containers in the house, "which provided us with an ample supply of drinking water for a week, during which time our less foresighted neighbors had to carry drinking water many blocks." He probably didn't mean for that entry to sound as smug as it seems today.

He rushed out to help with the rescue work. He watched with fascination as the fire worked its way out Market and California streets at the rate of "about one block an hour." It seemed certain that the Harrington house would be engulfed, so the family members busied themselves in saving as many of their treasures as possible. That done, Bill reported to the military authorities and was placed in charge of the Fort Mason dock, where refugees were embarked on various ships and taken to other cities on the bay where they could receive food, lodging, and medical attention. With little pause for rest, Bill and the other officers worked on the dock for three days and three nights until the crowds began to thin out. Tired as he was, he was still able to feel admiration for the majority who cheerfully endured their hardships. As for the others, the weaklings—he felt the city would be better off without them.

> The same self-reliance that was needed in the discovery days is needed now; the same weeding out of incompetents is going on. People who cannot live without luxuries will move out; new strong men will come to the front; and out of the universal wreck of an established social order should emerge a new and better people.

On 22 April, the *Boston* arrived in port, and Leahy returned aboard. By this time, the fires had been pretty well extinguished, and only looters and other criminals remained to be dealt with. As activity slacked, he was able to get some time off to inquire about his family. Happily they were all safe, and fortunately, the Harrington house had been spared from the flames.

Leahy's comments on the San Francisco earthquake mark an attitude of bygone days. Leahy's position, both as a naval officer and as a member of a prominent San Francisco family, ensured privilege, but it also demanded responsibility. Having seen to the safety of his family, he worked unceasingly to save those less fortunate, for he owed them a duty, just as he owed a duty to the enlisted men under him aboard ship. Such paternalism he shared with everyone else in his position. Today the term "noblesse oblige" is scorned, but to Bill Leahy it represented an almost sacred obligation. Physical assistance wasn't enough. It was his further duty to stiffen the moral fiber of the people. Those who failed to measure up should be got rid of, for the navy, the city, and the country would be better off without them. It was a stern, unyielding code that he set for others, and it was an even more stern and unyielding one he set for himself.

After a summer spent in various activities in the Pacific Northwest, Leahy returned to San Francisco in September, noting in disgust that little had been done to repair the earthquake damage, and that the city was overrun by professional criminals. "The local government is controlled by labor unions; and I am afraid that San Francisco will be set back many years before it begins to grow at a normal rate."

In February 1907, Leahy left the *Boston* and reported a month later to the superintendent of the Naval Academy for duty as instructor in the Department of Physics and Chemistry, known to the midshipmen in their unique slang as the "Skinny Department." "Skinny" is a corruption of "science," but it also stands for the inside word on anything. Here he would spend the next two years of his life learning the "skinny" on electricity and at the same time come to understand better the minds of young men a decade or more his junior.

On the whole, Annapolis duty was a disappointment. Clearly it was not one of his favorite assignments. He wrote of inadequate housing and of the necessity for officer instructors to go to sea with the midshipmen each summer. He did admit to learning a good deal about electricity.

On 14 August 1909, Leahy received orders to the armored cruiser *California*, then at San Francisco. A day or so after Leahy had reported aboard, Captain Henry T. Mayo took command, and Bill came under the wing of one of the most remarkable leaders of the navy at that time. To those who served under him, he became a teacher and a father figure who brought out the best in those of his junior officers in whom he saw real possibilities. Among other officers who came under his influence and later attained high command were Robert Ghormley, Jesse Oldendorf, and Ernest J. King. Captain Mayo and Lieutenant Leahy were scarcely settled on board before the *California* sailed in its squadron of eight armored cruisers for Japan.

Although he was interested in Japan and enjoyed the hospitality of the Japanese, Leahy felt reservations about them. Meeting Admiral Heihachiro Togo, the victor of the Battle of Tsushima, he was unimpressed, finding him "a very ordinary looking Jap with all his gold lace and decorations."

Captain Mayo soon set Bill Leahy on the path he would follow for years by making him gunnery officer. Leahy objected but later admitted the change was "a wise one, both in view of the experience to be obtained, and the insistence of the Captain." From that time forward, Leahy set about becoming one of the gunnery experts in the navy.

By the end of August, newly promoted to lieutenant commander, Leahy sailed in the *California* for a long cruise down the west coast of South America in company with the *Washington*, *Pennsylvania*, and *Colorado*. In Cimbote, Peru, their first stop, Bill was much interested in the Incan ruins. Always the romantic when it came to vanished peoples and ancient ruins, he lamented that it did "not seem possible that a handful of desperate Spaniards could completely destroy a civilization that irrigated valleys with engineering talent of a high order, that built great castles on the hills, and that used well-constructed roads more than 600 miles long."

For the rest of the year 1910, the squadron visited various South American cities. The social life in the different ports of call was a heady experience, and the officers were swept up into rounds of dinners and receptions, hospitality that had to be returned. Naturally there were no government funds for such affairs, so the officers of the squadron returned from the cruise considerably poorer than they had been when they left San Francisco.

On the way back, the admiral conducted annual inspections of the four ships. When Captain Mayo was detached, Leahy wrote that serving under Mayo was "perhaps the most valuable and certainly the most agreeable sea duty that I have had. Every officer on the ship regretted the departure of the splendid seaman who was also a considerate gentleman and a very capable naval officer." Leahy joined the staff of Rear Admiral Chauncey Thomas, newly appointed commander of the Pacific fleet, with his flag in the *California*. He became fleet gunnery officer, an important advance.

The new fleet gunnery officer found his job frustrating, and after six months, only one ship came up to his standards. "I have so far," he complained, "been unable to correct apparent faults. Much could be done by changing some officers that I have neither the rank nor influence to reach."

During the fall of 1911, after a yard overhaul, the *California* returned to San Francisco to be present during a visit of President Taft. Whether by reason of his previous associations with Taft or by chance, Leahy drew the job of naval aide to the president for the visit. Throughout the four-day stay, "I was with the President all the time, . . . learning much about how presidential visits are managed."

Still, the duty was not entirely to his liking. In view of his subsequent close association with Presidents Franklin Roosevelt and Harry Truman, it is somewhat ironic to read in his diary: "While it is interesting and instructive to be attached to the President's personal staff, I do not think a permanent assignment to such duty could be either agreeable or valuable."

In due course, Rear Admiral William H. H. Southerland in March relieved Admiral Thomas, and the easy-going routine of his predecessor became a thing of the past. At that time, the fleet was in Hawaiian waters, and Southerland wasted no time in undertaking a rigorous schedule of drills and inspections. Bill welcomed the increased application to discipline as a chance to improve gunnery performance in the fleet.

While Admiral Southerland led his fleet in a cruise around the Orient in that summer of 1912, President Taft was renominated by the Republicans, and a furious Theodore Roosevelt, who thought he had the nomination in his pocket, bolted the party to run for president on the Bull Moose ticket. In one of his rare political statements, Leahy analyzed the situation:

> Mr. Taft has certainly been an honest, dignified Chief Executive, and Mr. Roosevelt has certainly not been dignified. It may be that energy and personal popularity are preferable to dignity and honesty, and it may even be possible that the Republic founded by our fathers has progressed so rapidly on its way through history that it is in need of a dictator. I feel, however, that the conservative element of our people will not elect Theodore Roosevelt for a third term.

Leahy was no advocate of dictatorship, but if it came to a choice between dictatorship and near anarchy, he would always be found on the side of authority. But the authority he visualized was based on responsibility toward subordinates. He certainly did not have in mind an American Hitler or Mussolini. He thought of authority in terms of a benevolent father. He approved of the old saying of the cavalry officer: "You take care of the horses before the men, the men before the officers, and the officers before yourself."

The fleet's return to San Francisco in late summer led to only a brief stay, for insurrection was brewing in Nicaragua, and the ships of the Pacific fleet were ordered to assemble at Corinto to preserve order and protect American interests. Soon after they arrived, their orders were changed; American forces would assist the Nicaraguan government in putting down the rebellion. For Bill Leahy that was a singular change, for Admiral Southerland put him in charge of the defenses of Corinto. So there he was, with an inexperienced squad of ten seamen, expecting immediate attack by some two hundred rebels known to be in the area. Happily the attack never came, and in a few days, he was given a deputy commander and enough troops to do the job.

The whole thing seemed futile to Leahy, who believed that as soon as the Americans left, the rebels, supported by the people, would rise against their weak and tyrannical government.

During this time Leahy worked closely with the spectacular marine, Major Smedley Butler. He spent more time describing Butler's exploits than he did his own. They had to work together keeping a railroad running between Corinto and the interior. Butler and his marines managed the interior terminal, while Leahy and his troops were responsible for the rail head at Corinto. When the rebels derailed a train, which they did frequently, Leahy or Butler had to get it back on the tracks again. At one of their meetings, Butler presented Leahy with a brace of pearl-handled revolvers taken from a captured guerrilla leader. "These may come in handy," he said. "Keep them with you." Leahy believed him and kept them with him for the rest of his life.

When in October, the rebellion was put down, Leahy had a few days in Managua. He recorded in his diary a meeting with an American minister who told him, among other things, "Instructions issued by the State Department to an officer in the field must always purposely be vague and capable of different interpretations in order that the Department may always in case of necessity unload responsibility for its mistakes upon some subordinate." This was the kind of thinking Leahy found abhorrent, and ever afterwards, he made sure that orders were as clear as he could make them.

When the rebellion was put down, Leahy was detached to return to the United States for new duty. He found that he was slated for another tour at the Naval Academy, but, as second choice, he was offered assignment as assistant director of target practice and engineering competitions in the Division of Operations of the Navy Department.

He eagerly accepted the latter assignment. Since Mrs. Harrington was suffering from terminal cancer, Leahy left his wife and son in San Francisco and reported for duty in Washington on 10 December 1912. His superior was Lieutenant Commander Thomas T. Craven. "Our office was in the Mills

Building, were with almost no clerical assistance we organized, tabulated, and reported on the gunnery and engineering performances of combatant vessels of the fleet."

Great expectations were in the air as the Leahys moved to Washington in the dying days of the Taft administration. Soon the family found a house at 1751 Que Street, Northwest. Her mother having died, Louise was able to bring young Bill and join her husband for the Washington tour.

The election of Woodrow Wilson as president in 1912 brought changes to the navy, many of them resulting from the appointments of Josephus Daniels as secretary and of Franklin D. Roosevelt as assistant secretary of the navy. In those days, the civilian politically appointed secretary exercised almost command functions, and he was fiercely jealous of any effort on the part of naval officers to challenge his authority.

Since 1842 the navy had been organized by bureau system. The heads of the various bureaus—Navigation, Ordnance, Operations, and others—were directly subordinate to the secretary. Most navy men felt that the system had outlived its usefulness and that the seagoing officers should have more say in high-level decisions affecting operational matters.

The army's performance in the Spanish–American War caused it to institute a general staff to strengthen the entire command system. But the navy was a victim of its own success at Manila Bay and at Santiago. Why change a winning system? The victor of Manila Bay, the prestigeous Admiral of the Navy George Dewey, was named to a newly created General Board, but the secretary of the navy saw to it that the board had only advisory functions. The power of the bureaus was pretty much unchanged.

When Theodore Roosevelt became president, he brought up the idea of a naval general staff, but entrenched bureau chiefs managed to sidetrack the scheme. Under Taft, the new secretary, George von L. Meyer, acting when Congress was in recess, organized the Navy Department into four divisions— Operations, Material, Personnel, and Inspection—each run by an aide to the secretary. These effectively bypassed the bureaus, but the overlapping functions of bureaus and divisions were highly inefficient.

Josephus Daniels, President Wilson's secretary of the navy, began to phase out the divisions, which he felt threatened the supremacy of the secretary's office. As each division aide's tour was completed, he was not replaced. The last survivor, Rear Admiral Bradley A. Fiske, aide for Operations, had particularly upset Secretary Daniels by his use of contacts on Capitol Hill to induce Congress to establish in 1915 the post of chief of naval operations. Unable to stop Congress from passing the law, Daniels nevertheless managed to weaken the post so that the chief had no assistant and very limited authority. As time went on, assistants were provided, but authority remained limited.

These changes were in various stages of evolution during Leahy's tour in Washington in 1913 and 1914. Some touched him not at all at the time, but they would all affect him in the years to come.

In August 1913, Leahy's former mentor, Rear Admiral Mayo, aide for Personnel to the Secretary, asked Bill to become his assistant. The new job brought him into frequent contact with Secretary Daniels, but more important, into even more frequent contact with Assistant Secretary Franklin Roosevelt.

Josephus Daniels was perhaps the last man who should have been chosen as secretary of the navy. A pacifist, he was determined to reform the naval establishment according to his puritanical views. His most famous action was General Order 99, effectively ending the consumption of alcoholic beverages on shipboard. A small, mild-mannered man, he dressed simply, wearing pleated linen shirts and black string ties, but he had iron in his soul. Leahy found him "a man of very superior energy, of calm judgment, devoted to his work, and loyal to the President, but not in sympathy with the Navy."

There was a real danger that Leahy could have ruined his career by openly ignoring the secretary and taking his orders only from the assistant secretary, Franklin Roosevelt, for FDR felt that his boss was incompetent. On one occasion he recounted to Eleanor how he and Daniels had slaved all day

> on all the things he *should* have decided and as I expected *most* of them were turned over to me! The trouble is that the Secretary has expressed half-baked opinions on these matters and I don't agree. I know that he would decide right if he'd only give the time to learn. However, he has given me *carte blanche* and says he will abide by my decision.[4]

Leahy managed to sidestep the danger, and when Admiral Mayo was relieved a little later, and his relief departed to become superintendant of the Naval Academy, that left Lieutenant Commander Leahy the only officer in the Personnel Division. There he remained, completely alone, doing a rear admiral's job, with only occasional clerical assistance. Thus he handled assignments and courts-martial of officers.

He found himself drawn more and more to the young, athletic Roosevelt, generally held to be a man with a bright future in politics. Franklin and Eleanor lived only three blocks from the Leahys at 1733 N Street, and in the rose garden in the back the assistant secretary and his wife entertained, as their office required them to do, the officials and social leaders of Washington. When the weather was inclement, the old-fashioned house afforded ample room for the frequent social functions. The Leahys received their share of invitations, for the Roosevelts were determined to get to know the officers on duty in Washington. Even though Leahy was comparatively junior, he was performing an important job and was working under the eye of the brilliant young assistant secretary. While FDR was primarily concerned with civilian appointments, he knew what was going on in the officer side. The knowledge was to stand him in good stead two decades later when he became president. He had an incorrigible curiosity, "I get my fingers into everything, and there's no law against it."[5]

In Leahy, FDR found a man of integrity, sound judgment, and common sense. Their association developed into friendship which extended beyond the office. Leahy was formal, respecting their different offices and ranks. The genial FDR always called him "Bill." Leahy would answer, "Mr. Secretary," or "Mr. Roosevelt."

Early in 1915, as his tour was drawing to a close in Washington, Leahy asked FDR for command of the new destroyer tender *Melville*. Roosevelt agreed, but Josephus Daniels overruled the assistant secretary and ordered Leahy to command of the *Dolphin*, the secretary's personal dispatch vessel. Though Leahy looked on his new job as a kind of glorified messenger service, it had its brighter side. The most frequent user of the *Dolphin* was the assistant secretary, so the friendship that had developed between the two men had an opportunity to deepen during days at sea. As Roosevelt loved to handle ships, his habit of taking the con in tight spots may have given Leahy some tense moments, but FDR always came through.

Lieutenant Commander William D. Leahy, USN, commanding officer of USS *Dolphin*, about 1916. (Courtesy, National Archives)

At that time Roosevelt was thirty-four years old, vigorous, handsome, and athletic. He made friends easily, and his affability enabled him to carry off any social occasion. As he renewed his association with the future president, Bill was able to find the strength of character behind the extrovert from Hyde Park. In the course of taking FDR here and there, Leahy often found himself transporting the Roosevelt children as well.

As the election of 1916 began its fall campaign, Wilson being opposed for reelection by Republican Charles Evans Hughes, there was a polio outbreak in the country. The Roosevelt were naturally concerned for their children, thinking, as everyone did, of the more familiar name of the disease: infantile paralysis. No one dreamed that it would be Franklin, himself, five years later, who would be the victim.

While the children were summering on Campobello, FDR sent the *Dolphin* to pick them up and take them around past New York City and up the Hudson to Hyde Park on the east bank. Thirty years later, Leahy recalled how the vigorous Roosevelt youngsters were all over the decks, sticking their noses in places they had no business to be. But he really didn't mind, so long as they left him in peace on the bridge.

For a year the *Dolphin* ran the routine of a dispatch vessel, until in 1916, Leahy was ordered to take her to the West Indies to serve as flagship of Rear Admiral William B. Caperton, commanding the cruiser squadron of the Atlantic Fleet. This was just in time to deal with the revolution in Haiti.

Admiral Caperton appointed Commander Leahy as chief of staff, an interesting assignment, Bill felt, which brought him in daily contact with Haitian officials who were sustained in office by the American presence. Since none of the Haitian officials knew any English, and Admiral Caperton knew no French, it fell to Leahy to "intensively apply myself to the acquistion of a French vocabulary applicable to the business of a government." This application would pay dividends years later in Vichy.

Leahy felt that the American occupation of Haiti was beneficial. In his view it was the responsibility of stronger powers to take care of weaker ones. International paternalism was, in Leahy's mind, as important as domestic and was for the good of the small nations concerned.

> Our occupation performed miracles in improving the condition of the poor inhabitants who were poverty- and disease-stricken beyond words, but it was bad fortune for the ruling caste, most of whom were taken off the payrolls and none of whom could, under their social system, accept any employment that did not carry with it official rank. I know that many of this official class suffered acutely. There was little that we could do to help them.

No sooner was the Haitian situation in hand than revolution broke out at the other end of the island of Hispaniola. The squadron moved over to Santo Domingo, where Leahy witnessed his first amphibious operation.

The USS *Dolphin*

This picturesque performance was accomplished during one night when, in the light of ship's searchlights, we landed more than three hundred men and field guns without loss of a man or serious damage to material other than the smashing of a few boats. . . . We were entirely prepared to smash any resistance with gunfire from the ships, but fortunately, that was not necessary.

Once Santo Domingo was settled, the *Dolphin* resumed her duties as dispatch ship for the secretary of the navy and more especially for the assistant secretary.

In April 1917, she was sent to help install the first American governor in the Virgin Islands; while the ceremonies were going on, the United States declared war on Germany. As soon as the festivities were over, Leahy sadly gave the order to paint the ship a dull, drab gray, covering all the beautiful bright work and mahogany which had made the ship so distinguished in appearance.

Leahy's first wartime duty was to run down the steamer *Nordskav*, which was suspected of being a German raider. The chase took him all over the Caribbean, and each time the *Dolphin* entered port, there were the obligatory calls to be made and returned before she could get to sea again. Leahy fretted impatiently because these calls were so irrelevant in wartime. On 4 May, he located the *Nordskav* in Santa Lucia. She turned out not to be a raider, but her papers were not in order. Until the international lawyers made up their minds, she had to stay where she was and that meant that the *Dolphin* had to stay and watch her. It was more than seven weeks before the *Dolphin* was able to leave.

Late in his stay, Leahy gave a dinner party aboard his ship, in return for the hospitality of the islanders. One of the guests read a poem to enormous applause. Among its many verses:

The gallant gunboat *Dolphin*,
She sailed the Spanish Main.
She went into St. Lucia
And ne'er came out again.

The reason why she stayed there
Was never clearly known.
She nearly fell to pieces;
Her crew were skin and bone.

And when I asked the Captain,
He shook his hoary head.
"My friend, I have no orders;
No orders, yet," he said.

On 26 June, the orders finally arrived, and Leahy sailed for the United States, where he was ordered to the battleship *Nevada* as executive officer. It was a disappointing tour, for the ship missed the opportunity of going with Rear Admiral Hugh Rodman to Scapa Flow to operate with the British Grand

Fleet. While the battleships *Texas*, *New York*, *Florida*, and *Delaware* steamed out of Hampton Roads, Leahy resignedly helped take the *Nevada* into the yard for overhaul. When the ship came out, she went back to the "usual drudgery" as Leahy ached to get where the action was.

His hopes seemed to be fulfilled when he was relieved by Lieutenant Commander James O. Richardson so that he could proceed to New York to take command of the transport *Princess Matoika*, a former German liner named *Prinzess Alice*. She was being refitted to carry thirty-five hundred troops and five-hundred sailors "if," as Leahy wrote disgustedly, "all are packed in like sardines. Four six-inch guns are being installed, and the ship is a mess of dirt and dirty workmen."

Leahy almost didn't make it to sea in the *Matoika*, for the CNO, William S. Benson, wanted him in Washington as director of Gunnery and Engineering Exercises. When Leahy expostulated, Benson coldly informed him that personal preferences had no meaning in wartime. He finally agreed to allow Leahy to make one voyage to France in the *Matoika*.

Bill Leahy soon had cause to wonder if he had made a mistake in undertaking that one voyage.

No sooner had they cast off than the port engine began to make sounds of distress. With a poorly trained crew, the ship loaded with green troops, the river jammed with shipping, and the weather turning nasty, he managed to work her into Gravesend Bay without accident and drop an anchor. There they effected repairs and managed to sail with the convoy.

After a thirteen-day crossing, they arrived safely at Brest. A pilot, characterized by Leahy as "entirely unnecessary and almost entirely useless," came on board, and Bill scorned the French for having the gall to collect pilotage fees from those who had come to save them from the Germans.

The return voyage was devoted to dodging U-boats, but the ship reached Hampton Roads safely and as soon as he docked, Leahy was relieved to go to Washington for his new job as director of Gunnery and Engineering Exercises. He barely had time to find his office before CNO Benson sent him on an inspection trip to Britain and France to study their methods of naval gunnery.

Reaching London in July 1918, Leahy reported to Vice Admiral William S. Sims, one of the more controversial officers in the navy. Having become a disciple of Sir Percy Scott, the Royal Navy's gunnery expert, Sims had openly criticized the performance of American gunnery in the Spanish–American War. This impertinence might have ended a promising naval career. If galled senior officers had had their way, Sims would have been promptly retired, but President Theodore Roosevelt heard of him and his ideas. The upshot was that Sims was appointed inspector of target practice. The gunnery reforms he imposed on the U.S. Navy paid off, increasing the effective range of battleship guns from about 6,000 to over 20,000 yards. In 1917, Sims was assigned as Commander United States Naval Forces Operating in European Waters, and he had arranged a lively program for his visitor. Leahy profited greatly from his meetings with Sims and was inspired to become one of the navy's leading gunnery experts.

Then came a visit to the American battleship division with the Grand Fleet at Scapa Flow. Assigned as a staff member under Admiral Rodman, Leahy was delighted to have the opportunity to go to sea for a five-day exercise aboard the British battleship *Queen Elizabeth*. He was able to make valuable comparisons between British and American gunnery practices.

Moving across the Irish Sea, he visited the land of his ancestors and was moved to distress by the history of oppression by former British governers. But he saw no excuse for talk which seemed to him to be highly treasonable.

> I occupied a compartment on the train with a British major, an Irish priest who lived in England, and a native Irishman. The Irishman talked rank treason whenever he said anything. I advised him to get it all out of his system before by any chance he should come to America, because if he talked that way on an American train, it would stop long enough to let the other passengers hang him to a telegraph pole.

Leaving Queenstown in the company of young Commander Ernest J. King, Leahy returned to London and went on to Paris, where he looked with a jaundiced eye on the frivolity of Gay Paree while their soldiers were fighting for their lives in the trenches.

He was not impressed by the state of the antiaircraft batteries defending Paris. He noted that the guns almost never hit the planes, "but they frequently frighten them away." Leahy tended to blame the French for their own misfortunes, an attitude he was to retain years later as ambassador in another world war.

> The people's nerves are very much on edge, and there is a feeling that a little success by the German army followed by reasonable peace terms might terminate the war to the fatal disadvantage of France. The population of Paris seems ready to evacuate, if necessary, at an hour's notice, and I believe that an evacuation of Paris at this time would end the war in Germany's favor. Great hopes depend upon the American troops who are reaching the front fresh and in great numbers. Great hopes also hang on the availibility of American money.

Leahy took passage home in the captured German liner *Leviathan*. Sailing on 13 August 1918, he experienced his quickest passage of the Atlantic, crossing in seven days. The first day out, the news arrived by radio that Commander Leahy had been promoted to captain. In celebration of that happy event, the executive officer transferred him to the "Kaiser's Suite, [a] combination of two sleeping rooms, a dining room and a library, all superbly furnished and equipped."

The voyage home ended Leahy's participation in World War I. For the next few months, he was occupied with his gunnery and engineering duties. Looking forward to an extended tour in Washington, the Leahys purchased a house on Connecticut Avenue, and when the war ended, the fact that the United States had more ships in its navy than ever in history meant that Captain Leahy was kept busier than ever.

CHAPTER 3

# Conforming to the Channel

Following the armistice, President Wilson called for an increase in the size of the American navy, doubling the number of capital ships in commission at the end of the war. But he was going through the motions; he knew that Congress would never approve. Wilson hoped to indicate to Britain, France, Italy, and Japan that the League of Nations would be supported by the armed might of the United States, suddenly the most powerful nation in the world.

It never happened, of course. On Capitol Hill, now that the war was over, they were more interested in deep cuts in appropriations for the army and navy. Wilson's plan was rejected by the Congress and by the American people. The election of Warren G. Harding on an essentially isolationist platform was followed by powerful pressure for disarmament and the demand that America keep her nose out of European affairs.

The Washington Naval Conference of 1921 resulted in the famous agreement by which the United States, Great Britain, France, Italy, and Japan agreed to a "holiday" in capital ship construction and to the scrapping of existing ships. At length a general agreement emerged, and the principal naval powers accepted the ratio for capital ships: the United States, 5; the United Kingdom, 5; Japan, 3; France, 1.75; Italy, 1.75. Some variation was permitted, and the United States was allowed to convert two 33,000-ton battle cruisers, the *Lexington* and *Saratoga*, to aircraft carriers.

During these years, Leahy was kept busy in a variety of jobs. As he became more expert in gunnery matters, he made sure that successful new experimental procedures became standard practice in the fleet. He made frequent trips to sea to observe target practice and to inspect the organization and efficiency of gunnery departments. In June 1919, Vice Admiral Clarence S. Williams asked him to serve as his chief of staff in the Pacific, but unwilling to uproot his family again, Leahy was glad that CNO Benson refused to let him go. The following September, Admiral Benson was relieved as CNO by Admiral Robert E. Coontz, "a much brighter man," who "should be a great success."

Admiral Benson's shortcomings as chief of naval operations were not entirely of his own making. Josephus Daniels had consistently undercut his authority. On leaving office, Benson urged that the chief of naval operations, under the secretary of the navy, "should have the authority to coordinate all the technical activities of the Navy Department, and he should be held responsible for their efficient coordination and cooperation." The chief should be kept "fully informed as to the policies of the Government—I mean the political policies of the Government; what international problems were

Captain William D. Leahy, USN, about 1921.
(Courtesy, National Archives)

pending, what the international policy of the administration is at the time, and any changes that might involve the distribution of forces."[1]

Largely unaffected by these matters at the moment, Leahy went about his own business. In November, when the Prince of Wales visited the United States, the Leahys had an opportunity to meet him informally at a tea given by the Niblacks, who had known him in London. "The Prince," Leahy observed, "at this most informal gathering appeared to be what we like to think is the very best type of a young English gentleman." He would have much harsher words later when the same "English gentleman" forgot his duty and abdicated his throne to marry Wallis Warfield Simpson.

Before he left Washington in January of 1921, Bill Leahy had the mournful duty of paying his last respects to the man who had done most in launching his naval career, the former skipper of the *Oregon*, Rear Admiral Charles E. Clark. Several officers who had made the long passage around South America gathered to honor their former commanding officer. "It was," Leahy wrote sadly, "the last anniversary dinner given to our beloved commander of the *Oregon* that I was privileged to attend."

In late February, having sold their house on Connecticut Avenue and leaving young Bill in school preparing for the Naval Academy entrance examinations, Bill and Louise had a day or two in New York before he sailed for Europe to take command of the cruiser *Chattanooga*. After almost a month, of leave spent in Belgium, the Netherlands, and Great Britain, he made his way to Plymouth, where he relieved Captain Lyman A. Cotten on the morning of 2 April, sailing that afternoon for Lisbon to represent the United States at the ceremonial funeral of Portugal's Unknown Soldier. Other navies were represented by the *Alphonso XII* of Spain, the *Jeanne d'Arc* of France, and the *Cleopatra* of Great Britain. The Portuguese foreign minister whispered to Leahy that Spain had not been invited to participate but had sent a ship anyway. "He did not," Bill observed wryly, "seem to care much for the Spaniards."

Ceremonies completed, the *Chattanooga* went to Antwerp, where Louise and Bill joined him for a week. The pleasure of the occasion was marred by the news that his father had died on 23 April. "Being in the sea service has resulted in my being in foreign countries when both of my parents . . . departed this life."

Leahy's stay in the *Chattanooga* was brief. Early in May he was detached with orders to proceed to Constantinople and take command of the cruiser *St. Louis*. Once again, he had delay written in his orders, and he and his family were able to spend time in Paris and in the French countryside.

The visit gave Louise her opportunity to take the lead in family affairs. As a young woman, she had spent two years studying in France and living with a French family. She loved the people, and her fluent command of the language enabled the Leahys to get around better than most Americans. Thus it came about that they were permitted to see a private "wonderful collection of art treasures made by the duc d'Amlé and willed by him with the Chateau to the Institute de France." At length, all leave must come to an end, and leaving Louise and young Bill in Paris, Leahy set out on the Simplon Express for the long journey to Constantinople. Passing through Italy, Yugoslavia, Bulgaria, and European Turkey, he arrived in the early evening of 30 May and reported to Rear Admiral Mark L. Bristol, USN.

At that time, Turkey and Greece were engaged in war, and many western powers maintained naval forces at Constantinople to protect their interests. Leahy, in command of the *St. Louis*, was to be American senior officer present afloat, while Admiral Bristol acted as American high commissioner in charge of both military and diplomatic activities.

This assignment was Leahy's first post in which diplomacy was more important than naval skills. He had to work with representatives of other nations, Frenchmen, Englishmen, Italians, Turks, Greeks, Armenians, Russians, Serbs, Yugoslavs, and many more who inhabited Constantinople, the city that was the link between Europe and Asia.

Because the duty in the Turkish metropolis was likely to be extended, no navy was anxious to tie up her best ships to ride idly at anchor in the Golden Horn, so a good many of them were old and decrepit. The *St. Louis*, it is certain, was the most decrepit. Fortunately not much naval activity was required of her. "This cruiser of 9,500 tons, with its 14 six-inch guns and a crew of 650 men, would be admirably suited to the duty of senior ship in Turkish waters if her speed had not been spoiled by the deterioration of the boilers." She could barely make 11 knots instead of the 23 she had once boasted.

Leahy was soon caught up in the diplomatic and social life of the city as it existed in 1921.

> I find it a necessary part of my efforts to acquire information to attend many dinner dances and receptions at the residences of the diplomatic and military officials. These social affairs are invariably interesting because of the different antagonistic and friendly nationalities represented and because of the exchange of gossip and misinformation that can best be accomplished in a gathering that apparently has no official status.

Constantinople was then the capital of Turkey, and despite the war, social life in the diplomatic corps was extensive. Exiled White Russians seemed to be everywhere, each with his tale of daring escape from the old family palace or estate, accompanied by the usual faithful servant, carrying just enough food to enable them to reach the next village, where loyal peasants harbored them from their ruthless pursuers. Everyone was a prince or a princess, or at least a count or a countess, and they spent their days moving in the best society of

Constantinople, supporting themselves at the expense of sympathetic patrons or by selling some of the treasures they had smuggled out of Russia.

How much of these stories Leahy believed can be left to the imagination, but as an intelligent man of the world, he must have heard them with a good many reservations. Still, there *were* White Russians, and they *had* escaped from Mother Russia, smuggling out some treasure, but leaving more behind, and, while most of them dreamed of a triumphant return to their own country, some were anxious to establish roots elsewhere. For there was evidence that the Bolsheviks were actively pursuing the expatriates. On one occasion while Leahy was there, he recorded that eighty Reds were arrested for smuggling arms into Turkey, whether to kill White Russians or to stir up trouble for the Turks is not clear.

Nor were the White Russians the only ones wishing to make their way to the west, more especially to the United States. The wife of a Turkish official let it be known to Captain Leahy that she had a great desire to see America and would be glad to marry Captain Leahy in order to gain passage to the United States. Captain Leahy presented his compliments to the lady, expressing his personal regrets and explaining that American law permitted a man only one wife at a time. He went on to point out that he was happily married. If he could be of any other service. . . . Not to be daunted, the lady offered to become the wife of any of the officers aboard the *St. Louis*. To her disappointment, there were no takers.

Toward the end of September, as Leahy was in his cabin dealing with the never-ending paper work of the navy, his orderly entered and reported, "Sir, the officer of the deck reports that a bear is coming alongside the officers' gangway to starboard."

Intrigued and amused, Leahy went on deck just in time to see a large bear climbing up the ladder and stepping onto the quarterdeck. He seemed used to such surroundings, looking around and shaking the water out of his fur. As he lumbered forward, sailors and marines scattered up the ladders and ducked behind hatches. Eventually the bear made his way to the crew's quarters and sat down in a corner, quite at home and satisfied with life.

A few minutes later, a British boat came alongside and a very small midshipman requested permission to come aboard. When he had done so, the midshipman stated that he was from the battleship *Iron Duke*, and that one of the ship's company, Mr. Bear, was absent without leave. Intelligence having reached the commanding officer of the *Iron Duke* that the absentee was aboard the *St. Louis*, he had sent the midshipman to make inquiries.

With equal formality, as he sought to restrain his laughter, Captain Leahy assured the midshipman that Mr. Bear was indeed aboard the *St. Louis*, and that he would be obliged if the midshipman would remove him as soon as possible. Thus encouraged, a party of British sailors came on board. Seeing his friends, the bear accompanied them to the gangway but balked at getting in the boat. This led to a lot of British profanity and pushing and shoving. Finally, using a borrowed line, the British sailors managed to get a bight around Mr. Bear, who was tugged to the boat. Realizing that all was lost, he sat quietly in the stern sheets with the midshipman for the ride back to the *Iron Duke.*

The next day the British admiral, whose sense of humor matched Leahy's own, sent his flag lieutenant to apologize for the unauthorized visitation of the bear. Further the officer desired to express the admiral's regrets at the behavior of the bear, who had been so presumptuous as to use the officers' gangway when he came aboard the *St. Louis.* The flag lieutenant assured Captain Leahy that Mr. Bear would incur proper punishment for unauthorized absence and for conduct unbecoming a member of the crew of one of His Majesty's ships.

Leahy requested the flag lieutenant to convey his respects to the admiral and to inform him that while "there had been at one time in the distant past some serious question about the propriety of permitting the search of American warships for refugees from foreign services, this appeared to be a special case between friends in which I was very much pleased to have been of assistance to him."[2]

But there were more serious sides to the stay of the *St. Louis* in Constantinople. At one point the ship was sent into the Black Sea to investigate a report at Samsoun that authorities there were preparing to send Greek women and children who lived in that Turkish city into the barren, mountainous country to the south where it was certain that many of them would die from starvation and exposure.

As the representative of a neutral power, Leahy had to be careful to avoid taking sides in the war between Turkey and Greece. The only possible argument he could use was that of humanity. He pleaded this case earnestly to the local Turkish commander, who was polite and friendly, but firm in his determination. The Greek women and children had been harboring spies and had been giving them valuable military information.

Leahy persisted in his arguments, and eventually the local commander agreed to postpone the order of exile to the interior so long as Leahy remained in Turkey. "So far as I know the Greek women and children were never deported from Samsoun, although they were from other cities, and many of them who were deported perished en route from cold, hunger, and exhaustion."[3]

Before he left Samsoun, Leahy was presented with another problem involving trust, this time requiring him to break his implied word to the local commander. One night, just before the *St. Louis* was to get under way to return to Constantinople, a sailor spotted a boy swimming near the ship in the rough, cold water. Hauled aboard, he turned out to be a Greek, about fourteen years of age. Shivering from the combined effects of cold and fear, he blurted out his story. He had escaped from an inland town with another boy his age. Traveling by night and hiding by day, the two had eventually reached Samsoun, where they had become separated. In desperation, the boy had seen the lights of the *St. Louis* and plunged into the water to swim out and beg for asylum.

If the Turks discovered he was hiding the lad, the agreement so laboriously reached for the safety of the Greek women and children might well be repudiated. If, on the other hand, Leahy turned him over to the Turks, he would undoubtedly be shot as a spy. So, "we dressed the youth in sailor's clothes, gave him perhaps the only adequate food he had seen for months, and in plain but very secret violation of all the rules of neutrality, made him an honorary member of the crew." Fortunately everyone cooperated, and when Leahy later confessed to Admiral Bristol, the admiral told him, "Forget all about it."[4]

Good faith, as Leahy saw it from these experiences, could bring many rewards in dealing with peoples of other nations. On the other hand, there were occasions when it became necessary to temper justice with mercy, and that there was no rule to be followed blindly. Perhaps in some way this experience atoned for one in the Philippines many years before. Then he had been forced to stand by helpless as a fifteen-year-old Filipino boy begged in vain for his life before American soldiers shot him as a spy.

Early in October 1921, the *St. Louis* got under way from Constantinople with the "Homeward Bound" pennant flying. The old wreck of a ship was scheduled for decommissioning, and high time, thought her skipper.

In mid-November, the *St. Louis* arrived in Philadelphia. Leahy was dog-tired from having to spend every night on the bridge, since all his experienced officers had been detached before the ship left Turkey. The fatigue was forgotten, however, once he saw Louise standing on the dock waiting for him.

At this stage in his career, Leahy should have had a year at the Naval War College in Newport, but in spite of repeated requests, he never got there. Instead he was sent to sea in a minelayer, but it was not such a dead-end assignment as might have been supposed. He was to have his first experience of commanding a number of ships together, and the assignment brought other items of importance both professionally and in diplomatic experience.

His executive officer having relieved him of command of the *St. Louis*, Leahy took over Mine Squadron One with additional duty as commanding officer of the flagship, USS *Shawmut*.

The *Shawmut* was one of a number of coastal minelayers of 4,200 tons displacement. Laid down in 1907, she was not completed until 1917. Nearly 390 feet long, she could travel at 20 knots, which made her ideal for a flagship of a mixed bag of vessels of various duties, sizes, and speeds.★

★The *Shawmut* was later renamed *Oglala* and was sunk during the Japanese attack on Pearl Harbor. She was raised and converted to a gasoline engine repair ship, ARG 1.

His new assignment permitted the Leahys to celebrate Christmas together in their Washington apartment at 2400 16th Street NW. Early in January 1922, the *Shawmut*, in company with the other ships of the squadron, sailed for Cuban waters, where exercises were conducted in fits and starts until April. Then Leahy took the ship to San Juan, Puerto Rico, where he made his official call on the governor, little realizing that some eighteen years later he would be the one receiving calls from captains of visiting naval vessels. His impression was that after twenty years of American occupation, "San Juan is in appearance the nearest approach to a Spanish city, and the few people that I spoke to on the streets did not understand English."

Further exercises followed, and during them he was flattered when the admiral in tactical command asked Leahy to accept a position as his chief of staff. He didn't really want the job, for he disliked the admiral "who has an ungovernable temper." Stalling for time, he replied that he was under orders to take his squadron back to the United States soon, and he would discuss the matter with the Navy Department. To his intense relief, the chief of the Bureau of Navigation advised him to refuse the position. "Independent command, such as I now have, promises better prospects for advancement than staff duty and provides more opportunities for useful sea experience."

In mid-June he was overjoyed to learn that young Bill had passed the physical examination for entrance to the Naval Academy and was now Midshipman Leahy. From New England, where the squadron was spending the summer, he wrote, "He is probably experiencing the same adjustment to new conditions and strange environment that I found difficult 29 years ago."

The summer months went quickly, with Louise having rooms in Rockport, where the squadron was based for those months. Visits to Gloucester, which he detested because of the citizens' rapacious claims on sailors' wallets, and Newport, which he liked, took up his time until early September when the *Shawmut* was designated to supervise the international six-meter yacht races off Oyster Bay. Visiting the grave of Theodore Roosevelt, Leahy mourned that "America produces so few men of the type."

In November, Leahy got the thankless job of conveying home the body of the minister of Honduras. On arrival, he had to represent the United States at the funeral, and while he was so engaged, some of the crew got into trouble. He had plenty to say about that. A quarter of a century later, J. N. Mueda, who had been a messboy in the *Shawmut*, still remembered it. Leahy decided that the dressing-down must have put the fear of God into him, for Mueda had become a missionary, serving with the Filipinos who lived around Sacramento, California.[5]

Soon after his return from Central America, Leahy was saddled with another unusual job, that of shepherding flights of aircraft from Norfolk to Panama in experimental exercises to determine the usefulness of aircraft in long-range operations. The task was a unmitigated headache. On 8 January

1923, MineRon One got underway from Chesapeake Bay and ships took life guard stations between there and Charleston, South Carolina, where Bill waited with his flagship. Eighteen torpedo planes left Hampton Roads, and sixteen of them made it as far as Charleston. And so it went. The shepherds moved down the coast in stages, to Fernandina, Florida, to Miami, and finally to Key West, as the struggling planes endured one vicissitude after another. It was not until 25 January that the fifteen surviving aircraft arrived in Key West. Every plane had had trouble en route; two had turned back. One had been lost at sea.

Three days later, Leahy had to begin it all over again, this time with a dozen large scouting planes, which were supposed to fly in stages from Key West to Panama. The situation had not changed. As plane after plane broke down, Leahy concluded that naval aviation had not yet come of age. In Panamanian waters, he was infuriated and amused when, during an exercise, naval planes were presumed to have a "constructive radius" of eight hundred miles. He had just spent nearly a month with the best planes the Navy Department had been able to find, and he knew better.

Late in March, Leahy participated in a target exercise he found highly distasteful. The old battleship *Iowa*, which had fought alongside the *Oregon* in the Battle of Santiago, was to be expended as a gunnery target. She had been equipped as a radio-controlled drone, and Leahy was responsible for handling her during the forthcoming exercises. The crew, which had been placed on board to start the engines and set her on her initial course, was evacuated, and the *Iowa*, steaming at 8 knots, received the fire of a battleship division, the ammunition being especially selected to minimize damage. Five-inch shells did little harm, and three 14-inch projectiles succeeded only in flooding spaces above the protective deck forward. The ship settled by the head a trifle, and the night after the first day's firing, Leahy's men were able to correct the trim with a little judicious pumping.

The following day it occurred to the admiral that unless they sank the *Iowa*, General Billy Mitchell would be able to claim that naval guns couldn't sink even a twenty-five-year-old battleship. Since Mitchell was at the height of his influence, the navy could ill afford to give him any more material for his propaganda.

Although several of the special shells fired early in the day did little harm, when the *Mississippi* opened fire at 15,000 yards with armor-piercing shells, the second salvo inflicted fatal damage. Other hits finished her off, and she went down in fifty fathoms of water. "In Spanish war days, when I was a midshipman, the *Iowa* was the highest development in naval construction and the pride of the fleet. There was something very sad about seeing the old veteran destroyed by the guns of its friends."

Routine duty followed for the next few months until the end of June when Captain John W. Greenslade relieved Leahy in Boston. The next day, Bill and

Louise set off for Washington, D.C., in a Buick coupe they had purchased and returned to the Meridian Mansions at 2400 16th Street, where they still had their apartment. The next day Leahy reported to the chief of the Bureau of Navigation for duty as detail officer, a job he would hold for the next three years. Leahy began his new duties in the summer of 1923 about the same time that the new chief of naval operations, Admiral Edward W. Eberle, began his.

Although Leahy and Eberle had been shipmates in the *Oregon* during the long voyage around the Horn and in the Battle of Santiago, their paths had not crossed since. As CNO, Eberle was particularly concerned with problems in the Pacific—the defense of Guam and the Philippines in the event of war between Japan and the United States. He also had to worry about maintaining the fleet in view of the appropriations doled out by a parsimonious Congress. Admiral Hilary P. Jones ruefully remarked that the navy was "laboring under economy run wild."

Working in the old State, War, and Navy Building, later to become the Executive Office Building to the west of the White House, Leahy had to help see to it that each ship had enough officers to do the jobs assigned. He also had to look after the career of each officer—that he had a proper mixture of sea and shore duty, of engineering and deck experience, of school and practical work, whether afloat or ashore. The job required the utmost tact and judgment, and he performed it practically alone. In Harding's time, officers did not have dozens of assistants.

Over a quarter of a century out of the Naval Academy, Leahy had lived up to the promise he had shown as a naval cadet aboard the *Oregon*. He had established a reputation for attention to duty. Utterly reliable, devoted to his family, a loyal friend, he found his pleasure in seeing things and meeting people. He enjoyed the pomp of official functions, and he enjoyed simple things like fishing, going to baseball and football games, hiking, golf, good talk with friends, picnics, and a day at the beach. He had a subtle sense of humor, which he could use in writing and in conversation. He was especially fond of atrocious puns. He was able to set his ideas down on paper with clarity and forcefulness if without literary distinction. At the same time he was not given to reckless confidences, and he tended to keep his thoughts to himself.

Louise was a great help to him in Washington society. Although she was from San Francisco, she had attended school in Baltimore, and this gave her an eastern outlook. "Miss Somebody-or-other's School," as her son put it, gave her not only the academic subjects, but also the social graces and an appreciation of the arts and of music which filled gaps in Leahy's own education. She taught him to go to concerts, to visit museums, and her example caused him to look with a keener eye on the places and people he saw in the course of his duty.

He inspired his crews to their best behavior, and he was free with praise for jobs well done, just as he was uncompromising in the face of ineptitude or carelessness. Politically he was conservative, believing in the right of a man to enjoy the property and money he had earned. Repeated remarks in his journal show his scorn for liberals who reward the unfortunate for being unfortunate, but he was as ready as the next man to help in times of real need. In an era of excess, the Roaring Twenties, he was a model of rectitude, a bit of a prude, but during the period of Prohibition he did enjoy his occasional forbidden drink. He did not record employing a bootlegger, but he did not confide everything to his journal, and he certainly knew those who did patronize them. In common with most of his class, he knew little about Jews and Negroes. He had probably never met a Jew socially. His experience with Negroes was as mess boys on naval ships, bellhops in hotels, or as porters on Pullman cars. It did not occur to him that other groups were inferior or superior, but that they were just different.

This was the time of the Red scares. Attorney General A. Mitchell Palmer's notoriously savage investigations were not long in the past. The International Workers of the World, popularly known as "Wobblies," were believed to be exporting the Bolshevik revolution. At secret meetings, so rumor had it, they plotted assassinations, rebellions, strikes, sabotage, arson, and all manner of evil things. Leahy obviously knew better than to believe the most extreme of these tales, but he did frequently note in his journal that so-and-so seemed to be socialistically motivated.

While Leahy was settling down in his new job, President Harding set out on a trip to Alaska and the western states. The happy confidence which had marked the beginning of his administration was disappearing. The trip was supposed to be a good rest, a time of poker-playing with cronies, an opportunity to see new things, and to "bloviate," to use his own term for the oratorical excesses he enjoyed rendering. Somehow things never quite worked out. One crony after another was resigning under a cloud. Washington insiders and members of the press were beginning to suspect that something was wrong in the government. Although no breath of wrongdoing was yet attached to the name of President Harding, in a few months there would be scandals on a level unknown since the Grant administration nearly half a century earlier. For Harding, the great tragedy was finding out how his friends had betrayed him.

On 3 August 1923, Leahy recorded that Harding had died of apoplexy in the Palace Hotel in San Francisco. The nation mourned, even as the story of misfeasance and malfeasance spread itself in the newspapers and as the sternly righteous Calvin Coolidge moved into the White House. None of this, of course, touched Leahy directly, but it did tarnish the reputation of a man he admired, Secretary of the Navy Edwin Denby.

Harding's Secretary of the Interior Albert B. Fall, formerly senator from New Mexico, precipitated the scandal when he proved unfaithful to his trust. From the beginning Fall, who was heavily in debt, determined to use his office to clear his debts and line his pockets to ensure a comfortable old age. He saw his opportunity in oil. He persuaded the unfortunate Denby, who suffered more from stupidity than anything else, to transfer control of naval oil reserves at Elk Hills and at Teapot Dome to the Department of the Interior. Then by devious routes, Fall acquired large sums of money for licenses which permitted oil companies to exploit those reserves.

Although Denby was never charged with any crime, the revelations of the Teapot Dome scandal forced him to resign. Leahy defended him in the pages of his journal.

> Mr. Denby, acting on the advice of the Engineer in Chief, J. K. Robinson, was entirely innocent of any guilty knowledge or intent, as was also the Engineer in Chief. Mr. Denby held and still holds the full loyalty of the Naval Service.
>
> He was replaced by Mr. C. D. Wilbur of California, a judge of high attainments in the legal profession, and a thorough believer in national defense. His wife is a fanatic on the subject of liquor and tobacco.

In addition to the national tragedies, the last half of the year 1923 nearly brought tragedy to the Leahy family. The run of bad luck began on 1 August when the family Buick coupe was stolen from a parking place on C Street, next to be seen, two and a half months later, wrecked, in a garage in Wilson, Virginia. Friends of many years' standing were dropping by the wayside. Two members of the class just senior to his died that year. Captain Arthur MacArthur, brother of the famous general, died of a ruptured appendix. Leahy would later be closely associated with Arthur's son, Douglas II, in Vichy. But, much closer to home, they almost lost young Bill.

Bill had returned from Youngster Cruise, and the family was spending leave at Squam Lake, New Hampshire. In those days, roads were not well mapped, and motorists traveling in New England had to depend on a "Blue Book." It gave precise instructions, such as, "Pass a red barn on your right, go 3.7 miles to a white silo, and turn left on dirt road. . . ." Following such guidance, the Leahys reached Camp Rockywold on the evening of 3 September. But they were not fated to enjoy their stay. "When we arrived . . . Bill went to bed with a temperature of 104." There followed a series of mis-diagnoses and poor treatment. After a week of claiming it was only the "grippe," the local doctor finally decided it was bronchial pneumonia. The Leahys then moved their son to a hospital in Plymouth, New Hampshire, where an intelligent nurse made the correct diagnosis of pus in the pleural cavity.

Fed up with civilian doctors, Leahy moved Bill to the Chelsea Naval Hospital near Boston, where the nurse's diagnosis was confirmed by X-ray examination. Having great confidence in her, Leahy brought her to the hospital to take care of his son. After a single day, she left, a victim of the inflexible routine of the hospital. "I had too many other troubles at that time,"

Leahy wrote wrathfully, "to do what I would like to have done to the administration of that hospital."

This being before the days of antibiotics, an operation was necessary to remove the pus. Following it, the patient began to improve, but it was the middle of November before he was able to transfer to the naval hospital in Washington, where further examination disclosed that the pus had not all drained and another operation was necessary. The effect of the two operations and the lingering disease kept him out of the academy for the entire academic year. He returned to Annapolis in the fall of 1924 and was turned back to the class of 1927, to graduate a year after those he had started out with.

While the younger Leahy was recuperating from the second operation, Leahy's Uncle Stephen was killed in an automobile accident in Montana.

Thoroughly worn down by grief and worry, Leahy collapsed from exhaustion and tension. The symptoms began with violent abdominal pain, first diagnosed as appendicitis. Four days of being tested, poked, prodded, and examined in the Washington Naval Hospital led to a verdict that nothing was wrong with him but two infected teeth. Removal of the offending molars effected a cure, and the Leahy family celebrated Christmas at the hospital around a small tree in the room of the younger Leahy. Leahy wrote optimistically in his journal, "We start the New Year with hopes for better luck."

That same day, 1 January 1924, Leahy attended the annual reception held by the president for army, navy, and marine officers in the rank of colonel or navy captain and above. "The President," he wrote, "is a small man with a sour expression."

Assignment to Washington gave the Leahys opportunities to take advantage of some of the cultural activities of the city. Together, he and Louise enjoyed the music of the romantic composers: Tschaikovsky, Brahms, Wagner, and even Beethoven and Mozart. But Leahy never could cope with Schoenberg, Hindemith, or any other of the moderns. Of the Strauss family, he liked Johann and Oscar, but he could find no use for Richard. He enjoyed the theatre, and sometimes his remarks were perceptive. On 7 January 1924, for example,

> Dined with Captain and Mrs. [Charles F.] Preston and went with them to see a production of *Hamlet* at the Polis Theater by John Barrymore, an exceptionally gifted actor, and he was supported by competent assistants. It is likely that nobody can possibly play Hamlet as well as Shakespeare wrote it, and that, therefore, its presentation must always be a little disappointing. The performance attracted a fashionable audience, including President Coolidge, Ex-President Taft, and Mrs. Woodrow Wilson.

Nearly a month later, on 3 February, Leahy's twentieth wedding anniversary, Woodrow Wilson died. Considering the widespread adulation Wilson has since received, Leahy's remarks are surprisingly critical.

Thus ends the career of a man who had the greatest opportunity that has ever been presented in the cause of world peace, and who failed completely to take advantage of it. It may be correct, and it certainly is charitable, to charge his failure to bad health, the exact nature of which has never been made clear to the public. . . . Many people of intelligence say that this most conspicuous failure will go down in history as a great national hero.

During this time, the navy was fighting off new economy measures imposed by President Coolidge. It wanted to modernize six coal-burning battleships, to complete the two carriers *Lexington* and *Saratoga*, and to bring the navy up to treaty strength by adding eight heavy cruisers. President Coolidge allowed the completion of the two carriers, cut battleship conversions back to three, allowed only two heavy cruisers, and gratuitously added six gunboats for the Yangtze Patrol, which no one in the navy wanted, but which had been put in to appease the China lobby. One of those gunboats came to world fame a dozen years later: the USS *Panay*.*

A problem which faced Leahy more directly was how to maintain an adequate number of officers to man the ships in the fleet. At the instigation of Captain Charles F. Preston, a plan was established to give college students some training in naval subjects in addition to their regular courses of study at various colleges and universities. Thus the Naval Reserve Officer Training Corps (NROTC) was born. Backed by the CNO and by Leahy, the NROTC established a source of junior reserve officers who could serve in time of war or national emergency. Of course, when the Great Depression came along and the navy was not able to commission every Naval Academy graduate, the NROTC seemed to be rather superfluous. But the organization existed, and it would be expanded when the need arose.

One unusual item that came to Leahy's attention during this tour was the task of supplying then Commander Richard E. Byrd with people to assist his explorations of the Arctic. This association began a friendship which lasted until the great polar explorer died in 1957.

By the spring of 1926, Captain Leahy had completed three years of shore duty, and his next sea duty was crucial for his career. If he were given command of some minor naval vessel, he could begin laying his plans for retirement in twelve months when he would have been thirty years out of the academy. But to his joy, for he was the quintessential black-shoe sailor, his orders directed him to San Pedro, California, to assume command of the battleship *New Mexico*. He and Louise proceeded by train across the continent, and on 6 June, he moved his gear aboard the ship. He was a man whose future was assured in the navy unless some catastrophe blocked his way. All

---

*Japanese aircraft bombed and sank the *Panay* on 12 December 1937 in the Yangtze River near Nanking. Leahy, who was then CNO, recommended strong measures against Japan in retaliation.

things before had been but preparation for the moment when he would assume command of the battleship *New Mexico*.

The USS *New Mexico* (BB 40) was laid down 14 October 1915, at the New York Navy Yard, launched 23 April 1917, and commissioned 20 May 1918. She had two sisters, the *Idaho* and the *Mississippi*. Displacing 33,400 tons, she was 660 feet in length with a draft of 34 feet. Her beam of 106½ feet gave her a clearance of only 21 inches on each side for passage of the locks of the Panama Canal. Her main battery included twelve 14-inch 50-caliber rifles in four turrets; twelve 5-inch 51-caliber guns constituted a secondary battery. She had an experimental turbo-electric power plant. Oil-fired boilers generated steam for the turbines which drove generators for the motors which turned the screws, two on each side. Maximum speed was 21½ knots. She also carried two scouting aircraft and a crew of 72 officers and 1,323 enlisted. Equipped with flag quarters, she flew the flag of Commander Battleship Division Four during Leahy's term aboard.

On 9 June 1926, after the customary thorough inspection of the ship, Leahy stood with Captain Frank H. Brumby on the quarterdeck. Reading his orders to the assembled crew, he relieved Captain Brumby who, according to naval tradition, departed immediately after the ceremony. The formalities continued as Leahy made the necessary calls on the various admirals under whom he would be serving.

San Pedro was surprisingly cool for that time of year, and no bad weather interfered with Leahy's becoming acquainted with his new command. His executive officer, Commander Halsey Powell, was thoroughly efficient and presented him with a smoothly running ship so that Leahy was free to concentrate on a captain's statutory duties of "command and morale."

A few days after the change of command, Louise went to San Francisco. The family house at 2129 California Street had been sold, so she took an apartment at the Hillcrest, 1200 California Street, where her brother Tennant and his wife Minnie also lived. Thus, when the new skipper of the *New Mexico* could get ashore, there was a pleasant family gathering awaiting him.

Most of the summer was spent in exercises off the Pacific coast, largely in the northwest where Leahy had spent so many months early in his naval career. Toward the end of July the battle fleet moved to Seattle, and Louise joined him in time for the pulling boat races which were the rage in those days in both the British and American navies. Large sums changed hands over the outcomes of the races, and boat crews prepared with all the care of a professional football team contending for the Super Bowl. Coaches tried various combinations at the oars; boat hulls were waxed to reduce drag in the water; different styles of oars, strokes, moves were all assessed until the great day came. In early August, the *New Mexico* managed to put up a creditable performance. Following the races, the navy people celebrated with a dance at the Hotel Olympic, while the *California* hosted a reception and dance on board for the citizens of Seattle.

Leahy had a good eye for a racing stroke, and, under Louise's tutelage, was developing a good eye for art as well. As in the case of music, his tastes were conventional; he preferred the realists to the impressionists, and he did not go for the cubists and abstract impressionists at all. But he did like literal representation, and was therefore delighted when he had the opportunity to have as his guest on board the *New Mexico* the well-known marine painter, Charles R. Patterson of New York, who wanted to make a series of paintings of naval ships under various weather conditions. Leahy observed that Patterson knew his business and that he knew the sea as well, having spent a good many years on sailing vessels. Patterson accompanied the fleet during its move in late August from Seattle to San Francisco and on down to San Pedro.

Annual overhaul in the Bremerton Naval Shipyard a few weeks later gave Leahy and his wife time to spend a few days in the Mount Ranier area, a seven-hour drive over dangerous roads from Seattle. The Paradise Inn afforded them only primitive accommodations, being a collection of wooden buildings "with beaverboard partitions and unheated sleeping rooms that in this season of the year are bitterly cold at night. We slept in our clothes and overcoats."

They were bitterly disappointed in one way, for during their entire stay, Mount Ranier was shrouded in clouds and fog. The leave, on the other hand, was a great success, for young Bill was able to join them, and father and son had opportunities to get off together, climbing up to a height of 7,000 feet and observing spectacular vistas whenever there was a rift in the clouds. All too soon it was time for the younger Leahy to return to the Naval Academy for his First Class year.

During the period in the shipyard, Commander John Sidney McCain relieved Halsey Powell as executive officer. Like any good exec, McCain, who became famous in World War II as one of the foremost carrier task force commanders, kept things humming so that Leahy was able to enjoy the hospitality of the people of Bremerton. Louise was especially helpful in these social situations, for she made friends easily and enjoyed the round of teas, receptions, dinners, and parties where the forbidden cocktails were served. After working hours, Leahy liked to get away for nine holes of golf before dinner. His average score, he noted was 43.

Leaving Bremerton on the afternoon of 23 October 1926, the *New Mexico* encountered heavy fog, navigating her way out by radio bearings. Off Cape Flattery, the weather worsened, and when the ship reached Swiftsure Bank, she encountered heavy seas, which rolled her far over to port. As usual after an extended spell ashore, the crew seemed to have forgotten how to secure gear for heavy weather, and there was considerable breakage before Leahy was able to heave to and permit disgusted officers and chiefs to supervise the errant crewmen in lashing and stowing.

While they were on the way to San Francisco, an unfortunate whale blundered across the bow of the *New Mexico* one night and, unable to get free, was pushed through the water until daylight. Inspection then revealing no damage to the ship's bows, Leahy stopped and backed clear, noting regretfully that the "whale, which I estimated to be about sixty feet long, was evidently badly hurt by its long ride on the ship's ram, but it seemed to be alive."

Now began a time in the story of the *New Mexico* which caused her to be known, by her crew at least, as the "Wonder Ship." With Leahy and McCain leading, the officers kept their men up to the highest standards, and rewards began to come to the ship and men. According to Marine Bugler Harry Reece, writing Leahy many years later, there was only one unpopular officer, who partially redeemed himself by befriending a wet, bedraggled kitten outside a hotel in Bremerton. Feeling sorry for the animal, the officer took it aboard ship and fed it. He enlisted the carpenter's aid in making a bed for it "large enough to house a tiger." It was just as well that the bed was large, for the cat grew and grew. It was, however, so friendly that it often tired of its quarters and, looking for company, "it frequently in the middle of the night," Leahy wrote, "used to crawl under the bed covers with me in my cabin."[6]

Unfortunately, however, the unpopular officer's good intentions toward the cat did not long raise him in the esteem of the crew, for one Saturday morning, wrote one of the crew years later, "just before inspection, one of the men on the galley deck threw an egg and hit him as he was standing on the forward deck. I have never seen any man as angry as he was at that time! He just stood there and pleaded for the man, whoever he might have been in the crowd, to come down and fight."[7]

Leahy replied that he did not remember the incident of the egg. "Of course, nobody would tell the Captain about that."[8]

When the ship joined the fleet for six weeks of exercises at sea early in 1927, her crew managed to win the "meatball" for gunnery and the General Efficiency Pennant. During the voyage, Leahy again enjoyed the company of Charles Patterson, the artist, and also that of Associated Press reporter W. B. Jessup. He took them both into his mess, and the stories Jessup filed with AP did nothing to hurt the reputation of the ship.

After a simulated attack on Balboa, the fleet transited the Panama Canal and exercised in the Caribbean, ranging as far east as Haiti. When the drills were over, the fleet put into Guantanamo Bay, Cuba, for a fortnight's rest and recreation. On a trip ashore with Patterson, Leahy watched him paint by moonlight an ancient bronze cannon. "This cannon," Leahy observed, "bears a legend telling that it was manufactured in 1748 for the duc d'Amalie and that its name is Le Bourbon. It has a grotesque face carved on the breech and is

The USS *New Mexico*

altogether a beautiful example of the artistry of gun makers in the early eighteenth century. I think it is the same gun that I saw mounted at the Morro de Santiago in 1898."

The voyage back to Bremerton was uneventful for the *New Mexico*, and on arrival the battleship once more entered the yard for overhaul. Leaving the ship in the capable hands of McCain, Bill and Louise crossed the country to Annapolis to attend the graduation of young Bill from the Naval Academy. Alfred and Mary Niblack came as well, traveling all the way from Monte Carlo, where they had been living ever since the admiral had retired in 1923.

The class of 1927 was more than a dozen times larger than that of thirty years earlier to which Bill Leahy had belonged. With nearly six hundred members in the graduating class, the traditional celebration of the cheers "for those we leave behind us," accompanied by the tossing of the midshipman hats in the air, made a colorful ceremony. In addition to the pleasure of seeing their son graduate, the Leahys enjoyed the festivities of June Week with friends and classmates.

Soon after their return to Bremerton, they received a letter from their son

telling us of his engagement to marry Elizabeth Marbury Beale, eldest daughter of Dr. Robert S. Beale of Washington. Elizabeth Beale is acceptable as a daughter-in-law by any standard, but with my observation extending over many years of the difficulties encountered by young married officers without an independent income, I am acutely disappointed by the boy's decision to marry at this time. It will almost certainly adversely affect his career as a naval officer.

In the thirty years since the elder Leahy had graduated from the Naval Academy, great changes had come about. No longer did graduates have to serve two years as naval cadets before they were commissioned. And no longer did they have to wait the same length of time to marry. Young Bill was not intending to waste any time.

The wedding of William H. Leahy to Elizabeth Beale took place on 23 July in Christ's Church, Georgetown, in Washington, where Elizabeth's grandfather had been rector for many years. The senior Leahys were unfortunately unable to attend, for the *New Mexico* was just returning to service after her period in the yard.

In early August, Tennent Harrington and his wife Minnie came to Seattle to help celebrate Fleet Week. The racing cutter of the *New Mexico* was able to run away with the honors in the pulling boat race on Lake Washington, the cutters of all the battleships competing. "Racing crews had been in training all summer for this particular event; thousands of spectators watched it from the shore and from the boats, and it was a particular pleasure to me to accept the cup. . . ."

When the *New Mexico* reached San Francisco, there was a kind of family reunion, for Ensign Leahy was assigned to the USS *California*, flagship of the

Battle Fleet. "Louise, Bill, and Elizabeth took rooms at the Bellview Hotel, where we had a happy week together."

Captain Leahy's last major activity with the *New Mexico* was to conduct full power trials, needed both because of the recent overhaul and because of the fleet competition. Everything went well for the first twenty-two hours of the scheduled twenty-four, when suddenly the ship began to vibrate terribly, indicating a bent or broken propeller.

> As we had an excellent chance to win the annual engineering trophy for the year if the full-speed trial should be successful and no chance if the trial failed, I decided to take whatever chance was involved and maintain the required speed. The vibration was so bad as to make us fear for the safety of the masts, . . . but we were permitted to finish the run without penalty.

After the trial was successfully completed and the engineering trophy won, Leahy learned that his rash decision had been lucky indeed. Divers found that each starboard screw had lost a blade. "No ship," he marveled, "other than one with electric propulsive machinery could have maintained speed with propellers in that condition. It was not wise for us to try to do it, but we succeeded and probably have the highest score in engineering for the year."

At the end of September, Admiral C. F. Hughes, commander in chief of the U.S. Fleet (CINCUS) arrived in the *Texas*. When Leahy went aboard to make his formal call, he was delighted to learn that Hughes had recommended him for appointment as chief of the Bureau of Ordnance.

The appointment was a crucial one for Leahy's career. If an officer hoped for high command in the navy, it was important for him to have the job of either chief of the Bureau of Navigation or the Bureau of Ordnance. As it turned out, Leahy would hold both positions.

The new post would carry with it promotion to the rank of rear admiral. Neither an aviator nor a submariner, Leahy, a staunch member of the "Big Gun Club," was heading for the top of his profession in the classical way, through duty in the big surface ships and in the two most powerful and influential bureaus in the navy.

The day after learning the good news from Admiral Hughes, Leahy received orders to report as soon as relieved to Secretary of the Navy Curtis D. Wilbur. On 10 October 1927, Captain Edgar B. Larimer took over, and Leahy departed after saying farewell with many regrets to the officers and men who had helped him make the *New Mexico* the "Wonder Ship."

Leaving immediately after the change of command, the Leahys reached Washington on 14 Ocotober 1927, where "I reported to the Secretary of the Navy, Mr. Curtis D. Wilbur, and assumed the duties of the Chief of the Bureau of Ordnance, with the rank of Rear Admiral, the first of my Naval Academy date to reach flag rank, which is either something to have accomplished or extraordinarily good luck."

# CHAPTER 4

# The Rear Admiral

When William D. Leahy returned to Washington to assume his duties as chief of the Bureau of Ordnance, he was entering a new world and yet one as familiar as though he had known it all his service life. It was the world of the senior officers of the Navy Department in Washington.

There are two real watersheds in the career of a naval officer. If he reaches the rank of commander, he is virtually assured of retention to retirement age; he becomes a "senior officer." The second is promotion to flag rank, by which he joins a small, select group. In Leahy's day, every member of that group was a graduate of the Naval Academy. All of them had known similar lives in the thirty or so years that had elapsed since their graduation. Their duties had taken them all over the world, and they had encountered peoples of many nations and many races.

Still, they clung to their own society, seeing the same people, whether in Manila or Panama, Hong Kong or Guantanamo, Bremerton or Washington. This life bred a kind of provincialism that separated them not only from their own countrymen but also from a real understanding of the ideas and cultures of other nations. In 1927, when Leahy returned to Washington, the Roaring Twenties were still in full swing, but the professional officer corps of the navy, especially the senior officers, were not a part of it. Civilians might frequent speakeasies, dance the Charleston and the Black Bottom, and brew bathtub gin, but the senior naval officer, while he might like his private tipple now and then and might serve mixed drinks to his friends in the privacy of his own home, avoided the extravagance associated with the Roaring Twenties. Or, if he did not, he was very discreet, shunning notoriety and the press. There was an old navy saying: A naval officer never drinks. If he drinks, he doesn't get drunk. If he gets drunk, he doesn't stagger. If he staggers, he doesn't fall. If he falls, he falls flat on his face with his arms under him so no one can see his stripes.

The world of "Main Navy," which Leahy was joining, was one of its own, and the ground rules were well known. The officers of "Main Navy" were those who had come to the top. The U.S. Navy had been the dominant force in their lives, setting standards of behavior and values of judgment. Strictly speaking, "Main Navy" referred to the Navy Office Building on the corner of Constitution Avenue and Eighteenth Street in Washington, but the term was as much an idea as it was a building. Here the senior officers, their futures assured until they reached the statutory retirement age of sixty-four, ran their various domains, contending with one another for funds and influence, subject to the general direction of the secretary of the navy and the chief of naval operations.

Because of the loose organization which still persisted from the days of Josephus Daniels, each of the bureau chiefs was almost supreme in his own bailiwick. The position of chief of naval operations was seen as that of *primus inter pares*—"first among equals." The bureau chiefs, having no direct connection with operations, were coordinated and supervised by the CNO and not directed by him. In 1927 there were eight bureaus: Aeronautics (BuAer), Construction and Repair (BuC&R), Engineering (BuEng), Medicine and Surgery (BuMed), Navigation, (BuNav), Ordnance (BuOrd), Yards and Docks (BuYard), and Supplies and Accounts (BuSandA). Of these by far the most important were the Bureau of Navigation (later the Bureau of Personnel (BuPers)), and the Bureau of Ordnance. Since naval aviation had not yet come of age, the Bureau of Aeronautics under its controversial leader, Rear Admiral William A. Moffett, had not yet gained the influence it would later enjoy. Also the functions of the later Bureau of Ships were divided between BuEng and BuC&R, so that those two offices had less to say than they would later.

In "Main Navy" in those days, the battleship was king, and coming from command of one of the first-line battleships, Leahy as chief of the Bureau of Ordnance was in the inner circle by virtue of both job and experience. BuOrd provided ships with guns, ammunition, torpedoes, and all other offensive weapons. As a gunnery expert, the new chief was secure in his position, and his great competence ensured that he would succeed. He was entering a phase of his career that would in ten years bring him back to "Main Navy" to the office held in 1927 by Admiral Edward W. Eberle, chief of naval operations.

When the Leahys arrived in Washington that fall, they had to put themselves up temporarily in the Hotel Martinique. "The city is crowded, rents are high, and we finally decided to purchase a house at 2168 Florida Avenue,

N.W. . . . We paid $20,000 for the property, a very high price, but the best
we could do."*

As an assistant, Leahy had the dependable, service-oriented Captain
Andrew C. Pickens, who was of special help in giving testimony before
the numerous congressional committees that are a fact of life in official
Washington.

Soon after taking over, the new chief summarized his understanding of his
duties in a memorandum to the staff. As finally revised, it gives a clear picture
of his concept of his job:

> My essential part in this extensive undertaking is to obtain the necessary
> funds from Congress, to endeavor to so allocate available money as to produce
> the best advantage to the National Defense, to direct Ordnance effort along lines
> that will provide the Navy with weapons that are at least equal in efficiency to
> those possessed by any other Nation, and to exercise the economy and insure the
> accurate accounting that is required by the Congress that appropriates the
> money.
>
> If I seem to refer frequently to "expense," it will be for the purpose of
> stressing for your benefit the fact that funds are limited and that careful economy
> in every line of expenditure must be practiced if the Navy is to continue in an
> efficient condition. Given unlimited funds, it would be easy to provide superior
> armament, but with the money available, many promising prospects must be
> neglected, and effort must be spread over much time in order to find the
> wherewithal.
>
> All Ordnance matters are considered more or less CONFIDENTIAL, and it
> is therefore desired that anything I tell you will not be discussed with any person
> who is not an officer of the Navy.[1]

These lines were written before the collapse of the stock market and the
onset of the Great Depression. Later he would have reason to stress even more
strongly the problems of economical use of funds.

During the time of Leahy's tenure as chief of BuOrd, the navy was still
under the constraints of building because of the Washington Treaty, and,
when it was concluded, the London Treaty of 1930. A moratorium prevented
the construction of new battleships, but certain numbers of other vessels were
allowed under treaty limitations.

Much controversy arose in the Navy Department over what the Washington Treaty really meant. To the General Board, the treaty defined the size of
the various navies of the contracting powers, and therefore it was essential to
build the navy up to treaty strength immediately. To President Coolidge and

---

*As it turned out, the house proved to be an excellent investment, and Leahy owned it until
the end of his days. Then it was sold to the Cosmos Club with the understanding that it be used
for overflow space for club activities. As soon as the club took title, however, it had the house
demolished for a parking lot.

later to President Hoover, the treaty represented a ceiling which might be approached gradually as economic conditions permitted.

Admiral Eberle remained in office only a month after Leahy reported for duty. His successor was Leahy's old friend and mentor, Charles F. Hughes, who assumed the post on 14 November 1927 and kept it until 17 September 1930.

This period was for the armed forces one of those times when they are looked down on by the public as dangerous at worst and as useless at best. Harding's isolationist policy had grown stronger in succeeding administrations, and it would remain a powerful force in the United States right up to the time of Pearl Harbor. Armies and navies seemed simply irrelevant to a large section of the population. America, they said, would not be fighting overseas wars, and moneys spent on the armed services were moneys denied better things. A spirit of optimism reinforced this national isolationism, for most Americans were convinced that "Yankee know-how" could solve all problems. There was no point in looking toward the decadent countries in Europe which had so recently brought war and revolution to a suffering world. The Old World had little to offer the New, and, therefore, armed forces were a thing of the past. In Washington, military leaders felt it was better not to remind the public of the existence of admirals and generals. This led to the absurd situation wherein senior officers of the army and navy were ordered to wear civilian clothes instead of uniforms in the office. It was as though the country's uniforms were something to be ashamed of instead of something to be worn proudly. Uniforms were saved for ceremonial occasions and parades, where the spirit of patriotism could be exploited safely without arousing criticism.

In addition, an article in *The Saturday Evening Post* by Rear Admiral Thomas P. Magruder, commandant of the Philadelphia Navy Yard, charged the navy with sloppy management practices, and a subsequent congressional investigation confirmed the opinion of many people that the entire military establishment was riddled with graft, waste, and corruption. Although the offending admiral was promptly relieved of his assignment by an indignant Secretary Wilbur, the charges did nothing to help the navy so far as the public was concerned. All this meant that naval budgets were in grave danger from the Congress, and that fact affected every branch of the service. In Leahy's domain, for example, it was vital to know how many ships of what kind were going to be built, for the proper guns had to be designed and manufactured for them.

Part of the difficulty in planning during those years arose from a controversy between the Americans and British over the number and kind of cruisers that each navy would be permitted under treaty quotas. These were expressed in tonnages rather than in number of ships. While the British wanted a large number of 5,000 to 6,000-ton light cruisers mounting 6-inch guns, the American navy felt that what best suited them for the vast distances of the Pacific was a heavy cruiser of 10,000 tons, mounting 8-inch guns. The question was not easily settled, however, for during the first year or so of Leahy's tenure in BuOrd, certain senior officers, especially War Plans Director Rear Admiral Frank H. Schofield, were so Anglophobic as to insist that Britain be considered as a possible enemy and that war plans be laid accordingly. Thus the Joint Army and Navy Board added Plan Red, for war against Great Britain, to its others: Orange, against Japan, and even Red–Orange, a coalition of unlikely allies.

The details of these plans need not concern us, but the fact that they existed at all kept naval planning in a state of flux. Recognizing this, Secretary Wilbur directed the General Board to produce a five-year building plan for the navy to ensure that it kept up with other navies of the world. The General Board, by this time, had more authority than in the past, because by statute the chief of naval operations was a member. His presence meant that the board was no longer simply a group of overage admirals who had no responsibilities.

Under the leadership of Rear Admiral Hilary P. Jones, the board recommended that the navy build twenty-five 8-inch-gun cruisers, five to be laid down each year until the total of old and new reached forty-three, with an overall cruiser tonnage of 396,000. In addition, the board recommended that the moratorium on building new battleships be lifted in 1931, and that five small aircraft carriers, thirty-seven destroyers, a number of submarines, and a floating drydock be added as well. President Coolidge knocked out the battleships, the dry dock, and most of the destroyers, but approved the rest. Soon, however, President Hoover would pare the list even further.

During 1928, the problems of modernization of the battleships occupied the attention of naval planners. Besides the obvious moves of converting them to burn oil rather than coal and adding "blisters" to their hulls to decrease their vulnerability to torpedoes, two changes came under Admiral Leahy's purview. The first was the provision of proper antiaircraft guns. That was a knotty problem, for the navy did not have a good design for an antiaircraft gun. The Bofors 40mm. and the Oerliken 20mm. guns, which were to play such a big role in World War II, were not yet available. The other major problem was modifying the main batteries to increase the possible angle of elevation to lengthen the range. The technical and design problems were enormous. Thus it was with a feeling of pride that Leahy was able in January 1929 to note in his journal, "During the past year, an extensive building program of new cruisers and modernization of battleships has taxed the ordnance manufacturing establishment of the Navy, but we have succeeded in meeting delivery dates."

There was another kind of delivery in December of 1928, when Elizabeth and Bill presented him with a granddaughter, Louise Harrington Leahy. Her adoring grandfather always called her Louisita.

President Herbert Hoover was sworn in 4 March 1929, and the notation in Leahy's journal is laconic, describing the new chief executive as "a Quaker native of Iowa, resident abroad most of his adult life, and claiming citizenship in California." He was much more favorable about the appointment of Hoover's cabinet, especially praising the selection of Charles Francis Adams as the new secretary of the navy.

> Mr. Adams, by his superior character and his knowledge of the sea, at once attracted and held the full loyalty of the naval service. . . . Mr. Hoover's cabinet seems to be composed of individuals who have been successful in big business affairs. It is said by the President's political opponents that he himself is a promoter and that he has never done any successful work as an engineer. He has admittedly accumulated a fortune in some way.

During July 1929, Leahy received a practical lesson in politics as it affected his department. An explosion having destroyed the main naval ammunition depot near Lake Denmark, New Jersey, the main facility was moved to Yorktown, Virginia. Powerful Nevadans wanted a secondary one in the desert near Hawthorn in a $2,500,000 facility which Leahy had little use for.

> It would be cheaper to throw our accumulated explosives into the sea, but Nevada probably needed the money, and the station will be a lovely oasis when it is finished. We expect to produce from the desert a golf course, trees, lawns, truck gardens, and flowers. All of these should materialize when we get sufficient water by damming two very small mountain streams, the only fresh water within reach.

After a short leave, Leahy returned to Washington to face a whole new group of problems. In October, Wall Street crashed, and the Great Depression had begun.

The implications of the depression lie beyond the scope of a biography, and it is certain that Leahy was concerned only as the economic collapse affected the navy. In general, service people were better off than the rest of the population. While they did not earn large sums of money, their jobs were secure, and benefits such as free medical care, commissaries, and military exchanges reduced the cost of many items they had to buy. In addition, the depression brought general deflation, so the take-home pay of servicemen went further than it had before. Later, however, when servicemen had to take pay cuts, the situation changed, but that lay in the future.

In January 1930, Secretary Adams led the naval contingent to a conference in London to help resolve the naval limitations problems and to revise the Five Power Treaty which had established a 10:10:7 ratio for cruisers among the

United States, Great Britain, and Japan. The chairman of the entire American delegation was Secretary of State Henry L. Stimson.

The main problem was that American naval leaders could not agree among themselves. The General Board defined the official navy position, which was represented in London by Admiral Hilary P. Jones. The board still looked on Great Britain as a potential enemy and stuck to the idea that the U.S. Navy should emphasize heavy cruisers as most suitable to use in the Pacific, where their greater size and endurance could cope with the vast distances. Whether in the Atlantic or Pacific, those bigger cruisers would be valuable, no matter who the enemy was.

President Hoover, however, was not convinced, and he sent Rear Admiral William V. Pratt to London to represent the administration. Pratt favored compromise with the British. The General Board wanted twenty-three heavy cruisers; Pratt recommended eighteen and that the remaining tonnage available to the United States be made up in light cruisers. As Jones and his supporters saw it, Pratt's plan could have no other purpose than to weaken the U.S. Navy vis-à-vis the Royal Navy.

Pratt, who was to become the next chief of naval operations, was considered a defector from the naval ranks. He always insisted that he was working for the good of the nation as opposed to the narrow view of what was good for the navy. He felt that any conflict with Britain was the remotest of possibilities and that the failure of the United States and Great Britain to reach an understanding would only play into the hands of the Japanese militarists. Pratt viewed Japan as the most probable future enemy, but he was not convinced that light cruisers were unsuited to Pacific service. There was even a short-lived plan during his term as CNO to put flight decks on cruisers, an idea which had been discussed in London as a possible compromise. Fortunately those ships never came into being.★

Leahy paid close attention to the progress of the conference in London, and when it was over he joined others in expressing general dissatisfaction. He felt that Pratt had sold out to President Hoover's pacifist views, and that the decisions of the conference gave Britain and Japan

> naval advantages that they had not previously possessed by treaty rights. . . . The navy was generally disappointed in the treaty for the reason that it was not advantageous to our national defense. Admiral Pratt seemed to align himself with the administration point of view."

While the discussions in London were in progress, the chief of naval operations, Admiral Hughes, suffered a stroke, brought about, many of his friends thought, by overwork. After he left the hospital, he took a cruise aboard the new cruiser *Pensacola* to Panama and back, arriving in Washington

★The only two such ships ever built were the Japanese battleships *Ise* and *Hyuga*. They were weakened as battleships and total failures as carriers.

in time to review the treaty with the General Board and leading officers. He emphatically disagreed with Admiral Pratt. Far from feeling rebuked, and believing that he had the support of President Hoover, Pratt promptly put in a request to be named CNO in relief of the ailing Hughes.

The split threatened to divide senior naval officers into warring camps. Hughes had been a particular friend to Leahy, having named him to his present job as chief of the Bureau of Ordnance, and Hughes's retirement could be a setback to Leahy's advance to the higher grades. The prudent thing would have been for Leahy to keep quiet or even acclaim the rising star of Admiral Pratt. But, in keeping with his convictions, he supported the majority position in Washington in defense of Admiral Hughes.

The opposition to Pratt was useless. Because he had loyally supported the administration position at the London Conference, Pratt had the backing of the two men who counted—Secretary Adams and President Hoover. Pratt would be the next CNO, and the navy would have to live with it.

Learning that the president proposed extensive budget cuts for the coming fiscal year and deciding that his successor ought to be the one to make the decisions on the cuts, Admiral Hughes requested early retirement. The secretary was glad to oblige, and accordingly on 17 September 1930, the brief ceremony took place in the office of the chief of naval operations in "Main Navy" to the accompaniment of a tense and stiffly formal atmosphere. All the bureau chiefs attended; many of them, like Leahy, had been protégés of Hughes, and they shared feelings of disappointment and bitterness.

> In September, 1930, Admiral Hughes, after having been ill for some weeks following a paralytic stroke, was retired and Admiral Pratt was appointed Chief of Naval Operations. Admiral Hughes was in complete disagreement with all of Pratt's ideas and was much disappointed with his relief.
> The entire year was one of retrenchment in naval ordnance construction because of delays in ship construction and the executive withdrawal of available money.

As the weeks went by, Leahy was finding himself more and more frequently at odds with the new chief of naval operations, and he decided he would be better off not so close to Admiral Pratt. He had become a permanent rear admiral with rank dating from 6 April 1930, so he was secure from any reversion to the rank of captain. On the other hand, if he remained in Washington, he might well have a serious clash with the CNO, with fatal results to his career, so he was happy when commander in chief U.S. Fleet (CINCUS), Admiral Jehu Chase, formerly ComBatDiv 4 in the *New Mexico*, asked him to go to sea in the spring of 1931 as his chief of staff. This idea was smashed when Admiral Chase, a backer of Hughes, was abruptly relieved, and his successor, Admiral Frank H. Schofield, a Pratt man, had his own ideas about his chief of staff. As a result, Leahy had to look for another job. He wound up as Commander Destroyers, Scouting Force.

Returning to sea pleased Leahy after the hurly-burly of Washington politics. He left behind the hard feelings that had developed between him and Admiral Pratt and the parsimonies inflicted on the navy by President Hoover. On 1 June 1931, "relieved as Chief of Bureau by my friend, Captain E. B. Larimer, I departed from a difficult but very interesting tour of shore duty to take command at New York of the destroyers of the Scouting Fleet."

The world was moving ineluctibly toward war. In spite of the efforts in the London Conference in 1930, the following year the Japanese began aggressive operations on the mainland of Asia. Soon Japanese extremists were denouncing the London Treaty, even as they continued their operations in the part of China known as Manchukuo, which was being more and more referred to by its Japanese name—Manchuria. The rest of Leahy's regular naval career would be spent in preparing for the war that he would not be able to fight.

On 6 June 1931, Leahy became Commander Destroyers, Scouting Force. Because of shortages of funds, the ships did not go to sea enough to satisfy the wishes of their commanders. Nor were the promises of promotion bright. Of all the officers under his command, only a few reached flag rank, the best known being then Captain William F. Halsey, Jr., whom the press later insisted on calling "Bull." Friends knew him as "Bill."

Halsey's father had been an officer in the *Constellation* when Leahy had made his first ocean cruise in her in 1893. It was, therefore, appropriate just then, when he had the son under his command, for him to think of those days so long gone when he had known the father. The old frigate was moored at the Naval Training Station in New York, and on 4 July he paid a nostalgic visit, finding it

> a colorful picture of the Old Navy in this latest celebration of Independence Day. . . . My first cruise and the *Constellation's* last were made 37 years ago. On the fourth of July we were in Horta in the Azores Islands, and the National Salute was fired from the old muzzle-loading guns of the *Constellation's* broadside battery.
>
> Some repair work has been done from time to time to keep the old ship from falling apart, . . . A visit to the *Constellation* is particularly interesting in showing the living accommodations and conditions for officers and men in naval vessels a hundred years ago.
>
> "It's a great life if you don't weaken," must have been particularly applicable then.

Following exercises in the Atlantic and in Chesapeake Bay, Leahy in the cruiser *Raleigh* took part in the celebration of the 150th anniversary of the surrender of General Cornwallis at Yorktown. A French delegation included the descendants of those Frenchmen who had fought to help the American cause: the Marquis de Rochambeau, the Marquis de Chambrun, a descendant of Lafayette, and the Marquis de Grasse, whose ancestor commanded the fleet that had defeated the British under Admiral Graves off the Virginia Capes. Also present was Marshal Philippe Pétain, victor of Verdun, and then at the height of his esteem and honor in his own country and abroad.

Each day, all flag and general officers dined together in a tent with the foreign guests. On this occasion Leahy was presented to Marshal Pétain. Neither of them could have then imagined the circumstances under which they would meet again in Vichy in the cold January of 1941.

President Hoover reviewed the ships present and then delivered an address appropriate to the occasion. Leahy, whose opinion of the president had not improved during his years in Washington, confided:

> He read a very mediocre address that referred lightly, if at all, to the combatants at Yorktown. During this reading, a puff of wind blew away some of the President's prepared address, and he stood mute and apparently uninterested while aides secured the disturbed manuscript, after which he proceeded with his reading. A more vigorous wind would not have annoyed the spectators.

Late in November, Leahy relieved Rear Admiral William H. Standley as Commander Destroyers, Battle Fleet, while keeping his old job as Commander Destroyers, Scouting Force. The new command was a step up and was to prove to be a path to promotion, for Standley was to precede him in the post of chief of naval operations.

Entries in Leahy's journal for 1932 take on a more somber note than previous years had shown. Concerned with the threat of war, he devoted less space to places and people he had seen and more to his ideas of proper policies and strategies for the United States. He was then a most thoroughgoing isolationist, believing that America should stick to her own affairs and not seek out any "foreign entanglements," a phrase he was to use a good many times in the years ahead. On the other hand, he disliked the "pacifists," who urged that the United States reduce her military forces unilaterally in the hope that other countries would be inspired to do the same. Such a hope defied growing evidence of unrest in Europe, where Mussolini was beginning to talk of a new Roman Empire, and where a dynamic speaker, Adolf Hitler, was coming ever closer to power in Germany. On the other side of the world, Japanese troops in China engaged in open war with the Chinese, and Japanese soldiers there were publicly humiliating foreigners, including Americans, with taunts, insults, jostlings, and even blows.

In the summer of 1931, Chinese troops blew up a railroad near Mukden. The incident gave Japan an excuse to proclaim the independence of Manchuria. The following year the Japanese occupied several Chinese cities, such as Shanghai and Nanking, after a *pro forma* declaration of war. It was *pro forma* because for some time Japan had been doing just what she pleased in China.

The following January, Secretary of State Stimson announced that the United States would not recognize the independence of Manchuria, a move infuriating to Japanese militants. Isolationists in the United States immediately sounded the alarm. "The United States," the *Atlanta Constitution* protested on the heels of Stimson's actions, "is treading on dangerous ground in becoming involved in the Manchurian situation to the extent of joining other nations in notes of warning which are tantamount to threats. It is none of our business until some of our rights have been infringed upon."[2]

American interests soon were concerned. As Japanese outrages continued, even to the extent of threatening the International Settlement in Shanghai, the United States beefed up its naval strength in the Pacific, and when the Japanese occupied Shanghai, more ships were sent to reinforce the U.S. Asiatic Fleet. In a few weeks the battle fleet would be ordered to the Pacific, and Leahy's destroyers would remain in that ocean as long as he was in command. He was alarmed:

> Meagre information available here indicates that the American government is interfering in an affair that does not concern us and that such interference may drag the United States into a destructive Oriental war.
>
> A war with Japan at the present time would be of sufficient length to almost certainly destroy the existing social order in America, and it would seem that some strong character must appear in our political organization to bring us back to the fundamental principal of "no entangling alliances."

He found the man he was looking for in his old friend, Franklin D. Roosevelt. On 1 July, after the Democratic Party had nominated FDR, Leahy wrote:

> Franklin Roosevelt is a gentleman by all standards of comparison, he is honest, and is what politicians term progressive. Given continued good health, he should, if elected, perform very satisfactory service as President of the United States.
>
> In any event he would start with the advantage of facing a situation and an executive organization where any change will be an improvement.

Two weeks later, in what some claimed as President Hoover's response to the optimism of Roosevelt's acceptance speech, the Navy Department announced that all officers would be required to take one month's leave without pay each year, and that the president had proclaimed a 10 percent reduction in the allowances for quarters and subsistence. "This is a hardship on officers," Leahy observed, "because they did not during prosperous times receive any increase of compensation, and now in times of distress they are required to contribute to the country's deficit."

Because of cutbacks in fuel allocations, Leahy's ships spent most of the summer in San Diego, giving him unaccustomed leisure to ponder the world situation. At this time he began the practice of writing an occasional summary of strategic and political conditions, an exercise he continued on and off for many years. Early in September he wrote:

New accounts of international relations are alarming, and conditions in Europe point toward a war in the not distant future.

Germany is almost certainly going to refuse to pay reparations and other debts to the victorious Allies, and Germany has also demanded equality in armaments with other European powers. Mussolini, dictator of Italy, is reported to be in full agreement with Germany.

The League of Nations has failed in Europe to maintain friendly relations between the powers and has failed to restrain Japan in Manchuria. . . .

There is some danger of America getting involved with Japan if our State Department continues to take an active interest in Oriental affairs.

We will probably not continue to interfere in the Orient if the present [Hoover] administration is thrown out of office by the November election. . . .

Europe seems to be rapidly approaching agreements and understandings, both open and secret, made with the purpose of reaching "a balance of power" similar to that which existed prior to the World War.

Another war in Europe seems inevitable, and while predictions of future diplomatic developments are always inaccurate, appearances now point to the probability of an alliance of Germany and Italy against France with Great Britain neutral.

As the election drew closer, Leahy sourly commented on a Navy Day address delivered by President Hoover on 27 October in which the president threatened that, unless other naval powers agreed to reduce their fleets, the United States would have to build up its own navy to the strength allowed by the London Treaty, "'with resulting injury to cherished ideals of the American people.' He did not explain these 'cherished ideals,' unknown to me."

Following the election, Leahy believed that Roosevelt would "use his office more directly for the benefit of the United States," and that he would be "less solicitous" of the welfare of "the international bankers and stock promoters" than Hoover had been. "The country and the navy undoubtedly face a bad period, but I believe their policies will now be directed by a man whose point of view is wholly American."

That bad period was not long delayed. While the ships in the Pacific limited exercises, in late March the new administration cut the pay of all government workers, including the military, by 15 percent. This action, coupled with a reduction in the number of men authorized for the navy, worried Leahy, who had just learned that he was slated to be the next chief of the Bureau of Navigation. He felt that "pacifist influences" had weakened the fleet, and only hoped that when American ships were "called upon for war service in the not distant future, . . . our personnel is in a better state of training than that of any possible enemy."

On 6 May 1933, Leahy, with Louise, boarded a train for Washington, where he would embark upon duty that "will probably be as full of controversy and as disagreeable as it is important." It turned out to be both controversial and disagreeable, and it was certainly important. It was to bring

Leahy into direct conflict with the next chief of naval operations, Admiral Standley.

Franklin Roosevelt's famous Hundred Days were more than half gone when Leahy arrived in Washington to serve on a board appointed by Secretary of the Navy Charles A. Swanson to consider changes in the command structure and to save money. The president of the board was a distant cousin of FDR, Assistant Secretary of the Navy Henry Latrobe Roosevelt. Leahy was senior officer, serving with Rear Admiral Ernest J. King, chief of the Bureau of Aeronautics, and nine other officers. The board met off and on through the remainder of 1933.

Assistant Secretary Roosevelt was a remarkable man. A classmate of King at the Naval Academy, he had served in the Marine Corps, becoming a lieutenant colonel by the end of World War I. He then left the Marines to enter business. He was assistant secretary from March 1933, until his death some three years later.

The thorniest problem before the board was that of the relationship between the chief of naval operations and the chiefs of various bureaus. His exact authority had never been defined by statute, and Article 433 of Navy Regulations adopted in 1924 did not have the force of law. It simply stated that the CNO "should so coordinate all repairs and alterations to vessels and the supply of personnel thereto as to insure at all times the maximum readiness of the Fleet for war." That was not very helpful, but it did satisfy Admiral Pratt, the current CNO, who remarked, "I'd rather sit around a table with a group of men, everyone of whom is perfectly independent and king of his own domain, and to get a man to work with you rather than tell that man what to do. I have found that all I have to do is to make a suggestion to them, and they will complete the job. If you can't get a man who will do that, get somebody else."[3]

Admiral Pratt, however, was to be CNO for only another few weeks, and Standley, his successor, wanted a clearer definition of the relationship and tended, once in office, to treat the bureau chiefs as though they were subject to his command authority. Perhaps they should have been, but the law didn't say so.

This attitude brought him head-to-head with the two strongest-willed bureau chiefs, Rear Admirals Leahy and King. They succeeded in convincing Secretary Roosevelt to report that "while the board felt that drastic changes were not necessary or advisable at this time," the relationship between the bureau chiefs and CNO needed redefining. They recommended, to the extreme displeasure of Admiral Standley, that the authority of CNO over the bureau chiefs, if it had ever existed, be discontinued. The situation should be corrected by "requiring the Chief of Naval Operations to advise the Secretary of the Navy as to the needs of the Navy, and by placing the Bureaus and Offices directly under and responsible to, the Secretary of the Navy."

That idea was completely unacceptable to Admiral Standley, so the matter was referred to the president for decision. FDR replied in a letter of 2 March 1934.

> My thought, therefore, on this question is that Article 433 of the Navy Regulations should remain in force. By this, I mean that the Chief of Naval Operations should coordinate all repairs and alterations to vessels, etc., by retaining constant and frequent touch with the heads of bureaus and offices. But at the same time, the orders to bureaus and offices should come from the Secretary of the Navy. In actual working out of this method, we come down to what should be a practical plan of procedure. The Chief of Naval Operations through his meetings with the bureaus will be able to carry through ninety-nine per cent of the plan and actual work by unanimous agreement. This constitutes the "coordination" expected. In one per cent or less of the problems involved, there may be disagreement or objection. The Secretary's council is the place to work out these cases after full and free discussion, the final decision resting, of course, with the Secretary of the Navy himself.[4]

Admiral Standley did not take kindly to this decision which seemed to be a case of "hang your clothes on a hickory limb, but don't go near the water." As he saw it, he had the responsibility but not the authority he needed to do his job. He blamed his defeat on Leahy and King and never forgave either of them. Later, when Leahy was ready to move on to other duty, Standley tried to end his career and force him into retirement.

Work on the Roosevelt Board was only a part-time job for Leahy, for he faced major problems when he took over the job of chief of the Bureau of Navigation on 1 July 1933. There was the responsibility of providing officers and enlisted men to the fleet and shore stations and of ensuring that they were trained to do their jobs. He had to see to it that they were properly rotated so that their experience would enable them to qualify for promotion to higher rank or rate.

When he took over BuNav, the navy was at a low ebb, as both Coolidge and Hoover had consistently refused to build the fleet up to anything approaching treaty strength. But in the Congress, one of the best friends the navy has ever had on Capitol Hill was acutely aware of the weakness of the United States Navy and was not afraid to support the service in the face of widespread isolationism. He was Representative Carl Vinson of Georgia. First elected to the House in 1914, his abilities and his seniority ensured that with the Democratic victory, he would chair the House Naval Affairs Committee. He and Leahy were to become friends and collaborators in the years that lay ahead.

Shortly after the election of 1932, Vinson briefed the president-elect, who was relaxing at Warm Springs, Georgia, and gave him a crash course in the problems of the navy. He pointed out, for instance, that since 1922, Great Britain had built 148 naval ships. Japan had built 164, and Italy, 144. France had led the construction boom with 196 new ships. As for the United States—it had built 40. Even worse, most of the fleet was overage, and many of the ships were completely obsolete. It might seem comforting to the public to think that the United States had 15 battleships to Britain's 12, but no new American battleships had been laid down since the *Maryland* class, and the last of them had been commissioned in December 1923.[5]

Leahy, too, had hopes that the new administration would recognize something of the difficulties the navy was experiencing. As he saw it, there was a great deal wrong and a great deal to be done.

He considered the navy to be in a chaotic state, morale at a low ebb because of the 15 percent pay cut and the freeze on promotions. The worst of all were the "repeated, persistent attacks" by "fascists leagued with economists." He felt the president and Secretaries Swanson and Roosevelt were friendly and surely would come to the aid of the navy when its case was presented, so that "the persistent attacks of enemies of our national defense will be repulsed."

> Today the President announced that $238,000,000 of the $3,000,000,000 Public Works appropriation will be used to build new naval ships.★ The purpose of this appropriation is to provide employment for people in distress, but if it is carried out in accordance with Sunday's announcement, the Navy may be materially improved in its strength as compared with the navies of England and Japan. It is intended that work will start at the earliest practicable date, and that 20 destroyers, 2 aircraft carriers, 4 10,000-ton cruisers with 6-inch guns, 4 submarines, and 2 gunboats will soon be in process of construction.
>
> The program will probably cause a vigorous attack by the pacifist element in politics, but some of the projected ships, if not all of them, will be completed. . . .
>
> A hurried estimate of the prospects before those of us who will be charged with administering the navy during the next few years promises well. . . .
>
> The work will be difficult at times and very discouraging sometimes, but I expect good results from the favorable consideration of high administrative officials.

If Leahy's hopes were not realized in every respect, enough good did happen so that the navy slowly began to rebuild. President Roosevelt proved unexpectedly slow to spend money for the navy, and Leahy was soon to lock horns with Admiral Standley over the recommendations of the Roosevelt Board on the matter of the bureau system.

The most immediate need in Leahy's bailiwick was reform of methods of officer selection, promotion, and retention. As conditions were, Leahy pro-

---

★These ships were funded under the Public Works Administration, administered by Secretary of the Interior Harold L. Ickes. This is not to be confused with the WPA under Harry Hopkins, which was not yet in existence. When it came into being, WPA worked mostly on small projects, with a theoretical ceiling of $25,000. PWA built large things, such as dams, buildings, airports—and naval vessels.

jected that in a very short time Naval Academy graduates would not reach the grade of captain until they were sixty years of age. Since statutory retirement came at sixty-four, one wondered where new admirals would be coming from. He and Secretary Swanson persuaded Congress to permit the navy to use selection boards for all promotions from the rank of lieutenant (jg) and above, with forced retirement for those twice passed over. This legislation permitted the navy to eliminate long waits for promotion, waits which were destructive of morale and which doomed the navy to be run by the "Old Fuds," instead of the "Young Studs," as the old navy saying has it.

Meanwhile, Congress had appropriated only enough money to man the existing fleet to 80 percent of authorized complement. This policy enormously reduced fleet efficiency. Even worse, it made no allowance for obtaining the number of men that would be needed when the new ships came along. The Naval Academy simply would not be able to supply the numbers of aviators and line officers that the navy would require in a few years.

Leahy, therefore, speaking for BuNav, proposed increasing the number of appointments at the Naval Academy allowed each congressman and senator from three to four in 1936 and from four to five in 1937. Additionally, to produce naval aviators, Leahy instituted a program for naval cadets, selected on graduation from civilian colleges and universities, who were given a year's flight training at Pensacola, Florida. On completion of training, cadets had an obligation to serve three years as junior officers.

Similar programs for staff officers—doctors, dentists, supply officers, civil engineers—were undertaken, with the grudging concurrence of a Congress reluctant to spend a penny more than it had to on the army and navy. Leahy wryly noted that members of Congress seemed to like individual admirals very much, but they hesitated to increase the number of them, for they all winced at the word "admiral."[6]

Soon after being sworn in as chief of the Bureau of Navigation, Leahy made a trip to Annapolis to address the Post Graduate School, then located in the Academy grounds. Entering through Gate 3, and being received with full honors, he contrasted his treatment with that he had received when he had entered for the first time in 1893.

> It is not altogether strange that memory has persisted in going back forty years to when I first passed through the same gate, embarking on an adventure into a totally unknown life that was strange, and, in a way, forbidding to me. The gate is unchanged. Everything inside is as entirely different as the two receptions separated by forty years. Whether forty years have worked much change in my point of view, I do not know, but memory seems to say that then as now I considered personality more interesting than prestige, and that I thought the Commodore Superintendent a friendly old fossil. It is hoped that the midshipmen of today are equally kind in their thoughts of us.

Ever present in Leahy's mind was the prospect of war, which, in common with a majority of Americans, he hoped to avoid by keeping out of European and Asiatic affairs. When, in October, Germany announced her withdrawal from the League of Nations, Leahy noted with apprehension:

This seems to definitely mark the beginning of the League's dissolution. Now, if America can so arrange its affairs as to remain aloof from European politics, there seems to be a prospect of returning to a condition of self-sufficiency and of industrial, financial, and political independence. The League's collapse at this early date brings much nearer the inevitable European war.

In spite of President Roosevelt's love of the navy, his determination to balance the budget kept that service on very short rations. As a matter of fact, at one point Secretary Swanson realized that on a "checks written" basis, he would actually have less money to spend under the first Roosevelt budget in 1934 than he had had under the last Hoover budget in 1933. The modest rebuilding program would not bring the fleet into anything like parity with the Japanese, let alone with the British. Even at that, the Japanese were worried. Ambassador Joseph Grew reported from Tokyo:

The Japanese press varies in its reactions to the American plans for naval construction, but the dominant theme is that America is making a thrust toward Japan. . . . Back of all agitation over American naval plans is the determination of the Japanese to better their relative naval standing at the next conference in 1936. It is highly unlikely that they will submit to a further extension of the 5:5:3 ratio after that date.[7]

Leahy, of course, was not directly concerned with naval appropriations as he would be when he became CNO four years later. He had enough to worry about in his own department. He spent a good deal of time before various congressional committees justifying his own budget proposals. The fact that authorized personnel of the navy increased during his term in BuNav was not so much the result of his own eloquence as it was the natural consequence of the gradual build-up of the navy. The new ships coming out as a result of the PWA program had to be manned. Then the efforts of Carl Vinson and Senator Park Trammell of Florida, both strong advocates of navy interests, promised more ships later.

In mid-November, the simmering differences regarding the question of authority over the bureaus between the Roosevelt Board and Admiral Standley came to a boil. The situation worsened to the point of super-heated steam when Standley demanded that the report of the board recommend that the chief of naval operations also have command of the fleet.

History is replete [Leahy wrote after an "almost acrimonious discussion with the Chief of Naval Operations"] with failures of campaigns caused by confusion of understanding and conflict of authority between administrative officials and military commanders in the field, and I am thoroughly convinced that the duty of the Chief of Naval Operations should be definitely limited by law and regulation to administrative control of the naval establishment.★

One of the most sensitive tasks the chief of BuNav had each year was making up the annual list of flag appointments. Although the president approves the list, it is prepared in the office of the chief of naval personnel, successor office to the Bureau of Navigation. Preparing the list is a delicate matter, with consultation on all levels, for the officers to be assigned are often senior to the man doing the assigning. And frequently a president, especially such a man as Franklin Roosevelt, will have his own ideas.

A letter from Admiral David F. Sellers, then CINCUS, to Leahy in December 1933 reveals some of the kind of thinking and discussion that went on:

> Both [Joseph M.] Reeves and I agree that it would be highly desirable from the standpoint of efficiency of the Fleet if [John] Halligan could be retained in command of the [naval] Air Force for another year. This opinion is based on the fact that there doesn't seem to be anyone of the proper caliber available for his relief just at present. [Henry V.] Butler, [Frederick J.] Horne, and [Alfred W.] Johnson seem to be the only ones available, and none of these three can reasonably be expected to get the same results out of the Air Force that Halligan has. Neither Reeves nor I have a very high opinion of Butler's ability; Reeves relieved him in command of the Air Force, so has an intimate knowledge of his capabilities in this respect. Of course, it may be said that even if Halligan is retained afloat for another year, you will be confronted with the same problem as to his relief at the end of that time, but it would mean that in a year and a half (if we start now) some officer of appropriate rank could be found who could qualify as an [aviation] observer and thus be eligible under the law.[8]

Because of the legal requirement that commanding officers of carriers and of other aviation activities in the navy must be aviators, it was sometimes necessary to send senior officers to flight school. Most of them did not qualify as full-fledged pilots; most became "observers," which fulfilled the law, but did little else. Leahy didn't think much of the system, believing that if a man was going in for naval aviation, he should be a real pilot and not a half-baked substitute called an "observer."

---

★Leahy clung forthrightly to this position when he became CNO, but he obviously came to understand that it was unworkable in wartime to have the commander in chief U.S. Fleet (CINCUS) at sea, directing operations without direct contact with Washington. With the establishment of the Joint Chiefs of Staff as the source of strategic planning, it became necessary for its members to have command authority. This was made evident when Admiral Ernest J. King was given both jobs of CNO and CINCUS. He changed the title of the latter after the Pearl Harbor attack to COMINCH, since CINCUS ("Sink Us") was a sensitive word in the early stages of the war.

One of the men who started for the observer route was Halsey. Offered the command of the carrier *Saratoga* if he would take the observer course, Halsey accepted quickly, but his wife raised a storm of objections; finally she said she would let him go if Leahy, "for whose judgment we both had enormous respect, agreed that the idea was sound. Bill Leahy not only agreed, he was enthusiastic."[9]

The year 1934 opened with no apparent change in the state of the world as Leahy perceived it. He saw the depression easing slightly but the threat of war in Europe in no way abated; he hoped that there was no reason for American involvement and felt that the president's determination to build up "an adequate sea defense" would "keep us out of war for the year at least." The biggest naval news of 1934 was the passage of the Vinson–Trammel Act which was approved by the Congress on 22 March and signed into law by the president five days later.

The Vinson–Trammel Act was more an expression of intent than it was a real program. It merely provided that the president should have the authority to build the navy up to treaty strength. It did not force him to do it. It defined the tonnages of each category needed for such a building program, and it demanded that any excess profits be returned to the Treasury. It required the secretary of the navy to recommend each year what ships should be built and what funds Congress should appropriate to pay for them.

In spite of the Vinson–Trammell Act, the administration continued to drag its feet on building new ships. President Roosevelt tried various schemes to cut back expenses. He even had the strange idea of a forty-hour work week for crews of operating ships, which was obviously impracticable. Another rejected scheme was to rotate crews from ship to ship so as much as a third of the fleet would be laid up at any given time. Promotions were still held up, pay cuts remained, and only the upper half of the graduating class of the Naval Academy was commissioned. If, in Leahy's mind, conditions around the country were seeming to improve, they weren't in the navy.

Asked one day to speak at the Naval Academy, Leahy gave a whimsical statement of how education had changed since his time. On being informed that a new course called English and Public Speaking had been established, he suggested that it would give all the midshipmen proficiency in getting out of

the kind of predicament that I find myself in tonight.

It is unnecessary to say . . . that in the ancient days when I was a midshipman, the final result of our misnamed English course approximated to what we call an absolute zero.

It did force us, with threats of disaster, to memorize portions of uninteresting, badly written naval history, and it did include a pamphlet on the correct usage of the auxiliary verbs "shall" and "will," which was completely beyond the comprehension of EVERYBODY in the class.

It is hoped that your equipment in the use of the spoken and written word is better, because I can assure you that . . . skill in the use of written English is one of the most valuable of all the accomplishments that can be possessed by an officer of the Navy.[10]

A good bit of time that spring Leahy spent testifying before congressional committees. He felt a great sense of triumph when he won the authority to commission all members of the Naval Academy class of 1934, which gave special satisfaction to the lower half of the class who otherwise would have faced bleak employment prospects in the depths of the depression.

In May 1934, Leahy addressed the graduating class of the Naval War College in Newport. He spoke of the many times he had made application for duty there as a student but always something had stood in his way. His speech was largely a summary of the activities that had concerned him for the eleven months he had been chief of BuNav, but near the end he touched on his philosophy of the functions of the War College and on his view of the naval educational system as well.

Senior officers of the navy differed on what the purpose of the War College really was. One group held that it was a kind of testing ground, where ideas of strategy and tactics could be wargamed without the expense of actually using ships. Supporters of this view held that it would therefore be an influential power in actual naval operations. The other view was that it was a school for senior officers who might be leaders of the navy in future years. In other words, the dispute was over whether it was an extension of the War Plans Division of the Navy Department or a school where future flag officers could study tactics, strategy, logistics, and planning.

Leahy came down squarely on the educational function of the War College. As he saw it, there were four formal steps in a naval officer's career, interspersed with practical experience and learning at sea. At first the Naval Academy gave the primary education and background. Then the General Line School, which was primarily technical, was able in its tactical course to lay a good deal of groundwork for further study in strategy and tactics. The Junior War College was intended to deal with minor tactics, such as "the handling of individual units and small type groups." The War College Senior Course built on everything that had gone before to a "study of major tactics and strategy covering everything in the art of command at sea which falls within the probable duties of naval officers afloat."

Leahy felt, however, that there was no need for a separate school where officers of the other services and civilians of the State and Treasury departments would study together. He felt that it would be much better to send those advanced students to Newport or to the Army War College, rather than build a "so called College of National Defense wherein they might educate us."[11] Of course the other view prevailed when the National War College was established.

During the summer, Leahy expressed unusual interest in the political campaign. He felt that the Democratic party had succeeded beyond expectation when the Republican gains in November were minimal. To him the election represented a peaceful political revolution, but the consequent social revolution was yet to be realized.

If the cultural revolution was not yet at hand, neither was the personnel revolution in the navy. In face of the administrations's economies, Secretary Swanson informed the president that CNO, CINCUS, and the chief of BuNav had made a study which indicated that "eighty-five percent of war complement is the minimum allowance for satisfactory peace-time operations."[12] Such an increase from the current 80 percent manning policy meant that the navy, by fiscal 1936, had to bring the enlisted strength up to 93,500 men, some 4,500 more than original projections. After some grumbling, FDR went along with the increase and, in a gesture of goodwill, permitted reopening of the naval training station at Newport.

The departure of Admiral Standley in early October for London to take part in a disarmament conference made life easier for almost everyone in the Navy Department. While Standley got along well enough with Secretary Swanson, he and Assistant Secretary Roosevelt were barely on speaking terms, and his dislike of Leahy and King had been unrelenting ever since the report of the Roosevelt Board. Standley was gone for the rest of the year, but his job required that he keep in touch with Leahy over the flag officer list which was under preparation.

When Standley the previous year had persuaded President Roosevelt to appoint Admiral Joseph M. Reeves as CINCUS, he had expected him to be a Standley supporter in the political game of the navy. To his fury, Reeves had proved to be as independent as Leahy and King. Thus, when Leahy sent the proposed flag officer list to Standley in London, and it included a second year for Reeves as CINCUS, the CNO replied, "I am not sure I would want to keep Reeves. He seems to be running wild with the schedules, etc., and his attitude toward War Plans was rather disturbing."[13]

President Roosevelt, nevertheless, appointed Reeves to another year, as Leahy reported in a letter to his classmate Leonard Sargent, going on to say, "There isn't much cheerful news about the sea defenses except that the President apparently does not intend to permit any foreign nation to dictate our naval policy. He seems to be sound in the matter of national defense."

Bill added hopefully that Secretary Swanson had suggested that Leahy might soon be able to go back to sea, and "this really is one H--- of a job, and I will trade it for anything at sea, unseen, at any time."[14]

Things looked bright for an early return to sea for Bill Leahy when Reeves, making a visit to Washington in December, told Secretary Swanson that he would like to see Leahy named Commander of the Battle Force. When, however, Standley returned from London early in January he tried to keep Leahy from getting any good job. Bitterly, Leahy wrote that Standley

> is now persistently and vigorously opposing this nomination with the purpose of eliminating me from any prospect of promotion to the fleet or of succession to his office when he retires.
>
> Secretary Swanson wants me to succeed Admiral Standley, which is undoubtedly the cause of the latter's attitude.
>
> In view of the fact that Admiral Standley has officially questioned my professional competency, it is pleasing that a decision as to future prospects will not be made by him, and that he will not find it easy to remove me from the picture. It is my present intention to obtain an appointment as vice admiral in the fleet.

Fortunately for Leahy's career, Secretary Swanson did not share the opinion of Admiral Standley. On 12 February 1935, when President Roosevelt approved the flag officer list, Leahy was scheduled to relieve Vice Admiral Thomas T. Craven in command of Battleship Divisions, Battle Force, with the rank of vice admiral. Leahy in turn would be relieved as chief of the Bureau of Navigation by Rear Admiral Adolphus Andrews. As Leahy wrote Admiral Reeves a few days later, "It will certainly feel good to escape from this desk, even if it does involve dumping the load on my good friend Adolphus. However the navy needs him here and will need him badly for the next couple of years."[15]

After his performance of duty as chief of BuNav, Bill Leahy had every right to expect a good seagoing assignment. His success in dealing with Congress and the reforms he accomplished stood him in good stead when the time came for him to leave. As he made a farewell appearance before the House Subcommittee on Naval Appropriations, the chairman, Grover H. Cary of Kentucky, welcomed him:

> Admiral, we understand that you cannot resist the call of the sea and will not serve your full tour of duty as Chief of the Bureau of Navigation. If that is your wish, of course we are glad that you will be able to realize it; but we shall miss you up here. It has been a genuine pleasure to know you and to do business with you. You will carry with you our best wishes.[16]

One man who did not go to sea then in spite of Admiral Reeves's best efforts was Rear Admiral Ernest J. King. In view of the Japanese withdrawal from the Washington Treaty at the end of 1934, Reeves wanted a tough, no-nonsense officer in command of naval aviation in the Pacific. Accordingly, Leahy's list for 1935 gave King that job and the president approved it, but Swanson, who objected to losing his two best bureau chiefs at the same time, persuaded FDR to change his mind. The upshot was that King had to stay another year, not getting out of Washington until 1936.

One by-product of the announcement of Leahy's new job was a statement about him by the Japanese, which he copied with amusement in his journal. It said, falsely, that he had been appointed to head the "Combined Fleet," which was a Japanese term, and, correctly, that he was a big-ship, big-gun advocate, but that he also understood air power. It termed him a "suitable candidate" for commanding the "great fleet in the approaching emergency." It concluded by prophesying that he would succeed Standley as CNO, and "it is no mistake to predict a splendid future for this young and spirited admiral."

On Monday, 30 June, Adolphus Andrews relieved Leahy as chief of the Bureau of Navigation. FDR asked him to drop by the White House before leaving for the West Coast, and "We had a half hour's talk about the navy, naval affairs, and things in general. He had nothing of importance to tell me, but apparently just wanted to have an informal talk to wish me good fortune in my new command."

During the long trip by train across the continent, which included stops to see family and friends in Chicago and Wausau, Bill Leahy had ample time to reflect on what he had achieved as chief of BuNav:

> In thinking of the two long, difficult years in Washington, now happily concluded with a promotion to the rank of vice admiral, the following are among the accomplishments that assist in justifying the efforts expended:
>
> Legislative authority and funds to increase the enlisted force of the navy from 82,000 to 93,500.
>
> Provision of funds with which to start building ships up to treaty strength.
>
> Legislative authority to increase the authorized number of officers from 5,499 to 6,531.
>
> Extension of the process of selection for promotion down to the rank of junior lieutenant.
>
> Change of Navy Regulations restating the duties and responsibilities of subdivisions of the Navy Department by the so-called Roosevelt Reorganization Board of 1933.
>
> Establishment of a group of aeronautical engineers.
>
> Legislative authority to employ "aviation cadets" in active service for periods of four years.
>
> Provision of a limited number of enlisted servants for officers stationed ashore.

Leahy had good reason to be satisfied with his tour in Washington. By this time he had successfully run two of the navy's most important bureaus, and he had had service in many types of ships over the years, but none in aircraft carriers or in submarines. For Leahy was strictly a surface sailor, and now, in the summer of 1935, he was returning to his first love—battleships. And it was remarkable that he was given the job of commanding battleship divisions without first having had command of a single battleship division.

The USS *West Virginia*

Vice Admiral Leahy reads orders assuming Command Battleship Divisions on board the USS *West Virginia*, 1935

On 13 July, with "appropriate ceremonial formality, I relieved Vice Admiral T. T. Craven and assumed command of the Battleship Divisions of the Battle Force, with the rank of Vice Admiral, flying my flag on the U.S.S. *West Virginia*, commanded by Captain R[oscoe] F. Dillen, USN."

The battleships of his day were not the sleek, fast, powerful ones that would be coming out in a few years, but they were formidable, and they would be the mainstay of the navy's planning until the Japanese, by their air attack on Pearl Harbor, changed everything.

# CHAPTER 5

# In Time of Peace . . .

Pleased to be back at sea after two years ashore in the "grilling" duty as chief of BuNav, Vice Admiral Leahy felt that the frosting on the cake was to be under Admiral Reeves, who had been a shipmate on the old *Oregon* and a firm friend ever since.

At sixty years of age in 1935, Leahy could look forward at best to four years of further naval service. If all went well in the present tour of sea duty, he was in line to become the next chief of naval operations. After that he would retire, unless the war that seemed more probable every day demanded further service from him. .

Following routine drills and a visit to San Francisco, where he marveled at the partially completed bridges from San Francisco to Oakland and across the Golden Gate, he took the Battle Force to sea, using the cruiser *Houston* as the "enemy fleet." Battleship guns trained on her, and destroyers and aircraft made mock attacks. The exercise was chiefly noteworthy because aboard the *Houston* was Franklin D. Roosevelt and a party of friends, including Secretary of the Interior Harold Ickes and WPA Administrator Harry Hopkins. FDR enjoyed the exercise enormously, and when it was over, the *Houston* took the politicos on a fishing trip-cruise through the Panama Canal to Charleston, South Carolina, while the navy went back to work.

The fishing trip almost died aborning, for just then Mussolini ordered his troops to invade Ethiopia. Characteristically, Leahy felt contempt for the timidity of the League of Nations, which failed to accuse Italy of unprovoked

aggression. Instead the league weakly "found that Ethiopia took no aggressive action." He did not, however, seem to see Italy's adventurism as particularly ominous.

Shortly after the *Houston* had parted company, Leahy was infuriated that
October when Walter Winchell, the radio broadcaster and gossip columnist,
predicted that he would be the next CINCUS. "There is no basis for such a
statement," he wrote furiously, "and its dissemination is just exactly of no
help whatever." Fortunately the misguided prediction did no harm, as he
found out in a trip to Washington for service on a selection board. There he
learned that according to present plans, he was scheduled to relieve Admiral
Standley as chief of naval operations in December 1936. Thus Leahy's final sea
duty would last little more than a year.

In 1936, Leahy summarized the gloomy situation of the world, noting such
things as Mussolini's formal annexation of Ethiopia and the outbreak of the
Spanish Civil War. Hitler's occupation of the Rhineland gave the admiral
occasion to note the inability of the nations of Europe to "reach a decision as
to which side of the inevitable conflict they would take." In common with
most naval officers, he saw the greater danger in the Far East where the rapid
growth of Japan's military power pointed to the "probability or the certainty
of a war in the western Pacific between eastern and western powers at some
time in the future."

As the fleet sailed for a week of battle maneuvers in February, unpleasant
news came in by radio. The death of King George V of Great Britain Leahy
felt would have "no effect whatever" on affairs of the world, but he was
considerably more disturbed by the condition of Secretary Swanson, "desperately ill in the Naval Hospital in Washington." A week later came the news
of the death of Assistant Secretary Henry Roosevelt, who had "been an
intimate acquaintence of mine, . . . in his death I lose a valued and reliable
friend, while the loss to the navy in the present unsettled conditions at home
and abroad is serious beyond estimation."

It seemed likely that Swanson's illness and Henry Roosevelt's death might
give Admiral Standley the opportunity to torpedo Leahy's prospects, but if he
had any such ideas, they didn't work out. On 19 February Leahy received an
order from the president directing him to assume command of the Battle
Force on 30 March with the rank of admiral.

At that time the navy was limited by statute to four admirals: CNO;
CINCUS, who was commander in chief Pacific Fleet; commander in chief
Asiatic Fleet; and Commander Battle Force.★

A surprise drill in mid-March sent all ships in the San Pedro–San Diego area
rushing out to sea in a test of fleet readiness. One of the battleships was caught

★Actually, the title CINCUS was assumed by the senior officer whenever two of the three
combat fleets got together, but in practice CINCUS commanded the Pacific Fleet. Shortly
before Pearl Harbor, the CINCUS and Pacific Fleet commands were separated.

with her main propulsion plant down, and her embarrassed skipper had to do a good deal of explaining to his division commander and to Leahy. In view of his certainty that war was coming, Leahy believed that there could not be too many drills, and if some officers were embarrassed, it was a small price to pay for fleet readiness.

On 30 March Leahy put on the four stars of an admiral and at 10:00 Rear Admiral Clarence S. Kempff, a classmate and shipmate from the *Oregon* days, relieved him as Commander Battleships. At 10:30, having moved to the *California* from the *West Virginia*, Leahy then relieved Admiral Harris Laning as Commander Battle Force. His new command consisted of four divisions of battleships, for a total of fourteen, two divisions of light cruisers, eight in all. Some forty-three more ships composed a destroyer flotilla, with a light cruiser as flagship. Also included were the only aircraft carriers in the navy: *Saratoga*, *Lexington*, and the much less satisfactory *Ranger* and *Langley*.

At Pearl Harbor, Leahy had eight mine-laying destroyers, whose flagship was his old *Shawmut* of 1923, now named *Oglala*. In all, he commanded a total of seventy-eight combatant ships, manned by 2,762 officers and 30,370 enlisted. Among the officers to serve under him who later rose to high command were Claude C. Bloch and Ernest J. King.

On 27 April the fleet went out for a fleet problem. Leahy's classmate, Vice Admiral Arthur J. Hepburn, known to all by his middle name "Japy," commanded the WHITE fleet, which was defending the Panama Canal against Leahy's BLUE fleet. It was, in Leahy's mind, a simple matter of evasive tactics. Much more worrisome to him was the fact that his smaller BLUE fleet would be all that was left in the Pacific if the amateur strategists in Washington had their way and divided the fleet between the two oceans. "A fleet at least as strong in all essential areas as any possible enemy must be kept together to avoid probability of disaster. Its geographic location at the time war is declared can have little effect on the final outcome of the war, but must not at that time be widely separated."

When the Battle Force returned to Long Beach, the annual changes of flag officer assignments were announced. One of Leahy's classmates, Rear Admiral Thomas Hart, who would command the slender American forces in the Far East after the attack on Pearl Harbor, was being sent ashore after a successful tour in command of the heavy cruisers in the Scouting Force. Another officer, widely believed to be slated to become CNO some day, Rear Admiral Joseph K. Taussig, took over a battleship division. He never did get the job of CNO, for FDR turned him down. Another of Leahy's classmates, who had been his junior, now, in the wonderful way they shuffled flags in those days, became his boss. "Japy" Hepburn became CINCUS. Since Leahy was slated to become CNO in another six months, there was no reason to move him from where he was.

Of course, if FDR lost the election that fall, a new president might have different ideas as to who should be CNO, so it was with considerable interest that Leahy turned on the radio to hear the Democratic Convention nominate Franklin Roosevelt and John Nance Garner for second terms. The Republican slate consisted of Alfred Landon of Kansas and Frank Knox of Chicago. "At the present time, it appears almost certain that the Democrats will be successful in the election to be held in November."

On a cruise to Pearl Harbor that summer, Leahy found things much changed since his previous visits. Honolulu had become a prosperous city of 150,000 with "attractive residences stretching miles into what was before unoccupied worthless land." Amid the various luaus, exhibitions of tree climbing and the hula, and the formal dinners, Leahy found that "social obligations are demanding from flag officers so much time as to make burdensome the kindly intentions of the inhabitants."

The main problem in the islands, as he saw it, was the large number of unassimilated Japanese who "do not admit of an inferiority in any respect," and their increasing numbers seemed to make "serious racial clashes . . . inevitable."

Curiously enough, at almost the same moment, President Roosevelt was also worrying about the Japanese problem in the islands, and in a memo to CNO, he proposed that "every Japanese citizen or noncitizen of the Island of Oahu" who was observed fraternizing with crews of ships calling at Honolulu should have his name placed on a list for being placed in a "concentration camp in the event of trouble."[1]

While in the islands, Leahy had an unpleasant interview with classmate Harry Yarnell, who "expressed to me sharp disappointment and disapproval of everybody" because he had not won one of the top jobs in the fleet. He apparently blamed Leahy for not doing enough for him when he was in BuNav. "It did not appear either useful or polite to inform an angry person of the efforts made without success by several of his friends, including myself, to obtain for him a high command in the fleet."

Yarnell, however, was crying before he was hurt, for in the not too far distant future, he would take over the Asiatic fleet with the rank of admiral. And he and Leahy would have a great deal of work together as the Japanese stepped up their activities in east and southeast Asia.

In September, another prickly character, Admiral William S. Sims, died, and Leahy recalled his brief service with him in the last months of World War I. He had thought highly of Sims for his success in winning friendly cooperation between the British and American navies, but later, "his arbitrary employment of publicity for his own ends alienated most of his following, even in the junior ranks of the navy. . . . For those of us who are familiar with his service history, Admiral Sims provides a splendid example of what not to do. He came very near to being a great naval officer."

Following the reelection of Roosevelt, Leahy spent his remaining time as Commander Battle Force (ComBatFor) in routine exercises. He made one cruise aboard the *Ranger* in order to learn more about carrier operations. Although he was a fully paid-up member of the "Gun Club," he was not blind to the potential power of carrier forces. "There is no doubt whatever," he wrote as he completed the *Ranger* cruise, "that America's carrier-based air planes have reached a marvelous efficiency."

Perhaps to bring his thoughts together as a result of his latest experience with carriers, Leahy recorded a long entry on the good sense of the American services and Congress in not making the same mistakes the British had made following World War I. At that time, listening to the air enthusiasts, the British had transferred all naval aviation to the Royal Air Force for "efficiency and economy." Since the naval aviators were greatly outnumbered by their land-based colleagues, they learned to conform or keep quiet if they wanted to be promoted. Carrier planes in the RAF tended to be cast-off land models, hastily modified for use at sea. Promises made to give naval aviation equal support with land-based air were quickly forgotten when peacetime budget crunches came along.

In spite of the air zealots, the U.S. Navy managed to keep control of its own air operations, and the marines held on to their own air arm as well. The efficiency of American naval aircraft, Leahy argued, "is largely, if not entirely, due to the fact that they are operated exclusively by sea-going personnel instead of by a separate air force as is the case in England and other naval powers."

A week after the election, the *New York Times* carried a story about changes in the naval high command. Leahy, of course, was to be the new chief of naval operations, and Claude Bloch would take over as ComBatFor. Admiral Standley, the current CNO, would retire.[2]

Leahy's appointment was generally well received by the press. The *Literary Digest* stated that his subordinates thought of him as "a sailors's admiral," one who "wears his honors lightly and never lords it over the mess."[3] *Newsweek* called him "gruff in voice, a strict disciplinarian, he drives himself and everybody else. During fleet maneuvers, when high-ranking officers must remain almost constantly on duty, Leahy's tremendous physical endurance enables him to wear down younger assistants. His men say: 'Old Bill can stick on the bridge for six weeks without sleep.'" Then, descending to cliché, *Newsweek* concluded, "off duty he is kindly, friendly, and as comfortable as an old shoe."[4]

Leahy's reaction to his appointment was characteristic, a mixture of pride and regret:

> Pleasure for this selection to the highest office in the navy is at least tempered by a realization that it brings to an end a service at sea that commenced on board

the frigate *Constellation* in June 1893, and that has in the forty-three intervening years provided splendid opportunities for service in peace and war in many parts of the world.

On the last day of 1936, Leahy was sworn in as chief of naval operations, to be effective 2 January 1937. His friend Secretary Swanson was well enough to attend, along with all the high-ranking naval officers in Washington. The prospect of his new job seemed to him "more than difficult," but with the "splendid talent" available, he hoped that with "an efficient and adequate sea defense," the United States could avoid "being drawn into any foreign wars."

Bill Leahy took over the office at a singularly fortunate time for himself and for the well-being of the navy. He was not fated to be its war commander, but he would be the one who prepared the way for the two-ocean navy and helped to provide the ships and planes which made it possible.

Of immeasurable importance would be his friendship with President Roosevelt reaching to those days in Washington when they had nearby offices in the old War, State, and Navy Building, and when his *Dolphin* had served as a dispatch boat for FDR. It was evident by this time that Roosevelt was most comfortable working with those he had known in the days when he was assistant secretary. Three consecutive CNOs, Standley, Leahy, and Harold R. Stark, were men he had known well back then.[5]

Another plus was the fact that the flamboyant former chief of staff of the army, Douglas MacArthur, was safely in the Philippines, a long way from the power center in Washington and an equal distance from the Washington press corps he was wont to play as on a musical instrument. The present chief of staff, General Malin Craig, was quieter. Although he had the president's respect, he had none of the close personal relationship enjoyed by the new CNO. Although it is a myth that Roosevelt's interest in and love for the navy meant that the sea service had unlimited budgets and a vast building program, it is true that FDR, who could talk to anyone at any time about almost everything, felt more comfortable in dealing with navy men, just as his successor, Harry Truman, preferred the army.

In Roosevelt's overwhelming victory in the recent election, the presidential coattails had pulled into office large Democratic majorities in both houses. The navy's good friend, Carl Vinson, to no one's surprise, had retained his seat and his chairmanship of the House Naval Affairs Committee. Senator Park Trammell, co-sponsor of the Vinson–Trammell Act for rebuilding the navy, had died the previous May, but his place as chairman of the Senate Committee on Naval Affairs had been taken by David I. Walsh of Massachusetts. While the senator was an isolationist, so to some extent was Leahy. Walsh was a strong big-navy man. His convictions were as firm as those of the late Senator Trammell, and he was far more eloquent in speaking out for the sea service. He had a ready means of pro-navy publicity through a special sympathetic relationship with the Washington *Evening Star* and *Sunday Star*, as well as with the local NBC radio station.

Leahy's position in Washington was also immensely strengthened by his long friendship with Secretary Swanson. But the secretary was a chronically ill man and frequently had to name an acting secretary. Although in January 1937, Roosevelt appointed as assistant secretary Charles A. Edison, son of the famous inventor, Edison was more interested in the technical side of the Navy Department, so Swanson usually picked Leahy to appear for him, largely because the new CNO had a larger view of the job.

Soon after he took office, Leahy summoned the chiefs of the bureaus and offices to a conference "for the purpose of discussing policy of the office in relation to other offices of the Department." Some officers expected Leahy to abandon his previous attitude of the independence of the bureaus and adopt Admiral Standley's position of the supremacy of the CNO. It might have been tempting, but Leahy remained faithful to the conviction over which he had risked his career in opposing the former CNO. Now that he held that post, he saw no reason to change. He was dedicated to the principle of *primus inter pares*.

Of course, his job by its nature could not be limited entirely to that role. He was chief of naval operations, with duties defined in Navy Regulations, and there was a limited command function attached to his position. No matter how much he asserted the independence of the bureaus, in the end he knew that the president and the secretary would hold him responsible. To him the privileges and to him the brickbats, if any.

The president did not wait long before sending for Leahy. On 4 January, only two days after he had taken over, the new CNO reported to the White House for a conference which lasted for an hour "until disturbed by the arrival of a foreign minister with urgent business."

The talk ranged over a wide variety of subjects, the Caribbean, Central and South America, and means of preventing European nations from extending their influence in the western hemisphere, in violation of the Monroe Doctrine. FDR toyed with the idea of transferring the Coast Guard from the Treasury Department to the navy, an act normally done only in time of war.

The most important feature of their talk involved plans for building a new navy, constructing new ships to replace the venerable veterans of World War I vintage. And, once built, the ships would have to be manned, supplied, and maintained.

The building program was by no means extensive. Just four days after his talk with Bill Leahy, FDR announced at a press conference that he was directing the Navy Department to proceed with the construction of two battleships, the *North Carolina* and the *Washington*, replacements for the *Arkansas*, *Texas*, and *New York*, which would be twenty-six years old by the time the new ships would be ready for service. Replacement of three ships by two could scarcely be called a rush to rearm.

FDR went on to remind the reporters that the United States had faithfully observed terms of the London Treaty that forbade laying down any battleships before 1 January 1937. In fact, he stressed, the only reason the United States was moving now was that Great Britain, France, Italy, and Germany were already building new ships. The United States, unfortunately, had to follow suit.

> We had hoped [the president concluded] that the date of replacement would have been deferred for another term so as to avoid the building of these new ships. However, agreement could not be reached, although the United States delegation did everything in their power to get an extension of new building, replacement building, agreed to by other nations, but it did not go through. That is much to our regret and I think that is all we can say.[6]

Considering this inauspicious beginning and the reluctance of the commander in chief to spend money, the building program begun during Leahy's stewardship is remarkable. To be sure, the headlong rush of world powers toward war was more persuasive to the administration and to the congress than any of Leahy's most compelling arguments.

When, on 12 January, the president's authorization for the new ships was officially received in Leahy's office, it was a long way from beginning construction. At the earliest, it would be March before the plans and specifications could be checked and readied for builders. Two months would be allowed for the bidding process. Secretary Swanson wanted one ship built in a private shipyard and the other in a naval shipyard, either at Brooklyn or Philadelphia. If this schedule could be met, Leahy hoped that actual construction could begin about 1 June.

Meanwhile a huge winter storm caused calamitous flooding in the Mississippi and Ohio river valleys, and President Roosevelt summoned the army and navy to assist the federal agencies and the Red Cross in disaster relief. This activity brought together, apparently for the first time, Leahy and the controversial WPA Administrator, Harry Hopkins. Almost the only thing they had in common was the fact that they were both born in Iowa and both had tremendous admiration and respect for Franklin Roosevelt. During World War II, these men—the cynical, pragmatic, informed Hopkins, and the formal, reserved Leahy—would work side by side as FDR's closest advisors.

In the office of the CNO, the able assistant CNO, Rear Admiral William S. Pye, minded the routine business, enabling Leahy to concentrate on other aspects of the job, which included wooing congressmen and presenting a favorable view of the navy to the public.

The requests that crossed his desk ranged the world in geography and in

WDL with Harry Hopkins about 1939 (Courtesy, National Archives)

variety. The State Department wanted to borrow some destroyers to assist South American nations in developing their own naval tactics. A congressman from San Francisco wanted the navy to send a fleet to help celebrate the opening of the Golden Gate Bridge. The Russians wanted to have one or two battleships built for them in American shipyards. The State Department and even the president thought it a good idea, but Leahy objected. He knew that America had limited shipbuilding capacity, and he hoped to fill the available building ways with ships for the American, not the Russian, navy. He managed to drag his feet throughout his term, and when he left office, the Russian ships were still only on paper.

In his plans to rebuild the navy, Leahy had to contend with a powerful adversary, his own commander in chief. Roosevelt simply was not ready to move rapidly in rebuilding the armed forces of the United States. He loved the navy, but he was going to keep it on short rations. From Bill Leahy's point of view, it was a starvation diet.

At a House subcommittee hearing on 21 January, Leahy pleaded for adequate naval funding. He had often testified when he had been chief of BuOrd and of BuNav, but this was the first time he had been in the witness chair as CNO. He wanted to leave the subcommittee in no doubt that he considered the world situation dangerous.

> I need only to refer to the political conditions in the world at this moment, both in Europe and in the Far East, to emphasize the fact that the Navy must be prepared for eventualities that may develop from the international situation and that our Government may be brought suddenly face to face with a situation that it had no part in creating and over which it may have no control. For this reason, in considering the estimates of the Navy, conditions in the world on all sides of us must be considered, together with the strength of our Navy as compared with the strength of other great naval powers.

In reply to the president's latest cutbacks, which had already trimmed $75 million from the navy's budget, he added:

> The Navy Department has already pruned the preliminary figures submitted by its various agencies to the minimum with what it considers are the needs for reasonable national security. I can therefore state that it would, in my opinion, be jeopardizing that security to reduce our present number of vessels and aircraft in full commission, to delay or reduce our shipbuilding or aircraft programs, or to fail to build up our shore establishments and reserve stocks in support of the fleet.

Leahy concluded his presentation by pointing out that at the rate of shipbuilding going on in 1937, it would be 1942 before the United States Navy would be equal in size to that of Great Britain.[7]

This wisdom of using the British as a point of reference was proved in mid-February when the Royal Navy announced that it was adding two battleships to its building program. Two days later, Leahy broke precedent by calling a press conference. Previous CNOs had been content to let the secretary do the talking. But Leahy had something to say, and he felt he could say it better than the ailing Secretary Swanson could.

As he faced the reporters, he pointed out that the new British ships were, unlike those ordered for the United States, additions, not replacements. That statement put pressure on the administration, as Leahy hoped it would. It might have cost Leahy his job, for FDR had fired people for less, but Leahy got away with it, largely because the naval appropriation bill, as finally passed, came closer to Roosevelt's views than to Leahy's.

As a sop to the navy, the president did give the nod to a few small projects, about $19 million worth, to be paid for out of public works funds, but the major public works improvement projects—the modernization of the carriers *Saratoga* and *Lexington* and five battleships—never saw the light of day after being referred to congressional committees. In April, FDR turned down a ten-year building program for auxiliaries, but Leahy hoped he could talk him into a one-year program and the modernization of the carriers, "essential if these two ships are to remain in active service with the fleet." Leahy had to wait over a year before the modernization of the *Saratoga* and *Lexington* was authorized.

When he was not appearing before the Congress, pleading with the president, or dealing with the problems of the Navy Department, Leahy had to face the inevitable social life of the capital, much of it obligatory for high officials. In this activity Louise took full and active part. "Mother was a great help to him in his social activities," recalled their son. "She was an expert at it."

On 27 February, Leahy attended a dinner of the Society of the Carabao, an order composed of American army and navy officers who had served in the islands during the Philippine Insurrection. The four hundred members and guests heard President Manuel Quezon give a speech of appreciation of the good that the United States had done his country since then. No one had opposed the Americans any harder than he. His "two controlling passions at that time were to kill American soldiers and to avoid being killed by the same soldiers, and that preoccupation with the business of avoiding the latter made it impossible for him to indulge himself in the pleasure of the former."

The following day at a reception for Quezon, Bill Leahy saw for the first time in many years the former army chief of staff, General Douglas MacArthur, now serving in the Philippine army with the rank of field marshal. As usual, the outspoken MacArthur was trying to be a major policy maker. He told Leahy that in return for a few patrol boats given to the Philippine navy, he saw no reason why the U.S. Navy should not retain its bases in the islands. "I did not inform MacArthur," Leahy confided to his journal, "that the present policy of the government seems to be to eventually remove all naval bases except for one unfortified station for the maintenance and upkeep of the ships of the Asiatic Fleet as may be necessary to take care of America's peacetime interests on the coast of Asia."

The continuing battle between Leahy and President Roosevelt led in due course to a luncheon meeting of the two men in the White House. On 15 April, FDR and Bill Leahy sat down in the Oval Office to discuss, of all things, calibers of battleship guns.

> Lunch in the President's office was served by servants placing the little table equipment necessary on the President's working desk, wheeling a cabinet containing the hot food, and then withdrawing. The President, sitting in his chair, serves the different articles of food from the cabinet without interrupting the conversation which may be of a secret or confidential nature, as it was in this instance, as there are no persons in the room other than the President and his guest. President Roosevelt transacts confidential business in this way during his

lunch hour nearly every day. The lunch today consisted of green soup, eggs with mushrooms, and strawberries for dessert.

During the lunch, FDR tried to persuade Leahy to accept 14-inch guns as the main battery weapons in any subsequent battleship. Leahy protested, even though he knew that the new British battleships, the *King George V*-class, were being so equipped. FDR's reasons were simple: 14-inch guns cost a lot less and weighed a lot less than 16-inch guns. That meant that smaller ships could be built, and the reduction in tonnage would save additional money. The new CNO argued forcibly, pointing out that the Japanese had given no assurances on limiting the caliber of their guns, and therefore, all new battleships ought to be provided with 16-inch guns. It took a good deal of argument over the coming months, but Leahy won in the end. All new battleships had 16-inch main batteries. And, as predicted, the Japanese did not stick to the 14-inch size. In fact, their new battleships were rumored to have batteries even larger. Naval intelligence had heard of the "special 16-inch gun" ships the Japanese were building. Of course, these were the new battleships *Yamato* and *Musashi*, which were equipped with 18.1-inch guns.

Leahy had long since learned that decisions on national defense are not always made solely on strategic or wholly military reasons. On 19 May, Secretary of State Cordell Hull inserted himself into the debate on the caliber of battleship guns. While officials from State fretted over Japanese reaction to American 16-inch guns, Leahy laid it on the line.

> I informed the conference that in the Navy Department there is no difference of opinion regarding the necessity of installing 16-inch guns on our new ships, and that any action leading toward the reduction of American battleships of gun caliber below 16-inch would have to be taken by some other department of the government, which department must assume responsibility for providing less efficient units of sea defenses.

As far as Leahy was concerned, the matter was settled. While State continued to dither, and while FDR wavered, the chief of naval operations continued to act on the assumption that the new battleships would have the larger caliber guns. He was right.

On 22 May, Leahy accompanied the president and a goodly number of his friends on a cruise from the Washington Navy Yard to Quantico, Virginia, aboard the presidential yacht *Potomac*, an ancient sidewheel steamer, with hand-operated engine valves."* Among the guests were Vice President Garner, Senators James F. Byrnes of South Carolina and Claude Pepper of Florida, Congressmen Sam Rayburn of Texas, and Carl Vinson of Georgia. Also present was Harry Hopkins, who by this time had became FDR's closest friend and confidant.

---

*This *Potomac* was soon replaced by a newer diesel-propelled vessel, 165 feet in length, also named *Potomac*.

The cruise itself is unimportant, but the fact that Leahy was invited to come along to witness a review and attend a baseball game is significant. In his position as CNO, Leahy had a good many dealings with the White House, but for him to be included on a yachting trip or any of the other informal activities set up by FDR meant that he was moving toward the inner circle. On such occasions the guests were of two sorts: those FDR felt could be of political assistance to him, and those he liked. There was no conceivable way that Leahy could be of political assistance; he had to be there because the president liked him.

On this occasion, the outing was not a success. The heavens opened and the review and the ballgame were rained out. Leahy and the others joined the hoi polloi who had driven down and ate in the mess hall with the marines. Leahy had been forsighted enough to have an automobile waiting for him at Quantico, and making his excuses to the president, took his leave, providing transportation back to Washington to three grateful guests who wanted to get away.

The end of May marked the fortieth anniversary of Leahy's graduation from the Naval Academy, and of the fifty-nine members still living, twenty-one appeared in Annapolis for the festivities. The Class of 1897 took time out to present to the academy

> with appropriate ceremony a stone seat correctly called an Exedra. This very handsome stone seat, for which we paid about $4,000, is located just behind the statue of Tecumseh, which was some years ago presented by the Class of 1891.

On 23 July, serving as acting secretary of the navy, Leahy attended his first cabinet meeting. Since President Roosevelt was one of the few chief executives to make his cabinet a working, consultative body, Leahy's description of a meeting is of some interest.

> Friday at two p.m. is the routine time for meetings of the President's Cabinet. By that hour the Secretaries of the Executive Departments have congregated in the Cabinet Room, which contains a long table, chairs marked for each member of the Cabinet, and on the walls inferior portraits of Jackson, Jefferson, and Woodrow Wilson.
>
> At about two o'clock, the President arrives in a wheel chair and takes a seat at the head of the table. The Vice President's seat is opposite at the end of the table, and the Secretaries of the Executive Departments are seated on both sides of the long table in order of precedence of their Departments, as follows: State, Treasury, War, Justice, Navy, Post Office, Interior, Commerce, and Labor.
>
> After a very free discussion of general subjects, the President asks each Cabinet officer in succession to report on any business of his Department. The conference today lasted from two until four o'clock.

The entry quoted is typical of Leahy's infuriating reticence for the rest of the time he kept his journal. He relates what he did, but he carefully refrains from telling anything of background, of reasons, or of his own feelings. He tended to carry his reticence to the point of self-effacement.

During the summer, with Congress in recess and only routine matters in the office, Leahy decided to take a few days leave. But in August he was summoned back to Washington in order to deal with the unexpectedly serious developments in the Shanghai and Nanking areas of China.

The International Settlement in Shanghai was still, as it had been when Leahy was there during the Boxer Rebellion, a city within a city, its forty thousand residents governed by an elected council representing all nationalities in the settlement. Each nation, however, claimed that its particular area was part of its national territory, and each had a small military force to protect its interests. When one of their officers was killed in Shanghai, the Japanese sent in reinforcements. Harry Yarnell, finally having his top job in command of the Asiatic Fleet, was to find no smooth sailing. For starters, he asked for one thousand additional marines.

American strength in the area was rather less than met the eye. Marines in Peking and Shanghai and army troops in Tientsin, totalled just under three thousand men, far too weak to do any good if Admiral Yarnell's mission was to be anything more than showing the flag. From his comparatively new flagship *Augusta*, he commanded a motley group of some dozen destroyers, six submarines, and six river gunboats, especially designed for operating on Chinese rivers. One of them was named *Panay*.

High level conferences following Leahy's return to Washington were aimed, on the one hand, at keeping the United States from taking sides in the argument between Japan and China and, on the other, at protecting American nationals, especially those in Shanghai. The forty thousand residents of the International Settlement were being guarded by some three thousand European and American troops, while playing involuntary hosts to some two hundred thousand terrified Chinese refugees. "It appears likely that the International Settlement will experience rioting by the starved refugees, possibly looting by troops of either of the belligerents, and epidemics of disease."

No one wanted a war over the issue, even though the Japanese seemed to be spoiling for a fight. At a cabinet meeting, which Leahy attended for the navy, the president asked him where the American marines were located in the crisis. At the point of maximum danger, replied the CNO. FDR then wanted to know why they were there instead of, say, the British. That, replied Leahy, was because the British are smart.[8]

The State Department's expert on far eastern affairs, Dr. Stanley K. Hornbeck, moderated the strong call for action urged by Yarnell and Leahy and its near avoidance recommended by his superior, Secretary of State Cordell Hull. Yarnell, for openers, asked for four additional cruisers; Hull felt that "sending additional naval vessels at this time might have an irritating effect on some of the belligerents, might cause international complications from

accidental or intentional injury to one of the ships, . . . and would also bring
alarming headlines in the American press."

Hornbeck recommended two cruisers, and, accepting the compromise,
Leahy, on 1 September, traveled up to Hyde Park to try to sell the idea to the
president. FDR turned him down cold. While Hull had been afraid of adverse
public reaction, Roosevelt was afraid of losing ships the navy could ill afford
to lose with no compensating gain. He may have been influenced by the
bombing of the American liner *President Hoover* by an unidentified plane,
probably Chinese, while she was anchored in the Yangtze River. Roosevelt
told Leahy to have Yarnell charter a merchant vessel if he needed it for the
evacuation of Americans.

"I tried my best to get the cruisers for you," Leahy postscripted in a letter to
Yarnell.[9]

When the Japanese admiral at Shanghai demanded that he be informed of
the movements of American merchant ships in and out of the Yangtze River,
whether bound to or from Shanghai or Nanking, Admiral Yarnell wanted to
refuse, but Hull cut the ground from under him by cabling the consul general
that there was no objection "to the giving of such notifications, but if and as
notifications are given they should be given on the basis of courtesy and
practical expedience rather than on the basis of waiving the right to immunity
from interference which the giving of an express promise on our part would
imply."[10] Furthermore, both the Japanese and the Chinese were to receive the
"courtesy notice."

From that welter of obscurity, Yarnell properly decided that Hull was
trying to give him orders which should have come through the Navy Department. He proceeded to raise some hackles by notifying Leahy that he had
authorized his ships to fire back if attacked by aircraft. They were also to
protect merchant ships from similar attack. This was bad enough from Hull's
cautious viewpoint, but Yarnell made things worse when he issued a statement to the press, which he summarized in a telegram to Leahy.

> The policy of Cincaf [Commander in Chief Asiatic Fleet] during the present
> emergency is to employ United States naval forces under his command so as to
> offer all possible protection and assistance to our nationals in cases where
> needed. . . . Most American citizens now in China are engaged in businesses or
> professions. . . . these persons are unwilling to leave until their businesses have
> been destroyed or they are forced to leave due to actual physical danger. Until
> such time comes our naval force cannot be withdrawn without failure in our
> duty and without bringing discredit on the United States Navy. In giving
> assistance and protection, our naval forces may at times be exposed to dangers
> which will in cases be slight but in any case these risks must be accepted.[11]

FDR was annoyed with Yarnell's statement and directed Leahy to telegraph
him "that hereafter any statement regarding 'policy' contemplated by the

Commander-in-Chief Asiatic Fleet must be referred to the Secretary of the Navy for approval."[12]

The Japanese announced that Nanking would receive a heavy bombing on 21 September and advised all foreigners to leave the city. Leahy's wrote furiously,

> This threat by Japan to conduct a bombing raid against the civil population of China is another evidence, and a conclusive one, that the old accepted rules of warfare are no longer in effect. . . . There is today an urgent need for a restatement of the international rules governing the conduct of war. No other possible action seems to me to be so important to the future peace of the world. . . . Some day Japan must be called to account, . . . and from all indications, the present splendid opportunity will be lost through lack of decision on the part of the major powers.

With Fluellen in Shakespeare's *Henry V*, Leahy believed, "'Tis expressly against the law of arms!"

The world would soon learn that the twentieth century was even more barbaric than the fifteenth century of Henry V. The subsequent Rape of Nanking shocked people everywhere. Unhappily, it was only the first of horrors—the Bataan Death March, Lidice, Belsen, Auschwitz—the list is too long and too sickening to continue.

Most Americans looked the other way. Nanking was on the far side of the world, even more distant than Europe, and two huge oceans protected the North American continent. To Leahy such a view was folly. The democratic nations needed to band together "in opposition to those violations of treaties and those ignorings of humane instincts" which he felt were "creating a state of international anarchy and instability from which there is not escape through mere isolation or neutrality."

He therefore approved President Roosevelt's "quarantine speech" in Chicago on 5 October. The CNO was happy that the president had called for cooperation with those who would oppose the aggressive actions of Germany, Italy, and Japan. Leahy felt that such a policy would inevitably lead to war but that it was better than supine surrender. For a time FDR seemed to have joined the hardliners in opposing the powers soon to be designated as the Axis.

But if Leahy approved FDR's quarantine speech, he was one of the few who did, judging from the screams of outrage from conservative newspapers and isolationists. At once Roosevelt backed away from his position. The lack of any understanding of what he meant by the word "quarantine" gave him the opportunity. In the labyrinthine logic for which he was famous, he insisted that his speech by no means signaled the end of neutrality. It might even, he confided to a reporter, be an "expansion of neutrality," but only FDR knew what that phrase meant.

Roosevelt was really frightened by the reaction of the isolationist press. His speech had received support from a good many papers, particularly in the east, but the vehemence of the others caused him to put on the brakes. "It's a terrible thing," he later confided to Sam Rosenman, one of his closest aides, "to look over your shoulder when you are trying to lead—and to find no one there."[13]

Such subtleties as "expanded neutrality" were too much for a sailor like Leahy. Like others, he wondered and watched as American foreign policies that autumn were fraught with ambiguities, with uncertain responses to the actions of aggressor nations. There were, however, some encouraging signs. The president began to take over more and more major decisions in foreign affairs, shunting Hull more and more into peripheral matters. By the time World War II came along, Roosevelt was almost his own secretary of state, with the assistance of Undersecretary Sumner Welles, and of Harry Hopkins, who became general go-between with Churchill. In later years Leahy would be a part of this activity.

In November, Leahy had a long talk with FDR in the Oval Study on the second floor of the White House.* It ranged over the entire international situation, which soon led the formerly parsimonious Roosevelt to approve the idea of requesting four battleships to be laid down in fiscal 1939. FDR proposed that the annual fleet exercise be held in the Caribbean and South Atlantic in order to reassure Japan. Although to Leahy, this seemed to be giving in to those who wanted the major part of the fleet in the Atlantic, he went along. On the personal side, it seemed to him that Roosevelt was tired but well despite an abcessed tooth, which was extracted shortly after Leahy's visit.

The next day Leahy and Harry Hopkins left with FDR on a fishing trip aboard the *Potomac* in the Gulf of Mexico. The voyage was not a success. Leahy thought that FDR looked so listless that he even appeared ready to let Congress have its own way. All this was caused by an infection where the offending molar had been removed. In considerable pain, FDR cut the trip short to return to Washington for treatment. He arrived just in time to face what was the worst military crisis of his presidency to date.

On 12 December, Bill and Louise were dining with Secretary of War and Mrs. Harry H. Woodring at their residence on S Street. Summoned to the telephone, Leahy learned that the Japanese had sunk the American naval

---

*A good many writers mistakenly use the terms "Oval Office" and "Oval Study" interchangeably. The Oval Office is in the Executive Wing of the White House, while the Oval Study is on the second floor of the main building in the president's private quarters. FDR usually worked in the Oval Study in the evening, and it was there that he received his closest friends and advisors.

gunboat *Panay* in the Yangtze River above Nanking. Loss of life was unknown. Making his excuses to his hostess, he sped to the apartment of Secretary Hull in the Carlton Hotel. Dr. Hornbeck, who by this time had joined the hardliners, and several other State officials were present, but their deliberations did not impress the admiral favorably. "The Department of State seems," he wrote witheringly, "to be interested principally in getting the written record of this incident so complete as to provide defense against criticism."

Details were sketchy. The *Panay* was at anchor some distance above Nanking with three Standard Oil tankers nearby. All four ships were flying American colors; the *Panay* had a large flag painted on her awning, which was rigged horizontally over the deck and clearly visible from the air. Flags were painted on the superstructures of the three tankers. There was no possibility of their being seen as anything but American.

About 1:30 P.M., 12 December, at least six Japanese planes attacked, diving in succession and dropping about twenty bombs. The *Panay* suffered at least five hits and began to settle by the starboard bow. Her gravely injured commanding officer was taken ashore in a small boat with other wounded. The Japanese machine-gunned the boat.

After the air attack, two Japanese army patrol boats came down the river and pumped machine-gun bullets into the wreck of the *Panay*, which by this time had been abandoned. Soon the *Panay* sank in thirty fathoms of water. Two of the Standard Oil tankers were total losses. The British gunboat *Ladybird* had also been attacked, but she was not seriously harmed. The Japanese searched for survivors, but it soon became apparent that they wanted to dispose of witnesses when they began spraying the reeds near the river bank with machine-gun fire.

"It is, in my opinion, time to get the fleet ready for sea," Leahy wrote furiously, "to make an arrangement with the British Navy for joint action, and to inform the Japanese that we expect to protect our nationals."

Indignantly, President Roosevelt demanded an apology from the Japanese government, compensation, punishment of the perpetrators, and assurances that the incident would not be repeated. This response, in Leahy's view, did not go far enough. In talking with the president on 14 December, he urged "sending ships of the fleet to navy yards without delay to obtain fuel, clean bottoms, and take on sea stores preparatory for a cruise at sea." The president, he regretted, was not ready "to take that action at the present time."

To Leahy the issue was clear; the Japanese had challenged the United States, and the answer had to be firm and unmistakable. He was prepared to risk war by joining with the British in a blockade of Japan and all the territories she held in the Far East. But he was not president of the United States. Franklin Roosevelt was, and he vetoed Leahy's ideas. FDR was, however, considering seizing Japanese assets in the United States. Prompt Japanese disavowal of the actions of their planes in Nanking led to a settlement. They paid $2,214,007.36 as an "indemnification for losses to American property and injuries of American citizens." And so the incident was allowed to die away. But for the rest of his life, Leahy wondered whether the United States had made a mistake.

The odd thing is that the affair brought no cries of "Remember the *Panay!*" from the American people. The *Panay* was not the *Maine*, and the Yangtze River was not Havana Harbor. Few people wanted to send the fleet to China. Many more demanded that Americans get out of China altogether. Instead of rousing the country to anger, the *Panay* incident strengthened the isolationists and the pacifists. The incident enabled Representative Louis Ludlow of Indiana to get his proposed constitutional amendment out of the Judiciary Committee, where it had been languishing for months. Ludlow intended his bill to provide that, except in cases of direct attack, a declaration of war by Congress would have to be confirmed by a national referendum!

It took all the big guns of the administration and of congressional leadership to defeat the Ludlow proposal. When the vote was taken in the House in January it lost by the uncomfortably close margin of 209 to 188.

Yet the *Panay* incident, as the culmination of a year of Japanese aggression in Asia, jolted Roosevelt out of his habit of economy. He was at last prepared to build up the armed forces, especially the navy as the "First Line of Defense," a slogan intended to make his actions a bit more palatable to the isolationists. As one of FDR's biographers put it, his Christmas message to the people was "love thine enemy," but in his support of a limited rearmament program, it was "love thine enemy but carry a big stick."[14]

# CHAPTER 6

# . . . Prepare for War

In spite of Japanese promises, their soldiers continued to abuse and humiliate American and British subjects in China. Furious, the British planned to announce the "completion of naval preparations," which was only a step short of mobilization. On 8 January 1938, they asked the American navy to support them. The cautious Roosevelt agreed only to set an earlier date than mid-March for U.S. naval maneuvers and to send a few cruisers to visit Shanghai. This was so far short of what the British had in mind that Prime Minister Neville Chamberlain backed down, and told Washington that His Majesty's Government would respond to Japanese acts of brutality only with stiff verbal protests.[1]

In view of such cross-purposes, Leahy decided to send his chief of War Plans Division, Captain Royal E. Ingersoll, to meet with Captain Tom Phillips, RN, his opposite number in the Admiralty. Leahy wanted him to find out what the Royal Navy would be willing to do in a showdown with Japan. FDR agreed that Ingersoll's trip was a good idea and even gave him a personal supplemental briefing after Leahy had given his own instructions.

Captain Ingersoll set off just as the year was ending, and Leahy saw even greater danger in the coming one, with the increasing risk of "a world war between the 'Fascist' and the 'Democratic' nations." In his annual appraisal of the world situation, he summed up: "All naval powers, England, France, Japan, Italy, Germany, and Russia, are constructing navies to the limit of their resources in an effort to prevent a world war or to be secure against invasion if such a war cannot be avoided."

Captain Ingersoll's mission to London was one step Leahy took in an effort to avoid war or to strengthen a possible Anglo–American alliance if one should come. He obtained "agreement in principle" that in the event of hostilities between Japan on the one hand and Britain and the United States on the other, the two navies would cooperate in the Pacific, the British arriving at Singapore and the Americans at Pearl Harbor simultaneously. It was a vague agreement and soon overtaken by events.

Soon after Ingersoll got back, Leahy, on 29 January, took him to the White House for a meeting with FDR, and there the three of them kicked around plans for further cooperation with the British. As it turned out, however, Chamberlain refused to go along with any further moves against Japan. He felt he had enough to worry about in Europe without taking on the Far East as well. But neither in Europe nor in Asia were his appeasement policies fruitful.

On a lower level than president–prime minister, Ingersoll's mission did have an important consequence. Over the next few years, the two great navies came closer to a mutual understanding of means, methods, problems, tactics, and strategic views. Thus, when war came, they were better able to work together in the oceans of the world.

The comparative failure of Ingersoll's mission did, however, confirm Roosevelt in his decision to seek an increase in naval construction, and late in January he asked Congress to authorize an increase of 20 percent in naval appropriations. Leahy had already appeared before Congress on the same subject.

> The present moment is not one when the United States can safely reduce its means for national defense without jeopardizing our national security. The political conditions in the world, both in Europe and the Far East, are more threatening than at any time since 1918 and are distinctly worse than a year ago.
>
> In China a major conflict is in progress involving grave danger to American citizens. The civil war in Spain continues unabated and the possibility of a general European conflict is ever present.
>
> We must continue to maintain our existing national defense establishments at their highest efficiency, complete as soon as possible and practicable the projects now under way to improve or augment the existing establishments, and provide those features which are still lacking and which are vital to the efficiency of the national defense at sea.[2]

In a letter to the new CINCUS, Admiral Claude Bloch, Leahy wrote ruefully how the House Naval Committee

> has had me thoroughly grilled for the last three days on the question of the naval increase proposed by the President in his letter of a recent date. The opposition in Congress, which after all does not amount to very much in the way of votes,

appears to be preparing material which they can use as a political issue in connection with the President's desire for a moderate increase in the Navy.[3]

Republican members of the committee, eager to exploit weaknesses in the administration, grilled him further about the Ingersoll mission, but backed down when Leahy replied, "I will not answer that question here, but I will make a statement in executive session—of course on the basis that it is absolutely secret."[4] Since there were no headlines to be made out of an "absolutely secret" session, no more was heard of the matter. In those days, government leaks had not been developed to their present state of a fine art.

Existing treaties among the naval powers contained escalator clauses which permitted them to build battleships larger than the 35,000-ton limit, providing they gave due notice to the other signatories. Since the Japanese would not say what sizes of battleships they intended to build, the British announced that they were invoking the escalator clause and intended to build 39,000-ton ships. On 3 March, Leahy informed the State Department that the navy wished to build 45,000-ton battleships, in addition to the 35,000-ton *Alabama*, *Indiana*, *Massachusetts*, and *South Dakota* already authorized in fiscal 1939. In a move that surprised some officers, who thought of Leahy as one of the most hidebound members of the Gun Club, he pushed for aircraft carriers as well.

Of course, with war clouds threatening, all the services wanted as big a cut of the budget pie as possible. Reviving the attitude of Billy Mitchell in the 1920s, airmen began attacking naval building programs on the ground that ships were too vulnerable. Any bomber, they argued, could sink a ship with no difficulty. As Leahy wrote Bloch:

> My recent session in Congress was very largely devoted to explaining why we need ships in view of allegations that they can easily and quickly be destroyed by torpedoes or bombs, particularly when these annoying weapons are manipulated by ARMY aviators. The Naval Authorization Bill at the present moment is in the Senate where the opposition is trying to talk it to death. Some observers here feel that it may fail of enactment in the Senate because of persistent opposition, but it is my opinion that it will pass in due time in just about the form we proposed.[5]

Leahy still believed that the navy needed more ships, for the politicians wanted to be strong in both oceans, and he realized that unless there were enough ships, such a notion was suicide. The term "Two Ocean Navy" had not yet gained popularity, and, as long as he was operating a "One Ocean Navy," Leahy felt strongly that its main strength should be kept together in one ocean. Since general understandings had been worked out with the British and French to take care of the Atlantic, Leahy believed the U.S. Navy should be concentrated in the Pacific to deal with Japan. In the event of war with Japan, Plan Orange called for the American navy to advance through the

Marshall Islands and seek decisive battle with the Japanese in or near Philippine waters.

With the support of Vinson in the House and Walsh in the Senate, and with President Roosevelt finally committed to a buildup and modernization of the navy, Leahy was gratified to win more than he expected on Capitol Hill. "Congress is today approaching its final agony," he wrote Bloch, "after having provided the Navy with practically everything we could think of as necessary or desirable within the next fiscal year."[6]

The appropriation bill finally out of the way, Leahy was able to accept an invitation to visit Wisconsin and address the American Legion convention, where he criticized those who still called for disarmament and diplomacy. "To expect that modern diplomacy will safeguard the property of a nation is to expect too much," he warned. "A record of tragic failure to prevent wars by collective action lies open for inspection."[7]

That same day, Bill Leahy was ceremonially inducted into the Red River Tribe of the Chippewa Indians. "My Indian name," he wrote proudly, "is 'Kitchi-Be-Ba-Mash,' which in English is 'Great Man Sailing Around.'"

That evening, Leahy was forced to listen to a Northwestern University professor who held forth for an hour on the necessity of international understanding and of keeping out of war. The unimpressed chief of naval operations, while agreeing with the professor's objectives, found his proposed methods wanting: "He did not give me any useful information as to how we might accomplish any of the purposes which he pointed out as necessary."

By the time Leahy returned to Washington, another gunboat in China, the *Monocacy*, was keeping radiomen busy with messages between Admiral Yarnell and the Navy Department. On 27 July, the ship had been present when the Japanese captured Kiukiang, a city on the Yangtze some 250 miles above Nanking. A Japanese gunboat rendered honors. That was the last friendly action accorded the vessel for a long time to come.

A few days later, Japanese officials denied the *Monocacy* permission to refuel at the nearby Standard Oil dock. They next refused her permission to sail down river. Again Leahy recommended firm action.

> It is my opinion that this action by Japan is for the deliberate purpose of injuring the prestige of America in the Orient, and that it has no other purpose. I believe that it should be answered by strong, positive action on the part of this government. . . . Sending the ship down river might result in its loss by accident or design, but some strong stand by this government is, in my opinion, necessary to preserve what little prestige America now has in the Orient.

In the end, the *Monocacy* incident faded away after two months of correspondence and dispute. It revealed to Leahy the lengths to which the military controlled the Japanese government and that in many cases high officials in

Tokyo were actually powerless to curb the actions of the officers—especially those in the army—when they were determined on a course of action. Later in an interview with a Japanese newspaper correspondent who was trying to trap him into making an indiscreet statement, "I told Mr. Ito that this country differs from some others in that naval officers have no voice whatever in the formulation of national policy, that the only task of the navy is to be prepared to defend that nation against aggression from any direction, and to support the policy of the nation which is established by Congress."

This, of course, was a somewhat disingenuous statement, intended for public consumption. As well as any other high-ranking officer, Bill Leahy knew it was not only his privilege but his duty, to make recommendations on matters of policy in such cases as the *Panay* and *Monocacy* incidents. But once the decision had been made, then naval or any other officers had no business opposing it.

> Yarnell is having a heck of a time on the Yangtze, [he wrote Bloch at the end of August] and about all I have been able to do so far with great effort is to send him sympathy. Our [army] friends across the street are lavish with sympathy but not strong on the punch. There is much doubt about their ever getting any better unless somebody should attack Cheyenne or some nearer place.[8]

Of much graver concern was the Sudetenland crisis in Czechoslovakia. Hitler threatened military action unless the Czechs ceded that German-speaking part of their country to the Reich. Day by day war seemed closer. The British and French made preparations; the Royal Navy placed its reserve officers on thirty-day notice for mobilization. The next day, Treasury Secretary Henry Morgenthau asked Leahy to send a cruiser to England in case she was needed to transport $116 million in gold to America for safekeeping.

Oddly enough, Leahy, who had been predicting a European war for many months, was not particularly concerned just then. He had no confidence in the ability of France to stand up to Germany. He predicted the big powers would compromise with Hitler at the expense of Czechoslovakia.

The next two weeks were filled with conferences with the president, with Secretary Morgenthau, Secretary Hull, and other high officials considering how to evacuate Americans in the event of war in Europe. The president told Leahy to beef up the Atlantic forces with ships from the Pacific and to be ready for any eventuality. Although he still considered it folly to split up the fleet, Leahy realized that FDR meant what he said and directed Bloch to send three light cruisers to the Atlantic.

While the major European powers moved ever closer to confrontation, British Prime Minister Chamberlain met several times with Hitler and other leaders. The upshot was the famous Munich Agreement, which Chamberlain proclaimed meant "peace in our time." Bill Leahy didn't think much of it. In fact, his comment was caustic.

30 September. Yesterday evening the Prime Ministers of England, France, Italy, and Germany signed an agreement which . . . postpones the prospect of war by a virtual partition of Czechoslovakia in almost exact agreement with the reiterated demands of Germany.

As the fall progressed, tension in the Far East eased as it had in Europe. In November the Japanese agreed to allow foreign war vessels to move down the Yangtze River with the minimum of restrictions. There was a brief crisis when the Japanese refused to permit the American liner *President Coolidge* to sail from Shanghai, but tension disappeared when the vessel off-loaded $4.5 million in Chinese-owned silver.

No one was convinced that tensions with Japan would go away so easily, so planning for possible conflict continued. If the United States was to oppose Japanese expansion in the south, and if it was to carry out the Orange Plan of an advance through the Marshall Islands to the Philippines, it needed bases farther west than Pearl Harbor. Since the army and navy had disagreed on where those bases should be located, who would run them, and what equipment they would have, Congress attached a rider to the Naval Expansion Act of May 1938 which established a board headed by Leahy's classmate, "Japy" Hepburn. Congress wanted the board to come up with some sort of answers to those questions by the end of the year.

The Hepburn Report, which crossed Leahy's desk en route to Congress, called for bases in the Atlantic, Caribbean, and Pacific, with a price tag of $287 million. Eighty percent of them were in the Pacific, the six most prominent being Kaneohe Bay in the Hawaiian Islands, Midway, Wake, Johnston, Palmyra, and Guam. All were crucial keys for the implementation of Plan Orange. The most important was Guam, which sat athwart Japanese supply routes to the South Pacific and the Philippines. The Hepburn Board argued that a minimum of $39 million would be needed to set up air and submarine bases. Ideally, they said, a major fleet base should be established there. Failing adequate facilities, the board recommended that Guam be dropped entirely from the list, since in that case the island could be captured easily by the Japanese, and it would require an unacceptable number of casualties to retake it. That, of course, was exactly what happened.

By this time Roosevelt was fully committed to rebuilding the navy, and he told Leahy that he wanted to expand the naval air arm to three thousand planes. He urged Congress to adopt and fund the recommendations of the Hepburn Report. But FDR would only go along with $5 million for Guam. Throughout the long debate, Leahy supported the conclusion of the board about Guam—either do it right or don't do it at all. Leahy's position carried, but in an unexpected way, for Congress deleted even the $5 million that Roosevelt proposed, and Guam became one of the issues politicians could blame each other for when the Japanese were overrunning the Pacific in the early months of World War II.

On 13 December, Leahy substituted for Secretary Swanson at a National Press Club luncheon in honor of Anthony Eden, who had quit the cabinet of Neville Chamberlain in protest against his appeasement policies. Leahy, who would get to know Eden better in the coming years, was more impressed by his appearance than by his substance. Eden "made a very pleasing half-hour talk without saying anything that we did not already know."

Eden's presence emphasized the president's growing interest in Europe. While the navy, Leahy in particular, emphasized the Pacific, FDR correctly saw the graver danger arising in the Old World. He still insisted that the annual fleet problem be held in the Caribbean and Atlantic early in 1939, and he was determined to view it himself, combining inspection with a fishing trip aboard the cruiser *Houston*.

Leahy, his mind concentrated on the Japanese, agreed reluctantly to the formation of an Atlantic Squadron of seven cruisers and seven destroyers, but he balked at an Atlantic Fleet. More than anything else he feared splitting the fleet so that it was too weak in both oceans. He felt the Atlantic Squadron was strong enough to enforce the Monroe Doctrine, and for anything more serious, he counted on the assistance of the British and French navies.

Since Army Chief of Staff General Craig and Leahy disagreed over this strategy, in November they directed the Joint Planning Committee to consider "(a) violation of the Monroe Doctrine by one or more of the Fascist Powers, and (b) a simultaneous attempt to extend Japanese influence in the Philippines." The assumptions ignored any possible aid the French and British navies might give, so the planners had to choose: fight in the Atlantic; fight in the Pacific; or split inadequate forces between the two.

In February 1939, Rear Admiral Robert L. Ghormley made his own report. As director of the War Plans Division in the office of CNO, he said the navy could do one of three things:

(1.) It could defend Hawaii, the West Coast of the United States, and the western hemisphere.

(2.) It could wage offensive war against Japan while defending the Panama Canal and the East Coast of the United States.

(3.) It could defend both the East and West Coasts of the United States and the Panama Canal.

It could not wage "an offensive naval war simultaneously in the Atlantic and the Pacific."[9]

Leahy was disappointed with the conclusion of the report of the Joint Planners. They recommended hemispheric defense, with emphasis on an Atlantic war. In the Navy Department, Leahy and a number of other thoughtful officers thought this was a tragic mistake. He believed he was correct in emphasizing the Pacific and in keeping only a small Atlantic Squadron as a kind of outpost in case of trouble. FDR, however, bought Ghormley's recommendation of adding four battleships and a carrier to the fourteen cruisers and destroyers currently in the eastern ocean. In the Pacific, the fleet would be headed by twelve battleships and four carriers, as well as the cruisers and destroyers presently there.

For all his good relationship with Roosevelt, Leahy found when the president revealed his prospective budget that the navy had once again come out on the short end. In addition to the funds set aside for new ships, he recommended $48 million for the navy, of which $19 million was for aircraft. In glaring contrast, the army was allocated $150 million for expansion, and an additional $300 million for aircraft. As Leahy expostulated, FDR gave him verbal authority to ask for $65 million more for the shore establishment, with the understanding that not more than $44 million would be spent in the first two years.

On 9 January, Joseph P. Kennedy and William Bullitt, ambassadors respectively to the United Kingdom and to France, called on Leahy. They were both prophets of doom and gloom, Kennedy the worse. Neither of them "expressed any hope of solving the problem without a destructive international war" that would involve America, and in their opinion "present civilization is in danger of destruction."

Leahy's last tour at sea as a naval officer on active duty was Fleet Problem XX. It was, as the president desired, held in the Caribbean and Atlantic. Admiral Bloch brought his fleet through the Panama Canal in time to rendezvous with the *Houston* from whose flag bridge the commander in chief would observe the maneuvers.

President Roosevelt loved a sea voyage. On board ship he could relax and get away from the hourly pressures of his office. There was time for fishing and for good talk. And in President's Country, General Order 99 did not apply, so he could enjoy his ritual cocktail hour with friends. The *Houston* was a favorite of his. He had on several occasions enjoyed its comfortable flag quarters.

For the voyage in February 1939, FDR took with him the customary mix of officials and political cronies. On this cruise the party was a small one, the inner circle consisting of the president, Leahy, FDR's personal physician and friend, Rear Admiral Ross McIntire, Naval Aide Captain Daniel J. Callaghan, Military Aide Brigadier General Edwin M. "Pa" Watson, and his personal secretary, William D. Hassett.

POTUS, as the train was invariably called (from the initials of *President Of The United States*) left Washington just before midnight on Thursday, 16 February. As always, POTUS took a great deal longer to make the trip than most trains would, for Roosevelt's infirmity would not permit him to brace himself in his berth. Thus he could not stand the lurching of higher speeds. He liked to watch the scenery, and while Leahy and others might fret over the 35-mile speed limit, they at least knew the reason for it.

Reaching the southernmost limit of the rail line at Homestead, Florida, the party embarked in cars for the long drive down Ocean Highway to Key West. After arrival, the usual photographs, and a short speech by Roosevelt, the party set off in motor boats for an hour's fishing. They had not a single strike and, disgusted, they went aboard the *Houston*, which was anchored about a mile out from the fleet landing.★

The president occupied the admiral's quarters aboard the flagship, and Leahy had the equally comfortable quarters of the chief of staff, which he found spacious and far above the average for ships he had known.

As soon as the presidential party had come aboard, the *Houston* got under way for Columbus Bank near Crooked Island passage in the hope of finding better fishing grounds. Everyone turned in early after two nights on the train.

Leahy described the routine aboard as "simple and restful."

All members of the party have breakfast in their rooms. The President usually comes out to his cabin between ten and eleven o'clock and works on his papers until noon. We lunch together at 12:30 and there discuss the Fleet Problem and the news received by dispatch from Miami where a White House staff office is maintained.

After lunch those who wish to do so take a nap, after which, when the ship was at anchor, we have gone on fishing expeditions in the ship's motor boats.

To meet the President's inability to walk, he is lifted into a motor whale boat at the rail and lowered in the boat.

Returning, he is hoisted in the boat. The President's boat is always provided with a boat officer, a signalman, and an armed Marine. The President is an experienced, enthusiastic small-boat sailor and fisherman.

We have dinner together after an "aperitif" as 6:30, and after dinner join in conversation about everything, usually going to bed at an early hour.

The President is a charming host, and he has a fund of interesting small talk.

After several days devoted to fishing, the *Houston* was "sunk" by a WHITE fleet submarine, but the "sinking" did not count because the submarine had jumped the gun and "sank" the flagship before the exercise officially began. On 26 February, the *Houston* joined the BLACK Fleet under Vice Admiral Adolphus Andrews. The BLACK Fleet steamed eastward to do battle with Admiral Edward C. Kalbfus's WHITE Fleet.

When it was all over, there was a parade of flag officers coming aboard the *Houston* to pay their respects to the president and the chief of naval operations. Following the amenities, the *Houston* departed for Charleston, South Carolina, where POTUS was waiting.

During the exercises, while the flagship was steaming through the placid waters of the Caribbean, Leahy went over with the president the forthcoming

★For many years the trains ran as far as Key West, but the tracks were destroyed in a hurricane in 1936. When repairs were made, Florida authorities decided to build a road instead.

Leahy with the president aboard the USS *Houston* during the Fleet problem, February 1939. Standing, left to right, Captain Daniel Callaghan; General Edwin "Pa" Watson; Admiral Ross McIntire, MC, USN; and Lieutenant Commander G. N. Barker. Seated, FDR and WDL. (Courtesy, FDR Library)

changes in flag officer appointments in the navy. For his own relief, he recommended Rear Admiral Harold R. Stark, known by his Academy nickname of "Betty." When they had finished the list, Roosevelt told Leahy that after his retirement as CNO, he intended to appoint him governor of Puerto Rico, replacing Governor Blanton Winship, who had asked to be relieved after six years in the job, during which he had been the target of two assassination attempts.

All in all, Leahy enjoyed the trip. "This cruise has really been essentially a restful yachting trip, during which the President has had a fully-earned vacation from the trials of his office."

In mid-March, Hitler brazenly scrapped the Munich pact and took over all of Czechoslovakia. This time there was no general feeling of a rush to war.

President Roosevelt confers with Admirals Edward Kalbfus, Claude Bloch, WDL, and Vice Admiral Adolphus Andrews during the Fleet Problem in the Caribbean, February 1939. (Courtesy, FDR Library)

The Munich agreement had denuded Czechoslovakia of any power to defend herself, and none of the western nations was in any position to take action. On 17 March, Leahy, as acting secretary of the navy, attended a cabinet meeting which took up the coup in Czechoslovakia.

Harold Ickes, who attended as secretary of the interior, reported that FDR considered declaring a national emergency, so he could seize the assets of Germany in the United States. Turning to Leahy, the president asked

> what he would do if he were given orders to seize the [German liner] *Europa* while she was sailing out of New York Harbor. The Admiral said that he would carry out the orders and then the President asked him what he would do if the *Europa* refused to heave-to under orders. To this the Admiral replied: "I'd sink her." He went on to explain that, of course, he would first fire a shot or two above the waterline, going lower until the *Europa* surrendered.[10]

But in the end, FDR backed away from any action, and Leahy was not happy with indecision.

> It appears to be the consensus of opinion of those present, including the Vice President, that America should exercise some leadership to assist in an effort to stabilize political conditions in the world, and that any action taken by America should be short of war.
>
> It does not seem to be fully realized that any action whatever that interferes with bandit nations points toward war.
>
> In other words, if we are going to meddle in European politics, we had better get ready for the war we are not ready to wage.

By the time of the Czechoslovakian coup, Leahy had just over four months remaining of his tour as chief of naval operations. Most of his important work had been done. The expansion of the fleet, for which he had fought since taking office, was well on its way, now that the president had been persuaded of its necessity. Faced with the Munich crisis the previous year and Germany's naked aggression in March, Congress was unlikely to upset the building program which had been worked out. On 27 March, Leahy spent the day testifying before a subcommittee of the House Appropriations Committee, speaking in defense of the naval budget. "The Committee was very considerate, and even the opposition members appeared friendly. I left with an impression that all requests for funds will be granted and that 45,000-ton battleships will meet with no serious difficulties."

Following one of his sessions with President Roosevelt in the early summer, after the others had left, FDR called Leahy to his desk. "Bill," he pronounced solemnly, "if war breaks out in Europe, I'll want you right back here advising me."

The crisis over Czechoslovakia caused the British to request further naval staff talks with the United States. The upshot was that the Royal Navy declared that in the event of war in Europe, they would be unlikely to be able to reinforce the Far East by transferring ships to Singapore. The French went even further, stating that they would seek accommodation with Germany if the British transferred ships to Southeast Asia on the outbreak of a European war.

This caused a great deal of discussion and reevaluation of strategies on both sides of the Atlantic. While Leahy believed that the British and French positions reinforced his own desire to concentrate the fleet in the Pacific, Roosevelt was not convinced. He wanted a powerful force in the Atlantic to preserve American neutrality if war came. As president and commander in chief, he naturally had his way, and when war broke out in September, the Neutrality Patrol was established.

Leahy, on the other hand, was convinced that the place for the main strength of the U.S. Navy was the Pacific. In secret conversations held at his own home to avoid leaks, he and Ghormley discussed possibilities with the British. In the event of a two-front war, Leahy emphasized to his Royal Navy colleagues his belief that the British and French navies could take care of the Atlantic and Mediterranean, while the U.S. Navy operated in the Pacific, reinforced by whatever token forces the British could send out. In return, American forces in the Atlantic would cooperate by reporting movements of German shipping.[11]

All of these events and consequent discussions led to a rethinking of American strategy, and on 30 June, the Joint Board recommended that Plan Orange be scrapped and replaced with five possible Rainbow Plans, the new name reflecting the probability that the United States would be fighting more than one enemy.

RAINBOW 1. This was based on the concept of single-handed defense of North and South America north of 10° south. This took account of the probability that Germany might try to establish bases in the "bulge" of Brazil.

RAINBOW 2. This was basically the plan that Leahy had discussed with the British, contemplating war in the western Pacific while allied with Britain and France.

RAINBOW 3. This assumed that the United States would be fighting in the western Pacific without allies. Rainbow 3, thus, was indentical with the old Orange Plan.

RAINBOW 4. This plan included the defense of all of North and South America, including the parts of South America south of the "bulge" of Brazil, by the United States alone. It also gave the fleet responsibilities in the eastern Atlantic.

RAINBOW 5. This plan assumed that the United States would be fighting in the eastern Atlantic and on the continent of Europe and Africa in alliance with Great Britain and France against Germany, or Italy, or both. It also assumed a simultaneous war in the Pacific against Japan, but under that plan, the strategic defensive would be employed in the Pacific until forces could be spared from Europe to mount an offensive against Japan. This plan, which anticipated the ABC-1 Staff plan, agreed to by America, Britain, and Canada in March 1941, placed emphasis on defeating Germany first.

In common with most naval officers, Leahy was not an advocate of the "Germany first" strategy which was later adopted. In the end, there would be a good deal of revison of the Rainbow plans before the war came and Pearl Harbor sent the planners back to the drawing board.

But, thanks to Leahy's constant efforts, the United States Navy was going to be better and larger than anyone had dreamed possible when he began the job of CNO. In spite of everything, it was a formidable force. There were fifteen battleships (five of postwar construction), and eight more were in various stages from the drafting board to the builders' ways. There were five big carriers and another abuilding. In addition, there were thirty-eight cruisers of all types, seventy-three modern destroyers, and 153 four-pipers left over from World War I.[12]

As Leahy's service career was drawing to its end, another man was about to rise to the top of his profession, and he would have many close associations with Leahy in future years. On 27 April, the president nominated Brigadier General George C. Marshall as chief of staff of the army to relieve General Malin Craig on 1 September. Marshall, of course, would go on to win the highest acclaim as a member of the Joint Chiefs of Staff and later, under President Truman, as secretary of state and secretary of defense.

For the next few months, Leahy spent a good deal of time preparing himself for his new job as governor of Puerto Rico. In a letter to Claude Bloch, he confessed he had little idea of what he was getting into.

> I have almost no news whatever in regard to the job that the President has been complimentary enough to offer to me. Some of the recent visitors to the Spanish Main assure me that the office is sufficiently full of grief to keep even an old sailor moving rapidly. However, as you and I know so well, old sailors will try anything once, and we will endeavor to survive, if not to enjoy, such incidents as may come to us while trying to administer one of the islands of the Spanish Main.[13]

A few tasks of a more pleasant nature came his way during the closing weeks of his term as CNO. He delivered the commencement address at the Naval Academy, and he helped the Roosevelts entertain King George and Queen Elizabeth of Great Britain. Festivities included a garden party and a cruise to Mount Vernon aboard the yacht *Potomac*. Both Leahys were impressed by Their Majesties who had spent some little time in conversation with them.

About this time a rumor began going around Washington that Leahy would not be going to Puerto Rico after all. Instead he would replace the ailing Claude Swanson as secretary of the navy. The rumor began when Leahy's name as governor-designate had been crossed out on the list FDR had sent to the Senate for confirmation. According to the United Press story, "The President has collaborated closely with the Admiral in laying down his huge naval construction program. During the next two years, when the tremendously complex program reaches its peak, he is said to be desirous of having in his Cabinet a man of Leahy's known ability and qualifications."[14]

At any rate, if FDR had considered Leahy for the job of secretary of the navy, he changed his mind. But the idea kept recurring during the time Leahy was in Puerto Rico.★

On the morning of 20 July, while Leahy and the president were discussing Puerto Rican problems, FDR surprised him by calling in photographers and all the high-level naval people in Washington and pinning a Distinguished Service Medal on the breast of his retiring chief of naval operations. "All of this last was a complete surprise to me, although it must have been known in advance to a number of officers in the Navy Department."

Then came a bittersweet entry in Leahy's journal:

> I August. At 10:00 a.m. I turned over the Office of Naval Operations to Admiral Harold R. Stark. The formal ceremony of the oath of office . . . was attended by moving and still picture photographers, and a sound picture was made of the actual assumption of office by Admiral Stark.

At the bottom of the page, which had been neatly typed by his yeoman, Bill Leahy added an entry in his own handwriting:

> This brings to an end forty-six years of active service in the Navy of the United States.

At the end of a formal letter to Leahy ordering his retirement, Roosevelt also added a handwritten comment:

Dear Bill

I just HATE to see you leave.

FDR

---

★When Swanson died in July, Roosevelt appointed the assistant secretary, Charles Edison, as acting secretary. He apparently already had in mind the bi-partisan cabinet he achieved the following year when he appointed Republicans Henry L. Stimson and Frank Knox as secretaries of the War and Navy Departments.

PART TWO

Civilian Interlude

## CHAPTER 7

# Governor of Puerto Rico

Today San Juan is a stark contrast between the gleaming city of modern hotel and resort areas and the labyrinthine streets of the old Spanish calles and barrios. Traffic is heavy; thousands of tourists arrive each day in the winter season, stepping off the jets at Isla Verde International Airport or off the many cruise ships that call there bringing passengers to the sunshine and the casinos.

In 1940, San Juan was a much smaller Latin-American city. Tourism was virtually nonexistent, and although Puerto Rico was a possession of the United States, the attitude of the people was insular in nearly every sense of the word.

Traditionally the post of governor of Puerto Rico had been a sinecure for retired army officers, and the man Leahy was replacing, Major General Blanton Winship, had not been kept very busy. To be sure, Winship had twice been the target of an assassin's bullet, and while he had escaped injury, some of the people standing near him had not. In the general view, the attempts on Winship's life had been dismissed as normal events in the volatile politics of Puerto Rico. No one, except for the victims and their families, took them very seriously.

So there was widespread feeling on the part of a good many in Washington that Leahy's appointment was another case of putting a good man out to pasture, letting him enjoy a few more years of activity and authority in a place that would not tax his energies too greatly. Certainly the post appeared to be of far less importance than the one he had just left as the head of the nation's navy.

On the other hand, there is no evidence that Leahy himself shared that view. He prepared for the assignment with customary care and thoroughness, for he knew that the war in Europe could spread and that the Caribbean was vital for the defense of the Panama Canal. San Juan would be the center for expanded military preparations in the Caribbean. And the island itself, with its own special brand of politics and its widespread poverty would require an active governor. For a politically unstable island offered a poor site for large-scale military facilities.

As the *Washington Post* put it, Leahy would "encounter on that tropical island a set of problems which will require as much energy, resourcefulness, and worry as any post he ever filled as a naval officer."[1]

What the *Washington Post* did not know and what most people did not know was that the post of governor of Puerto Rico was being upgraded because of the certainty of war and the importance of the Caribbean to the United States. Unlike Winship, who had been a staff officer and far removed from strategic planning, Leahy's recent job as CNO had brought him to the center of global affairs, and he was bringing that knowledge and experience to his new job. FDR selected him because he wanted a strong, dependable man in the Caribbean. In addition to spending $30 million for bases there, as recommended in the Hepburn Report, the navy was planning to establish the Tenth Naval District with headquarters in San Juan. Although, as governor, Leahy would have no direct responsibility for these bases or for the Tenth Naval District, it was more than coincidental that he should be at hand at just that stage in history.

Even as the Leahys were making their preparations to leave for Puerto Rico, German troops, on 1 September 1939, crossed the Polish border and began their Blitzkrieg aimed at the double envelopment of the Polish army. Two days later, Britain and France declared war on Germany, and World War II had begun.

To President Roosevelt, to Leahy, and to all responsible officials, it was time to look to America's defenses. And the Caribbean was an important part of those defenses, for at the southwestern end of that sea lies the Panama Canal.

No one could be sure just what Germany would do, but a widely held view was that when she had had her way in Europe she would move south through Spain and Africa and cross the Atlantic narrows to Brazil. Thus she would be in position to threaten the United States from the south. So it was that when Leahy received his briefing from the president, he received a lot more than the usual talk about the economy, politics, and social conditions that might have been given to any new governor. FDR laid it on the line.

He also gave me oral instructions to keep myself adequately informed in regard to progress on the military and naval installations under construction on the island with the purpose of preserving United States neutrality in the Caribbean Sea, to protect America against possible attack by any of the belligerent European nations, and to give such assistance as was available in the territory under my control.[2]

That was all that Leahy could set down at the time without including classified information. While there is no other record of the conversation between Roosevelt and Leahy, it seems safe to assume that they talked about more than the sugar-cane crop. As it turned out, the governor's house became the unofficial center of military activity and intelligence in the Caribbean. Naval etiquette required captains of visiting naval ships to call upon the governor. If, during those calls, they told him what they had learned of affairs in Martinique, in Curacao, in Barbados, in Aruba, was it not the governor's duty to pass that intelligence on to Washington?

Just before leaving for Puerto Rico, Leahy had one final conference with the president, who

informed me that if the United States becomes seriously involved in the European difficulty, it will be necessary for him to recall me from Puerto Rico and assign me to membership on a four-man War Board, with the duty of coordinating the work of the State, War, and Navy Departments.[3]

Even at that early date, FDR was obviously toying with some kind of organization to coordinate strategy if the United States became involved. As commander in chief, Roosevelt wanted to have around him the top leaders whom he knew and trusted.

Like his commander in chief, Leahy believed in the cause of Britain and France against Germany, and he listened with approval as FDR proclaimed American neutrality but added, "I cannot ask that every American remain neutral in thought as well."

Shortly before sailing, Leahy received a visit from the pacifist Oswald Garrison Villard, whom the admiral considered a busybody. When his appointment as governor was announced, Villard had opposed it on the ground that no such post should go to a military man. This time Villard asked Leahy to show mercy to some terrorists, self-proclaimed nationalists, who had tried to assassinate Governor Winship. Usually those nationalists got off scot-free by intimidating judges and juries. These men, however, had come up against a courageous judge and had been sentenced to long prison terms. For no reason that Leahy was able to discern, Villard believed they deserved executive clemency and pleaded with him to grant it once he reached San Juan.

Restraining his disgust with what he felt was woolly thinking, Leahy informed his visitor:

When I related to him Governor Winship's account of the assassinations, he said that much could be said in justification of their being only patriots.

I then assured Mr. Villard that if any of the "patriots" attempted to assassinate me, they would have no further trouble in this world, because they would be dead before they could move their feet. He expressed horror at this barbarous attitude of mine, saying that he did not believe an American could so deliberately dispense with the due processes of law.

Throughout his life the admiral had only contempt for "do-gooders" whose theories defied practical events, and who, in face of overwhelming evidence to the contrary, considered their theories as ranking with the Ten Commandments. He clearly regarded Villard as one of those, and there are a good many references to him in Leahy's journal, none of them very kind.

The new governor and his lady arrived in San Juan aboard the SS *Coamo* early on the morning of 11 September. On hand to greet them was the acting governor, Jose E. Colom, accompanied by his wife, other officials, and "the newspaper fraternity."

His inauguration took place that same day, and although the Puerto Rican officials made lengthy speeches, most of them in Spanish, Leahy spoke briefly and in English. After promising to put all the pressure on Congress to remedy the many ills marring Puerto Rico's economy, he went on to say that most problems could be solved by people working together. He then made a statement that many citizens found hard to believe and which the politicians cynically assumed was window dressing. But Leahy meant every word of it.

> Your Governor has no political affiliations and will not become affiliated with any particular political group as compared with any other.
> He will ask for advice on the conduct of his executive office from the leaders of those groups who hold different views of the local political aspect, and he will respect their counsel and advice to be an expression of their considered opinion as to what is best for the general welfare of the people of Puerto Rico, regardless of any other consideration whatever.
> We can make no serious errors in the performance of the duties of our office if our only consideration is the welfare of Puerto Rico, and if our official action is taken with that purpose in view.[4]

Listening to the speech, one commentator described the new governor as a "sour puss without a sense of humor." Those nearby denied that, noting the twinkle in his eye as he tried to manage his top hat during his speech. The hat was performing with all the perversity objects can attain at especially awkward occasions, and when he had finished his speech, he gave it to his aide, Lieutenant Commander Ralph H. Wishart and said, "Throw it away. I won't need it any more."[5]

After an hour-long parade of national guardsmen, police veterans, school children, war veterans, civic groups, and anyone else who could find an excuse to join the procession, the Leahys were driven to La Fortaleza, a

Governor William D. Leahy delivering his inaugural address at San Juan, Puerto Rico, September 1939. (Courtesy, National Archives)

400-year-old castle which served as the official residence of the governor.
Apparently no repairs had been made since it had been built, and it was nearly
falling to pieces, but that evening it hosted some fifteen hundred people,
"presumably the official and social elite of the island," in a reception to meet
their new governor.

"This ended a very long, tiresome day."

It was obvious that La Fortaleza simply would not do as a governor's
residence. It was, in fact, scheduled for a complete overhaul to begin in a few
weeks, using WPA funds, which Leahy had been able to win for the purpose
before he left Washington. In return, he had been saddled with supervising
how those funds were spent. He also had the *ex officio* job of director of the
Puerto Rican Reconstruction Authority. PRRA was another relief organization and would have its part in the restoration of the castle.

All this meant that the Leahys had to find some other place to live. Officials
had lined up a list of possibilities. Leahy rejected them all. There were some
attractive houses for long-term lease, but the rents were too steep. A few
families offered furnished homes at no cost at all, but the admiral clearly saw
the trap if he accepted their hospitality. He would no longer be free as

governor, for he would have obligations to his hosts. He wasn't going to owe anybody anything as he governed Puerto Rico.

A Puerto Rican admirer wrote in later years:

> While he was walking through the gardens of Fortaleza, a little pavillion caught his attention, built of concrete and wood, which in the course of time has served as a storehouse for old furniture, residence of the chief of the palace guard, and lodging for guests of the Executive. Also it had been for several months the house assigned to the official chauffeur of Fortaleza. Admiral Leahy, after inspecting it inside and out, turned to those who accompanied him and said, "Gentlemen, here, I believe, is the answer to the problem of where I am to live while the palace is being restored. This pavillion is enough for my wife and me. We will stay here."

When informed of the humble origins of the structure, he was unimpressed. "What of it? Let us say no more about the matter."[6]

There was one bright side to living in such modest quarters. The Leahys had the perfect excuse to duck much of the entertaining they might have been expected to do. Perhaps that was what he had in mind when he picked the guest house.

Finally settled, he turned vigorously to the problems of the island. He saw a natural strength in the people who, after four decades under the American flag, had kept their Spanish traditions, customs, and language, but who had also adopted many of the "social, political, and industrial accomplishments of our Anglo-Saxon civilization."

Society was dominated by people of pure Spanish blood, descendants of the original settlers. Into that group had been grudgingly allowed other white Europeans and Americans. All others were rigidly excluded. But this exclusion, as Leahy pointed out, existed only in social matters. During day-to-day life, the elite rubbed elbows with Indians, Negroes, and those of mixed blood. "In politics, the professions, business and trade, no perceptible distinction was made because of race and color."

Because tourism was not developed in Puerto Rico in 1939, its economy was largely dependent on sugar exports to the United States. Unfortunately, lobbying by sugar interests in America had resulted in strict quotas on Puerto Rican sugar imported to the States. Many American sugar producers had large investments in Cuban sugar, so that independent island had a larger quota than did Puerto Rico, an American possession.

Since Puerto Rican plantations, largely owned by American absentee landlords, supplied more than enough sugar to use up the quota, independent farmers were pretty much out of luck. Laborers on the large plantations lived "in abject poverty such as is not known on the continent except perhaps among Negroes in some of the most distressed areas of our far south."

The generosity of the climate contributed to the poverty of the people.

They saw little reason to work hard to improve their lot while the land produced their basic diet of fruits, vegetables, and coffee. Occasionally some of the poorer people would save up a few coins to buy some luxuries. One of their favorites was, oddly enough, salted codfish from New England.

Soon after Leahy took over, a major crisis erupted. The Department of the Interior, which was responsible for the administration of all American territories, decreed that the minimum wage requirement of 25 cents an hour would apply to Puerto Rico. This wage scale was so wildly at variance with the prevailing pay that the island's economy came close to complete collapse. If they paid the minimum wage, the plantation owners could not produce sugar which would compete in the United States with Cuban-grown sugar, where no minimum wage applied.

While the Puerto Ricans were still reeling from that blow, the Supreme Court decreed that the minimum wage applied to people doing piece work at home. Since many of the island women were accustomed to making embroidered place mats, table cloths, napkins, aprons, and blouses in their homes, their source of income dried up. The goods they made could no longer be sold at a profit in the Caribbean market.

While low wages in the Caribbean islands were deplorable, they were a fact of life, and a unilateral attempt by the United States to raise them in Puerto Rico could only price Puerto Rican producers out of the market, given the fact that the islands of the Caribbean were an economic entity. Unhappily the problem of the minimum wage never was solved during Leahy's tenure, and his repeated reports of the harm it caused in the island fell on deaf ears and before blind eyes in the Department of the Interior and the Department of Agriculture.

Puerto Rico had the outward signs of democratic government, but in practice the legislature was completely dominated by Senator Rafael Martinez Nadal, leader of the Union Republican Party. Nadal was accustomed to picking his own people for the governor to appoint to judicial and executive positions. Previous governors, either uninformed or unable to decide on the merits of the men concerned, had usually rubber-stamped Nadal's list. It came, therefore, as a considerable shock to the senator when Leahy informed him that the practice had to stop. Unbelieving, Nadal sent up the name of one of his cronies to be named a municipal judge. "I found upon investigation," Leahy wrote in amazement, that the man "was on parole after conviction on a charge of murder." Feuding between Nadal and Leahy continued, and things reached an impasse. Leahy refused to appoint men proposed by Nadal, and Nadal kept the Senate from confirming those nominated by Leahy.

As might be expected, during his first few months in Puerto Rico, the admiral spent quite a bit of time on the road, inspecting hospitals, municipal institutions, sugar plantations, and schools, including branches of the University of Puerto Rico. This activity naturally gave him an opportunity to inspect as well some of the military facilities, such as Puenta Borinquen, on the western end of the island, where the army was building a huge air base. Later, of course, many more installations would be built, including the vast naval base at Roosevelt Roads.

Although most of the work on military bases was going reasonably well, the same could not be said for the relief projects. Most of them had been taken over by politicians, who had the attitude that they could divert what money they desired to their own pockets on the assumption that they could control any auditors and that there would always be more available from the federal government. Leahy set out to stop these abuses, but he was fighting an ingrained system, and the few months that he was governor were not enough for him to make much progress.

Meanwhile there were the obligatory activities which any governor had to perform. On one trip in November, the Leahys stopped at Barranquitos so that the admiral could lay a wreath on the grave of Señor Muños Rivera, one of the early patriots of the new Puerto Rico. His son, Luis Muños Marín, who died in the summer of 1980, was to become a leader of the legislature while Leahy was governor.

Another ceremonial occasion which was particularly difficult, since he had known the man only slightly, was the funeral of the Resident Commissioner in Washington, Santiago Iglesias. The remains arrived in mid-December, and because Señor Iglesias had been so adored by his people, there was a pro-tracted state funeral, which gave the people ample opportunity for paroxysms of grief.

These included a two-day funeral, complete with lying in state in the Senate chamber. The governor was required to make a speech—in Spanish—which lasted three minutes. Other orations went on much longer, so that the entire affair lasted five hours. Then, at the funeral procession a minor riot erupted as two groups of Señor Iglesias's friends of opposite political parties struggled for possession of the coffin and the honor of bearing their hero to his last resting place. According to Leahy, the contest was finally settled by "weight of numbers," and, borne on the shoulders of the triumphant party, Señor Iglesias was carried to the cemetery and duly interred.

There were so many problems in the island, and there was a great deal to report on the progress of military facilities there, so the governor decided to go back to Washington to try to sort some of them out. There was the matter of the minimum wage, and there were many bottlenecks in the bureaucracy which was supposed to provide relief funds for Puerto Rico.

Just as the year ended, Leahy was in the offices of people in Washington who might be able to help. Interior Secretary Ickes listened but did nothing. Budget Director Harold Smith wanted to help, but he had no money. As far as the sugar quota was concerned officials of the Department of Agriculture were downright hostile, wanting to do nothing to offend domestic sugar growers.

He found the president sympathetic, and he "with a full knowledge that sugar was and probably always would be the only saleable product of Puerto Rico, indicated the possibility of his personal assistance in my effort to obtain an increase in the sugar quota."

Only in the office of WPA could Leahy find any concrete help. Colonel Francis "Pink" Harrington, who had succeeded Harry Hopkins as administrator, promised sufficient money to put twenty thousand Puerto Ricans to work.

Shortly before returning to the island, the Leahys lunched in the White House with President and Mrs. Roosevelt and a few others. Dryly the admiral observed, "The President entertained friendly but practical views of what might be done to assist the distressed people of Puerto Rico. The ideas of Mrs. Roosevelt were equally sympathetic but less practicable."

Back in Puerto Rico by the end of January 1940, Leahy was in time to open the legislative session, calling for economy in all branches of the government. Since it was an election year,

> little or no attention was paid to the Governor's demand for economy, nor was any serious attention to the demand expected, but the Governor's power of veto made it possible to prevent the final enactment of appropriations made for the benefit of political supporters without regard to the public interest.

Elections that year were unstable because the leader of the dominant Union Republican Coalition Party, Rafael Martinez Nadal, Leahy's old adversary, was suffering from an incurable disease, and his loss meant that other parties, the Tripartista, the Nationalist, and the Socialist, all saw opportunities for gain. By far the most important, however, was the new Popular Party, formed by Luis Muños Marín, whose father's grave Leahy had honored a few months earlier. Marín had been born in San Juan, but he had spent many years in New York trying to make up his mind whether he was a writer or a politician. In 1931 he decided on a political career and returned to Puerto Rico for good. Of all the candidates, Marín most won Leahy's respect.

> Luis Marín was a far left liberal. He advocated subdivision of the great sugar estates to give small landholders opportunities to become self-supporting, and he also contended that it was practicable, with insular financial assistance, to build up an industry on the island that would eventually support itself and improve the living conditions of a great number of laborers who had always been dependent upon employment in the sugar industry. . . .
>
> I took the occasion to inform him that the election would be free and under adequate police protection, to which he replied that was all he needed to win the election.

The legislative session which ended on 8 April had been dominated by the efforts of the dying Nadal to challenge once again the authority of the governor. He made repeated attacks on Leahy's executive council, which corresponded to a cabinet, and he forced the resignation of the treasurer by repeated death threats from unknown persons, but who were clearly known to be his supporters. Nadal also blocked the appointment of Supreme Court Justice Martín Travieso as a member of the board of trustees of the University of Puerto Rico, thus temporarily frustrating Leahy's efforts to bring the merit system to faculty appointments.

Determined to have the judge as a trustee, Leahy reappointed him after the legislature had adjourned. The English-langauge newspaper of the island approved: "The Governor made a statement which only a strong man would make. Few governors in the continental United States would have an assurance like that. Few would have the courage, the determination, the intestinal durability to carry the idea out. Yet, the Governor on Monday showed that he meant to keep his word by appointing Judge Martín Travieso to the board of trustees of the University of Puerto Rico. . . . It took guts for the Governor to stand up before the dominant party of the island."[7]

While the governor was winning some and losing some in the political game, his wife was making her mark in Puerto Rico as well. Not content to be First Lady and preside over the social life of the capital, Louise busied herself in charitable works, assisting such institutions as the Red Cross and the School for the Blind. She believed that participation in such activities was important, and she kept herself busy even as she studied Spanish and fulfilled her duties as the governor's wife and hostess.

On 9 April, the so-called Phoney War ended with a vengeance as German troops invaded Denmark and Norway, and the following month, the long-awaited Blitzkrieg through the Low Countries into France began. The symbol of appeasement, Neville Chamberlain, was replaced as prime minister by Winston Churchill.

Just a few weeks later the Leahys were on board the SS *Angelina* en route to New York. The stay in the United States lasted six weeks, and there were conflicting stories as to its purpose. *Newsweek* reported that FDR wanted to make Leahy secretary of the navy but backed down when the admiral became too bellicose. It also disapprovingly charged that he wanted to get rid of the minimum wage law.[8] He did, but only in Puerto Rico where it was unworkable. Another story reported that he would head some "new division of national defense coordination."[9]

Probably there was a grain of truth in all these reports, for Leahy and Roosevelt met many times during the six week period, and all possibilities, from Puerto Rican to military and foreign affairs, were discussed. Apparently the time was not ripe for FDR to pull Leahy out of his job in San Juan and bring him back to Washington, but the idea was not dead, as Leahy later recorded. FDR hoped the United States could stay out of the European war, but that hope did not prevent him from "making every defensive preparation for which he could obtain authority and funds from the Congress." Leahy, however, thought FDR was far too optimistic.

> With only England offering effective resistance to the Nazis, and with China fighting alone and almost hopelessly against Japan, I could see little or no prospect of our not being attacked on one side or the other sooner or later.
>
> At our last conference before my return to Puerto Rico, all this subject was gone over again in friendly disagreement, and upon my departure, he directed me to be ready to return to Washington at any time, because in the event of my being right and our becoming involved in the war, he would recall me by telegraph.

It seems clear that in spite of stories and rumors spread by his detractors, Bill Leahy had not fallen out of favor with the president. He went back to Puerto Rico because he was doing a good job and because FDR needed him there during the time of the buildup of military and naval strength in the Caribbean.

While the Leahys were in the United States, Italy, on 10 June, declared war on Britain and France, even as the latter was reeling from the Blitzkrieg. In his famous speech at Charlottesville, an infuriated Roosevelt declared, "The hand that held the dagger has struck it into the back of its neighbor!" Leahy thought the president's charge "seems to be about as close to a declaration of war as it is possible to reach without actually making such a declaration."[10]

Back in Puerto Rico, Leahy devoted considerable time to trying to keep the opposing candidates from killing each other in the campaign.

About that time a federal parole board released two Puerto Rican terrorists from prison in the United States. The terrorists promptly returned to Puerto Rico and proclaimed they were patriots. They did not, therefore, consider themselves bound by the conditions of their parole. The United States government, they went on, had no jurisdiction over them because they were patriotic Puerto Ricans seeking freedom for the island. "I informed President Roosevelt of the situation," Leahy penned dryly, "telling him that I did not particularly like the prospect of being assassinated, even by a self-styled patriot out on parole." The upshot was that the paroles were revoked and the "patriots" were quietly returned to prison in Atlanta.

During the summer, Leahy made an inspection trip of other islands in the Caribbean, a trip which was outside his jurisdiction as governor but which came under his loosely defined responsibilities as senior military officer in the area. He kept in close touch with Rear Admiral Raymond A. Spruance, commandant of the Tenth Naval District, recently established at San Juan.

Soon the huge naval base at Roosevelt Roads would vastly increase American strength in the Caribbean. When the British agreed to exchange bases in the Western Hemisphere for fifty overage destroyers, Leahy wrote, "Franklin Roosevelt by this exchange made the greatest single contribution to the safety of America from overseas attack since the construction of the battle fleet of the United States."

On yet another trip to Washington, Leahy on 8 October had lunch with President Roosevelt. Also present was Admiral James O. Richardson, who had been for a time assistant CNO under Leahy. Now serving as CINCUS, he was having a major difference of opinion with Roosevelt. FDR wanted the Pacific Fleet based at Pearl Harbor to impress the Japanese that the United States meant business if the Japanese continued to expand in east and southeast Asia. Richardson objected. He claimed that Pearl Harbor could not support the fleet for an extended stay and, in any case, the crews of the ships were suffering loss of morale because of long separation from their families. FDR brushed these arguments aside and insisted that in his view the fleet should remain in the Hawaiian area. In a statement that almost surely cost him his job, Richardson charged:

> Mr. President, I feel that I must tell you that the senior officers of the Navy do not have the trust and confidence in the civilian leadership of this country that is essential for the successful prosecution of a war in the Pacific.

With a look of pained surprise, Roosevelt shook his head and said wearily:

> Joe, you just don't understand that this is an election year and that there are certain things that can't be done, no matter what, until the election is over and won.[11]

In testimony after the war, Leahy told a congressional committee that the president had been right and that "neither he nor anybody else at that time anticipated a Japanese attack on our ships in the Islands."[12]

> The conference lasted two hours. When I left with the Admiral, I told him that the country believed the fleet was always ready for war, and that he must obtain fuel ships and make every other possible preparation for hostilities that could be made wherever his fleet was stationed.
> I have no doubt that upon his return to the fleet, he did just that.[13]

Obviously Richardson did not do "just that," for on 1 February 1941 he was relieved by Admiral Husband E. Kimmel and ordered to duty in Washington.

The Leahys returned to Puerto Rico with only eight days remaining before the election of 5 November. Because of the history of violence and threats of violence in Puerto Rican elections, Leahy was determined that the people should be free to vote their consciences. With the full cooperation of the chief of police, guarding the polls was as carefully worked out as though it were a battle plan, which in a sense it was. No policeman guarded his own district. Leaders of all parties were notified that the police had been instructed to keep order and ensure free elections, and that anyone who tried to start riots or intimidate voters would be dealt with. "Police with orders to shoot," commented Leahy dryly, "have a quieting effect on political rioters anywhere."

When the ballots were counted, the Popular Party of Luis Muños Marín had won by a large majority. Marín was to become leader of Puerto Rico for many years and would after the war be the first native-born Puerto Rican to become governor, a post he was to hold for sixteen years.

> I was . . . told that this election was the most peaceful and free from disturbance of any in the history of Puerto Rico. . . .
>
> While not entirely satisfied that the results of this election were the best that could have been obtained under competent political leadership, it was a matter of high personal satisfaction to me that I had managed to keep entirely free from association with any political party and to have been able to provide the electorate for the first time with an opportunity to choose their elected representatives freely and without being intimidated.

Great as his satisfaction with the results of the Puerto Rican election, he was equally pleased when the voters returned Franklin D. Roosevelt to the White House for another four years.

It was not long afterwards, on the morning of 17 November, that Commander Wishart interrupted the Leahy breakfast with a confidential telegram from the president:

> We are confronting an increasingly serious situation in France. . . .

That afternoon the Leahys attended a picnic "as planned, with sadness in our hearts over a certainty that we were soon to be taken away from a host of Puerto Rican friends for whom we had acquired an affectionate attachment."

Then began a hectic week of packing, taking care of last-minute affairs, seeing friends, briefing the acting governor-to-be, and attending to the myriad other details of the sudden upheavals known to naval officers and to others in the government service.

In the few months that the Leahys had spent in Puerto Rico, they had become popular with most of the people of the island. Leahy could look with satisfaction on his work in the islands. His even-handed enforcement of the law had much improved the conditions of the working people. Too long had the established politicians had their own way in matters of land, prices, and working conditions just because previous governors had found in simpler to let them run things. When they tried that game with the admiral, he had brought them up short with a few well-chosen words.

Now that the moment of departure had come, it was a time of mixed feelings. He felt a sense of loss at parting from the new friends he and Louise had made during their tenure. At the same time, he looked with anticipation on the new job in France, which promised to be both challenging and frustrating. As he prepared to leave, he reflected that he knew no more about conditions in Vichy than he had been able to read in official messages and in the Puerto Rican and American newspapers which were regularly received in the office. Like the late great humorist Will Rogers, he only knew what he read in the papers. There would be a good deal to learn in Washington briefing before Bill Leahy felt ready to undertake his new position.

The Leahys sailed from San Juan on 28 November 1940 aboard the steamer *Borinquen*. The four-day voyage to New York gave the admiral ample time to think about what lay ahead and to reminisce about what had passed. Since he was not yet ready for pipe and slippers before the fireplace, he gave the past short shrift while he was considering what was to come.

This new appointment was no mere change of station, such as he had undertaken countless times in the past. It marked a real watershed in his life, for he was to begin functioning in a manner to affect the grand strategy of the United States. As ambassador to France he would be in immediate and daily contact with events which could shape the course and outcome of the war.

As the SS *Borinquen* steamed slowly north from San Juan, the weather grew colder with each passing day. On board, the Leahys, their cabin still crowded with flowers sent by friends and well-wishers left behind in Puerto Rico, enjoyed the last days of complete freedom from responsibility that either of them was to know for a long time to come. They even had time on 30 November to listen to a broadcast from Philadelphia of the annual Army–Navy football game. The admiral was delighted with Navy's 14 to 0 triumph.

The Puerto Rican tour was over. Vichy France would be next.

## CHAPTER 8

# Ambassador to Vichy France

The weather grew colder with each passing hour as the *Borinquen* made her way northward. The sullen Atlantic waters hid U-boats, unknown numbers of British warships, and the vital convoys carrying the goods Britain needed to survive.

American ships could still safely travel those waters, even though the Germans occasionally stopped and investigated a vessel flying the Stars and Stripes. These problems were no part of the worry of the former governor of Puerto Rico. They belonged to the navy he had left behind him. Still, it gave him a pang to think of others doing the job he had spent his life preparing to do.

But now he had a new job. He knew that he was not the first choice for it, for he had learned that President Roosevelt had first offered it to General John J. Pershing, whose ties to France were unequaled by any American. But Pershing had had to refuse for reasons of health. And so, the job had come to Leahy. It had to be important, if Roosevelt had tried to bring "Black Jack" Pershing out of retirement. So what challenge did it offer Bill Leahy?

Leahy wondered each day over the problems he would face in captive France. France, a nation loved by his wife, yet one he scarcely knew, was divided by her conquerer, and in Vichy a few tired, discouraged men tried to govern. At the top was Marshal Philippe Pétain, hero of Verdun in World War I, but now a tired old man of eighty-four, who strove to keep the men under him from selling out completely to the Germans.

While Leahy was musing the problems of France, a steward approached. He was bearing a radiogram from President Roosevelt.

Admiral Leahy SS *Borinquen*
Info COMTHREE Stop Arranging disembark you upon arrival quarantine and thence by navy plane Laguardia field to Washington Stop Essential you arrive Whitehouse prior eleventhirty Monday two December if time of arrival at New York permits
OPNAV[1]

It seems that President Roosevelt was departing at noon on 2 December for a cruise in the Caribbean, and if he and Leahy were to have a proper talk, it had to be before the presidential train POTUS set out for Miami.

Accordingly, at 7:10 on the morning of 2 December, ten minutes after the ship had arrived at quarantine, Leahy embarked in a Navy patrol boat. He was quickly whisked to the Battery, whence a police-escorted navy car took him to La Guardia airport. At 8:10 a navy transport plane lifted from the runway and arrived at Anacostia Naval Air Station in Washington fifty minutes later. A waiting car took him directly to the White House, and for two hours he and the president conferred on American foreign policy vis-à-vis France and Leahy's part in carrying it out.

When France had been defeated in June of that year, the brutal armistice terms imposed on her by Germany and Italy had divided the country into two zones. About 60 percent of the nation, including the entire Atlantic coast and the city of Paris, was occupied by the Germans. A heavily patrolled line of demarcation separated the Occupied from the Unoccupied Zone in the south-eastern part of France. When the French government officials abandoned Paris in June to escape the conquering Germans, they had set up a temporary capital in Bordeaux, but since that city was to be included in the Occupied Zone, the French moved their wartime capital to the famous mineral spa, Vichy.

Chief of state was eighty-four-year-old Marshal Henri Philippe Pétain, who had taken over the demoralized government in June in order to negotiate an armistice with the Germans. He had become virtual dictator of France. But in the number-two spot was the unabashedly pro-German Pierre Laval. Known in the diplomatic cables as "Black Peter," Laval had the reputation of being an untrustworthy pragmatist, whose aim in life was to be on the winning side in all matters. Equally, he was determined to have France on the winning side in all matters as well. Many times an office-holder in prewar France, he had risen from the state of a poverty-stricken peasant to a rich man and a powerful politician.

The third most powerful man in Vichy France was Admiral Jean Louis Xavier François Darlan, commander in chief of the French fleet and the marshal's heir apparent. When FDR selected Leahy for the post of ambassador, he expected him to talk to Darlan as one sailor to another. Darlan, after all, commanded the only potential fighting force remaining in France. The problem was that Darlan hated the British and was widely held to be an Axis sympathizer. No one really trusted him to keep the French navy from supporting the Axis.

As ambassador, or course, Leahy would have much wider responsibilities than keeping Darlan and the French fleet in line. Roosevelt shrewdly guessed that Marshal Pétain was no willing collaborator. Pétain, according to Roosevelt, was a man who thought of the French people as *mes enfants*, who used the royal "We" in his decrees, and who sincerely desired an Allied victory. While Laval and Darlan thought of their own positions in the new France as she took her place alongside a triumphant Germany, Pétain thought only of France. A true patriot, he was to win the respect and friendship of Leahy in the sixteen months of their association.

Roosevelt also felt that there was some fighting spirit left in the French people, that there was some contribution they could still make, despite the bitterness of their defeat, despite the occupation of most of their country, and despite such leaders as Laval and Darlan.

While Leahy encouraged any signs of French independence, he was, at the same time, to stiffen the backbone of Pétain and keep him from giving Germany anything more than the armistice articles demanded. His ministers, and not only Laval and Darlan, might deceive the marshal, and it would be one of Leahy's tasks to keep him informed of the truth insofar as it was possible. "I was to tell Pétain anything I learned that his ministers might be keeping from him."[2]

An ominous event had taken place in October when Marshal Pétain had met with Hitler at Montoire, near Paris. Although few details had reached Washington, the State Department feared the meeting presaged closer collaboration between France and Germany. The presence of Laval at the meeting added a sinister note.★

As events were to prove, there was rather less than met the eye in the Montoire meetings, for Marshal Pétain drew no closer to collaboration with Germany after he had met with Hitler than before. But Leahy would have to reinforce American influence and remind the marshal of the strength of the United States. It would be difficult, for the Germans were on French soil, while the United States was across an ocean, and many American leaders spoke loudly for neutrality and noninvolvement in the European war.

French North African colonies were largely beyond the influence of the

---

★It is now known that the Montoire meeting led to a *procès verbal* in which the two leaders agreed that the "Axis Powers and France have an identical interest in seeing the defeat of England accomplished as soon as possible. Consequently the French Government will support, within the limits of its ability, the measures which the Axis powers may take to this end."

Germans. Under General Maxime Weygand, they offered opportunities for opposition to Hitler, even though the risk of reprisals in France itself was staggering. Most of the contacts in North Africa and the negotiations there were to be done by Leahy's first counsel, Robert Murphy, but Leahy, of course, would be in overall charge.

At the end of two hours of conversation, Leahy felt he had a good understanding of what the president wanted him to do.[3] But to be on the safe side, he wanted the instructions in writing. With Roosevelt's approval, he and Secretary of State Cordell Hull prepared a letter for the president's signature, FDR's crisp instructions being translated into State Department verbiage. [The complete text appears in Appendix A.]

Perhaps Leahy's mind went back to an occasion in 1912 when he heard an American diplomat in Nicaragua remark, "Instructions issued by the State Department to an officer in the field must always purposely be vague and capable of different interpretations in order that the Department may always in case of necessity unload responsibility for its mistakes upon some subordinate."[4] No one was going to make Bill Leahy a scapegoat for anything. If he was to make a mistake, it would be his own and not one made because of fuzzy instructions.

In any case, Leahy realized that his job was a political hot potato. A good many Americans believed that the Vichy government was too pro-German, that the French had cravenly yielded to the Germans while the British fought gallantly on. Since he had a considerable suspicion that the critics of Vichy were right, he wanted to make it very sure that he was not to be identified with the Vichy regime.

It was inevitable, of course, that he would be. Later in the war, after his return to the United States, a good many newspaper correspondents hinted that he was a sinister influence in strategic deliberations because he was too pro-French, that he supported French goals at the expense of other considerations. These attacks did not succeed because, like General George Marshall, chief of staff of the army, he was above criticism on personal grounds. Also FDR knew better than to take any notice of such ill-informed journalists and commentators.

For the next several days, while the president was enjoying his cruise aboard the *Tuscaloosa*, Leahy spent his time trying to learn as much as he could about France, about American policy, about the state of the war in Europe. He talked to State Department officials, to M. Camille Chautemps, onetime premier of France, and to William Bullitt, whom he was replacing as ambassador. He met Gaston Henri-Haye, French ambassador to the United States. He had a medical checkup and his teeth filled. Then, on 19 December in company with Under Secretary of State Sumner Welles, he had a final conference with the president.

Tanned and refreshed by his cruise in the Caribbean, Roosevelt had just promulgated his plan for Lend-Lease, selling it to the public with his famous analogy—"suppose my neighbor's house is on fire and I have a length of garden hose. . . ."

Although Secretary of State Cordell Hull had assisted in drafting the written instructions to Leahy, he was to have little part in the new ambassador's subsequent dealings with Washington. Throughout the war, Roosevelt preferred to work directly with his important representatives and diplomats abroad. He dealt personally with such men as Churchill and Stalin, or he entrusted the relationships to a faithful agent, most often, Harry Hopkins. At the time Leahy was sent to France, however, Hopkins had not yet made his mark in foreign affairs.

Cordell Hull had for the most part to content himself with routine matters of the State Department. For jobs such as Leahy was to undertake, FDR preferred to get his reports direct or through someone who spoke language more akin to his own. For this reason, while Leahy was expected to submit routine cables through normal channels to the State Department, he was to feel free at any time to correspond directly with the president and with Sumner Welles, FDR's fellow Grotonian and fellow patrician.

Leahy's selection as ambassador was part of a general realignment of American diplomatic representatives in the major European capitals. For some time, as a mark of American displeasure, there had been no ambassador in Berlin. Ambassador William Phillips had recently returned from Rome and submitted his resignation. He would not be replaced. Ambassador Joseph P. Kennedy, who had filed one gloomy report after another from London, was in the United States and would soon be replaced at the Court of St. James's by John G. Winant. The previous ambassador to France, William Bullitt, had been too closely associated with the regime of former Premier Paul Reynaud. Of other major capitals, only in Moscow was there an active ambassador, Laurence A. Steinhardt.

In general the American press approved Leahy's selection for the post in Vichy. Anne O'Hare McCormick, writing in the *New York Times*, had a perceptive comment:

> The appointment of Admiral Leahy as Ambassador to France . . . is the first move in a diplomatic counter-offensive. It is clear that the President is the only democratic leader with the power and position to check Hitler's moves; Mr. Churchill is a war leader completely absorbed in military strategy. It is equally clear that the first aim of democratic diplomacy at this moment is to prevent Hitler from sewing up the Continent and to undermine his influence in every way among those nations in which the hunger for freedom and the tradition of self-government are strongest.
>
> The first of these is France. Whether it succeeds or not, the effort to save and stiffen France should be made. Hitler's setback in winning the full cooperation of the Pétain government is an opportunity Washington seizes to send an

Ambassador to Vichy—a gesture made more significant because the envoy
chosen knows naval strategy, knows the Caribbean and may be able to help the
French to guard their interests as they are affected by the present anomalous
position of France. It is not a spectacular move, but it announces the President's
intention to take a hand in Hitler's game of shaping the peace while the war goes
on. Others are expected to follow.[5]

*The United States News*, which ran Leahy's picture on the cover of its issue
of 13 December 1940 commented:

> Mr. Leahy, as admiral-ambassador, will be especially well fitted to deal with
> such men as Marshal Henri Pétain, premier of France; Vice Admiral Jean
> Darlan, the right-wing head of the French fleet, and General Maxime Weygand,
> now in North Africa. Admiral Leahy will be able to talk in terms these men
> understand. He can discuss the problem of Martinique from first-hand knowl-
> edge. He can talk about Gibraltar, and what it means to the future peace of the
> Western Hemisphere. He can discuss the French colonies in North Africa, in
> Syria, in Indo-China. He may be able to keep those colonies from becoming
> part of Hitler's war machine. . . .
> From his public utterances of the past and from his conversations with
> friends, it is known that he believes that only a policy of firmness will keep this
> nation safe from the dictators abroad. He is opposed to any policy of appease-
> ment. He is said to be going to Vichy with no illusions about the hold which the
> Nazis have upon the Pétain government.[6]

These comments are typical of those in the press. Everyone stressed Leahy
as the military man. No one seemed to realize that as an ambassador, he would
have to talk the language of diplomacy, not the language of guns. He was to be
no Gauleiter. He was to persuade, not demand. He was to influence, not
coerce. In short, he was to be an ambassador.

On 22 December 1940, Leahy and his wife embarked at Norfolk in the navy
cruiser *Tuscaloosa*. As soon as they had come aboard, the ship got under way
and set course for Lisbon. It was a rough crossing. On Christmas day the
Leahys opened their presents while sitting on a settee in the admiral's cabin,
bracing themselves against the lively motion of the ship.

The *Tuscaloosa* continued at 20 knots, arriving late in the morning of 30
December at Lisbon, where the new ambassador and his wife were met by
Commander Roscoe H. Hillenkoetter, who was to be the admiral's aide in
Vichy, and by Commander James L. Wyatt, attaché to the embassy in
Madrid. After spending the night in the legation in Lisbon and obtaining
additional food stores from the *Tuscaloosa*, the party embarked on the over-
night train to Madrid. Their hosts, Ambassador and Mrs. Alexander Weddell, made the most of the arrival of their guests to welcome members of the
diplomatic corps to the embassy to meet the Leahys. The admiral was impressed by the excellent staff work of the French embassy in Spain when the

WDL, with Mrs. Leahy, inspecting honor guard of Marines aboard the USS *Tusca-loosa* before sailing for Lisbon to take up duties as ambassador to Vichy France, December 1940. (Courtesy, National Archives)

French ambassador accurately quoted some testimony that Leahy had given to a congressional committee three years earlier.

On 3 January 1941, accompanied by Commander Hillenkoetter, the Leahys caught a morning train for Barcelona. The journey was supposed to last about twelve hours but that proved to be wildly optimistic. Although they had reserved a private compartment, the Leahy party did not enjoy it to themselves, as three uninvited Spaniards crowded in with them. Other people jammed the aisles, filling every available space with themselves and their baggage, which included wilting vegetables and live chickens. The mass of beings in the aisles made it practically impossible for the American party to obtain food from the restaurant car. Every so often, for no reason anyone

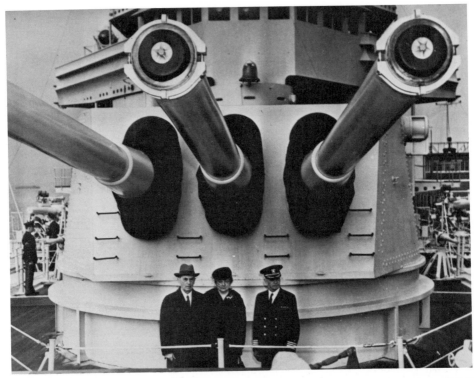

Ambassador and Mrs. Leahy with Captain N. C. Gillette, USN, aboard the USS *Tuscaloosa*, December 1940. (Courtesy, National Archives)

could discern, the train would stop. Once it stood stock-still for over three hours. The miserable journey, made worse by the cold both inside and outside the train, took twenty-five hours instead of the scheduled twelve.

Reaching Barcelona at last, tired, cold, and hungry, the party had breakfast in a poor hotel bearing the mendacious name of the Ritz, and then "started in a small Hispano-Suiza motor car for France, our baggage following in an army truck. The weather was cold but bright, and in a closed car at midday not uncomfortable even to those of us who started chilled and fatigued by the train journey."[7]

Shortly before reaching the French border, they had a bad hour or so. A bridge had washed out, and the Hispano-Suiza got stuck trying to ford the river, and there the party remained until a peasant and his horse could be hired to pull them out. The rushing water around them made the experience much like that of sitting in a refrigerator. "While the temperature could not have been much below freezing, that time seemed to be the coldest hour in my experience."[8]

As they reached the French border, conditions improved. They were met by a French motorcade, a general in command of that district of the French army, and by three agents of the Sûreté. The motorcade proceeded to Mont-pelier, where rooms at the Hotel Métropole awaited them. Unfortunately the rooms were unheated, and that part of Europe was in the grip of a cold wave unmatched in a hundred years. Too tired to care, the Leahys bundled all the clothes they could around them and piled on all the blankets they could find. In spite of their fatigue and the bitter cold, they slept well. Rising late, they had an excellent breakfast and then continued in the motorcade to Nîmes, where the private railway car of Marshal Pétain awaited them. It was warm and well provided with food and drink. As soon as the American party had boarded, the train departed, reaching Vichy about midnight. There they were met by Henri Lozé, chef de protocol, and by members of the embassy staff and were conducted to the residence "where we began our tour of duty in France with a hot supper that had been provided by Mr. H. F. Matthews, our Chargé d'Affaires."[9] The house, which belonged to the American, Frank Gould, was located, ironically enough, on the Avenue Thermale, named in honor of the warm springs for which Vichy was famous.

German propagandists and their puppet French editors in Paris lost no time in trying to discredit the new American ambassador to France, and not all Frenchmen endorsed Leahy's mission. In German-occupied Paris, Jacques de Lesdain, writing in *L'Illustration* on 4 January 1941, demanded to know why a daily visitor to the White House was sent to France, but he hoped he would be understanding. A few weeks later, the same writer accused Leahy of trying to force France to do America's bidding. He described how ministers of all ranks presented themselves at the American embassy in Vichy to do *humbles hommages* and to offer their service.[10]

The British, on the other hand, having no cordial relations at all with the French government at Vichy, welcomed American efforts to keep contacts open. Above all, they did not want the French driven by fear or desperation into the Axis camp, and they hoped that Leahy would be able to keep them leaning toward the Anglo-Saxon side. Yet characteristic British distrust of American diplomacy made them suspicious of the ambassador chosen. Harold Macmillan later expressed grave reservations. Although he approved of America sending an ambassador to the Vichy government, he considered Leahy less than ideal.

> Admiral Leahy was one of those men who, although unable to converse with any Frenchman in intelligible French, believed himself the supreme exponent of the French mentality. Even the keenest members of the Admiral's group had their doubts about his fitness for this post. The reports that he sent were not helpful and his action throughout was unfavourable to the British Government. But the American administration also suffered under the delusion, to some extent shared by the American people, that they were especially popular in France.[11]

It is not clear where Macmillan got the idea that the embassy staff had doubts about Leahy's fitness for the post. The evidence simply is not there, and certainly President Roosevelt and Sumner Welles felt he met their standards in his reports, even if he did not meet those of Mr. Macmillan. But the key to Mr. Macmillan's criticism is in his statement that his actions were not helpful to the British.

Since, by diplomatic custom, an ambassador is not recognized until he has presented his credentials to the head of state, it was important that Leahy arrange to meet Marshal Pétain as soon as possible. The day after his arrival, therefore, he called upon Foreign Minister Pierre Flandin and arranged to present his letter of credence to the French leader the following day, 8 January.

Bill Leahy knew quite well that if he was going to succeed in what was very nearly a hostile country, he would need the support of the local newspaper correspondents, particularly those who worked for major foreign newspapers and wire services. They often had better sources of information than he did, and what they wrote about him and his efforts would have effect in Washington, in Berlin, in Paris, and in London. Largely to make their acquaintance, therefore, although he had nothing in particular to say, he called a press conference.

> I was to grow very fond of these correspondents. They were nice lads and very useful. They had many sources of information and on occasion gave me much more news than I had for them. Among those who thus performed a valuable service for their own or adopted country were Paul Archembault (*New York Times*); Herbert King (United Press); Taylor Henry (Associated Press); John Elliott (*New York Herald Tribune*); Paul Ghali (*Chicago Daily News*); and, lastly, Ralph Heinzen (United Press).
> Archembault was the best informed. It was no secret that Heinzen was a "favorite" of Laval. The recently deposed Premier [Laval] and his son-in-law, René de Chambrun, were trying to use Heinzen to get favorable publicity by telling him many things the other correspondents did not get. However, I think Heinzen really used his informers and that his copy was accurate. I once asked him, "Is this propaganda they are getting out for Laval?" He replied it was not and he thought the story we were discussing was a statement of fact. Heinzen was very useful.[12]

On the morning of 8 January, Leahy woke with a sore throat and a bad cold, scarcely surprising in view of his experiences of the previous week. Swallowing aspirin and gargling, he dressed himself in his formal morning coat and waited for the promised arrival of M. Lozé, assistant to M. Flandin. Promptly at 11:45 A.M. Lozé arrived, and accompanied by members of his staff, Leahy set out by motor car to the Pavillon Sévigné.

The welcome was cordial from the moment they disembarked from the cars to be greeted by a guard of honor composed of matelots in acknowledgement of Leahy' naval rank. Marshal Pétain received him more warmly than strict protocol required. The new ambassador presented his letter of credence, the recall letter of former ambassador William Bullitt, and a personal letter from President Roosevelt to Marshal Pétain.

After the letters had been proffered and received, and the two staffs presented, Leahy and Pétain, accompanied by Flandin and H. Freeman "Doc" Matthews, withdrew to a small inner room for a few moments of polite conversation. Revealing either an excellent memory or even better staff work Pétain referred to their previous meeting at Yorktown in 1931, and they reminisced about how the French had assisted the infant American republic in the revolution against George III and his redcoats. The conversation was polite, proper, and nothing of substance was discussed.

> Maréchal Pétain, who is eighty-four years of age, gives every appearance of a remarkable virility and mentality. He appears to understand English, but spoke only French so clearly and deliberately that it was easy for me to understand it. We arranged for a conversation tomorrow at 4:00 P.M. on affairs of state.

The following day, when Leahy appeared for the promised discussion, Pétain appeared tired, worn-out, and feeble. He left almost all of the conversation to Flandin, who wanted to talk about relief shipments of food and medicine for the children of unoccupied France. From this experience, Leahy determined to schedule as many appointments as possible with Pétain for early hours before the work of the day had sapped the old man's mental and physical powers.

As soon as he had recovered from his cold, the new ambassador began, as the new boy in town, to make the obligatory calls on other members of the diplomatic corps and on French officials. One of the most important was one of several hours duration with Admiral Darlan, the minister of marine. As one sailor to another, the two men got along well enough, but as diplomat to government official, Leahy never developed full confidence in Darlan, whom he began to refer to as "Popeye," the sailor man. Frequently in his journal he observed, "You always had to keep an eye on 'Popeye.'"

He found Darlan hopelessly prejudiced against the British, especially against the Royal Navy and its leadership. Darlan swore he would never again clasp the hand of an Englishman and that he would gladly lead French ships against the British with every expectation of success.

Leahy appreciated that Darlan was biased toward the Germans and that he was determined to end up on the winning side in the present war. In this respect he parted company with Laval, who openly espoused collaboration because he knew the Germans were going to win. Darlan was not absolutely sure, so he tended to hedge his bets. He told Leahy he believed the Nazi regime would not long survive the death of Hitler. When the German government collapsed, then France would have her opportunity to regain her grandeur, power, and influence. The British, he added scathingly, would be happy to keep France forever in an inferior position. France, he added, had no intention of accepting such a subordinate role.

A fortnight after presenting his credentials, Leahy sent a detailed preliminary report to President Roosevelt.

The situation had changed since Leahy had been named ambassador. The despised Pierre Laval had been fired by Marshal Pétain. The infuriated Germans demanded that "Black Peter" be restored to power at once. It was up to Leahy to stiffen the spine of the old marshal and keep Laval out.

Pétain, Leahy felt, was very capable but caught in a job too big for him. Surrounded by a weak cabinet, Pétain tried to shoulder too much of the responsibilities of government himself. In particular, the marshal disliked and distrusted Laval, who, he suspected, was after his own job. Still, the ambassador predicted, the Germans would sooner or later force Pétain to take Laval back into the government. The Germans, Leahy reported, would wring the last concession from the French and would reinforce their demands with threats against the two million French prisoners of war, by withholding foodstuffs, and by threatening to move into unoccupied France.

Leahy saw no possibility whatever that Pétain could be persuaded to move his government to North Africa where it would be free of German pressure. Frenchmen as a whole had no faith whatever in a British victory, although they hoped for one. So they saw it as more logical and safer to make any necessary accommodations with the Germans.

As far as other personalities were concerned: Flandin was a weak compromiser, who leaned "pretty far over to the German side." General Charles-Leon Huntziger, war minister, was the strongest member of the cabinet, and Admiral Darlan was "not pro-German, but like all the others, he thinks the Germans will win." No one wanted to return to the prewar Third Republic with its ineffectual democracy. Many favored a fascist-style government, but without the ideas of foreign expansion pursued by Mussolini.[13] As the months went on, Leahy learned that German demands on Vichy were increasing, ruthless, and implacable. Only three days after he had written the president, he heard that Pétain was expecting fresh demands from the Nazis but that he had no idea what they would be. "The old Marshal's back was definitely stiff, and he expressed willingness to let the Germans do their worst rather than to help them in any way beyond the requirements of the present Armistice agreement." The marshal's determination was not always, as Leahy was to learn, so forceful and so indomitable.

The new ambassador soon realized that truth had very little relationship to what appeared in the newspapers controlled by the Germans or their puppets. In an early interview, Leahy forthrightly and strongly predicted a British victory. The local censor refused to let the Vichy press carry the story, and a

Belgian paper turned it completely around, reporting that Leahy had predicted the inevitable German triumph. His indignant denial was widely disseminated in the British and American press, and courageous citizens in occupied countries who listened to clandestine radios heard the BBC reveal the lie for what it was.

> Here, [Leahy commented in a letter to his successor as CNO, Admiral "Betty" Stark,] we are pretty thoroughly isolated from news and very thoroughly exposed to rumors that practically all turn out to be false. . . . We manage to keep pretty close contact with the Marshal's Government and we find the living conditions not too bad for us and probably for those others who have plenty of money. The general run of natives are already short of money and that will get worse as they use up their savings. There is a definite shortage of food.[14]

The routine at Vichy was soon established. Best known as a health spa, Vichy was unsuited to be the capital of a country. Normally the population had been around 50,000, rising to about 90,000 during the peak season. As capital of unoccupied France, it offered dubious accommodations to more than 130,000 government functionaries, bureaucrats, lobbyists, hangers-on, spies, *demimondaines*, and a few diehards who presented themselves for treatment at the various spas or sanitoria. And then there were the people who made their homes there, less, of course, the men who had been killed or captured in the war.

The Leahys were reasonably comfortable in the house on the Avenue Thermale, although they never succeeded in getting the place warm until the arrival of spring made further efforts unnecessary. Around the corner, the Villa Ica, previously a doctor's office, served the dual function of temporary embassy and chancellery. Leahy's office was upstairs in a former sitting room. The furniture already there had to do, for none other was to be had.

The embassy counselor, Robert Murphy, was seldom in Vichy, President Roosevelt having assigned him the special task of negotiating with the French commander in North Africa, General Maxime Weygand. Weygand, who was anathema to the Germans, and Murphy worked out an accord by which the United States undertook to keep the French in North Africa supplied with food, medicines, and other necessities. In return, Weygand agreed that the distribution of these shipments should be supervised by a number of American "control officers." Everyone knew that their nominal duties were far less important than their gathering intelligence useful to the Anglo-Saxon cause. The Germans fumed but they were powerless to do anything about the "control officers." Their contributions paid off in November 1942, when the Allies landed in North Africa. Leahy, of course, was fully informed of Murphy's activities, but kept his hands off, since Murphy was doing a splendid job.

In due course the Murphy–Weygand agreement was signed, and Bob Murphy came to Vichy to have it ratified by the ambassador. Murphy, a career diplomat, certainly did not agree with Macmillan's caustic comments about Leahy. Later he wrote that FDR had appointed Leahy because he hoped he could get closer to Pétain than any civilian diplomat could.

> Roosevelt's hopes were justified, [wrote Murphy] and the Admiral exercised great influence at Vichy for eighteen months. He told everybody there that he was no diplomat and that he knew very little about European politics, but that he did know something about military matters and that these were of major concern in wartime. He was keenly interested in the African project, and during our first meeting he put me through a detailed and critical examination. After that he supported my efforts at every stage.[15]

Approved in Washington at the end of February and by the Vichy government on 10 March, the agreement was adequate reason for Murphy to remain in North Africa were he could supervise the "control officers." Technically he remained attached to the embassy at Vichy.

In addition to Commander Hillenkoetter and Freeman "Doc" Matthews, Leahy found himself most drawn to Third Secretary Douglas MacArthur II. This MacArthur was the nephew of the famous general and the son of a naval officer, Arthur, who had graduated from the Naval Academy in 1896, a year ahead of Leahy. Although Bill Leahy and Arthur MacArthur had seldom crossed paths since leaving Annapolis, they had been friends until Arthur's death in 1923. Having known the father, Leahy was prepared to welcome the son into his circle of friends.

Of all the embassy staff, these three and their wives were closest to the Leahys. All went on to distinguished careers in their respective services, and whenever they met in later years, they had much to say about the years in Vichy.

Communications with the outside world were a major problem. Everyone assumed, correctly, that the Germans were intercepting and deciphering the official cables, so the most sensitive materials were sent by couriers who appeared at irregular intervals, having flown across the Atlantic to Lisbon and thence by car or train across Portugal, Spain, and France, and on to Vichy. The appearance of one of these couriers would result in a flurry of activity as mail was sorted, read, considered, pondered over, consulted about, and answered in the shortest possible time. Many letters were written while the courier stood first on one foot and then another, anxious to be off on the return journey.

News of the world came from American newspapers brought in by the couriers, always weeks late, from the BBC broadcasts, in spite of German efforts to jam them, and occasionally from a Boston radio station. The local French newspapers, whether from the Occupied or Unoccupied Zone, were heavily censored. Those from Paris often had highly scurrilous stories about the American ambassador. He felt that the more outrageous they were, the more they revealed Nazi displeasure and therefore that he was doing a good job. Jacques de Lesdain had another go at him in March, explaining how he had witnessed an *explosion de servilité de la presse vichyssoise*. It concluded with the note that in Vichy one no longer asks "What is best for the country?" Instead, he concluded, one asks, "What will the Admiral think?" And certainly, he added, "they are not talking about Admiral Darlan."[16]

Vichy residents made efforts to maintain normal social activities. The Leahys were regular patrons of the opera and other musical events. Food was always in short supply, but the various embassies had adequate stocks, although much was stolen from resupply shipments. Members of the *cours diplomatique* entertained each other often at formal and informal affairs. In season, there was the horse-racing schedule, when those in, and aspiring to be in, fashionable society dressed in their best and sauntered about the track, trying to pretend there was no war.

Of course, in Vichy, it was obligatory to take the "cure." This consisted of consuming exact doses of water from the various springs, the amounts from each carefully prescribed by a physician. Patients went from spring to spring, carrying their graduated glasses in little green baskets. The other part of the "cure" consisted of thermal baths, accompanied by massage under a spray of hot water centered on the liver for one minute precisely. The Leahys, who took the treatment in July, felt it accomplished little more than would a thorough massage.

In February, defying German pressure to reinstate Laval as vice president of the council, Pétain reorganized his government, appointing Darlan to that post, and also naming him heir apparent. In addition he gave him the additional duties of foreign minister and chief of the Department of the Interior. Darlan also retained his post as minister of marine, the most effective of the remaining armed forces of France.

German propagandists in Paris began a vigorous attack on these appointments, charging that Leahy, a "Free Mason, a representative of the Jewish bankers, and ex-British agent," was using "ultimatum methods" on the marshal to obtain the appointment of "his sailor friend, Admiral Darlan."

Leahy, who was not quite clear what an "ex-British agent" was nor had any idea what "ultimatum methods" meant, could only reflect that it was better for "Popeye" to have those departments than "Black Peter." The idea of Laval having authority over the Department of the Interior was enough to make anyone shudder, for that department had control of the Sûreté, which was already adopting some of the unpleasanter methods of the Gestapo. Still, he had no illusions that Darlan was wedded to the principles of democracy.

He duly reported to the president on a conversation with Darlan after his elevation to all those posts.

> The trend of development today in France seems to be to give Admiral Darlan all of the essential powers of the Government to be exercised for so long a time as he can retain the confidence of the Marshal and for so long as he can avoid being forced out of office by the German and pro-German influence.
>
> He expresses himself very freely as being in favor of economic collaboration with Germany.

After describing Darlan's threats to use force to break the British blockade if Churchill continued what Darlan called his deliberate starvation of women and children, "without any possible military advantage to Great Britain," Leahy concluded:

> Admiral Darlan is able, ambitious and, in my opinion, dangerous unless he is restrained by the Marshal in his intentions toward the British Navy and the British blockade.[17]

In a detailed letter written a fortnight later to Sumner Welles, Leahy described his belief that the reconstituted government would "be permitted to operate" in order to see "whether or not it could be induced to 'cooperate' properly with Germany." In describing reports of a journey Pétain had taken, he told of a man asking for more bread. The marshal, according to Leahy's source, replied, "How can we do anything when we are occupied by a horde of leeches who take everything?" On another occasion, in speaking of de Gaulle, he called him "a poisonous viper" that he had "warmed at his own bosom."

> The old gentleman, whom I hold in the highest regard as a patriot completely devoted to the welfare of his people, has of late been hitting on all cylinders. If he were assisted by a group of completely devoted, unselfish advisers, he might be able to slap back occasionally at the invaders who seem to be thoroughly detested by all those Frenchmen who are not in search of political advancement through German influence, or subsidized by the Germans. I have a definite feeling that he is not kept accurately informed by his ministers.[18]

One of America's principal hopes for France lay in old General Maxime Weygand, who continued to thwart Axis ambitions in North Africa. FDR and his advisors believed that he might be persuaded to make himself a focal point of French resistance outside of metropolitan France. If Weygand would take the leadership in North Africa, even if Pétain chose to remain in France, then the British and Americans would not have to deal with the Free French and their leader Charles de Gaulle, whose behavior had speedily gone from difficult to impossible.

Pétain promised Leahy that when Weygand next visited Vichy, he would invite the American ambassador to a dinner in the general's honor. When the visit actually took place, Pétain reneged on his promise because the men around him believed that such a dinner would be a dangerous challenge to the Germans. Instead, Weygand called at the embassy on 9 March. Leahy wondered why the call would attract any less attention than a dinner. There was not the slightest doubt in his mind that every German authority from the local Gestapo spy to the Führer himself knew of the meeting.

Weygand was glad to talk to Leahy because he knew that Pétain trusted him implicitly. The marshal, according to Weygand, never concealed the truth from Leahy, but perhaps he did not tell all of it.[19]

The general proved to be a tough old warrior. Like many Frenchmen, he was a pragmatist, and he hoped for a German defeat in the war, but he was first and foremost a Frenchman. He expressed appreciation of American aid arriving in North African ports, and he gave Leahy a great deal of information about the military and political conditions in the area. The Germans, he said, were spending a good deal of time and effort to turn the natives against the French and Americans.

But, he warned, North Africa was French, and he would defend that territory against an attack by anybody. He emphasized *anybody*, and Leahy clearly understood that he meant British and American as well as German forces. He also argued, and Leahy had to agree, that any attempt on the part of the French in North Africa to join the fighting against Germany would inevitably mean the occupation of all of continental France. That would reduce her people to a condition of slavery.

On the whole, Leahy was favorably impressed by the indomitable old general and hoped that he would be able to remain at his post for some time to come. "The only two persons here," he wrote in a letter to Roosevelt, "who have impressed me as completely devoted to France without thought of personal advantage are Marshal Pétain and General Weygand. While they possess an astonishing vitality, both are old, and both are irreplaceable."[20]

Admiral Darlan, whom Leahy trusted just so far, called at the embassy that same day. He had come to report on a visit he had made to Paris where, he boasted, he had wrung from the Germans a promise to release to unoccupied France 200,000 tons of wheat from their reserves in the north. According to Darlan, the Germans expected to reap their reward in the propaganda value Dr. Goebbels would be sure to exploit. "Admiral Darlan," commented Leahy wryly, "did not say what else the Germans expect in payment for his wheat."

Food shortages in Vichy France were caused not only by German occupation but by the British blockade, and anti-British sentiment was widespread. There were many causes for it. Universally the French believed, because their leaders wanted to believe, that the British had withheld vital reinforcements in the critical days of June 1940, reinforcements that might have turned the tide of battle. Then, after the French surrender, there had been attacks on the French fleet by the British, the seizure of French ships in British ports, a British–Free French assault on Dakar, led by the upstart Charles de Gaulle, who had already been condemned to death *in absentia* by the Vichy government. Worst of all, the British continued to fight on, against all reason. Weygand had predicted that in three weeks after the French surrender, Britain would have its "neck wrung like a chicken." To which Churchill replied as the bombs fell and British defiance continued, "Some chicken! Some neck!"

But hatred of the Germans was even more widespread. It was said that two prayers were said daily in France. Those who sympathized with the British, prayed, "Oh, God! Let the British win!" British-haters prayed, "Oh, God! Let the British swine win!"

A problem that plagued Leahy throughout his tour in Vichy was the German demand on France for gasoline and oil as called for by the armistice terms. So long as those supplies came from France herself, they were of no concern to the United States, but repeatedly the Germans or Italians insisted that Darlan supply petroleum products from stores in North Africa. Since those stores had been largely provided by the United States, American authorities naturally objected to seeing them go on to members of the Axis.

On 30 March, Darlan told Leahy that the Italians had ordered the French to deliver to Genoa 5,000 tons of gasoline, specifying that it come from their reserves in Algiers.

> I reminded Admiral Darlan of his statement made to me in the Marshal's presence on March 3 that he would not deliver any petroleum products from Africa to the Axis powers and told him that a delivery of this gasoline would, in my opinion, make it exceedingly difficult for America to give any further assistance in the provision of essential material to the African colonies and that it might prevent any further American assistance to either colonial or unoccupied France.

This was pretty tough language, and France found herself in the middle between two powers. America could threaten to cut off aid, but the pitifully small amount of supplies the British allowed through their blockade reduced the impact of that threat. The graver peril, and one which gave every Frenchman nightmares was that, if the French went too far, the Germans would occupy the entire country, send every able-bodied man to forced labor in Germany, and maltreat, starve, or enslave the prisoners of war they still held.

From March onward, Leahy was almost never able to see Marshal Pétain without Darlan being present and dominating the conversation. This fact he found most irritating, for the forceful Darlan was often able to overbear the old marshal and make him take positions Leahy believed he would not have taken if left to his own devices. These Darlan-induced positions were, naturally, not to the advantage of the United States.

One of the few ships allowed through the British blockade to French ports was the American freighter *Exmouth*, which was carrying a cargo of food and medicine, intended primarily for children. On 7 April, the Leahys set out by motor car to meet the ship at Marseilles.

During the reception ceremonies for the *Exmouth*, the cold, driving rain of the mistral forced them to move the gala affair into the shelter of a closed pier. Leahy made a speech, which was widely broadcast, to counter German propaganda that America cared nothing for the French people in their time of distress. Distribution was under tight control of the Red Cross in order to keep the milk, cheese, and other commodities out of the hands of Germans and black marketeers. Hearing expressions of gratitude from French parents as their children received fresh milk, Leahy decided that if anyone tried to divert part of these supplies to the black market, the aroused parents would kill him.

The next day the Leahys moved on to Toulon, "where we were greeted by thousands of children lining the streets," as well as by the more formal official reception by dignitaries. Everywhere they went it was the same story: thousands of children waved French and American flags; grateful parents tried to clasp their hands. In Marseilles, the ambassador was summoned *au balcon* and had to make a brief speech to the crowd in the Rue Canebière below. In Nice, Leahy was kissed by two "highly emotional old ladies."[21]

On their return to Vichy, the Leahys found they had traveled nearly 1,200 miles in terrible weather over slippery roads but that it all had been worthwhile. They had succeeded in bringing American supplies and American moral support to areas of France where the people believed they had been forgotten by their own government and by the world.

When he turned to the mail that had accumulated in his absence, Leahy was startled to read a report, sent by a Puerto Rican friend, that he had been assassinated. No one knew how the rumor had started and how it had reached San Juan. It was, in Mark Twain's word, "exaggerated."[22] But it might have happened, especially on the trip he had just concluded. That journey had given no joy to the Germans and the French collaborationists.

With their successes in Greece in April, the Germans began to tighten the screws on the Vichy government. In several letters to both Welles and to the president Leahy wrote how the Germans had refused to issue any further *laissez-passers* to any foreigners, thus effectively closing the line of demarcation between the two parts of France to members of the diplomatic corps as well as to business travelers. The Nazis claimed and exercised the right to search homes, factories, shops, and farm buildings in the Unoccupied Zone. They demanded that Germans control all coastal shipping in the Mediterranean. They pressured factory owners in Vichy France to work exclusively on German orders, which might or might not be paid for in occupation currency, which was generally useless to the French. They sent some two hundred men, mostly officers, to North Africa as an "armistice commission," and they sent large numbers of "tourists" there as well.

"We are unable," Leahy confided in a letter to the president, "to ascertain the purpose of Germany in these new activities, and the Marshal's Government is not able to offer any effective opposition."

He went on to advise FDR that Marshal Pétain asked him to come by often to hear his difficulties and lend a sympathetic ear, a clear proof that he had confidence in Leahy's good intentions. Those problems included the German policy of interpreting the armistice agreement just as they pleased, and that the Vichy government was powerless to resist.

> It appears from what the Marshal tells me of German methods that the only effective opposition would be armed resistance or the use of sabotage methods, and while the people of France are almost unanimous in their hatred of Germany, they have no arms, no organization, and very little fighting spirit at the present time.
>
> Sabotage or guerrilla warfare is discouraged by a knowledge of German methods of retaliation and by a fear of what would happen to the . . . war prisoners in German prison camps. . . .

But even as things seemed darkest for the French and for the western cause, Pétain saw a ray of hope.

> The Marshal tells me he is sure that Germany in the future faces trouble in all the occupied countries because of its wide dispersion of force, and he believes also that Germany cannot avoid a clash with Russia. He says that America is the only friend now remaining to France and is the only hope for the future of his country and his people.[23]

By the end of April, Leahy had cause to learn that not even Americans were immune to the aura of German success as the Nazis drove the British out of Greece, and Rommel in North Africa advanced toward Egypt. German demands on France became more arrogant, and the Vichy government yielded more and more frequently. About that time the Nazis demanded that the United States close the skeleton office it still maintained in Paris. The head of that office stopped in Vichy on the way home. As he paid his courtesy call on the ambassador, Leahy was unimpressed. In his view, the man had too high an opinion of Laval and too small regard for the policies of President Roosevelt. Fortunately for both men, the official's stay in Vichy was brief, and he was soon safely out of the country so his view could no longer do any harm.

The situation in Vichy rapidly grew worse. Darlan went off to confer with Hitler at Berchtesgaden, and Leahy had the gravest suspicions about the meeting. On delivering a letter from President Roosevelt to Pétain, he was further depressed, for the marshal seemed remote, and not at all friendly as he had been earlier. He insisted that General Huntziger be present at the conversation, and he refused to make any answer until Darlan returned from Germany.

"I received in the interview a definite impression that . . . the Marshal and his Government are moving rapidly toward 'collaboration' with Germany and that there is now likely to be no effective objection made by France to any demands that may be received from Germany."

Two days after Leahy had written those words, Vichy officially announced the signing by Hitler and Darlan of an agreement known as "The Paris Protocols." Their terms remained secret for a considerable time. Even the best efforts of Leahy, "Doc" Matthews, MacArthur, and the rest failed to reveal precisely what they were about, but everyone in the embassy knew they boded little good for Anglo-Saxon interests. As it was later learned, the protocols permitted the Germans to use French airfields in Syria to aid Iraqi rebels against the British. A few French trucks would be sent to Rommel. In return the Germans promised to relax travel restrictions, reduce occupation costs, and free a few prisoners of war.

These were relative minor concessions, but they showed trends in French thinking. Clearly American influence was waning. By this time Darlan was ever more convinced of the inevitability of a German victory and felt that France simply must be on good terms with the triumphant Nazis. Then a peace arrangement more favorable to France could be worked out. Ever vain, Darlan might even have fancied that he could outwit the Führer. Darlan's apologists state that he agreed to closer collaboration with Hitler in order to avert even worse conditions being imposed on Vichy.

Hitler had no illusions about Darlan's sincerity. He knew that both the admiral and the marshal would turn again to the British side if and when they could do so without harming France. Pétain, Hitler perceptively observed, was "an old fox, whose memory deserted him just at the moment when it best suited him"[24]

Unable to resist the temptation of having restrictions eased, and not daring to stand up to Hitler, Pétain and the cabinet gave the Paris Protocols unanimous approval on 14 May. Leahy took a most serious view of the protocols. Soon after they were signed, he noted that Pétain no longer promised that Vichy would give no military aid to Germany; now the Vichy government promised only no "voluntary military aid."

In a letter to Welles on 19 May, Leahy indicated how seriously he took the situation when he requested that "before America really begins to apply pressure on France, it will be helpful to my peace of mind if you can give us sufficient notice to permit of evacuating the women and children connected with the Embassy.

"The newsgatherers hereabouts," he added, "have had reports of our already being on our way out via Portugal, and the Berlin and Paris radio news yesterday started a 'build up' to have me recalled."[25]

In the absence of precise knowledge of the terms of the Paris Protocols, the United States had no alternative but to interpret them as indicating full-scale cooperation with Germany. An indignant President Roosevelt broadcast a stinging rebuke, which concluded:

> The people of the United States can hardly believe that the present government of France could be brought to lend itself to a plan of voluntary alliance, implied or otherwise, which would apparently deliver to France and its colonial empire, including French African colonies and their Atlantic coasts, with the menace which that involves to the peace and safety of the Western Hemisphere.

Pétain and his followers did not like that broadcast at all. Leahy went to great efforts to have translations of the speech disseminated widely, making sure that all French leaders received a copy.

In the United States, President Roosevelt's radio address was generally interpreted as an attempt to speak to the French people over the head of Marshal Pétain, as the *New York Sun* put it. The Richmond *News-Leader* and the *Baltimore Sun* agreed that it would be easy for the United States to take over French possessions in the western hemisphere if necessary. Other papers concurred that the United States should reconsider sending any further aid to France until the situation had been clarified.

"One can be certain," the Hartford *Times* concluded, "that Germany has seen to it that it has gained something important in the struggle against Britain. For that reason the new Vichy negotiations spell no good to the United States."[26]

Day by day the atmosphere in Vichy became more chilly for Americans. The Vichy press repeatedly attacked embassy personnel and policies and even censored American press releases for the French papers in the Unoccupied Zone. One illustrated story about the embassy appeared in a French magazine with the faces of every American blacked out.

Leahy was not sure how much the current attacks in the press would undercut his influence with Pétain, and he reported optimistically in a letter to the president, "There are many possibilities in this collaboration movement that will not meet with his willing acceptance."[27]

While Leahy still had hopes for maintaining a friendly relationship with Pétain, Darlan took every opportunity to discredit Leahy. Once he sent a stiff note accusing the ambassador of consorting with people "whose known hostility to the Marshal and his Government is well known."

It was a week before an indignant Leahy gained an audience with the marshal; then in the presence of his accuser, he protested Darlan's behavior as "contrary to customary diplomatic practice." If satisfactory relations could not be maintained, he went on, the "century-old friendship" of the two countries would be threatened. Darlan was visibly embarrassed, and Pétain, who had obviously known nothing of Darlan's note, went out of his way to be cordial. Still, he acquiesced when Darlan, attempting to justify himself, told Leahy that the British had worked tirelessly to turn France against Germany because British "security required that generations of Frenchmen should see in Germany their hereditary enemy."

Today, he added, France was paying the price for such "Machiavellianism." Pressing his point, he assured Leahy, France "had every right to reverse her policy and to collaborate with the victor. And who could alter the fact that, in any event, eighty million Germans would still confront forty million French?"[28]

As time passed, it seemed clear to Leahy that America's support of Britain would inevitably bring the United States into war with Germany. The sinking by a U-boat of the American freighter *Robin Moor*, Leahy thought, might very well "be the *Lusitania* incident of the present war." When American forces relieved British troops in Iceland, he wrote that the action "of the President appears to have moved America about a thousand miles toward the European war."

On the morning of 22 June, the Leahys picked up a BBC broadcast telling of the German invasion of Russia. The next day, he received Soviet Ambassador A. Bogomolov, who wanted to find out what the American attitude would be toward Russia under the new circumstances. Having received no instructions, Leahy could only fence and show that he had learned the practice of diplomacy by referring to the president's recent statements of "full sympathy with all those nations that are resisting Axis aggression."

When in doubt, quote the boss!

Leahy rather enjoyed Bogomolov. He was intelligent, well informed, and not given to spates of Marxist dialectic and party-line propaganda which characterizes so many Soviet officials. Still, the American ambassador was less than delighted when Bogomolov asked him to take over Russian interests when Vichy broke diplomatic relationships with the Soviet Union.

The break in relations was obviously inspired by the Germans, although Darlan gave the lame excuse that a few members of the embassy staff had engaged in "unfriendly activity." Such activity might have been reason enough to declare an offender persona non grata, but it was a feeble pretext for breaking diplomatic relations.

Leahy forwarded the Soviet request to Washington with the recommendation that some other government, preferably Sweden, take on the job. Leahy had no desire to be saddled with any new responsibilities; he had enough as it was, and his situation was not made any easier by the continued hostility of Darlan who, "through his press campaign and through instructions to subordinates," had succeeded in making "me look like poison ivy to his colleagues in the Government who seem to be principally concerned with the prospect of holding their jobs." He was much relieved when the State Department told him to refuse the Russian request.

In the same letter to Welles, Leahy summed up French feeling on the German invasion of the USSR. Most Frenchmen welcomed the new war, for they felt that it would divert the Germans who would then leave France more to her own devices. No one expected the German venture to fail, although nearly everyone hoped it would. "Most of my contacts of all classes feel that a successful completion of the German campaign in Russia will be followed by peace proposals that Great Britain will accept."[29]

The former national holiday, Bastille Day, 14 July, was observed that year in Vichy as a day of mourning. Embassies and legations were asked not to send customary greetings or to make calls, and they were pointedly not invited to take part in the only ceremony of the day, that of placing a wreath on a memorial to soldiers who had died in the 1914–1918 war.

On 16 July, Leahy delivered an oral message to Pétain from President Roosevelt regarding German efforts to obtain the use of French bases in North Africa. Although he had particularly requested a private interview, he was not in the least surprised to see the ubiquitous Darlan there. As usual, "Popeye" did most of the talking. He refused to confirm or deny that Germany had asked for the bases, saying it was unimportant because "as long as the present political arrangement with Germany based on the Armistice continued, no foreign power would be permitted to use the bases." To be sure that Leahy got the point, he repeated the words, "for as long as the present political arrangement with Germany lasts."

Changing the subject, Darlan added that Japanese forces would be moving into bases in French Indochina. Since that colony was so far away, there was nothing that France could do about it.

As Leahy was leaving, Darlan warned him, "Serious events may happen in the very near future." When Leahy asked if he referred to the Orient, Darlan replied, "Everywhere."

A few days later, Leahy wrote the president of his discussion with Darlan:

> Indications here point to a German move against the Mediterranean. . . . It is practically certain that Germany some time ago demanded the use of French African bases, and that Darlan was unable to deliver them because of the resistance offered by General Weygand. It is generally believed here that the

demand will be renewed and that Weygand will at that time not succeed in preventing use of the bases by Germany.

General Weygand may possibly resign rather than agree to give away the African Empire, but he is a thoroughly disciplined soldier, he is completely loyal to the Maréchal, and he may salve his conscience with an acceptance of "orders is orders."

Now that Vichy has without objection handed Indochina over to Japan, it will be difficult to refuse Germany a present of French Africa when a new demand backed by threats is made.[30]

With Vichy drawing ever closer to Germany, life for the people of the embassy became even more difficult. Most of the incidents were pinpricks. Frenchmen they had been accustomed to meet in the hotels and spas avoided them, having been warned not to become too friendly with any American. Leahy reminded his staff that they were under constant surveillance by the police and probably by the Gestapo as well. They were to assume that their telephones were tapped and their letters read unless they were in the diplomatic pouch, which was always in the custody of American couriers.

Then there was the appearance of a book written by a certain Georges Suarez entitled *Pétain ou la Démocratie? Il Faut Choisier*. The book, which could not have been placed on sale without the knowledge and consent of the Vichy authorities, was a scurrilous attack on the United States, on President Roosevelt, and on Leahy himself. For the first time in his journal of his days in Vichy, Leahy revealed discouragement. The French, he feared, would be deluded by such venom and therefore "unable to appreciate that I personally am making a considerable sacrifice to remain here in the service of the President as Ambassador, and that an early return home is the one bright hope."

That same day, Leahy learned that Darlan had been made minister of national defense, a move which placed the army and air force under his direct command. In the same shake-up of his cabinet, Pétain had named Pierre Pucheu, a known collaborationist, as minister of the interior. Again Leahy reminded himself that the minister of the interior controled the police and the Sûreté.

In an attempt to take his mind off a day where everything had seemed to go wrong, he looked forward to the opera that evening. For some time the Leahys had countered the attempt to isolate the embassy by appearing frequently in public. They regularly attended the opera, and in a little over a week had heard performances of *Carmen*, *The Damnation of Faust*, *I Pagliacci*, and *La Vie Breve*. That night, 12 August, they attended a memorable performance of Moussorgsky's *Boris Godunov*.

Between the fourth and fifth act, the opera was interrupted by a broadcast of Marshal Pétain which was piped into the theater. Pétain announced the end of parliamentary government in France, the prohibition of political parties, public meetings, distribution of political tracts and pamphlets, and the abrupt stoppage of salaries paid to members of the Senate and the Chamber of Deputies. He also announced an increase in the size of the police force so that all those decrees could be enforced.

A few samples of Pétain's speech as translated by the embassy:

> For the past few weeks I have felt an ill wind rising in various parts of France. Anxiety is growing in your minds; doubt is gripping your souls.
>
> My Government's authority is questioned; its orders are often badly carried out.
>
> In an atmosphere of rumor and intrigue, the forces of national recovery are becoming discouraged, and other forces, lacking the same nobility and disinterestedness, are trying to take their place. . . .
>
> Authority no longer comes from below. It is properly that which I confer or delegate.
>
> I delegate it in the first instance to Admiral Darlan, towards whom public opinion has not always been either favorable or fair, but who has not ceased to help me with his loyalty and his courage. . . .
>
> I have decided to make use of the powers conferred on me . . . to judge those responsible for our national disaster. . . .
>
> In application of the . . . Constitutional Act, all Ministers and high officials must swear an oath of fidelity to me and undertake to carry out the duties assigned to them for the welfare of the State according to laws of honor and probity. . . .
>
> I have inherited a wounded France. It is my duty to defend this heritage and to defend your hopes and our rights.
>
> In 1917 I put an end to the mutinies. In 1940 I put a stop to rout. Today I am going to save you from yourselves. . . .
>
> Remember this: a beaten country divided against itself is a dying country. A beaten country which can unite is a country reborn.
>
> Vive la France!

It is worth remembering that Hitler, too, demanded a personal oath of loyalty to him rather than to the Reich. It was, as Leahy later wrote the president, "discouraging from the point of view of those of us who are confirmed believers in representative government, to see France completely in the hands of a dictator, a benevolent dictator for so long as the Marshal survives."[31]

The depression that Leahy felt was greatly overcome three days later when he heard of the meeting between the president and Prime Minister Winston Churchill at Argentia, Newfoundland. In the secluded waters of Placentia Bay, the two leaders were hammering out the agreement later to be known as the Four Freedoms. Leahy combined these with other conclusions to come up with the six items he felt most important.

(1) Destruction of Nazi Germany.

(2) Disarmament of aggressor nations first, then reduction of all armaments.

(3) Right of all peoples to choose their own form of government.

(4) No territorial gains for the United States or Great Britain.

(5) No territorial changes without the consent of the people concerned.

(6) Freedom of the seas and free access to raw materials.

Thus, in the space of a few days, while the voice of tyranny had seemed most triumphant, the voice of freedom and hope was heard the more loudly, even in Vichy, where the American ambassador was encouraged to go on to try to salvage something from the ruins of the Third Republic.

# CHAPTER 9

# Winter of Sorrows

As a break from the unfortunate events of mid-August, the Leahys decided to take a short leave in Switzerland where they could breathe the air of freedom. Incidentally, they could get a few good meals in anticipation of the rigors of the coming winter.

Leahy being Leahy, he made it a working vacation. He consulted the U.S. minister in Berne on the Russian situation. He made the proper diplomatic calls. He and Louise visited several of the beautiful Swiss cities, and in Geneva Leahy was interviewed by Dr. Bernard L. Wyler, "an exceedingly attractive superior type of the newspaper profession." Certainly the interview, which appeared on 28 August in the *Oberlaendisches Volksblatt* of Interlaken, under the title of "President Roosevelt's Ear at Vichy," was a considerable change from the brickbats he was accustomed to receive in the French capital.

> The man who met me in the Geneva Hotel was anything but a sea-dog with broad shoulders and a rolling gait. . . .
> "I always had to swallow what the diplomats cooked up," the Admiral said, "and now at my advanced age I have been asked to become a diplomat myself. . . . All that I knew about France was that the country's situation was grave. The President had especially instructed me to strive to help the unhappy people. . . . This problem is still my first concern today. Politics takes second place. We diplomats have no special privileges either. My wife and I have taken advantage of our stay in Switzerland to eat a little more ourselves. They are in need of

everything in France. When one has lived for a long time in a defeated country, one realizes at once how fortunate Switzerland and America are."

As I took leave of Admiral Leahy, I believed I understood why President Roosevelt had not sent a career diplomat, but a sailor with a tender, good heart, a kindly countenance, and smiling eyes, to the France of Marshal Pétain and Admiral Darlan.[1]

Becoming complete tourists, the Leahys took the train to Montreux, where they enjoyed a fine lunch in the beautiful Montreux Palace Hotel. In the afternoon, the governor of the Castle of Chillon personally showed them the signature Lord Byron had scratched on a stone pillar in the dungeon where he had let his imagination conceive the poem "The Prisoner of Chillon."

Their stay in a world of sanity was over all too soon, and the Leahys found themselves back in the French capital, where, as the admiral reported in a letter to the president, things were worse than ever. Drumhead courts ruthlessly condemned those accused of communism. A friend, the Comtesse de Villeneuve, a descendant of the admiral who had opposed Nelson at Trafalgar, had been exiled. Any kind of a Bill of Rights had vanished, and *lettres de cachet* were freely employed.

In the end, Leahy felt, the French people would rebel, and after the Germans had been defeated, they would choose their own form of government "after the usual rioting, street barricades, etc., with which the French people are familiar and which to them appear necessary, or at least customary."[2]

Leahy had been back in Vichy for only about ten days when President Roosevelt requested him to go to Barcelona to meet Myron Taylor, the personal representative of the president to the Vatican. This time the trip was made in comparative luxury, the French placing a comfortable compartment on the train at his disposal. On the Spanish side, no arrangement had been made, and the cars were filthy and crowded, but Leahy and his aide did manage to gain privacy by purchasing all six seats in a "first class" compartment. At the Ritz Hotel, they found Ambassador and Mrs. Weddell waiting for them with the news that Taylor's plane had been delayed in Bermuda. He was expected to arrive the next day.

As promised, the Taylors appeared the following morning, and after a lavish lunch, Leahy, accompanied by Weddell and Taylor, drove to the heights of Tibidabo, where, free from wire taps and recorders, they discussed international affairs for two hours. A Memorandum of Conversation (Memcon in State Departmentese) prepared by Taylor confirms the impressions that Leahy had been conveying to Washington for months: that France was a badly beaten nation, beaten in spirit as well as on the battlefield; that Pétain was the only force holding her together; that Darlan was a dangerous, ambitious, and unreliable man; that Weygand was a good general but not a national leader, who would, however, be the focus of hope in North Africa if properly supported; and that American shipments of food to children had helped to sustain American influence in unoccupied France.

> The Admiral is very emphatic in asserting it would be a mistake to close the Embassy, as destructive to French morale, that if he is withdrawn the Embassy should remain. It is one of the few remaining hopes of the French people that America is sympathetic with them in their distress and renders some assistance. Germany takes from France all the "food she dares." "No doubt if America sent food generally, Germany would take the equivalent."[3]

It was not entirely clear to the admiral why he had been sent for; perhaps it was that FDR wanted to confirm through uncensored sources all that Leahy had been reporting in the usual fashion. At any rate, it was a change for a few days.

At frequent intervals, Leahy had to deliver in person a letter from the president to the marshal. This happened every time the Vichy government made a move suggesting it might be moving closer to collaboration. Roosevelt's letters usually demanded assurances that the North African colonies would not be yielded to the Germans and that the French fleet would not be turned over to them.

It was a ritual. The embassy staff would prepare a French translation of the presidential epistle. At the appointed hour, Leahy would present the original and the translation to the marshal. Pétain would read it aloud to Darlan, who was invariably present. The marshal would give the desired assurances about the colonies. Darlan would do the same about the fleet. Leahy would report that fact to Washington, and the process would be laid to rest for a week or a month. Then it would be repeated.

Although the game sounds childish, it was deadly serious. Each move Vichy made vis à vis Germany was of vital importance to Britain, and because of American support of the United Kingdom, it was of great importance to the United States as well. If there was any hint that the Vichy government was moving closer to Germany, it was essential to remind Pétain and his officials of the promises and commitments they had made and make them fully aware of the consequences of their actions.

About this time, Leahy began to believe that some members of the Vichy government were no longer quite so confident of a Nazi victory as they had been. Those favoring a policy of collaboration began to worry about their own skins, for a German defeat would, Leahy wrote in a letter to Under Secretary Sumner Welles, "bring to a timely, if not a violent end, the political future" of those who had supported German aims during the occupation.[4]

Massive German losses in Russia helped to account for this change. Leahy's letter continues:

Yesterday a French *Sous-Préfet* . . . told me that because of his perfect use of the German language he had in his area very close and agreeable relations with the officers of the Army of Occupation. These officers frankly admit to him that they have given up all hope for victory, that their numerical losses in Russia are appalling, and that they want a peace in order that they may return to their homes.

Leahy, of course realized that the Germans still held all the cards in France, and countered most of the optimism of his letter by concluding, "I have a feeling at the present time that Vichy will submit to Nazi demands without any show of resistance, and possibly without formal objection."[5]

Meanwhile life in Vichy went on much as before. In mid-September, Pétain gave a dinner for the chiefs of the diplomatic missions and their ladies. The affair was held in the grand ball room of the Hôtel du Parc. During daytime hours the hotel served as the seat of the Vichy government. For this occasion, every effort had been made to give the ball room a festive look, a pitiful attempt in that capital of a defeated nation. While seniority in the diplomatic corps in Vichy placed Leahy some distance down the table, Louise was seated on the right hand of the marshal. Leahy interpreted her being so honored as a mark of esteem and a possible hint of improved relations between the two governments. It was a tiny clue, and it might or might not be significant.

The warming trend toward the United States did not last long. By the end of the first week in October, the Nazis were doing better in Russia, and Leahy recorded that Vichy was again turning toward a policy of closer collaboration, observing that the "present Government of France is not essentially different from that of Nazi Germany." The marshal, at eighty-six, was devoted to the welfare of his people, but no one had any "desire to see a representative form of government established in France." Most were only interested in perpetuating their own power.

A few days later, Leahy warned the president that Minister of the Interior Pucheu, "an open collaborationist" who controlled the Senate, "is busy building up . . . a militant following" very similar in organization and methods to "the 'black shirts' and 'brown shirts' of other dictatorships."[6]

Even as Pucheu was preparing to crack down on his own countrymen, the Nazis were becoming more ruthless in the Occupied Zone. They began shooting fifty hostages for each German soldier killed. If the killings of Germans continued, authorities threatened to double the number of hostages sent before firing squads.

Roosevelt expressed his profound shock over the execution of hostages and felt that "the Marshal might have taken a more positive stand." He agreed with Leahy's appraisal, being "fearful that France will not be able to hold out much longer against increasing demands for what would correspond to military assistance on the part of the French."[7]

As October went on and the German drive into Russia gathered momentum, and as the "barometric French Government" turned correspondingly toward collaboration, Leahy sent his impressions of senior French officials, from Darlan who "hates everything British," to Huntziger, who "accepts the defeat with too much complacency," to Pucheu, "a young man of ability, force, and ruthless ambition." The list went on to include minor officials who were joining their seniors in making a good thing for themselves out of their country's defeat.

By this time Leahy knew perfectly well that it was only a matter of time before the Vichy government became a junior partner in the Axis, very junior, but still a partner, whether by choice or by coercion. Thus his reports to Washington became more and more gloomy. Nor did it seem to him that the United States would be able to stay out of the war very much longer. There was the U-boat attack on the American destroyer *Kearny*, which became the focal point of FDR's Navy Day speech on 27 October. Shooting had started, the president told his listeners, proclaiming that America's navy was at battle stations.

Leahy was so moved by the speech that he copied it in its entirety in his journal. He added, paradoxically:

> This frank defiance of the Nazi program by the President of the United States seems to be as nearly an open declaration of "undeclared" war as it would be possible to formulate, and here in France we await the German reaction with interest.

During this period, two of Leahy's principal staff members were relieved, Commander Hillenkoetter being replaced by Commander A. C. J. Sabalot, and "Doc" Matthews by J. Pinckney Tuck. There remained only the MacArthurs as close friends. Bill and Louise were particularly fond of Laura MacArthur, a daughter of Senator Alben Barkley of Kentucky, and known to her friends as "Wahwee."

Early in November, Leahy learned that a German general, indiscreet after too much drink, had bragged that Pétain and General Huntziger would be eliminated, and that a German consulate would be opened in Vichy for "the purpose of observing and neutralizing the pernicious activities of the American Ambassador."

One of those predictions came true a few days later when General Huntziger was killed in an airplane crash. At once rumors sprang up that Huntziger had been killed on German orders, who wanted someone more to their liking as minister of war. According to this rumor, Huntziger, who was returning with aides from North Africa, was carrying secret papers—the story did not say what kind, who they were from, nor to whom they were addressed— and that the French pilot, a suicide volunteer, deliberately crashed the plane, destroying the documents and the general together. Other versions stated that this Gallic kamikaze escaped from the crash and saw to it that the general was dead before he disappeared.

The truth was that the plane had circled the Vichy airport for over an hour in bad weather before going on to Nîmes, where the pilot hoped for better visibility. He had no luck; he crashed as he tried to set the plane down, and everyone on board was killed. Leahy was not particularly surprised, for he thought all French aircraft were unsafe. In addition, the Vichy airport was notoriously bad, and he never used it, and he didn't think the one at Nîmes was any better.★

Rumors had been heard more and more frequently that General Weygand would be replaced in Africa because of his ferocious anti-Nazi views. Leahy didn't think anything had really changed, and predicted that "General Weygand . . . will be the next to go." Because he had won the confidence of the "native population of the African colonies," and because he was on good terms with the Americans there, he had "attracted the unfavorable attention of the Axis powers."

If Weygand were recalled, Leahy was concerned that the American reaction would be to cut off all aid to the French colonies, which might "throw France, including the African bases and the Fleet, completely into the hands of the Axis powers." But it was a case of damned if you do and damned if you don't:

> At the present time, and until England or America is prepared to occupy North Africa with a sufficient military force to join with the natives in a successful resistance to an Axis invasion, it would appear the part of wisdom to surrender the initiative. . . . After the departure of Weygand, this will, of course, mean that Axis penetration will move much more rapidly than heretofore and that in the absence of a military effort in Africa by Great Britain or America, the colonies will eventually come completely under the control of the Nazis.

The fears that General Weygand would be recalled were soon realized. He came to Vichy to consult the marshal, and the day after his arrival Leahy had the word from a representative of Pétain. Weygand was out. Leahy immediately asked for an interview with Pétain to protest this craven yielding to the Axis.

> It appears to me that this abject surrender to a Nazi threat at a time when Germany is completely occupied in Russia is the kind of a jellyfish reaction that justifies the stoppage of all assistance to France and the recall, at least "for consultation," of the Ambassador and the Foreign Service officers in Africa.

★According to Miss Dorothy Ringquist, the admiral's long-time secretary and friend, he never liked to fly. His preferred method of transportation was by ship, then train, then car, and a long way last, airplane.

The next day Pétain told him and MacArthur that the Germans had sent a brutal ultimatum demanding Weygand's recall, threatening "among other things, to occupy all of France and to quarter and feed an army of occupation on French foodstuffs; they would take everything and the French population would die of hunger."

Accepting this, Leahy nevertheless informed Pétain that the action might well cause the United States to reconsider its entire policy toward the French. Pétain replied that the Germans had especially hated Weygand because he had been the one to dictate the armistice terms to them in 1918. If that seemed to be a childish attitude, it is worth remembering that the Germans had insisted that the French surrender in 1940 take place in the same railroad car, set at the same place, where they had capitulated at the end of World War I.

Much as he sympathized with the French in their agony, Leahy was beginning to tire of the Vichy government and the increasingly feeble leadership of Marshal Pétain.

> While the great inarticulate and leaderless mass of the French people [he wrote to Roosevelt] remain hopeful of a British victory and continue to hope that America will in the end rescue them from their present predicament without their doing anything for themselves, the Government of France today, headed by a feeble, frightened old man surrounded by self-seeking conspirators, is altogether controlled by a group which, probably for its own safety, is devoted to the Axis philosophy.

As his letter continued, Leahy warned that Pucheu was consolidating his hold, organizing a *Légion des Anciens Combattants*, which was the French equivalent of the Ku Klux Klan, to conduct a terror campaign against enemies of the state. He added that Pucheu and Darlan both were anxious to take Pétain's job and predicted that they would "be tearing at each other's throat in the relatively near future."

He ended his letter by asking FDR to let him tell Pétain in no uncertain terms that if France went any further toward the German camp, the entire U.S. policy toward France would be reviewed. To make it stick, Leahy would be recalled "for consultation." He added, however, if he made any such statement, the United States must be prepared to carry it out. It must not be caught bluffing.[8]

Leahy now believed that France was almost totally a captive nation, and he expected to be recalled from a situation where he was having less influence every day.

To his considerable disappointment, because he was daily more discouraged over what he was doing in France, Leahy learned that FDR did not intend to recall him. Instead, the president announced that, as a result of the firing of Weygand, he had ordered Lend Lease aid extended to the Free French of Charles de Gaulle. That move wasn't going to help Leahy much in Vichy.

Sunday, 7 December, was a routine day in the embassy in Vichy, and it was not until 9:00 P.M. that the Americans learned of the Japanese attack on Pearl Harbor. Knowing the peacetime habits of the navy, Leahy immediately began to worry that the fleet had been caught in port as a result of normal weekend routine. The next day, he listened by radio to President Roosevelt's "Day of Infamy" speech. To him it was "a dramatic picture of the most powerful nation of the world embarking on an all-out war to destroy the bandit nation of the Orient."

The only immediate change the Pearl Harbor attack made in Leahy's life was to do away with one of his more pleasurable associations, for he had enjoyed the company of Sotomatsu Kato, the Japanese ambassador, and had dined with him only two nights before the attack.

The news a few days later of the destruction of the British battleship *Prince of Wales* and the battle cruiser *Repulse* by Japanese air attacks made him revert to life-long habits of thinking and consider military matters ahead of diplomatic ones. He hoped he could be of service in the navy he loved and was encouraged by a story in the *New York Times* of 10 December which, quoting "usually reliable sources," reported that Leahy might be recalled to take over a high defense post, "thus reducing to a minimum American relations with Vichy."[9] Picked up by French news sources and broadcast over the Paris radio, the story lifted Leahy's spirits briefly, but nothing came of it.

On 11 December, Germany and Italy declared war on the United States, and that same evening Leahy had an interview with Pétain, Darlan being present as usual. The two Frenchmen repeated the usual assurances about the fleet and the North African colonies. They hoped that France could remain neutral, but if Germany put too much pressure on them, they would be helpless.

In other words, the entry of the United States into the war changed nothing. Germany was too close and the United States too far away. France had to look to her conquerer for salvation. The American ambassador was distressed but not surprised.

On his return to the embassy, he called Ray Atherton, chief of the European Affairs Division in the State Department, telling him bluntly that it might be necessary to withdraw embassy personnel if the German influence in Vichy increased. If normal rail transportation were cut off, Leahy assured him, they would try to get through by automobile, going toward Marseilles to evacuate by sea or to the Spanish border. Caches of gasoline and food had already been established along both routes, unknown to the French as well as to the Germans. Leahy had been around long enough to realize that anything known to the French would soon be known to the Germans as well.

On the morning of 21 December, Leahy learned that following the attack on Pearl Harbor, the president had shaken up the naval commands, appointing Ernest J. King as CINCUS.★ Bill's classmate, Tommy Hart, had become commander in chief of the Asiatic Fleet, and Chester W. Nimitz was the new commander in chief Pacific Fleet (CINCPAC). "These three admirals, all of whom I know intimately," Leahy approved, "are in my opinion the best qualified by experience, talent, and temperament of all the flag officers known to me for high sea command in war."

Christmas in Vichy was cold and damp. The Leahys gave a dinner for all the remaining embassy staff, the most elaborate they could provide considering the shortage of food in the country. Their Christmas presents, which consisted mostly of food and clothing , were able to contribute to the festivities of the occasion and enrich an otherwise Spartan meal.

The Germans, meanwhile, were growing bolder. On one occasion the French police informed MacArthur that a German officer had been seen attempting to enter the embassy through a basement door. When challenged, the officer had fled in a waiting car.

Some of the embassy staff believed that the German was drunk, but Leahy didn't think so. He took the incident as a warning that the embassy was no longer safe from German attention. If they felt like it, Leahy concluded, the Nazis would ignore diplomatic usage and take over the embassy building. He asked the French to provide additional protection for the embassy and, with the concurrence of the State Department, prepared for destruction of codes and ciphers and moved everything but a single cipher system to Berne.

> We keep two excellent code clerks in the building [Leahy reported to Welles], and they are provided with extemporized means of burning within ten minutes' notice the strip cipher, which is the only secret method of transmitting information that we have retained. If the enemy should descend upon us by force in the middle of the night, we might not have time to accomplish destruction of the strips or any of the remaining confidential papers.[10]

But in spite of French aloofness, in spite of German activity, and in spite of American losses at Pearl Harbor, as the new year began cold and bleak in Vichy, Leahy refused to be pessimistic, feeling that the prospect "of a future for free people are much better at the beginning of this year than they were twelve months ago."

The combined force of America, Great Britain, Russia, and China, in his view, made inevitable the final defeat of the Axis powers.

> Today Germany is suffering a military reverse of major magnitude in Russia, and the combined Axis forces of Germany and Italy in Libya appear to be completely defeated. Japan in the Orient is having much success in the Philippines, in Indochina, and in Malaya, which successes will, I believe, be reversed as soon as the American fleet can be brought into action.

★King promptly changed the abbreviation to COMINCH. There had been enough "Sink Us," he figured.

If Leahy's prediction of defeat of "aggressor nations" in 1942 was wide of the mark, he had not lost hope, as some had, that victory would ultimately come. His military judgment was faulty simply because he lacked enough information.

On 12 January, there arrived at the embassy Henry P. Levrich, of the embassy in Lisbon, bearing secret orders from FDR. Leahy was to undertake the job of persuading Weygand to go back to North Africa and assume command there. He would have the full military and economic backing of the United States.

Bill Leahy didn't think much of the idea and wrote the president, "It does not seem possible for me to personally see your friend, the General, without attracting unfavorable attention to him, as I am constantly under surveillance, and everybody with whom I associate is suspected of something"[11] But, he assured FDR, the message would be delivered, somehow.

The job fell to MacArthur, who set out for Nice to sound the old gentleman out on how he would react to several sets of circumstances under the basic idea.[12] Meanwhile, Leahy, using more conventional channels, warned the Vichy government against any French aid to Germany and promised, in case of any Axis move against France or the colonies, "every possible military and naval assistance we could bring to bear."[13]

It didn't take long to dispose of MacArthur's mission to Weygand. The general turned him down cold.

> The General was courteous and agreeable but declined to give any considera-tion to the possibility of his taking any action in the Africa problem. He said that he is now a private citizen with no official status, that he is completely loyal to the Marshal, and that if France should be so unfortunate as to lose the services of the Marshal, he would, under the legally designated successor, have no oppor-tunity to render service to the country.

Asked to keep the visit confidential, Weygand refused, saying it was his duty to inform Pétain, but would try to keep it from becoming known to anyone else.

> I cannot escape from a belief that it will come to the knowledge of others and that it may be transmitted to the German authorities.
>
> A brief of the General's attitude is that he will have nothing to do with the proposition, and that he will not offer a suggestion of any other person who might be interested.[14]

Toward the end of January, Leahy rose from a sickbed where he had been confined with a severe cold in order to cope with yet another crisis in Franco–American relations. Darlan on a recent trip to Italy had agreed to furnish French ships to transport war materials to Tunis for use by the Afrika

Korps. When the American ambassador charged that he had broken a promise to the United States, Darlan explained he had been forced to agree to
transport two hundred tons of food a week and five hundred trucks to the
Axis forces. Otherwise, the Axis threatened to seize Bizerte. Darlan asked
nastily whether the United States would prefer to see Bizerte in Axis hands or
to supply those trivial amounts. "I replied it would in my opinion be a more
friendly act toward the United States and better for France in the end to lose
Bizerte by enemy action than to voluntarily give aid and comfort to our
declared enemy."

Leahy didn't really believe a word of Darlan's tale. In his opinion, Darlan
thought he could slip those shipments past the eyes of the Americans. It was
all rather stupid in view of the number of informants Murphy had organized
in North Africa.

In the midst of his frustrations in France, Leahy was amused to learn that his
old adversary and predecessor as CNO, Admiral Standley, had been appointed ambassador to Russia. "The Embassy in Moscow," he wrote wryly,
"is perhaps the only American diplomatic post that appears more difficult and
less promising of success than this."

Frustrated at one turn after the other, Leahy was pleased to receive instructions on 11 February to deliver a very strong statement to Marshal Pétain.

> Received today cable instructions from the President to inform the Marshal
> . . . that unless official assurance is given that no military aid will go forward to
> any of the Axis powers and that French ships will not be used in the furtherance
> of their acts of aggression in any theater of war wherever it may be, Admiral
> Leahy will be recalled for consultation in a determination of American future
> policy with regard to the Government of Vichy.
>
> This note from the President is the first positive action taken by America in
> the matter of French–American political relations since my arrival in France. It
> very closely approaches an ultimatum.

The next day, Leahy presented the president's note to Pétain, who read it
aloud to Darlan. Both men seemed shaken. For the next few days, Leahy
worked to try to get firm commitments from the French, while the men of
Vichy stalled. Bill Leahy warned the president that he had better not be
bluffing in the matter. He could always return after "consultation," he
argued, "but in my opinion, Vichy should not be permitted to believe that
your statement . . . was a 'bluff.' Too large a number of the Vichy government now share a belief with Admiral Darlan that the United States may be
always depended on to take no positive action whatever.[15]

A few days later, Darlan backed down a bit. French vessels were no longer
shipping Axis goods to North Africa, and, as he told Leahy, the Japanese
promised not to use French ships in the Far East for "military purposes."
Leahy was not happy with this statement, but FDR decided to be satisfied, for
the moment, at least. He explained in a letter:

Dear Bill:

I have given careful consideration to the thoughts expressed in your letter of February 20, particularly as regards to your feeling that it would be detrimental to our policy to fail to carry out the expressed intention to recall you for consultation. . . .

On the other hand, the timing of such a step has now become of paramount military importance. In fact, the Joint Staff missions have very definitely urged that we postpone as long as possible any evidence of change in our relations with France, . . .

I want you to realize that I am fully aware of the problems with which you are confronted but must consider that you are in a vital strategic position. In these critical days we count not only on your presence there as Ambassador but upon your military knowledge and experience to give us, in so far as possible, estimates of the French position from this point of view.[16]

Disappointed by FDR's letter, Leahy still hoped for an early recall from "this defeated country where not only the material necessities of life but the spiritual values have been destroyed by an invasion of barbarians." As he looked on the scene around him, considering the eternal vigilance he had to maintain against deception and outright hostility, "the thought of returning to a free, undefeatable country is pleasing beyond the power of words to express."

It soon appeared that Germany did not want a rupture of Franco–American relations. France, Hitler thought, might be useful if a negotiated peace could be worked out with the western allies. Then Germany could devote her full attention to the destruction of Bolshevist Russia. In spite of everything, the Führer still permitted himself that hope. And, suddenly, Darlan was not so sure that Germany was going to win after all. "Admiral Darlan," Leahy wrote Welles, "may be expected to shift from side to side with the changing fortunes of war."[17]

At this critical stage in Franco–American relations, the American ambassador had a great deal more on his mind than sparring with Pétain and Darlan. Several times during the late winter, entries in the journal reveal that Louise Leahy was too ill to attend a dinner or a reception, or that she had stayed away from a luncheon on the advice of her physician. Something was wrong, and both she and Bill hoped she could hold out until they both could return to the United States for treatment of her condition.

Every day that return seemed closer. At first it was a hint, then a powerful rumor, and at last a near certainty: the Nazis were demanding the return to power of arch-collaborator Pierre Laval—"Black Peter"—to a major role in the government. On 28 March Leahy noted:

Received today a cable dispatch directing me to inform the Marshal that the President is of the opinion that the appointment of M. Laval to an important post in the Vichy government would make it impossible for America to continue its present attitude of helpfulness to France.

This message undoubtedly means that if the Marshal submits to German pressure and appoints Laval to a position in his Cabinet, I will be recalled or the United States may break off diplomatic relations with France.

Reliable sources of information tell us that Germany has threatened to impose a "Gauleiter" Government on unoccupied France unless a government is established in Vichy that will cooperate fully with the Axis, and that this threat has induced the Marshal to enter into negotiations with M. Laval. Our informants believe that the return of Laval to a position of power in the Vichy government is inevitable. . . .

Correspondent Ralph Heinzen reported that Laval believed he could win more concessions from the German government than Darlan could, that Hitler had no confidence whatever in Darlan and a great deal in Laval, and that he would like to see Frenchmen free to "volunteer" to fight against the Russians. A good many Frenchmen believed that Laval's sly and ingratiating methods might improve the situation, for they didn't see how it could get much worse.[18]

As the rumors flew back and forth, Bill Leahy was more and more concerned about Louise. Just as the Laval affair was coming to a head, her doctor declared she needed an immediate hysterectomy; in his opinion she could not wait for a return to the United States. On 6 April, Easter Monday, Bill and Louise took a long drive through the country, "now bursting into its spring activity." The next day, Louise entered La Pergola Clinic for the operation.

My own nervous tension in connection with this problem is indicated by an incident of last night at 1:45 A.M., when I was sound asleep in the residence and heard Louise call me so clearly by name that I became at once thoroughly awake before realizing that she had already gone to the hospital in preparation for the operation. . . .

At 11:30 this morning, Dr. Regnault called to inform me that the operation was completely successful, and that the patient has an almost certain prospect of full recovery which should require about a month's convalescence.

As Louise Leahy was recovering from surgery, Laval was coming ever closer to power in the Vichy Government. In high triumph, "Black Peter" refused to share any of the authority with Darlan. He wanted it all.

Harry Hopkins, who was in London consulting Churchill, cabled Roosevelt, "How about nailing the wood pussy Laval to your barn door?" Roosevelt replied "Your suggestion being studied but consensus of opinion is that odor still too strong for family of nations."[19]

On 16 April, a week after Louise's operation, Leahy received a cable from the president saying that he would be recalled as soon as Laval's appointment was announced. The cable added that Leahy could delay his departure until Louise was able to travel.

The following day, Laval's son-in-law, René de Chambrun, called at the embassy to explain Laval's reason for assuming power. Leahy refused to see him, so Chambrun explained to Pinckney Tuck that the sole purpose was "correction of internal order," that the Germans would have no part in forming the cabinet, and that Marshal Pétain would remain as chief of state. Laval's title would be Chef du Gouvernement, and, under Pétain, he would have the portfolios of Foreign Affairs, Interior, and Information and Propaganda. Darlan would not be allowed any political activity at all.

The same day, an official communique announced Darlan's appointment as supreme commander of national defense and his resignation from all other duties.

On 19 April, the new government of Laval was officially announced, and Leahy began to get affairs in order for their departure for the United States.

Suddenly, two days later, at 9:45 A.M., as she was talking to her husband, Louise Leahy died of an embolism. She had been making a fine recovery, and the embolism was a surprise to everyone. Her two doctors fought fruitlessly to save her.

"Her death," Leahy wrote, ". . . has left me not only crushed with sorrow, but permanently less than half efficient for any more work the future may have in store for me and completely uninterested in the remaining future."

Letters and telegrams of condolence poured in. Those Leahy felt worthy of preserving were from President Roosevelt, Pétain, and Papal Nuncio, and Admiral Darlan.

Roosevelt's cable read:

Triple priority twentyfirst personal for the ambassador from the president Quote Dear Bill My heart goes out to you in the overwhelming loss which has come to you in a difficult and distant post of duty so far away from the legion of friends who loved Mrs. Leahy dearly but you must find consolation in the assurance that your friends everywhere are mindful of your sorrow though helpless by word or deed to mitigate the grief which is yours. Mrs. Roosevelt joins me in this message of deepest sympathy Affectionately Franklin D. Roosevelt Unquote = HULL[20]

Petain wrote in his own hand:

Vichy, le 21 Avril 1942

Monsieur l'ambassadeur

La nouvelle de la mort de Madame Leahy m'a profondément attristé. Les circonstances ne m'ont pas permis de lui témoigner tout la sympathie que m'inspiraient son charactère génreux et l'interêt qu'elle portait â la France malheureuse. Je l'ai souvent regretté.

Veuillez accepter que je prenne part â votre douleur que je comprends si bien, et agreér l'espression de mes sentiments três dévouér.

Ph. Pétain[21]

There was nothing to do but carry on. Leahy continued to do his job as ambassador, and the work kept him from too much brooding. On 27 April, he made a farewell call on Marshal Pétain, listening in polite disbelief as the marshal put the best face he could on Laval's triumph. Following that conversation, Leahy returned to the embassy in time to receive the formal visit of Laval.

"Black Peter" told Leahy that he expected to act as mediator between the United States and Germany, so that Germany would be free to devote herself to the annihilation of Bolshevism.

"My policy," Laval declared, "is founded on reconciliation with Germany. Without this reconciliation, I can see no hope for peace, whether for Europe, France, or even the world."

Warming to his subject, he declared the present war was a "civil war" of which "Stalin will be the only victor if the democracies continue to fight the Reich."[22] There was much more in this vein.

> I am convinced [Leahy recorded] that M. Laval is fully committed to go as far as he can in an effort to collaborate with Germany and to assist in the defeat of what he termed Soviet-British Bolshevism.
> He definitely is not on our side in the war effort.

On 1 May the MacArthurs held a farewell dinner for Leahy, and at 9:30 that evening the party left for the railroad station. Louise's casket was already aboard the special private car which Pétain had provided, and it was nearly concealed by the floral tributes. "It was difficult to say goodbye to our friends," he wrote, "and particularly to my loyal officers of the Embassy." As the train gathered speed, Leahy could look out on the vanishing faces of the many French people who had come to see him off and wish him well.

On arrival in Lisbon he was gladdened by the arrival of his son Bill, on leave from his job as assistant naval attaché in London. They had ten days together, spent in talking, hiking, and supporting one another before the younger Leahy had to return to his duties. The father, at loose ends, had to wait until 22 May to sail aboard the neutral Swedish steamer *Drottningholm*, an exchange ship which had been guaranteed safe passage by all belligerents. After a leisurely crossing, the ship arrived in Jersey City early on the morning of 1 June. Leahy was the first to disembark, being joined by Mary Niblack, Elizabeth Leahy, his brother Arthur, and by Commander William L. Freseman, naval aide.

Soon after he arrived in Washington, as duty required, Leahy reported to Secretary Hull and Under Secretary Welles. The numbness occasioned by his loss prevented him from any real satisfaction when both men told him that his work in France had been of major importance and that no one could have done it better. They also told him that the president wanted to send him on an important mission abroad. What it was he would have to wait to learn until

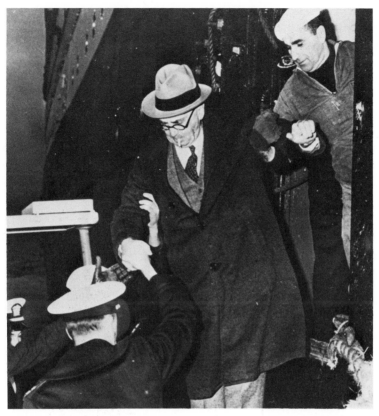

WDL is helped ashore from the Swedish exchange liner *Drottning-holm*, on his return to the United States "for consultation" as ambassador to Vichy France. (Courtesy, National Archives)

FDR returned to Washington in a few days. He never did find out what it was that Roosevelt wanted him to do, because, as so often with FDR's schemes, the mission vanished when a better idea occurred to him.

On 3 June, Louise Leahy was buried in Arlington National Cemetery, following services in St. Thomas Church, which was "filled with friends of Louise, and the altar was covered with floral tributes from friends and officials of foreign missions, the President, and the State and Navy Departments."

Two days later Leahy saw Roosevelt, who told him to take a rest, let the navy doctors give him a check-up, find out all he could about the military situation, and come to lunch next week when they would discuss what he was to do.

The promised lunch with the president did not take place for a month. He spent the interval taking physical examinations, arranging personal affairs, getting "debriefed" by members of the State Department, and getting "briefed" by military officials, including members of the Joint Chiefs of Staff.

Roosevelt put off the luncheon because he was too busy entertaining Prime Minister Winston Churchill, always a demanding guest. A major conference was in full swing, and Leahy had to wait until he knew enough to take part in one. In any case he was still technically ambassador to France, and it would be inappropriate for him to take part. He would have a lot to do with those that followed.

The long-delayed lunch took place on 7 July,. FDR said he was recalling him to active duty in his rank of admiral to serve as chief of staff to the commander in chief. This job would make him an *ex officio* member and chairman of the Joint Chiefs of Staff, the other members being Admiral King for the navy, General George C. Marshall for the army, and General Henry H. Arnold, for the army air force.

Once again Leahy would wear the uniform he loved. Having held the highest post in the navy, having been a governor and an ambassador, and, most of all, having the full trust and confidence of the president of the United States, he was about to embark on a job he was uniquely qualified to perform.

As it turned out, he would do this job for nearly seven years, under two presidents, who would rely on him for advice. He always gave it, and he never bothered to wonder whether or not it would be popular.

On 20 July, Roosevelt endorsed Leahy's orders to active duty as chief of staff to the commander in chief: "Reported this date."

PART THREE

# Chief of Staff to the
# Commander in Chief
# of the Army and Navy

# CHAPTER 10

# The Dimensions of the Job

When Leahy reported for duty as chief of staff to the commander in chief, neither he nor his boss, President Roosevelt, had any real idea of what his job would be. He had been on the sidelines during his job in Puerto Rico, and he had been far from the center of strategic decisions during the dreary year and a half in Vichy.

By the time he returned to the United States, the command organizations had been set up. While he was in France, the British and the United States in the ABC-1 Staff Agreement of March 1941 had provided that even if the United States and the British were drawn into a war with Japan, their policy would be to defeat Germany first, since she represented the greater threat. That decision was never changed, and it was one of the established facts that Leahy had to accept in his new post.

Another decision was to establish the Anglo–American organization known as the Combined Chiefs of Staff (CCS), which, under the direction of the president and prime minister, made the broad strategic decisions for coalition war. One of Leahy's duties would be to serve as chairman of the CCS when it met in the United States.

A third major agreement between the British and Americans was to have area commands. A designated officer in each of the major theaters of war, under the broad authority of the Combined Chiefs of Staff, exercised in his theater actual command of all forces, army, navy, air, marines, whether they were British, American, or of other allied nations. Thus General Douglas

MacArthur commanded the Southwest Pacific Area. The Pacific Ocean Area, which included everything in that ocean not under MacArthur, was the responsibility of Admiral Chester W. Nimitz. General Dwight D. Eisenhower had North Africa and later the European Theater of Operations, and General Sir Claude Auchinleck the Middle Eastern Command.

Within the limits of these very broad policies, Leahy would operate, and he would make of the job whatever he saw as suitable. The field was wide open.

The Constitution of the United States provides that the "President shall be Commander-in-Chief of the Army and Navy of the United States, and of the militia of the several states when called into active service of the United States." Under the president, the chief of staff of the army and the chief of naval operations exercised command functions over their respective departments. Together the two constituted the Joint Chiefs of Staff. Because of the vastly increased importance of air power in the war, the commanding general of the Army Air Forces, General Henry H. Arnold, also served as one of the Joint Chiefs although he was subordinate to the chief of staff of the army, General George C. Marshall.

As was true when Leahy was CNO, the chief of naval operations had only nominal authority over the fleet, which was the responsibility of commander in chief, U.S. Fleet (CINCUS). Following Pearl Harbor, Admiral Ernest J. King had been brought to Washington as commander in chief, U.S. Fleet, now called COMINCH. Admiral Harold R. Stark remained as chief of naval operations, and he and King both sat with the Joint Chiefs, which were then composed of Marshall and Arnold for the army and Stark and King for the navy.

In March, Roosevelt decided to send Stark to London to a largely meaningless post of commander in chief, U.S. Naval Forces, Europe. King took over the job of CNO, while retaining that of COMINCH. This left the navy outnumbered on the Joint Chiefs of Staff, two to one, a state of affairs which caused Marshall some misgivings. He and King did not always see eye to eye, and the outnumbered King was quite capable of demanding a showdown with the president.

Accordingly, Marshall proposed to FDR that Admiral Leahy be brought home and made chairman of the Joint Chiefs of Staff. This would place him between the other chiefs and the president, so that most disagreements could be settled without involving the Oval Office. On principle, King opposed the idea of a chairman until he heard it was to be Leahy. Then he withdrew his objection and became an enthusiastic supporter of the idea.

> I thought [Marshall wrote later] that it was very important that we, in effect, have a neutral agency. . . .
> I continued to press for Leahy being returned and made chairman of the Chiefs of Staff. The President always answered my proposals regarding Admiral Leahy by saying, "But you are Chief of Staff." But I said, "Mr. President, I

am only Chief of Staff of the Army, and in a sense, of the Army Air. There is not a Chief of Staff of the military services." "Well," he said, "I am the Chief of Staff. I'm the Commander-in-Chief." And I explained to him in great frankness that it was impossible to conceive of one man with all of his duties as President being also, in effect, the Chief of Staff of all the military services. . . .

But the trouble was he didn't quite understand what the role of the Chief of Staff would be. While I was in England [on July 21] Leahy . . . was announced as coming . . . on the Chiefs of Staff. But the President said he was going to be his "leg man." And when I arrived in Washington, Leahy was very much at a loose end. He didn't know quite where he stood. He called on me because he had learned that I proposed his name. I was the one who urged his return.[1]

Leahy's job evolved from those dubious beginnings into one of the most important in the Allied high command. In the press conference in which he announced Leahy's appointment, Roosevelt again used the term "leg man" to describe the job. He did go on to say that Leahy would absorb information from the armed services and transmit it to him and give him advice. In those words, he revealed that he did not know what a chief of staff was and what he did.

The term "chief of staff" as used to designate the highest ranking officers of the army and air force is confusing. In army usage, it derives from the concept of a general staff, such as was used by Germany. The general staff had command functions, and the head or chief is the overall commander.

In other areas of command, the chief of staff is head of the staff which serves a general or an admiral. This staff has only an advisory role; it can issue no orders except in the name of the flag officer. Its duty is to prepare plans and directives, but it cannot issue them until given authority to do so by the admiral or general.

This was the role that Leahy was to have. The commander was, of course, the president. Leahy was to advise him on military options, plans, intelligence, logistics—in short, on everything the commander in chief needed to know, without burdening him with thousands of details. Leahy would get his information from the army and the navy, through their staffs, so he had need for only a handful of people to do his job. He never believed in large staffs. He gave the lie to Parkinson's Law.★

I am amazed at the way he handled everything so efficiently and with such good judgment [recalled his administrative assistant of many years, Chief Yeoman Dorothy Ringquist]. Our office could have had three times as large a staff if we wanted it. And somebody else probably would. But the admiral said, "We'll get more work done with fewer people to handle it. And the fewer people that see it, the better.[2]

★Parkinson's Law states that in a bureaucracy an organization expands at a given rate each year, regardless of its function.

As time went on, the dual nature of Leahy's job grew less important. He presided at meetings of the Joint Chiefs of Staff. They met once a week as a rule. But he was every day in the White House, seeing the president, keeping tabs on things in the Map Room, and screening visitors and information. He put the president's ideas into action with notes or telephone calls.★

In this manner, he was doing very much the same sort of things that Harry Hopkins had been doing for almost two years. At the time Leahy reported on board, Hopkins was living on the second floor of the White House. Leahy never stayed in the White House, but his morning meeting with the president was as regular as clockwork.

As Bill Leahy learned more about his job, he began to work in tandem with Harry Hopkins. He never, of course, enjoyed the close, personal friendship that Harry had with FDR, but when it came to jobs to be done, they were equally trusted by the president. Hopkins's areas of activity were much more wide ranging: Leahy never made solo trips to see Churchill and Stalin as Hopkins did. Hopkins dealt with priorities, production, political problems with allies, strategy—in short with anything that might concern the president.

In the beginning Leahy's responsibilities were mostly military, but as time went on he came more and more to deal with foreign affairs and grand strategy. In the upshot, either Hopkins or Leahy could deal with almost anything that came up in connection with the war. Hopkins was special assistant to the president. Leahy was chief of staff. And the chief difference between them was that Harry Hopkins, because of his previous reputation as a big spender, got the publicity. And the brickbats. And when FDR had appointed Hopkins to his job, he had called him a "leg man" too.

In Bill Leahy and Harry Hopkins, FDR found two utterly dependable, loyal, dedicated public servants, who were both beyond personal ambition. They cared for nothing but getting the job done. Hopkins had long since given up any idea of public office because of his miserable health. His loyalty was personal, to the man, Franklin D. Roosevelt. In serving him, he served the country. Leahy's feelings can best be described as loyalty to the country. He liked and admired the president, but their relationship was more official than personal.

---

★The Map Room in the White House was a well-kept secret during the war. When he came to Washington shortly after the attack on Pearl Harbor, Winston Churchill brought his traveling Map Room. Much more than an elaborate series of status boards, it was a communications center, a reservoir of messages, policy papers, operation orders, and all manner of things necessary to direct the conduct of the war. President Roosevelt was so impressed that he ordered one set up in the White House and improved on the original. Everything the president needed to know, whether of military or diplomatic nature, was in the Map Room, which was manned twenty-four hours a day. Other than watch officers, only the president, Leahy, and Hopkins had regular access to the Map Room. Except for the president, Harry Hopkins was the only civilian.

Later Associate Justice James F. Byrnes gave up his seat on the U.S. Supreme Court to take over the job of director of the Office of War Mobilization. This appointment was described by the press as "assistant president," a title better applied to Hopkins. Byrnes, however, lacked the fierce drive that motivated Hopkins or the single-minded purposiveness of Leahy. He was too politically ambitious to give the kind of service rendered by the other two. His eye was on the White House, if not in 1944, then in 1948.

Of these three, Leahy was the only one who survived throughout all the remaining months of Roosevelt's administration and into Harry Truman's first term. Hopkins was too close to FDR to work with Truman, and his health was too far gone. Byrnes served Truman for a time as secretary of state, but their ways soon parted as Byrnes acted more and more on his own initiative without determining the policy of the president.

That left Leahy. In the same job, doing just as he had done earlier, he remained at his post until after Harry Truman was inaugurated in January 1949. Then he stepped down at his own request.

All this is preview of events to come, but an early understanding is essential to appreciating Leahy's part in the Roosevelt administration.

When Leahy first took the chair at a meeting of the Joint Chiefs of Staff on the afternoon of 30 July, he found himself in the midst of a dispute which had been settled after months of disagreement. Now that agreement had come unglued.

At the Arcadia conference in Washington immediately after Pearl Harbor, British and Americans leaders had generally agreed to make an all-out attack on Germany in Europe as quickly as possible. They also discussed the idea of American forces landing in French North Africa in an operation known as Gymnast. An alternative, which included British troops as well and had wider objectives, was known as Super-Gymnast. Both these operations appealed to the British who had a long history of peripheral strategy—hitting around the flanks of the enemy rather than attacking his main strength.

The Americans, on the other hand, preferred the straight, direct assault, and gradually over the next few months had won British concurrence "in principle" to the general plan of building up strength in Britain for an invasion of the continent of Europe in 1943. Originally given the code name Bolero, this operation appealed increasingly to the British. In particular the chief of the Imperial General Staff, Sir Alan Brooke, liked Bolero, for it ensured that nothing too rash would be done on the continent while giving the appearance of getting ready for the decisive thrust. The foolhardy Americans, in his view, would be prevented from undertaking operations on the continent which might well be fatal to the Allied cause. Meanwhile, he devoted his energies to promoting Gymnast.

General Marshall and the Americans generally had little or no use for the

North African venture, seeing it as a diversion that would suck Allied strength into the Mediterranean in an area that would not be decisive in defeating Germany. Worse, it would inevitably delay any possible invasion of Europe beyond 1943.

On this basis, the British and Americans accepted Bolero, and Gymnast was placed on the shelf. By April, while Leahy was still in Vichy, an outline draft of Bolero had been completed, and Marshall and Hopkins flew to London to obtain British approval.

As it developed, Bolero came to mean only the buildup of forces in the British Isles, while the operational part, the later invasion, was designated Roundup. But a part of the latest Bolero plan was, to Brooke's dismay, a provision for a limited beachhead in Europe in the fall of 1942. This would be undertaken only if Germany seemed about to collapse or if the Russians needed a sacrificial diversion to keep them from collapsing. This plan was called Sledgehammer and was for emergencies only.

The British approved the entire Bolero concept—Bolero, Roundup, and Sledgehammer—on 14 April, and Marshall and Hopkins departed believing they had a firm commitment. But by early May they were astonished to discover that the British were backing down. There were not enough landing craft and not enough men.

By the time the second Washington Conference took place in June, the British had rejected Sledgehammer in 1942 under any circumstances. They had even grown cool to Roundup. When the conference, broke up, however, the basic Bolero plan remained pretty much intact, with Sledgehammer barely a footnote. The Russians, however, were demanding that the Anglo-Saxon forces do something in Europe, and their supporters in the United States and the United Kingdom loudly called for "Second Front Now!"

The British were noncommittal about the second front in 1942, but when Foreign Minister Vyacheslav M. Molotov discussed strategy with Roosevelt in June, he persuaded an unwary FDR to sign a statement he had drafted. Both Hopkins and Marshall objected, but the president, in a rare moment of inattention, brushed their objections aside. The statement read that Molotov and Roosevelt had reached a full understanding "with regard to the urgent tasks of creating a Second Front in Europe in 1942." Although this was not quite a promise, it was good enough for the Russians, who proclaimed to the world that it was.

The conference ended with still a lot of work to do because Churchill had to dash home to face a vote of confidence in the House of Commons. But so far as the Americans were concerned, everything was settled. Bolero was on.

Not so, according to the British. Churchill wanted Gymnast in 1942, and he wasn't going to shut up about it. By this time, the code name Gymnast included Super-gymnast.

A disgusted Marshall proposed that the Americans abandon any thought of operations in the European theater in 1942 and throw their full strength into the Pacific war. He had an eager ally in Admiral King who had never been in sympathy with the Germany-first strategy in the first place. But Roosevelt killed that idea and sent Hopkins and Marshall back to London to work out something with Churchill and the British. This time King went along to remind the British that there was a war against Japan, too! They left on 18 July, just two days before Leahy reported for duty. They had been told to make a final effort to pin the British down on a cross-Channel attack. If no agreement could be reached, then they were to make other plans.

After much lively and even heated debate, the Americans accepted British arguments that Sledgehammer was impossible; as a trade-off, Marshall wanted a firm commitment on Roundup in 1943. Then President Roosevelt upset his advisors. He insisted that something be done in the European theater in 1942. It was, as Marshall came to understand, a political necessity that American troops be in action with the Germans and Italians before the year ended.

Out of all the choices open to them, the Combined Chiefs of Staff finally settled on Gymnast. On 24 July, they approved Combined Chiefs of Staff plan 94 (CCS 94), which scheduled Operation Torch, the distillation of Gymnast and Super-gymnast, for late fall. But it had an important reservation inserted by Marshall that the final decision of go or no go would be postponed until 15 September. FDR's cabled acceptance of Torch ignored the reservation Marshall had so carefully added, but the general did not forget it.

When Leahy sat down at the head of the table and gavelled the meeting to order on the afternoon of 30 July, he was not fully aware of all the background of vacillation and procrastination which had marked planning that spring and summer. And Marshall had fight in him yet. He still hoped for Roundup in 1943, and he wanted the president to be perfectly sure that Torch in 1942 would almost certainly delay Roundup until 1944. In fact, he argued, if the British had their way, it might never take place.

At the meeting, Marshall argued that the final decision on Torch, and thus the abandonment of Roundup, be postponed for a week in order to give the staff more time. That, of course, was specious, for there was barely enough time for Torch as it was. Any delay might kill it. That, of course, would have suited Marshall perfectly.

As soon as the session was over, Leahy reported the lack of agreement to the president. FDR immediately called a meeting of everyone concerned for that evening in the Oval Study. After hearing their arguments, the president told Marshall and King, the chief foes of Torch, that he, as commander in chief, had decided on the operation and it was up to them to carry it out. Brigadier General Walter Bedell (Beetle) Smith, at that time secretary of the Joint Chiefs of Staff, recalled that the president "considered that this operation was now our principal objective and the assembling of means to carry it out should take precedence over other operations as, for instance, Bolero."[3]

> It has been said [Leahy observed] that Roosevelt ordered "Operation Torch" in the face of opposition from his senior advisers. I never opposed the North African invasion. I told the President of the possibilities of trouble, but it looked to me like a feasible undertaking. Marshall did oppose it. He did not want to waste American troops in North Africa when he thought he could use them in a cross-Channel operation.[4]

Such was the manner of strategic decision. But normally it did not require repeated crossings of the Atlantic by senior officials nor presidential intervention to work out plans and strategy. Since the British Chiefs of Staffs needed to be in London, they established a Joint Staff Mission in Washington headed by Field Marshal Sir John Dill. The mission met regularly with the American Joint Chiefs of Staff, and most decisions could be worked out in those meetings with Leahy in the chair.

It would be easy to say that the Combined Chiefs of Staff, the Joint Chiefs of Staff, and the British Chiefs of Staff among them ran the war. To a limited extent, they did, but in another sense, it is entirely wrong to say so. Two strong willed, self-sufficient individuals ran the war, Prime Minister Winston Churchill and President Franklin D. Roosevelt. All other organizations worked under them, whether smoothly or not.

"The course of true love never did run smooth," said Shakespeare, and on that basis the United Kingdom and the United States must have had a true love indeed, for their path never was smooth, whether they were discussing strategy, tactics, leadership, politics, weapons, or anything else. They were too close in background and assumptions to agree perfectly. Their basic difference lay in the British fidelity to peripheral strategy and the American desire to drive straight to an objective, whether or not they were completely ready. In the long run, both sides were right. The British deserve great credit for holding the impetuous Americans back until the Allies had sufficient strength for the frontal assault; the Americans deserve great credit for pushing the cautious British into the assault at all.

Leahy's first experience in chairing a meeting had led to a showdown between the president and his advisors in favor of Torch. French North Africa, naturally, was an area of great interest to him because of his long association with some of the French leaders who would be involved either for or against the Americans. But in his new job, he could no longer limit himself to one area of the world. His view now had to be global.

While he had been in France, the Japanese had overrun most of southeast Asia, including Malaya, the Dutch East Indies, and the Philippines and had extended their conquests to the Carolines, the Gilberts, and the Solomons. In seizing New Britain, they advanced their forward base nearly a thousand miles from Truk in the Carolines to set up a huge advance base in beautiful Simpson Harbor at Rabaul. Following the loss of Bataan, Douglas MacArthur had been ordered to Australia and named commander in chief Southwest Pacific Area (COMSOWESPAC). Nimitz similarly had been named commander in chief Pacific Ocean Areas (CINCPOA), in addition to his earlier title of commander in chief Pacific Fleet (CINCPAC).

In early May Japanese forces had been stopped in the Battle of the Coral Sea which forced them to abandon their planned amphibious capture of Port Moresby, New Guinea. And in early June they had suffered a major defeat in the Battle of Midway. Each of these battles had cost the U.S. Navy a carrier, the *Lexington* in the Coral Sea, and the *Yorktown* at Midway. And in just over a week the first American offensive in the Pacific was about to get underway with the landing of American marines on Tulagi and Guadalcanal.

In the Atlantic, the war was going badly. Ship sinkings reached a peak in July. U-boat successes in the winter and spring off the East Coast of the United States, in the Caribbean, and in the Gulf of Mexico had brought gasoline rationing to the eastern states. It was not long before gasoline rationing was nationwide. In North Africa, Rommel's Panzer Armee, Afrika, had driven into Egypt and was threatening the British base at Alexandria and the Suez Canal as well.

At home, war production was beginning to hit its stride. Enormous problems remained in swinging the manufacturing capacity of the nation from making automobiles, bicycles, clothes driers, dishwashers, electric lights, Ferris wheels, golf clubs, hat racks, ice crushers, jams and jellies, kettles, lawnmowers, music boxes, nutcrackers, office machines, parasols, quoits, rip saws, silver spoons, toasters, umbrellas, vans, washing machines, xylophones, yawls, and zippers to producing for the armed forces and essential civilian needs. These included ammunition, boilers, caterpillar tractors, davits, earphones, fighter planes, generators, howitzers, ingots, jerseys, king posts, landing craft, machine tools, nozzles, oxides, parachutes, quinine, rifles and other guns, ships, tanks, uniforms, valves, warheads for torpedoes, x-ray machines, yarn, and zinc chromate. Not all decisions were wise, and not all production was smooth. Not all producers were honest, and not all were competent. But somehow the job was getting done.

Sometimes organizations tried to set their own policies, regardless of the administration. One such organization was the Board of Economic Warfare, with which Leahy locked horns soon after he took over as chief of staff.

French Ambassador Gaston Henri-Haye came to his office, asking for more milk and food for the children of France. The shipments had been suspended with the coming to power of Laval. Since the matter had already been discussed with the president and approved, Leahy was happy to be able to tell him that the shipments would soon be resumed. In this he was mistaken. Although President Roosevelt had directed Leahy to instruct the State Department and the Board of Economic Warfare to resume shipping supplies to North Africa and food and milk to the children in unoccupied France, the board knew better. "They clearly believed me to be pro-Vichy."

There were a good many in the government, especially in the State Department, but in other offices as well, who opposed Leahy simply because he *had* been ambassador to France. As such, he was associated with the Pétain government and thus an enemy of the Free French and their leader, Charles de Gaulle.

Matters dragged on for over a month. The board simply refused to obey the directive of the president. Leahy, of course, could not tell them the real reason for resuming shipping to North Africa: the forthcoming invasion, Operation Torch. Shipments to French Algeria and Morocco would encourage friends of the allies to help out when the time came. But Leahy knew that if he told them the real reason, some member of the board would be sure to blab it to the press.

"I had several meetings with this group," he wrote. "They did not want to send anything to anybody except Russia and England. I explained that the early shipment of necessities to the African colonies was desired as a propaganda measure. They took the view that such assistance would in effect be aiding the Germans."[5] Finally, Leahy told them that the order came from the president and was not a matter for discussion. Even then, the board members did not stop discussing and arguing, but they did carry out the order.

Soon after taking up his new duties, Leahy, who had been living with the parents of Elizabeth Leahy, his son's wife, moved to the Hay-Adams Hotel in order to be nearer to the White House. He then gave notice to his tenant that he wanted his house on Florida Avenue back when the lease expired in November.

Although informality was the keynote of White House life under FDR's administration, there were occasions when protocol, precedence, and proper form had to be observed. A precedence had to be found for the president's chief of staff, for no such job had existed before. He was placed just below the level of cabinet officers, but ahead of the chiefs of staff. In such a capacity he attended a state dinner and a luncheon at the White House on the occasion of the visit of Queen Wilhelmina of the Netherlands. One of the guests at the luncheon was Wendell Willkie, the 1940 Republican candidate for president, and more recently author of the book, *One World*, in which he made a case for internationalism. Leahy had only a terse comment: "Mr. Willkie, seen for the first time, appears physically awkward."

During the next few weeks, Leahy kept very busy, as there were decisions to be made in every theater of the war. In the Solomons, matters were going badly, starting with the Battle of Savo immediately after the landings. To counter the Japanese expansion into the south Pacific, especially the new air bases they had set up, Leahy sent his friend Richard E. Byrd to explore other

Grandfather shows his sword to granddaughter
Louise and grandson Bobby, September 1942.
(Courtesy, FDR Library; *Life*, T. McAvoy)

possible islands as bases and to look in on the situation in the Solomons. This
was another factor in the ultimate decision made by the Joint Chiefs of Staff
and the president to send Vice Admiral William F. Halsey to take over in the
South Pacific. Leahy went along with the decision, although he believed that
Halsey's predecessor, Robert Ghormley, had done all right considering how
little strength he had.

Then there were the questions of aid to China and Russia. The Lend Lease
expediter, Averell Harriman, who had been in Russia with Churchill, told the
president and the Joint Chiefs that he found Stalin and the Russians "exactly as
determined as ever. They are going to put up a hell of a fight for Stalingrad, as
already shown. They won't give any guarantee about it, but have not given it
up."

In spite of German successes, Harriman was optimistic.

If you can get them 10,000 trucks a month, it will have a very material effect
on the fighting power of the Russians this winter and next year. There is no

question there will be a Russian front. The question is how effective it will be, and the whole course of the war depends on that. The thing that strikes me as fantastic is the unwillingness of the military here and in the U.K. to recognize this. I will say that to any of them direct, but do not wish to be quoted on it.[6]

Soon after Leahy settled into the job of chief of staff, a French writer in *Le Matin* snorted at the president for taking on such a person, claiming that Leahy had merely adopted his name, changing it from Levy. "It is noted," the admiral wrote to Wahwee MacArthur, still in Vichy, "that the editorial does not insist that the ancient name is Jewish, but it does say that a Levy, meaning me, has assumed the ancient name. It seems to me that they may find difficulty in corrupting Doug's family name into anything faintly resembling a Biblical appellation. It is, of course, possible that Macenstein might be his real name, in spite of his well-known Scottish characteristics."[7]

It soon became apparent that Leahy's office in the Public Health Building at Nineteenth and Constitution was too far away from the White House to permit him to do the job that needed to be done. Since his function as chief of staff to the commander in chief was far more important and demanding than that of chairman of the Joint Chiefs, he moved on Sunday, 6 September, into new offices in the White House.

> My office in the unfinished East Wing addition to the White House consists of one large elaborately furnished room, an equally large adjoining room for my aide, Commander Freseman, and the stenographer–secretary, Mrs. Blaine, and a small but comfortable rest room that should be useful at times when we must be instantly available at night.
>
> This new wing is as yet far from finished, but my offices had been hurried to completion and are in a very satisfactory condition.

September 10 was a particularly busy day, but in a way it was typical of the kind of matters that came to Leahy's attention. In the morning, Lauchlin Currie, back from a fact-finding mission to China, stopped in to give Leahy a report. He said that Chiang Kai-shek insisted on taking Burma, which could be done with Chinese forces and "four or five American and British divisions," with five-hundred airplanes. "He does not expect any useful contribution by Great Britain," added Leahy, commenting on his visitor's attitude.

Then Bob Murphy, back temporarily from North Africa, came to see him. He and Leahy had faced the same kind of obstruction and suspicion. Many of the "best and brightest" in the State Department and elsewhere believed wholeheartedly in de Gaulle and distrusted men like Leahy and Murphy as "pro-Vichy." That made things especially difficult, for Murphy was being given a delicate assignment in preparing French leaders to accept the forthcoming invasion of Algeria and Morocco. Since de Gaulle's headquarters in London were known to leak like a sieve, his supporters in London and

Washington could not be told. There is no doubt that if any of them had known the secret of Torch, he would have revealed it to de Gaulle in order to "save the president from himself."

A major task was the preparation of a directive for Murphy. This time Murphy would be assigned to General Dwight D. Eisenhower, who had been selected to command Torch. Leahy was the principal architect of the directive, which spelled out Murphy's exact status on Eisenhower's staff and just what he could tell the French commanders in North Africa in order to ensure their cooperation. It was intentionally misleading, suggesting as it did, that the troops which would arrive would all be American and that their task would be that of keeping order.

> No change in the existing French civil administrations is contemplated by the United States. Any resistance to the American landing will of course be put down by force of arms. The American forces will hope for and will welcome French assistance. . . . The proposed expedition will be American, under American command, and it will not include any of the forces of General de Gaulle.[8]

Roosevelt approved of changes right up until the last moment and asked that "every effort be made to obtain either cooperation or at least neutrality in the interest of military success."[9]

Soon after Murphy's departure for North Africa, former Associate Justice James F. Byrnes moved into the east wing and set up an office as assistant for production. Leahy at that time thought Byrnes was probably the "most promising person in America for the job." Work on the new wing had progressed, and the admiral was very happy with the facilities. In addition to the office spaces already described, it contained a small movie theater and a bomb shelter which could accommodate up to a hundred persons. Harry Hopkins had a suite adjoining Leahy's offices.

The ensuing weeks saw many meetings to straighten out the strategy and tactics for Torch. Some were purely American and some involved the British Joint Staff Mission. Leahy, of course, presided at most of them. He spoke for the president and everyone knew it. If the group seemed about to be adopting a course he thought unwise, he would say quietly, "I don't think I can sell this to the boss." He was never fooled by anybody, according to one of his aides, and he made full use of the presidential power.[10]

> He didn't really use any pressure, but his technique was most interesting. . . . Marshall, for example, would start discussing some plan of his, something he thought we ought to be doing, and Leahy would say, "Well, George, I'm just a simple sailor. Would you please back up and start from the beginning and make it simple. Just tell me step one, two, and three, and so on."
> Well, Marshall, or Arnold, or whoever it was, kept falling for this thing and

they would back up and explain to this simple old sailor. And as they did it—which is what Leahy knew would happen—and went through these various steps, they themselves would find out the weakness or misconception, or that there was something wrong with it. So he didn't have to start out by saying, "This is a stupid idea and it won't work."[11]

During this time the British and Americans differed on where the forces should land in North Africa. The British wanted to land as far east as possible, in order to assist the Eighth Army under General Bernard Montgomery, while the Americans feared that Hitler might persuade Franco to close the Strait of Gibraltar and thus bottle up Allied forces in the Mediterranean. They, therefore, wanted to include Casablanca on the Atlantic coast as a target to ensure continuity of supplies. Eventually this view won out, and the final objectives were Casablanca, Algiers, and Oran.

On 14 October, in a sad homecoming without Louise, Leahy moved back into the house at 2168 Florida Avenue. Although he missed her keenly, the house was more of a home to him than anywhere else.

Three days later he was honored at the annual Convocation of Georgetown University with the honorary degree of Doctor of Military Science. The diploma, in both English and Latin, proclaimed the virtues of one who "stands four-square on the fighting bridge of Our Ship of State." The Latin text did not venture so daring a metaphor, but it was adequately complimentary.[12]

As the landings in North Africa drew closer, the Allies tried to smuggle General Henri Giraud out of France and take him to Eisenhower's headquarters. They hoped he would be able to win the support of the French officials in North Africa. In return they were prepared to offer him command of French forces in the target areas.

On 2 November, less than a week before the landings were to take place, Leahy learned that Giraud demanded that the landings be delayed several weeks so that he could organize the French forces. With that infuriating arrogance by which certain Frenchmen can forever alienate even their strongest supporters, Giraud declared that it would be impossible for him to leave France before 20 November, and when he did leave, he would consent to cooperate only if he were given overall command of the operation.

This demand upset Bob Murphy, for it threw awry all his careful cultivation of French leaders in the Algiers area. In what he later confessed was a ridiculous message, he cabled Washington, recommending that the landings be delayed two weeks.

> I am convinced that the invasion of North Africa without favorable French High Command will be a catastrophe. The delay of two weeks, unpleasant as it may be, involving technical considerations of which I am ignorant, is insignificant compared with the result involving serious opposition of the French Army to our landing.[13]

Without even bothering to consult FDR who was in Hyde Park, Leahy cabled Murphy:

> The decision of the President is that the operation will be carried out as now planned and that you will do your utmost to secure the understanding and cooperation of the French officials with whom you are now in contact.[14]

In his journal, Leahy added the comment, "I personally don't expect much enthusiasm on the part of the French African Army in opposing American troops, although the coast defenses under command of the Navy may be expected to oppose the landing."

The last few days before the landing were full of tension, for no one knew whether this first operation in the Atlantic theater would be a great success or a dismal failure which could extend the war for years in senseless fighting between Frenchmen and Americans.

In a move which Roosevelt hoped might lessen resistance, he proposed to send a personal message to Marshal Pétain. In view of his close association with the marshal, Leahy was naturally consulted, and with the assistance of Harry Hopkins and others, came up with a draft. When the text was cabled to Churchill, he rejected it as "much too kind." FDR took a look at it and changed the salutation from "My dear old friend" to "Marshal Pétain." He ran a pencil through the passages italicized in the following sentences:

> I am sending this message to you *not only* as the Chef d'État of the United States to the Chef d'État of the Republic of France, *but also as one of your friends and comrades of the great days of 1918. May we both live to see France victorious again against the ancient enemy.*[15]

Less than forty-eight hours before the landings were to take place, Leahy learned that Darlan was in Algiers to see his son Alain, who was desperately ill of polio. When he reported this to Roosevelt, FDR's first reaction was of sympathy as he recalled his own affliction. The two of them agreed that a letter to Darlan would be a nice gesture, but even more they worried how Darlan's presence would affect the landings.

British and American forces went ashore on 8 November, in the three North African target areas, meeting unexpectedly fierce resistance. Giraud finally came around and agreed to serve under Eisenhower's command, but the aftermath was ironic. The French refused to obey him. Instead they listened to Marshal Pétain, who ordered all-out resistance. To Roosevelt's message, Pétain replied:

> It is with stupor and sadness that I learned tonight of the aggression of your troops against North Africa.
>
> I have read your message. You invoke pretexts which nothing justifies. . . . France and her honor are at stake. We are attacked; we shall defend ourselves; this is the order I am giving.[16]

The next day France broke diplomatic relations with the United States.

With Darlan in Algiers, Eisenhower and Murphy saw an opportunity to end the fighting. With Giraud ineffective, they hoped Darlan could be persuaded to issue orders to his compatriates in North Africa to lay down their arms. On the afternoon of 10 November, Darlan issued the orders. He rescinded them, however, when he received a sharp rebuke from Pétain who ordered him to continue resisting American forces. The next day, however, news arrived that German forces were marching into unoccupied France. Darlan then changed once again and ordered the fighting to cease. He sent orders for the French ships in Toulon to sail to North African ports, but the orders were held up until it was too late. The ships were scuttled as the Germans approached. Darlan was able to reverse his course finally to the Allied side because, on the heels of his public order to resist the Allies, Pétain, using naval codes, sent another, approving Darlan's actions and expressing full confidence in him.

Eisenhower cabled the results of these various agreements to the president, arguing that in his opinion the arrangement had saved many lives and that the situation in the area was not remotely like what had been imagined before the troops had gone ashore. He ended by saying that the arrangement with Darlan had not involved the U.S. government, and if FDR disapproved, Eisenhower would be willing to place his head on the block.

Things were complicated enough when the British added fuel to the fire by sending representatives of de Gaulle to North Africa. Since there were already two highly volatile Frenchmen there, the arrival of representatives of a third, would be like lighting matches in a gunpowder factory.

Leahy objected to British ambassador to the United States, Lord Halifax:

> I expressed to him my personal opinion that any de Gaulle representatives in North Africa at this time would almost certainly be disadvantageous to our military effort in that area. He said he would inform his government of my opinion, and I asked him to make it perfectly clear to his government that I had expressed only my personal opinion, which I believe would be concurred with by everybody interested in the success of our African expedition.
>
> I have been unable to learn the reason for Britain's insistance on injecting de Gaulle into that already confused and difficult problem.

The Darlan deal caused such an uproar in the papers that some feared that FDR would have to repudiate it simply to silence the critics. Leahy, of course, was blamed for abetting the notorious Darlan, collaborator and fascist. He shrugged his shoulders. Such an attitude by the press was inevitable.

> Our expeditionary force in North Africa is making excellent progress toward Tunis, but we are here encountering political and press opposition to the arrangements made by General Eisenhower with Admiral Darlan. The latter has through his influence with the French army and navy succeeded in stopping all French armed opposition to our occupation. He had been out of favor for a

long time with the British government, and more than out of favor with the de Gaullists.

Having now assumed the duties of High Commissioner in North Africa, and having announced that he is on our side, he should, of course, be wholly taken into our camp—and watched carefully. This is not being done because of objections by de Gaulle and his few followers and the prejudiced press. If this stupid failure by America and Britain succeeds in alienating Admiral Darlan, it may cost us the lives of thousands of our soldiers, and it may add serious obstacles to the progress of our expeditionary force toward Tunis, and beyond, wherever that may be.

In spite of our full adoption of Stalin, even the president offers strong objection to any agreement with Darlan.

I am continuing and will indefinitely continue to try to use everybody, bad, good, and indifferent, who promises to be of assistance in reducing the length of our casualty lists.

This brings to mind Churchill's statement on the occasion of the German invasion of Russia: "If Hitler invaded Hell, I would make at least a favorable reference to the Devil in the House of Commons."

In *I Was There*, Leahy added, "You simply had to keep an eye on 'Popeye.'"[17]

Revisionist historians have made the statement that Darlan didn't do very much, that the fighting was pretty well over when he jumped on the bandwagon of the Allied cause. Leahy, the man who knew Darlan better than any other American, believed that Darlan could and would make good on his promises.

Even after Darlan had brought the fighting to an end and had been recognized by other French leaders as high commissioner, there was interference. On one occasion, FDR held up a message Darlan wanted to send through military channels, saying it should go through regular commercial communication systems.

"I told the president that I believe his decision in this matter is wrong in that he may alienate Admiral Darlan from our African adventure, and by so doing cost us the lives of many Americans."

"I'm a pig-headed Dutchman, Bill," FDR replied, "and I have made up my mind about this. We are going ahead with it, and you can't change my mind."

Harry Hopkins could occasionally persuade Roosevelt when he "got his Dutch up," but no one else could. Certainly Bill Leahy couldn't.

Of course, in Leahy's job, nothing ever came singly. While he was concentrating on the state of affairs in North Africa, a climactic battle was being fought for Guadalcanal. Two of Leahy's friends, Rear Admiral Daniel Callaghan, recently naval aide to the president, and Rear Admiral Norman Scott were killed in a furious night engagement near Savo Island. On 1 December, an American cruiser was sunk and four others damaged near Tassafaronga.

Meanwhile, Roosevelt resisted clamorous demands that he receive de Gaulle. The pressure came from the liberal press who seemed to fear Darlan's fascism more than any possibility that the local French might go over to the Axis. Finally the Joint Chiefs of Staff felt constrained to issue a statement that receiving de Gaulle at that time might "seriously hamper" Allied operations in North Africa.

Opposition to Darlan even made its way into the White House private rooms. On 1 December, Leahy dined with FDR and Eleanor Roosevelt, Harry and Louise Hopkins, Malvina Thompson, Mrs. Roosevelt's private secretary, and Brigadier General "Beetle" Smith, now Eisenhower's chief of staff.

"Mrs. Roosevelt," commented Leahy, "who is definitely opposed to Admiral Darlan's efforts in behalf of our African expedition, did most of the talking at dinner, and is an incurable uplifter and devoted to the task of arranging everything for everybody."

For the next few days, Leahy was frequently frustrated as FDR blew hot and cold on Darlan and de Gaulle. He was going to do nothing which might legitimize any claims of any French leaders to permanent positions in the postwar government of France.

During this time, Leahy came to appreciate fully the great abilities and devotion to duty of Harry Hopkins. He had, Leahy felt, "an understanding view of the whole problem" and "was from my point of view very helpful. . . ."

Leahy noted how Hopkins would remain quiet while others talked themselves out. Then he would unerringly put his finger on the gist of the discussion or point out the best solution to a problem they had been kicking around. This was the ability which caused Churchill to dub him "Lord Root of the Matter."

Up to this time, Leahy had had some reservations about him. They went back to the days when Hopkins had headed WPA and had been considered a radical who liked nothing better than throwing other people's money away on ne'er-do-wells who spent their time leaning on shovels. "That social worker in the White House" still drew a lot of criticism from people who did not understand that Hopkins's total energies were now directed at winning the war. "I frequently joked with him about those days," Leahy wrote, "and sometimes called him 'Pinko' or 'Do-Gooder.' He took it all in good spirit and we never had any major differences of opinion. By his brilliant mind, his loyalty, and his self-less devotion to Franklin Roosevelt in helping carry on the war, Harry Hopkins soon erased completely any previous misgivings I might have had."[18]

The wisdom of accepting the Darlan deal received strong support in a letter from "Doc" Matthews:

I'm sure that it is unnecessary to write you in detail the reasons why it was necessary to deal with Darlan instead of throwing him in prison. You and I have no illusions about Popeye, and it seems strange after our many problems and unpleasant hours with him in Vichy for me to be cast somewhat in the role of his defender! But the symbol of the Marshal and loyalty to their oath made it clear from the beginning that the bulk of the French army, navy, air force and civil government officials would only obey orders which came in Pétain's name and with his authority. However distorted this sense of duty may have been, it was very real, and there are still very few Frenchmen who feel that what amounted to suicide missions by the French warships at Casablanca and French military resistance in the early days could have been avoided without complete loss of "honor" and self-respect: they still argue that such useless waste of life and ships was necessary. Giraud, who in my humble opinion, had more real character and integrity that any other Frenchman either in North Africa or London, repeat London [where de Gaulle was located], quickly sensed the situation and himself *insisted* that Darlan be brought into the picture. (This, I think, is the clear answer to those here who imply that we let Giraud down.) There can be no argument as to the solid material gains which resulted from this move, whatever the moral indignation and public dismay which dealing with Darlan seem to have aroused. Briefly, Darlan alone was able to give the order to cease fire and have it obeyed throughout North Africa; he alone, with his secret private message from Pétain, was able to swing the French North African army from an attitude of hostility into fighting by our side in one week's time; he alone could keep the civil administration and public services functioning and actively cooperating with us, with all that it meant in those early days. . . . We would never have gotten Dakar at this stage without Darlan, I am quite certain. Bob [Murphy] and I sat in with [Governor General of Dakar] Boisson's delegates when they talked to Darlan after the President's statement of the "temporary" nature of our arrangements. (I can fully appreciate the need of such a statement to quiet the public both at home and here, but it certainly gave us some difficult moments on the spot and nearly resulted in the Dakar people going home and deciding not to play.) It was Darlan's secret message from Pétain, giving him the green light, which really convinced Boisson and his people that they would still be loyal to the Marshal by following Darlan and joining our team. Once their consciences were clear on this, Boisson and his people seemed eager to help.[19]

This letter accorded perfectly with Leahy's own views, despite the suspicions of American journalists who knew best what was to be done without having been there, and despite the British tendency to regard with suspicion anyone who "so much as set foot in the Hôtel du Parc."

At any rate, the Darlan deal was accepted; Leahy never wavered from his conviction that it was the only correct action given the situation in France and in French North Africa that November and December. "Popeye" had to be watched, but he had delivered.

On 24 December, Leahy received a long, handwritten letter from Darlan.

Ostensibly a thank-you note for Leahy's expression of sympathy on the illness of Alain Darlan, the letter went on to justify the actions he had taken while Leahy was ambassador, and in North Africa. [A translation of the letter appears as Appendix B.]

His motives, he said, were to prevent a ditch from being dug to separate France and the United States. He stated that the Marshal was in agreement with his policies in Africa, the word coming through secret messages from the French Admiralty, and that was how he had been able to rally the French in North Africa.

Leahy read that letter at home, nursing a severe cold. That evening he learned that Darlan had been assassinated. It was a severe shock, and Leahy found it impossible to stay in bed. Using his special telephone line to the White House, he talked to Roosevelt about what should be done to repair the damage and what the president should say to the press. For himself, Leahy noted in his journal:

> Admiral Darlan, who was the only French official in Africa with sufficient authority to exercise control of the French army and navy in that area, had recently joined with our effort in the African colonies to save France and protect ourselves from the barbarian hordes of Germans and Italians that now infest Europe.
>
> His death leaves the French in Africa without an accepted leader, and it may place our expeditionary force there in an extremely disadvantageous position. Darlan, in spite of his fanatical dislike for everything English, was, in my opinion, and I knew him well, an invaluable asset to the Allied cause in Africa.
>
> The British will probably make an effort to force General de Gaulle into his place as leader of the French. Such an effort will fail and will be harmful to the Allied cause.

Although final decisions had to wait until the forthcoming Casablanca conference, Giraud was named high commissioner soon after Christmas. A few days later, Leahy was amused to hear the crusty Tennessean, Secretary of State Cordell Hull, report that he expected in the "near future a press attack . . . by the de Gaulle 'polecats' in his department" for not pushing their hero.

On the last day of 1942, Leahy was surprised to read a column in the *Washington Post* by Constantine Brown, a correspondent he had known for years, to the effect that powerful persons were urging Roosevelt to get rid of Leahy, who was "too old, too reactionary and ultimately will prove a liability to the President in the 1944 elections."

Leahy's sound military advice, the article continued, was overshadowed by the drawbacks of his political weakness. The article claimed that he wanted to draw up a small war cabinet under himself. It also castigated him for his support of Darlan.[20]

The article was a mixture of truth and half truth, rumor, gossip, and hearsay, with little substance. FDR was not listening to Leahy's critics, and the admiral attributed the attack to "some of the civilian war agencies" which were "fearful of encroachment on their prerogatives by the military."

Leahy's journal reveals only routine entries until it was time to depart for Casablanca on 9 January. They left from a siding under the Bureau of Engraving and Printing in the *Ferdinand Magellan*. "The president's new heavily armored car with glass windows that are designed to keep out machine gun bullets is arranged with a sitting room, a dining room for ten or twelve persons, a small but well-arranged kitchen, and five staterooms. Dr. [Ross] McIntire, Harry Hopkins, Miss [Grace] Tully, and I occupied the staterooms, and Captain John McCrea [naval aide] joined us in the dining room. Other cars accommodated the Secret Service men, the apothecary, the communication personnel, and the president's valet [Arthur Prettyman]."

In Miami early on the morning of 11 January, the party boarded two Pan American Clippers, flying boats with limited capacity but luxurious accommodations. In the president's plane were Ross McIntire, Harry Hopkins, Captain McCrea, the inevitable secret service men, and Leahy. On the way, the pilot took them over Haiti, where they had an excellent view of Cap Haitien and Cristophe's Citadel.

On landing at Trinidad, Leahy found the cold he had been fighting for over two weeks had taken a turn for the worse, and the next morning he had developed serious bronchitis. Ross McIntire told him he would have to stay in Trinidad, and Roosevelt ordered him to "get a good rest, and be ready to rejoin" him on the return journey.

So it was that Leahy was unable to attend the one conference where he could have contributed the most. Decisions about the French had to be made in the absence of the one man who knew most about the persons concerned. It seems certain that had he been there, de Gaulle would not have gained the acceptance he did, at least not without a lot of argument from the former ambassador to Vichy France. As it was, he rested in the naval hospital and then took advantage of the hospitality of Rear Admiral Jesse B. Oldendorf, commandant of the naval base.

On 29 January, the president and his party returned to spend the night. The next morning at 7:00 A.M. the Clipper took off again, and at noon, as they were passing over the island of Haiti, Leahy, Hopkins, and Lieutenant Cone, skipper of the aircraft, shared a birthday party for President Roosevelt, who was sixty-one years old. Champagne, birthday cake, and presents contributed to the festivities, which FDR carried off with an air.

Late that afternoon the plane reached Miami. The party at once boarded the president's special train and left for Washington, arriving late the following afternoon.

Leahy concluded that he had missed little at the conference:

> Conversation with the president, General Marshall, and Admiral King leads
> me to believe that little of value to ending the war was accomplished by the

FDR and WDL inspect "Views of Trinidad" following the president's sixty-first birthday party aboard a Pan American Clipper flying from Trinidad to Miami, 30 January 1943. Mr. Roosevelt was returning from the Casablanca Conference, which Admiral Leahy missed because of illness. Others in the party included Harry Hopkins and Lieutenant Howard Cone, skipper of the Pan Am flying boat. (Courtesy, FDR Library)

conference in Casablanca. It appears that our British allies were forced to accept the necessity for some aggressive action against Japan in the Southwest Pacific and in Burma. In Europe the American plan to invade France via the Channel in 1943 failed of acceptance by Great Britain, and a decision to take combined aggressive action against the Mediterranean islands was substituted therefor.

Some small approach was made toward accomplishing a political agreement between General Giraud, who is fighting in North Africa, and General de Gaulle, who is talking in England and, through a partisan press, in America.

I am unable to see that any military advantage to us will be attained by an agreement between Giraud and de Gaulle.

Although Leahy minimized the accomplishments at Casablanca, the decisions reached there would lead to wider action in other parts of the world. The French in North Africa would remain a problem, but Leahy's attention was soon drawn to a more global view of the war.

# CHAPTER 11

# Grand Strategy

Although Leahy downplayed the importance of the Casablanca Conference, as he set to work following his return, he came to realize that several significant decisions had been made and that as go-between between the president and the Joint Chiefs, he would be responsible for keeping them all on track. As chief of staff to the commander in chief, he would need to coordinate the military decisions with the political ones, especially those involving France, China, Britain, and Russia. All presented thorny problems, and none could be dealt with in isolation from each other.

Agreements reached at Casablanca included a decision to give top priority to the Battle of the Atlantic against the U-boats, for if it were not won, Bolero, the buildup in Britain, would be imperiled. Perhaps Britain would even be driven out of the war. Successful U-boats could possibly cut off supplies and reinforcements to British and American troops in North Africa.

Operation Husky, the invasion of Sicily in July 1943, had been accepted, and Roundup for 1943 was off. In return for that major U.S. concession, the British agreed to permit the United States to allocate more of their resources to the Pacific. King estimated that Nimitz and MacArthur were getting about 15 percent of the Allied war effort. He wanted it upped to 30 percent. As a part of the package, the British agreed to operations leading to the recapture of Burma (Operation Anakim), in order to help keep the Chinese in the war. Marshall was the leading voice for that decision, for he feared that if Chiang

Kai-shek's forces collapsed, the Japanese would be able to send troops from China into other areas of the Pacific and Asia.

The Casablanca conferees, on the other hand, left a great many questions unanswered, and Leahy's journal for 1943 provides a partial account of how those problems were solved.

Soon after Leahy's return from Trinidad, Chief Yeoman Dorothy Ringquist reported for duty in the admiral's office at the Joint Chiefs of Staff headquarters. They soon developed a close working partnership and friendship which lasted until the end of his life. At first her work was confined to JCS and CCS matters, but Mrs. Blaine was not well, and soon "I was running back and forth, doing both jobs. . . . Then the admiral realized that I was working too hard." Mrs. Blaine soon left for reasons of health and Dorothy Ringquist was installed as his principal clerk in the White House office, with an assistant there and in the JCS office. She had not objected: "it was the admiral who felt that I was being overworked, and he did something about it immediately. That was typical of his concern for people."

With the small staff he preferred, Leahy insisted on and achieved efficiency. He seldom approved overtime work for his staff, and he usually left the office around five o'clock. "He was well organized," Miss Ringquist remembered, "and his mind wasn't cluttered, so we weren't cluttered. It didn't take him long to find out how much you were capable of doing, and he expected the utmost out of you, but nothing more than that. If you made a mistake you only made it once; he wouldn't be hard on you, but you didn't want to disappoint him. He made you feel that way. That was true from orderlies on up."[1]

By this time, Leahy and Hopkins were the two principal assistants to FDR in running the war. They emphasized different things, but either of them could and did cope with any problem arising about the conduct of the war, whether it dealt with production, strategy, manpower, diplomacy, or other national leaders. Hopkins, of course, was much closer to Roosevelt, but Leahy had wider experience. Hopkins dealt with matters as a civilian, emphasizing the political aspects; Leahy dealt with the same matters, emphasizing the military aspects. It was a matter of emphasis, not of area of responsibility. FDR accounted himself responsible for everything, and his principal assistants had to know everything as well.

In wartime, social life in Washington was greatly curbed, but some affairs could not be avoided completely. Nothing in his experience in Vichy had prepared Leahy for a reception in February held at the Russian embassy in celebration of the twenty-fifth anniversary of the founding of the Red Army. A good many of the guests, Leahy wryly noted, were more interested in their hosts' vodka than they were in the USSR. Ambassador Maxim Litvinov picked Leahy to clink glasses with for a toast. The ambassador downed his vodka with a single gulp. Leahy felt obliged to do the same. "It almost burned out my insides, but it was good training for the conference dinners . . . at Teheran, Yalta, and Potsdam."

A major problem which would not go away was how to support China in the war against Japan. The British seemed to resent every bullet, every man, every gun, every ship that went to the Far East, while the United States looked on the Chinese armies as vital forces keeping huge numbers of Japanese employed. Knowing that their friends were in the United States rather than the United Kingdom, the Chinese lost no time after the Casablanca Conference in stepping up a campaign for more support. In mid-February, therefore, Mme. Chiang Kai-shek made a state visit to Washington for that purpose. At that time, China was nearly isolated from the outside world, with the Burma Road cut off and the Japanese in control of the coast. Only the goods that could be flown over the "Hump" of the Himalaya mountains were getting through.

Lacking reliable leadership, Chiang depended on two American officers, Generals Joseph Stilwell and Claire Chennault. The latter was in charge of air operations, while the former, who spoke fluent Chinese, commanded Chiang's ground forces. Unfortunately, Stilwell had only contempt for Chiang, referring to him on all occasions as "the Peanut."

Mme. Chiang, a woman of great charm and intelligence, who spoke perfect English, made the most of her opportunities. She infuriated Mrs. Henrietta Nesbitt, the White House housekeeper, by insisting on using her own silk sheets and by otherwise suggesting by her manner that standards of living in the White House left a great deal to be desired.

According to Leahy, Mme. Chiang was impressive and answered questions with "quick wit and assurance." On 21 February, she asked the admiral to come to her apartment in the White House. He was never sure exactly what she wanted. She talked about the Burma Campaign and how the British had botched things in the Far East by refusing aid when Chiang Kai-shek had offered it.

She concluded the interview by asking Leahy to return to China with her so he could see for himself just what the situation was. If the admiral felt flattered by this offer, the feeling didn't last long. He soon learned that she had also invited Hopkins. Then, a little later, he told FDR about the invitation. "Don't get all swelled up about this, Bill," the president replied. "She also asked *me* to go back with her."

A few days after his invitation to China, Leahy recorded the story of a conversation between Mme. Chiang and the president. In his joking way, FDR accused her of being a "vamp" because she had so charmed Wendell Willkie during his stop at Chungking in his recent trip around the world.

"Mr. President," Mme. Chiang smiled in reply, "that does not qualify me as a 'vamp,' because Mr. Willkie has all of the emotional reactions of an adolescent."

Vamp or not, Mme. Chiang was so effective an advocate of her cause that she created some concern among the British that the Americans might go back on the Germany-first strategy and turn their major priorities to the Pacific.

Her visit to Washington was climaxed by a reception at the Shoreham Hotel. Leahy squired his granddaughter Louise to the affair. "There were thousands of invited guests," but apparently Mme. Chiang was fatigued, for she "was seated when we arrived," and the guests were being welcomed by the wife of the Chinese ambassador.

China, however, remained a problem that would not go away, and a few months later, in May , as the British were preparing to come to Washington for a conference, T. V. Soong, Chinese foreign minister, and generals Stilwell and Chennault arrived to give the Joint Chiefs of Staff ammunition to use against the British who seemed to be trying to wriggle out of the Burma commitment. Leahy felt the constant bickering of the two generals might result in the Chinese being driven out of the war.

> Chennault was up in China with the Generalissimo, and when the going got rough, he would drop some bombs on the Japanese and slow them down. He had a lot of courage, was a good airman, but knew little about other types of operations. Stilwell was down in the jungles far away from Chungking. Although tactless and with a tongue too sharp for his own good, he was an excellent fighter and knew what to do on the ground. I wanted this controversy straightened out and everything feasible done to keep China in the war. I knew that was the attitude of President Roosevelt.[2]

But there was really little Leahy could tell Soong. Only so much could be flown over the Hump, and any improvement in supply to China would have to await the reopening of the Burma Road. The campaign there was a British problem, and it was one they were anxious to neglect.

An American problem was the proper use of manpower. General Marshall wanted as large an army as possible. The navy and air force needed men to man the ships and fly the planes, and industry needed huge numbers to build the ships, the fifty-thousand planes a year insisted on by the president, and the myriad other products necessary for the war and for the people at home. Farmers were needed to grow the food to feed the soldiers and sailors as well as the men, women, and children in the cities and towns across the nation. Since everyone had a good case for his demands on the nation's manpower, the fact that no one could have all he wanted had caused considerable bickering in Washington as well as the rest of the country.

Labor had been restive because of President Roosevelt's "hold the line" order on wages, and during the year strikes by the coal miners and by the railroad workers were only the most obvious and dramatic examples of the inability of labor and management to subordinate their differences to the common cause of the war effort. Congress threatened to pass a "work or fight" act, but, even in wartime, most people opposed conscription of labor. Still the fact that men were being conscripted to fight in the armed forces left little room for sympathy for workers who held the safety of the nation at pawn over questions of wages and hours.

Accordingly, FDR appointed a special manpower advisory committee consisting of Bernard Baruch as chairman, Leahy, Hopkins, James Byrnes, and Samuel Rosenman. This was a high-level committee indeed. Barney Baruch had been a principal production advisor to President Wilson in World War I and had been consulted numerous times by Roosevelt in World War II. The three "assistant presidents," Hopkins, Byrnes, and Leahy, encompassed in their responsibilities every aspect of the war. Sam Rosenman, a justice of the New York Supreme Court, had recently joined the White House team as a general assistant and speechwriter. As a member of the "Cuff Links Gang," he had a close relationship with Roosevelt. All five were men FDR trusted, although he found Baruch a bit stuffy.★

The committee met irregularly over a period of several days, hearing witnesses, some of whom were more interested in preserving their own power than in getting on with the war. Secretary of Agriculture Claude Wickard "did not impress me as sufficiently efficient to meet the existing critical condition of food shortage."

Leahy saved his harshest criticism for William Green, president of the American Federation of Labor. "The A. F. of L. is definitely opposed to any legislation designed to control the labor market. It appears to be actuated more by desire to maintain its control of labor than to assist our war effort."

The final report of the committee faced the problem of conscription of labor, but concluded the time had not yet come.

> The report recommends 11,160,000 men for the military services, the utilization of women in industry, a radical, drastic change in the administration of the manpower commission and in the Department of Agriculture, and a further effort to obtain labor essential to the war effort by the volunteer system.
>
> The Committee agreed that if the war does not end in the near future, a draft of manpower and capital through legislative enactment of a national service act is inevitable. It believes, however, that the people are not at this time prepared to accept a national service act.

---

★The Cuff Links Gang was an organization consisting of some of Roosevelt's political cronies, to whom he had presented a set of cuff links. Some like Sam Rosenman and Louis Howe dated back to FDR's earliest political days. Others like Hopkins became members later. They exchanged birthday gifts and were poker-playing companions of the president. So far as I can determine, Leahy was never a member.

The limitation on the number of men in the services was not at all to the liking of George Marshall. He wanted a considerably larger army than was now possible. But the limit stuck, and this smaller army won the war in Europe and Asia, thanks to the vision of FDR and others in demanding fifty thousand airplanes a year. There was also the two-ocean navy that Leahy and his successors had fought for and which was now coming down the ways and entering combat in seas far from home.

Still, it was not easy going, and on the occasion of a visit of Foreign Minister Anthony Eden, Leahy remarked ruefully, "Anthony Eden knew what Britain wanted. There were times when I felt that if I could find anybody except Roosevelt who knew what America wanted, it would be an astonishing discovery."

What did America want? That would gradually emerge as the months went by. In the Pacific the struggle for Guadalcanal had ended in an American triumph, and in New Guinea, MacArthur had established his footholds in the Papuan peninsula. But no decisions had been made on where MacArthur and Nimitz would go from there. Nor were command arrangements clear.

Leahy, Marshall, and King occasionally met with Hopkins and the president to review the entire military situation. In the spring of 1943, the demands of the North African campaign were taking up more of the limited available resources than anyone had foreseen. Commanders in the Pacific, who had counted on larger allocations as a result of the Casablanca decisions, were understandably disgruntled when they saw the men, ships, planes, tanks, and other things go across the Atlantic to Algeria instead of across the Pacific to them.

MacArthur and Nimitz had widely different ideas of the strategy for the Pacific war, and in mid-March, their divergent views were dumped on the Joint Chiefs of Staff. It was a conflict of personalities, MacArthur against Nimitz, and a conflict of services, army versus navy. A good many people felt it was often MacArthur against the Joint Chiefs and the president as well.

When the Pacific theater had been divided up into area commands, MacArthur's bailiwick included the Solomon Islands. Since the Guadalcanal operation was to be largely a Navy–Marine Corps show, it obviously had to come under Nimitz in his capacity as CINCPOA. The problem of area command had been solved by moving the boundary between Nimitz's area and MacArthur's one degree of longitude westward, so that all of Guadalcanal would be Nimitz's turf. But with further operations planned for the Solomons, operations which would involve primarily naval and marine forces, the question of command and objectives arose all over again.

In March, therefore, the Joint Chiefs invited Nimitz and MacArthur to send representatives to Washington to thrash out those problems. From MacArthur came Chief of Staff Major General Richard K. Sutherland. Halsey, COMSOPAC, sent his mercurial chief of staff, Captain Miles R.

Browning. Representing Nimitz was quiet, brilliant Rear Admiral Raymond A. Spruance, who was sometimes looked on as Nimitz's alter ego. Leahy had last seen him in Puerto Rico when he had commanded the Tenth Naval District.

The discussions ranged widely over such areas as the allocation of forces between Europe and the Pacific, between MacArthur and Nimitz, on whether Pacific operations should be under a single command or two commands. If operations were to be unified, who should command?

General Marshall was out of town as these discussions began, but his deputy General T. T. Handy argued that all Pacific operations should be placed under MacArthur's command, and all forces consolidated in a single drive along the north coast of New Guinea aimed at the eventual capture of the Philippines. Leahy objected. He went along with the navy idea of a dual drive in which MacArthur and Nimitz "cooperated" in support of a common goal. MacArthur could have his strategy across the northern shore of New Guinea, but Nimitz was equally entitled to his through the Central Pacific. The proviso was that the two drives be "mutually supporting."

On 28 March, the issue was finally settled:

> Sunday. In the forenoon held a special meeting of the Joint Chiefs of Staff to decide upon command in the South and Southwest Pacific for immediately future operations against the Japanese invaders of that area.
>
> We decided that General MacArthur is to have full command of operations in New Guinea and the adjacent islands, and that Commander in Chief, Pacific Fleet [Nimitz in his capacity as CINCPOA], will have full command in other Pacific areas with full responsibility for defeating the Japanese fleet. This seems to fix unity of command in the Pacific areas where heretofore the Army and Navy have "cooperated."

This decision was clearly a triumph for King, who consistently had urged the Joint and Combined Chiefs of Staff to pay more attention to the Pacific. It confirmed the authority of Nimitz in the South, Central, and North Pacific, and it specifically authorized a Central Pacific drive which would be entirely under Nimitz's command.

It was not entirely a navy triumph over MacArthur, however; in the forthcoming operations against the Central and Northern Solomons, Halsey, while under the command of Nimitz, was to support MacArthur's northern New Guinea campaign. With Nimitz as his boss, Halsey was to operate under the "general directives" of MacArthur.

Leahy didn't think much of the arrangement. When Halsey was operating in MacArthur's bailiwick, he was "of the opinion that MacArthur should be given full command and full responsibility for results."

Still, the problems of the Pacific were less thorny than those between the British and Americans, who still held widely differing views of strategy. In spite of the best efforts of Sir John Dill and his people, it became evident as spring progressed that there would have to be a full-scale meeting between Churchill and Roosevelt, as well as an all-out set-to of the Combined Chiefs of Staff. On 2 May, Leahy recorded:

> Sunday. At noon the President held a conference in his study with the Joint Chiefs of Staff and Mr. Hopkins. This conference was called to discuss an impending visit to Washington of the Prime Minister of Great Britain and his military advisers, presumably with the purpose of making decisions on military objectives to be undertaken upon the successful completion of our combined effort to expel the Germans and Italians from North Africa. . . .
>
> It has become increasingly apparent of late that Great Britain does not wish to take the aggressive [sic—offensive(?)] against Burma, and that China has no confidence in British intentions or British ability.
>
> There have recently been many indications of a Japanese attack on India which probably accounts for the reluctance of the British to engage in a Burma campaign.
>
> Some of our officers have a fear that Great Britain is desirous of confining Allied military effort in Europe to the Mediterranean area in order that England may exercise control thereof regardless of what the terms of peace may be.

The Joint Chiefs had learned a bitter lesson at Casablanca. There, in discussions on whatever level with the British, they had been outdebated simply because the British were better prepared. No matter what the problem brought up, the British always seemed to have a position paper to which they could refer, while the Americans tried to argue matters off the tops of their heads. This time there would be adequate staff work. That was what they planned. In point of fact, it was several conferences later before the American staff work finally caught up with the British.

Then there had been the matter of interpretation. In a memo dated 4 May 1943, Joint Chiefs Secretary Major General J. R. Deane, soon to leave for Moscow, spelled out the necessity of nailing down the exact decisions of a conference. He recommended as a "ground rule" that "nothing shall be regarded as an agreed decision of the Combined Chiefs of Staff that does not appear in the conclusions of the minutes." He hoped to avoid such situations "wherein the U.S. believed that the British had concurred in the policy toward rearming the French, and wherein the British believed that the U.S. had concurred as to the naval forces allocated in the Mediterranean, which were set forth in a paper prepared by the British planners which only had been discussed."[3]

On Sunday, 9 May, the Joint Chiefs met with the president in his study to prepare to host their British counterparts. The sessions of the Combined Chiefs of Staff would be marked by an air of mutual suspicion. Each side believed the other would do its best to drag them into an unwise course of action. If the proposed action was merely indecisive, that wouldn't be so bad.

But, when each side thought of the other's proposals, they believed they would probably be disastrous.

General Sir Alan Brooke, the Chief of the Imperial General Staff (CIGS), as he prepared to embark in the *Queen Mary* for the Atlantic crossing, confided to his diary, "A busy time ahead, and am feeling uncommonly tired and weary before starting, but sea-journey should freshen me up before the hard work of the Conference starts. I do not feel very hopeful as to results. Casablanca has taught me too much. Agreement after agreement may be secured on paper, but, if their hearts are not in it, they soon drift away."[4]

Americans felt the same about the British tendency to "drift away." So far as the Americans were concerned, the minimum objective for the conference was to pin the British down on a firm commitment to a cross-Channel operation in the spring of 1944. The principal State Department expert on European affairs warned that Britain and Russia had totally different war aims than did the Untied States. The USSR, he predicted, would fight only as long as Germans were in Russian territory, and the British were so concentrated on postwar aims in the Mediterranean that they were blind to opportunities in northern Europe. Leahy wrote glumly in his journal that he believed "that the British Chiefs of Staff will not agree to a cross-channel invasion until Germany has collapsed under pressure from Russia and from Allied air attacks."

Thus, each side approached the Trident Conference warily, convinced that the other would try to dragoon it into unsound strategic decisions.

On the evening of 11 May, the British party arrived at Union Station in Washington by special train, having debarked earlier that day from the *Queen Mary* in New York. President Roosevelt, the Joint Chiefs, and Sir John Dill met the train and conducted their guests to a cocktail party before releasing them for a night in hot, steamy Washington.

The next day, the Combined Chiefs met for lunch before moving on to the White House for a conference with the president. Absent from the entire conference was General Henry H. Arnold, who two days earlier had suffered a heart attack, so during the conference, the Americans were deprived of their most knowledgeable spokesman for air operations.

Churchill employed his customary eloquence to urge forcing Italy out of the war in 1943, which sounded well, but which Leahy viewed with suspicion because the prime minister "made no mention of any British desire to control the Mediterranean regardless of how the war might end, which many persons believed to be a cardinal principle of British national policy of long standing." Similarly, Leahy noted that Churchill was again dragging his feet on the invasion of Europe, arguing that "adequate preparation cannot be made in the spring of 1944." In Leahy's later view, the prime minister favored the cross-Channel invasion only if "Germany should collapse as a result of the Russian campaign, assisted by the intensified Allied bombing attacks."

In reply, President Roosevelt argued that the United States had certain responsibilities in the Pacific, that China must be kept in the war, and that he did not favor further operations in the Mediterranean beyond Sicily and Sardinia, already approved. But the prime military effort of the allies must be the "destruction of Nazi military power before engaging in any collateral campaigns and before exercising our full effort against Japan."[5] Brooke sourly remarked that the president's opening address showed even less grasp of strategy than did that of Churchill.

The next day Leahy presided at the first meeting of the Combined Chiefs of Staff. In his diary, Brooke was contemptuous of Leahy's summary of American strategy, calling it "strategic innocence," since "they do not begin to realise the requirements of the European strategy and the part that Russia must play."[6]

In contrast to Brooke's arrogance, Leahy mildly observed the obvious, that in his belief the British would refuse to engage in any activity outside the Mediterranean and that they begrudged everything that the United States sent to the Pacific.

For the next several days, on both the presidential–prime minister level and the Combined Chiefs of Staff level, the same issues were debated over and over. The Americans opposed any further operations in the Mediterranean. The eloquent prime minister emotionally argued that knocking Italy out of the war would send shudders of fear through the German and Japanese peoples. King snorted that the idea was nonsense. Italy was only a drain on Germany. Let her continue to be so. The way to defeat Germany was through cross-Channel attack.

At the end, as always, the decisions were compromises. The British agreed

General George Marshall (second from left) and principal aides with WDL at a meeting of the Joint Chiefs of Staff, 22 May 1943. (Courtesy, National Archives)

"in principle" to a cross-Channel attack in the spring of 1944. The Americans reluctantly went along with the Italian campaign, largely because troops in the Mediterranean area would have nothing to do once Sicily was secured in the summer of 1943. King won his way so far as his Central Pacific drive through the Marshalls and Marianas was concerned, and the British once again pledged themselves to undertake the Burma campaign. At the last moment, Churchill nearly upset everything by insisting on rearranging the Mediterranean strategy in favor of operations aimed at Rhodes. Even his own countrymen opposed him, and the PM backed down.

In spite of everything, Leahy's final comment on the Trident Conference was optimistic.

> From four-thirty to seven P.M. [he noted in his journal for May 23] the British and American Chiefs of Staff presented to the President and Prime Minister their report of agreements reached during the present conference. The Prime Minister refused to accept the Mediterranean agreement. . . . The Prime Minister's attitude is an exact agreement with the permanent British policy of controlling the Mediterranean Sea regardless of what may be the result of the war. It has been consistently opposed by the American Chiefs of Staff because of the probability that American troops will be used in the Mediterranean area at the expense of direct action against Germany, which would, in our opinion, prolong the war. . . .
>
> It is my opinion that the agreements finally reached are more advantageous to the American cause than previous agreements. This is, of course, based on the assumption that the agreements will be carried out by our allies.

The major papers signed, Leahy, feeling considerable relief, saw the British off on 26 May on their homeward journey. Later that same afternoon, he took the train for Chicago and the next day inspected the huge Great Lakes Naval Station, where about 70,000 men and women were undergoing training. Continuing to Madison, he received the honorary degree of Doctor of Laws from the University of Wisconsin. It particularly pleased him to be granted the degree from his father's old undergraduate school, and it renewed his interest in the state of Wisconsin. For the rest of his life, he made frequent visits there.

In return for his degree, Leahy entrusted to the governor the silver service from the old battleship *Wisconsin*, to be held until it could be placed aboard the new 45,000-ton *Wisconsin*, then nearing completion in the Philadelphia Navy Yard.

He brought back from Wisconsin a bad cold, which may have colored his attitude expressed in a letter to classmate Orin G. Murfin, retired and living in California.

> Bill is stationed in Washington but is away most of the time travelling about the country. Elizabeth and the children are with me in our little house, which is very comforting to me. Little Louise, now fourteen, is as tall as her mother. She

WDL receiving an honorary degree from the
University of Wisconsin (Courtesy, National
Archives)

is a lovely girl, and her little brother, aged six, is a regular boy. They are my one
remaining interest in either the present or the future.

   Washington is a heck of a place these days. I spend my waking hours in this
office and almost never see any of our friends. Many who have been here
constantly since my return I have not laid eyes upon.

   Like the Captain of the Head, "I don't take no pride in my job," and I will
trade it with anybody, without sight or seeing.[7]

   It is more than possible that Leahy's grumpiness was caused by the recur-
rent problem of General Charles de Gaulle, whom Leahy never liked and
whose conduct grew more offensive with each passing day. It was one thing
after another. De Gaulle wanted to get rid of Giraud and did everything he
could to undermine him. At one time de Gaulle prevented a French supply
ship from sailing from Britain to Algeria because it was manned by a French

crew from North Africa instead of by his own "Free French." In exasperation Leahy growled that "M. de Gaulle is interfering with our war effort," and worse, the British declined to do anything about him, even as they financed his enterprise.

At Casablanca, the allies had agreed to rearming several French divisions. The Americans wanted to equip eleven French divisions to help in the North African fighting; the British feared that such equipment would divert too much shipping and too much strength from de Gaulle. Leahy and the other Americans felt that the real purpose of rearming the French was to prepare them for later use in France. In a meeting in May, he pointed out that although the French had been promised more, only three divisions had been armed, while eight others were forced to do almost entirely without modern equipment.[8]

Because Leahy steadfastly opposed de Gaulle, who had become the darling of the newspaper commentators, some claimed he was a secret supporter of the men of Vichy and therefore his advice to the president had to be tainted. Radio commentator and columnist Drew Pearson went so far as to argue that Leahy had been the sinister influence behind the Darlan deal. The resultant furor was too much for Dorothy Ringquist, and she went in to his office to say, "Admiral, the phone is ringing off the hook, and everyone wants you to answer what Drew Pearson has said." He told her to forget it. "Drew Pearson has to make a living with his column. He has a card file, and he just happened to pick my name. You just have to stand it. Eventually you forget about it."[9]

Drew Pearson aside, Leahy continued to go along with FDR in opposing the obnoxious French general who had captured the imaginations of so many. FDR felt that de Gaulle was actually harming French recovery in Africa by his constant sniping at Giraud and his scheming to elevate himself to the highest offices in France. Roosevelt had no idea of recongizing *any* French leader until the French people, after the war had been won, had a chance to choose for themselves. Giraud was no threat, for he wanted nothing better than to retire to his home after the war. But de Gaulle had his eye on higher things. He was determined to be the leader of his country some day.

The more pragmatic Churchill, while he considered de Gaulle's behavior to be little short of insufferable, continued to support the huge, haughty Frenchman, largely because he felt the Free French were a significant fighting force. But Roosevelt would have none of it. Leahy and Hopkins in June drafted a message for FDR to send Eisenhower designed to keep de Gaulle at bay. "For your exclusive information I want to state that we will not permit, at this time, de Gaulle to control through his partisans on any committee, or direct himself, the French army in Africa, either in the field of operations or training or supply."[10]

The Americans were fighting a losing cause. Giraud was too naive politically to have a chance against de Gaulle and his supporters in North Africa, as well as in London and Washington. Eisenhower worked out a temporary arrangement giving Giraud control of French land, air, and sea forces in North and West Africa and de Gaulle command everywhere else. Leahy didn't think much of the two-headed monster but felt it was probably the best that Ike could have done at the time. "It appears to me that Eisenhower is following a dangerous appeasement policy in his relations with the de Gaullists in Africa."

Whatever Leahy's opinion, the arrangements came unstuck in early July, just before the invasion of Sicily. De Gaulle's supporters in North Africa became so openly defiant of Eisenhower's authority that Hull suggested that delivery of arms to the French be halted until the situation improved.

On 7 July, hoping to retrieve an intolerable situation, Giraud visited the United States. In order to give the illusion that he was an important French leader, Washington rolled out the red carpet, giving him the full VIP treatment. Leahy met him at Bolling Field and accompanied him in a limousine to Blair House so that he could rest before a state dinner at the White House in his honor.

Leahy didn't think the treatment would work. He thought so even less when Ray Atherton showed him a letter from Doc Matthews, which said that the British had never had any idea of giving up their support of de Gaulle, whom Doc referred to as "this French Adolf."

Unless the United States was ready to break with Britain, Matthews continued,

> the only alternative it seems to me is to let de Gaulle gradually get control of the situation as we are now doing—offering just enough resistance to increase his irritation, his anti-American and anti-British feelings and his determination to run the show. When he does get control I am convinced that not only will General Eisenhower, who has been the long-suffering victim of the British Foreign Office policy, have far more headaches than he has before but from the long term point of view the French people will blame us. . . . Instead of having Adolf across the Rhine they will have Adolf of their own in Paris.[11]

Matthews was right. De Gaulle would be a problem for years, not only for Roosevelt but also for his successors.

If the United States lost with respect to de Gaulle, Leahy felt there was a real gain in another part of the world, when the British sent General Sir Claude Auchinleck to replace Field Marshal Sir Archibald Wavell in India. "Wavell while here last month with the Prime Minister," Leahy wrote, "consistently held such a defeatist attitude that the necessity for a change of command in India was apparent to everybody. There is now at least a possibility of some aggressive action against the Japanese in Burma."

Operations in the Mediterranean were meanwhile having a positive effect. Following the invasion of Sicily, King Victor Emmanuel of Italy fired Mussolini and replaced him with Marshal Pietro Badoglio. Leahy felt the move "may very possibly result in Italy's withdrawal from the Axis and mark the beginning of the defeat of Germany." Pursuing the thought, he added that the situation in Italy "may also necessitate a complete change in Allied strategy in Europe."

# CHAPTER 12

# Four Conferences

The war was rushing on, and major strategic decisions had to be made soon. The prime minister and the president planned to meet again in August, this time in Quebec. The Combined Chiefs of Staff would join them for their own sessions.

To prepare for the hard decisions to be made in the Quadrant Conference, FDR decided to take the closest members of his official family on a fishing trip to Canada. The party would include Pa Watson, Naval Aide Rear Admiral Wilson Brown, Ross McIntire, Jimmy Byrnes, and Leahy. Hopkins would join a little later. For the first time on one of the presidential fishing trips, it would not be entirely a stag party. FDR asked his two confidential secretaries, Dorothy Brady and Grace Tully, to go along.

> Dorothy and I [wrote Grace Tully] were never more surprised than when the President invited us to accompany him on this fishing trip. Of course, he would have work to do, but somehow I didn't expect to be asked because it seemed to me that a woman might be out of place in a group of men who intended to spend most of the time in fishing boats. We were thrilled to be included.[1]

After a stop at Hyde Park, which gave Leahy an opportunity to inspect the books, ship models, and pictures in the new Roosevelt Library, the party reached Birchwood on the northern shore of Georgian Bay on the afternoon of 1 August. There they found the USS *Wilmette* waiting to provide communications and the boats which took the fishermen into McGregor and

WDL fishing at Georgian Bay, August 1943. (Courtesy, National Archives)

Whitefish bays. For a week the party enjoyed the sport, sleeping in the train on a siding only a few yards from the landing where the boats picked them up each morning. When bets were paid off at the end, only Leahy and FDR were winners.

In general Leahy felt that the trip was a great success, "providing fresh air and sunburn for all of us," but he was kept busy most nights with messages "to and from our British allies." He felt very definitely that "on a vacation for relaxation we should have gone to bed earlier than midnight, which was the usual hour."

After a few days back in Washington for some intensive preparation for the conference, Leahy and Marshall, on the morning of 13 August, left National Airport in an army plane. Bad weather in Canada forced them to divert to Montreal, and they had to complete the journey by automobile. When they reached their hotel, Admiral King was waiting for them. He had come up in his own plane and had told his pilot to land at Quebec in spite of the weather. It was a definite plus for King, and he made the others very aware of his triumph.

Pending the arrival of the president and prime minister, Canadian officials entertained their military guests. That evening Leahy attended a reception given by Canadian Prime Minister Mackenzie King for all the dignitaries of the conference. As the highest military officer present, Leahy ate his supper at the head table with Clemmie (Mrs. Winston) Churchill, Mackenzie King, and a number of Canadian cabinet officials. After the reception he returned to his delightful suite in the Hotel Château Frontenac, a stately old structure on the high bluff overlooking the St. Lawrence River. The Canadian government had taken it over for the occasion, ousting the regular residents, except for 90-year-old Miss Alice Caron, who refused to budge. The authorities decided she was no threat to anyone and let her stay.

The next morning, the conferees got down to business in a preliminary session. The British had enlarged their top delegation by including Vice Admiral Lord Louis Mountbatten and Lieutenant General Sir Hastings Ismay, who was Churchill's personal chief of staff. Of course, Sir John Dill was there, helping keep the peace in face of widely differing strategic views.

As Leahy and Marshall feared, the British were backing away from their commitment to cross-Channel operations in 1944. While Churchill and Brooke both claimed they believed in the operation, they attached so many conditions that many Americans wondered if the British had any idea of undertaking a cross-Channel operation at all. The British insisted on further operations in the Mediterranean, and Leahy noted a "very frank discussion of a difference in opinion. General Marshall is very positive in his attitude toward the Mediterranean commitment, and Admiral King was very undiplomatic, to use a mild term for his attitude."

On 17 August, Roosevelt and Churchill arrived, having spent the last few days in private conversations in Hyde Park. Their arrival, of course, was the occasion for receptions, dinners, and picture taking before the two leaders got down to business.

Staff discussions became more amicable as time went on, for Brooke at last agreed to the cross-Channel operation, now known as Overlord. Target date was set for 1 May 1944, and, after a last British struggle, the Combined Chiefs of Staff agreed that Overlord would have priority over Mediterranean operations.

European affairs settled, the CCS turned their attention to the Pacific. The Americans enthusiastically accepted Lord Louis Mountbatten as commander in the China–Burma–India theater, and the British agreed that he would open the Burma Road. In the Pacific, the CCS agreed that while MacArthur continued his campaign along the northern coast of New Guinea, Nimitz would open a new one through the Gilberts, Marshalls, Carolines, Palaus, and Marianas. The two drives would bypass Rabaul.

As a sop to British desires for the Mediterranean campaign, Pacific operations would be carried out with what force was already there, on a not-to-interfere basis with activities in the European theater. And, at American insistance, an invasion of southern France would be staged concurrent with

Overlord. In all of these discussions, Leahy and Dill served as the catalysts, bring decisions out of discord.

Soon after the conference had ended, Churchill arrived in Washington just in time to learn that official representatives of the Italian government had agreed to the surrender terms dictated by Britain and the United States. As it happened, there were two documents, the "Short Terms," intended for immediate implementation, and the "Long Terms," which spelled out occupation policies, treatment of war criminals, and the like. The "Long Terms," as the Italians were to discover, were much harsher than the "Short Terms."

To keep the Soviets from claiming that the Anglo–Americans were leaving them out of consideration, the British telegraphed Stalin for his approval for Eisenhower to sign the "Short Terms" on behalf of Russia as well as Britain and the United States. "I personally," wrote Leahy who had no desire to coddle Russian sensibilities, "see no reason for having made such a request of the Soviets in view of the fact that they have already authorized signature of the comprehensive surrender terms, but a Soviet signature seems important to others."

On 8 September, with Montgomery's Eighth Army already ashore in southern Italy, and Mark Clark's Fifth poised to land at Salerno, the Italian government, fearing the Germans at hand more than the Allies at a distance, reneged on the surrender agreement. Eisenhower wouldn't let the Italians get away with it. He radioed them that he intended to broadcast the fact of surrender that very night; the Italians could keep their promise and broadcast the surrender, or they would be treated as enemies. In any case the landings at Salerno would go forward the next day as scheduled. The Italians could no longer have it both ways.

> It would seem that this failure of competent authority in the Italian Government to carry out its agreement for a formal surrender results from advance information reaching the German authority. It has appeared to me throughout the negotiations that American and British consultation with other members of the United Nations and the French Commission in Africa made it impossible to conceal the news from the German authorities.

The Germans did oppose the landings, and nine months of the most vicious, bitter fighting ensued before Rome finally fell to the allied forces.

But that September sat "expectation in the air," and wildly optimistic stories began to appear in the press and in the comments heard at cocktail parties on Embassy Row, in Georgetown, and along Pennsylvania Avenue. Constantine Brown, who had earlier predicted Leahy's dismissal, now estimated that the invasion of Italy meant that the war would be won by Christmas, this to be accomplished by a "negotiated peace between Germany and Russia, which will involve also Great Britain and the United States." Possibly Mr. Brown had not heard of the "unconditional surrender" policy proclaimed at Casablanca.

In an unusual move, perhaps worn down by his mercurial guest, FDR had gone to New York, leaving Churchill to make himself at home in the White House. Churchill presided at a meeting of the Combined Chiefs of Staff in the State Dining Room to consider steps to be taken in view of apparent disaster in Italy, where Clark's Fifth Army was in danger of being driven back into the sea. Leahy and Marshall were confident that the beachhead would be held. "Naples is today a critical area, and General Marshall is counting on our overwhelming air superiority to check the Germans."

Churchill's departure and the arrival of reinforcements in the Salerno area relieved tensions in Washington, and Leahy was able to resume regular duties.

Of course problems never stayed solved, and new ones kept presenting themselves. Admiral Standley resigned as ambassador to the Soviet Union and was replaced by Averell Harriman, who had been Lend Lease expediter in London. Leahy, Hopkins, and others had all joined in persuading the reluctant Harriman to take on the thankless job. Before leaving for Moscow, Harriman stopped in Leahy's office:

> He particularly requested that I keep him informed in regard to military plans and prospects that may be of interest to the Soviet Government in order that he may acquire credit for giving such information in exchange before the Soviet gets it from other sources.

About the same time Sumner Welles was forced to resign as under secretary of state. Leahy heard of Welles's removal from Hopkins on 23 September, who told him at the same time that FDR was considering firing King as chief of naval operations, allowing him to continue as commander in chief U.S. Fleet. This idea had come up several times before; it was unprecedented for one man to have both jobs, and no one else ever did. The idea of removing King as CNO was a favorite of Secretary Knox, who clashed with King on many occasions. The problem was that King was primarily interested in the COMINCH job, which involved strategy and its execution; the CNO job, which dealt with logistics and long-range procurement, bored him. He left the details of that post to Rear Admiral Frederick J. Horne, deputy CNO. Horne never had King's ear for very long periods, but he did his best to see to it that the goods and men were where they were needed to carry out the strategic plans King and the others worked out.

Although they lunched together once a week, the Joint Chiefs never developed a close relationship. Leahy and King in public addressed Marshall and Arnold as "General," and were in turn called "Admiral." In private, they may have used last names. Although Leahy thought very highly of King as a professional, he had scant patience with his personal pecularities. There is one

unconfirmed story that on one occasion, when King demanded to see the
president and refused to take Leahy's no for an answer, he was brought up
short when Leahy barked, as he would have to a plebe at the Academy, "Stand
at attention, mister!"

King thought Leahy was a "fixer," a term implying the very flexibility and
subtlety that had enabled Leahy to be successful in the peacetime navy and as
governor and ambassador. The very idea of King serving as an ambassador is
incredible. His entire character was undiplomatic, and he thrived on that
reputation. He and Leahy were simply different types. They complemented
each other. In the minutes of the Joint and Combined Chiefs of Staff, one
reads of King's vehement arguments, and then at the end of Leahy's statement
of a position, almost invariably the one finally adopted. Since the Joint Chiefs
operated only on the basis of unanimous decision, it was usually up the
president's chief of staff to secure that unanimity. If King was the "great
dissenter," Leahy was the great unifier.

As the fighting in Italy continued, the Italian government offered to enter
the war on the Allied side as a co-belligerent. The Americans and British
insisted that King Vittorio Emmanuele III, and not merely Marshal Badoglio,
formally declare war. Leahy drafted a message for Churchill:

> President to Prime
>
> On October 5 I informed Eisenhower as follows:
>
> The President and Prime Minister are in agreement that the King of Italy
> declare war on Germany as soon as possible. There appears to be no necessity
> for waiting until Rome is occupied. You will therefore put pressure on the
> Italian Government for an early declaration of war without waiting for further
> successes.
>
> Eisenhower informs me that he is using the above to reinforce his own efforts
> along this line.
>
> We can arrange to synchronize the . . . announcements immediately when
> war is declared.[2]

So passed the summer and fall. On Armistice Day, after wreath-laying
ceremonies at the tomb of the Unknown Soldier, Leahy went home to pack. It
was time to set off on another journey, this time to three conferences. First
Roosevelt and Churchill would meet Chiang Kai-shek at Cairo. Then Chiang
would go home, and the president and prime minister would go on to
Teheran to confer with Stalin. After those sessions, FDR and Churchill would
hold a final talk themselves in Cairo to wrap things up. It was a formidable
program.

On November 12, the admiral recorded in his journal:

> About nine-thirty last night the President's party left the White House and
> proceeded in a motor car cavalcade to Quantico, where we boarded the USS
> *Potomac* and sailed at once for the mouth of the Potomac River. The party

consisted of the President, Mr. Harry Hopkins, Rear Admiral Wilson Brown, U. S. Navy, Major General E. M. Watson, U. S. Army, Rear Admiral Ross McIntire, Surgeon General, and myself.

At nine-thirty this morning boarded the battleship USS *Iowa*, Captain John McCrea, commanding, and sailed at once for Hampton Roads.

We found already on board the *Iowa* General Marshall, Admiral King, General Arnold, Lieutenant General [Brehan] Somervell [Chief of Army Services of Supply], and about fifty American staff officers of subordinate rank and position in the Joint Staff organization.

The first of the navy's new 45,000-ton battleships, the *Iowa* had off-loaded fuel to reduce her draft for the trip up Chesapeake Bay to pick up the presidential party. As soon as she returned to Hampton Roads, she anchored and took on oil from tankers on either side. Meanwhile, the president's party was getting settled aboard. Roosevelt occupied the captain's in-port cabin, while Leahy was in the suite usually tenanted by the admiral embarked. Marshall, as next senior officer, had the chief-of-staff's cabin. Below that, the rest of the officers were assigned senior officers' staterooms, King, for example, in the room of a dispossessed commander. And so it went all down the line. Hopkins had a staff officer's cabin in Flag Country.

The president had his own mess. Members were Roosevelt, Hopkins, Leahy, Wilson Brown, Pa Watkins, and Ross McIntire. Meals were served in the sitting room, while the rest of the senior officers messed with the rest of the staff in Flag Country.

Because 12 November was a Friday, and the president shared the sailors' superstition that it was unlucky to begin a long journey on a Friday, he insisted that the *Iowa* not get underway until after midnight, preferring to brave the hex of the thirteenth to that of Friday.

Promptly at one minute after midnight, the *Iowa* picked up her anchor and stood out Thimble Shoals Channel, passed Buoy Two Charlie Baker, and then set course for Gibraltar at 25 knots with a heavy following sea. Her accompanying destroyers were making heavy weather of it.

Bad weather never bothered Roosevelt on a sea voyage, and of course Leahy and most of the other naval officers were immune, but as the voyage went along, there were some wan faces at the mess table. Roosevelt was in high spirits. He presided with his usual affability, and, as was his custom, suspended General Order 99 in the presidential mess. Cocktails were served before dinner in the ritual FDR loved. He mixed them himself and for seconds urged his guests to have "just another little sippy." Hopkins swore that FDR made the worst martini in the world, but not even he had the courage to tell him so.

On the second day out, while the *Iowa* and her escorting destroyers were exercising at drills, one of the destroyers accidentally let an armed torpedo slip out of her tubes and head directly for the battleship. Fortunately, she was able to warn Captain McCrea by radio, and the *Iowa* took emergency action so the torpedo missed. Admiral King stormed up to the bridge to find out what was going on. When he learned, he started proceedings to relieve the commandng officer of the destroyer, but FDR told him to forget it. Leahy must have agreed with FDR, for he failed to mention the episode at all!

Ever since the conference in Quebec, when it had been settled that the commander of Overlord would be an American, the question had been who it would be. Some Americans, Leahy included, wanted a single overall commander in Europe, having under him both operations in connection with Overload and in the Mediterranean. The British were adamant, however, that the two areas should have separate commanders. And since the Overlord commander was to be an American, then the British should command in the Mediterranean.

General Marshall was widely expected to be named for the Overload job. Stimson especially pushed for his candidacy as a man who

> . . . already has a towering eminence of reputation as a tried soldier and as a broad-minded and skillful administrator. This was shown by the suggestion of him on the part of the British for this very post a year and a half ago. I believe that he is the man who most surely can now by his character and skill furnish the military leadership which is necessary to bring our two nations together in confident joint action in this great operation. No one knows better than I the loss in the problems of organization and world-wide strategy centered in Washington which such a solution would cause, but I see no other alternative to which we can turn in the great effort which confronts us.[3]

Rather than follow British ideas for "committee control," Leahy, in a memorandum to the president, recommended that if Churchill and Brooke refused to accept the American idea of unity of command of Overlord, then the

> necessity for unified command, in our opinion, is so urgent and compelling that, in spite of the fact that the bulk of the forces, both ground and air, will ultimately be American, we are willing to accept a British officer as over-all commander for European operations[,] provided the man named is Sir John Dill. This indicates the weight we give to the matter of undivided command and responsibility.[4]

The memo went on to say that if this idea was adopted, then Eisenhower should remain in command in the Mediterranean. The matter of who would command Overlord would then be deferred until the decision of the president was known.

The final decision on the Overload commander was up to FDR, and he showed no disposition to make up his mind. Until a commander was selected, planning and decisions were limited. One such example was the insistence of the British in retaining their Bomber Command directly under the RAF and not under the supreme commander, whoever he might be. To Leahy's disgust, the British continued to demand that, when the time came, the supreme commander would make his wishes known to the commander in chief of Bomber Command, who then would "do his utmost to achieve the task given him by the Supreme Commander with the means allotted."

> This completely divided control of the essential air element of British expeditionary forces [Leahy wrote furiously] is sufficiently inefficient to account for most of the British failures in this war.
>
> Unity of command of all available forces, land, sea, and air, is essential to success in this war, and it is my intention if the British insist in exercising operational command of the Royal Air Force from England to insist that our American air arm be divorced from the British command, and its operational direction turned over wholly to the Supreme Commander of the area concerned.

On 20 November, the *Iowa* entered the French naval harbor of Mers el Kebir, a few miles west of Oran. The reception group, headed by Eisenhower, included two of the Roosevelt boys, Elliott, a colonel in the air force, and Franklin, Jr., a lieutenant in the naval reserve. FDR and his immediate party left immediately for the airport for a flight to Tunis. There, the afternoon being free, Leahy was able to get away from duty for a while. He explored the Roman ruins, including an amphitheater, a coliseum, and a theater. There were also Carthegenian ruins and graves which interested him.

The next day, Sunday, Leahy and a few others spent visiting the modern city of Tunis.

> The waterfront of this city was thoroughly destroyed by American bombers during the period when German troops were attempting to escape to Italy. Other parts of the city suffered very little damage.
>
> The streets on this Sunday were crowded with soldiers and sailors of many nations, and native Arabs. The very few women and children I saw on the streets appeared to be Italians or Jews or a mixture of white races and Arabs. Bar rooms, cinemas, and curio shops were doing a rushing business with the soldiers and sailors.
>
> I could not find any souvenier that appeared to be worth taking home.
>
> On my return journey to Carthage, the car passed a number of natives plowing their fields with oxen and the biblical plow with a wooden blade and one handle.

After dinner with the president, Leahy and the others departed for the airport and a night flight to Cairo. The plane was a new C-54 reserved for the use of the president, and it had already been given the irreverent but enduring name of "Sacred Cow." There were two bunks in the plane; one was given to Roosevelt by virtue of his position; the other by general consent went to Hopkins because of his precarious health.

Somewhat wistfully, Leahy noted that sleeping in the chairs of a transport plane was not restful, but somehow he endured the night, and at dawn the plane was coming in over the Nile some two hundred miles south of Cairo. "Flying over the desert gives one a picture of utter desolation; the Nile Valley is green fertility humming with industry, and a view of the pyramids from an altitude of 8,000 feet is disappointing in the reduction of their size by distance."

When they had landed, they learned that Chiang Kai-shek and Mme. Chiang had arrived earlier that morning and that Churchill and his staff had already been there for two days, probably arranging new worries for the Americans.

"I am looking forward," Leahy wrote, "to a very busy and to a probably controversial visit in Cairo."

The presidential party was taken to the residence of Ambassador Alexander C. Kirk, near the pyramids, which looked considerably larger to Leahy now that he was on the ground. The villa, in the Mena district, was of medium size and beautifully furnished. There was a flower garden in the rear, and it was there that FDR and some of the others spent their few leisure moments.[5]

Only FDR, Hopkins, and Leahy were quartered in the Kirk residence, the rest of the party being in nearby houses and villas. The sessions were held in the Mena House Hotel, near the base of the pyramids and about a mile from the Kirk villa.

That evening the president held a dinner for Churchill, Lord Louis Mountbatten, Hopkins, and Leahy. After the meal, Mountbatten outlined his plans for the Burma campaign. "Lord Louis made an excellent presentation of his problem, which I believe will be solved by his energy and his aggressive spirit."

The following day, Mountbatten repeated the performance for the benefit of Chiang Kai-shek. The generalissimo gave neither objection nor approval, but he did inquire as to the naval forces to be involved, "which information was not forthcoming from the British."

Leahy had never met Chiang before, although he could not forget his wife from her memorable visit to Washington.

> Chiang Kai-shek [Leahy wrote of their meeting] is a slight, studious appearing man, with no appearance whatever of being the bandit that he is reported to have been before this war commenced.
>
> Madame Chiang followed the discussion with attention and interest. She several times corrected the interpreter or amplified his translation.

That evening Leahy managed to escape a dinner given by Roosevelt for the Chiangs. Instead he joined Arnold and King to dine with the British Chiefs of Staff, a meal at which no business was discussed. Brooke gave an interesting

talk on the history of Malta, and Sir Andrew B. Cunningham, the new first
sea lord, told of his experiences in command of the Mediterranean Fleet.★

It was, Leahy noted, and "interesting evening."

Discussions began the following morning, but they were interrupted by
ceremonies and receptions. The next day was the American Thanksgiving
Day, but that fact did not keep the Combined Chiefs of Staff from their task. It
soon developed that the British wished to expand operations in the Mediterranean, even if they meant delaying Overlord, which they persisted in treating
as a possible objective rather than a fixed commitment. Leahy was depressed
over the backsliding. Nothing, however, could dampen the spirit of
friendship as everyone celebrated Thanksgiving.

> At six attended a Thanksgiving Service at All Saints Cathedral in Cairo,
> arranged by the British Chiefs of Staff in compliment to the Americans present
> at the conference.
> This gesture has been termed by one of our skeptics an example of "reverse
> lend-lease."
> The Cathedral, an enormous structure, was filled with worshippers, mostly
> soldiers and officers with a few ladies.

That evening the president hosted Thanksgiving dinner for twenty British
and American conferees and aides. Two large turkeys had been brought along
for the feast, and the traditional trimmings, including pumpkin pie, were
served. FDR did the carving himself, piling up such heaping servings that
Churchill worried that he would have none left for himself by the time he had
finished carving the second bird. But everything came out just right, and the
Thanksgiving feast was a great success.

No session being scheduled for the next morning, Leahy took an hour off to
see the pyraminds and Sphinx, "either of which would provide absorbing
interest for days of study, and the pressure of war business at this conference
which prevents an examination of these colossal antiquities will remain always a matter of sharp regret."

But the Sphinx gave no answers to the problems that beset them, and that
afternoon at a meeting of the CCS, Marshall and Brooke had what the later
termed "the father and mother of a row!" It concerned the British lack of
desire for naval operations in support of Burma and the British desire to divert
strength into the eastern Mediterranean. Leahy, in a rare show of temper,
informed the British bluntly that the Americans delined "to recede from our
present planned operations without orders from the President."

That was the last meeting of the Cairo Conference. Chiang Kai-shek
departed having been promised that a major campaign against Burma would
be undertaken. In a short time, that promise would be broken.

---

★Sir Dudley Pound, first sea lord from the beginning of the war, had died of a brain tumor
on 21 October, the 138th anniversary of the Battle of Trafalgar.

The next morning, everyone was up early for departure for Teheran. Takeoff was delayed, however, because of ground fog at the Cairo airport, and it was not until 7:00 A.M. that the "Sacred Cow" lifted from the runway, carrying its usual passengers, plus Averell Harriman and the president's son-in-law, Major John Boettiger. They encountered excellent weather, and since Ross McIntire would not allow the president to fly above 8,000 feet, they had ample opportunity for sight-seeing as the plane circled over Jerusalem, Bethlehem, Jericho, and the River Jordan before going on across the Dead Sea. Leahy was not impressed with the countryside, which looked barren and desolate.

> Perhaps after forty years wandering in the desert, any area containing even a little water would look like the Promised Land. One of our passengers expressed a thought that Moses, when he approached the end of his journey, committed suicide to avoid being charged with responsibility for what would be found upon arrival in the "Promised Land." It may, however, not have looked so bad to the travel-wearied Israelites after years in the desert.

Their way took them over the Tigris and Euphrates rivers a few miles south of Baghdad and on through the mountains to Teheran. On arrival they went at once to the American legation where they were glad to rest in preparation for the conference scheduled to begin the next day.

The American legation was outside of the city walls of Teheran, where the ancient and the modern vied for room in the crowded streets. Lend Lease trucks were jostled by patient burros, and biblical-era bazaars stood cheek by jowl with twentieth-century shops.

The following morning, Stalin sent word that his secret police had uncovered a plot to assassinate the Big Three. He offered the hospitality of the Russian embassy compound, which was well guarded. Harriman pointed out that if the Americans refused to accept the Russian hospitality, they would be responsible if any harm came to Stalin when he was traveling to meet the president. "Mr. Harriman emphasized that the city of Teheran had been under complete German control only a few months before, and that the risk of assassination of Mr. Churchill and Marshal Stalin while coming to visit President Roosevelt was very real."[6]

Roosevelt agreed to move. As a heavily guarded motorcade took off, armed men watched every possible hiding place and American and Russian soldiers lined the streets along the usual route from the American legation to the Russian embassy.

A few minutes later, Roosevelt, Harry Hopkins, and Leahy got into an ordinary-looking automobile, a secret-service driver at the wheel. The car took off at high speed, over a devious route, the chauffeur driving as wildly as the Iranians themselves drove, thereby attracting little or no attention. As it turned out, Roosevelt reached the Russian embassy well before the dummy caravan had made its sedate way along the two-mile route.

In the Russian embassy compound everyone learned to make no sudden movements, to move openly, and to halt immediately when challenged. All servants, except for the White House staff accompanying Roosevelt, were members of the Russian secret police, a fact that gave Mike Reilly, head of the president's secret service protection detail, a great deal of uneasiness. Happily, no untoward events took place.

Fifteen minutes after Roosevelt had arrived in his new quarters, Stalin dropped in for a visit, accompanied only by his interpreter V. N. Pavlov. Churchill was furious at this unscheduled meeting, for he had hoped to get Roosevelt to himself alone first. Roosevelt had no intention of granting any such interview, for he knew that the prime minister would again be asking for eastern Mediterranean operations. If he were not asked, FDR reasoned, he wouldn't have to say no.

The meeting of Roosevelt and Stalin went off famously and set a tone of cordiality between the two men which was to help the mood of the conference, even though Churchill showed more and more petulance at being relegated to a back seat in the deliberations.

The first plenary session of the Teheran Conference took place later that same afternoon. Churchill fumed to Harriman that he ought to be presiding because he was the oldest of the Big Three, because Britain had been in the war longer than the others, and because his name began with C. But he acquiesced when Stalin invited Roosevelt to take the chair. This was in accordance with strict protocol, because Roosevelt was the only head of state present; Churchill and Stalin were heads of government, subject, theoretically, to King George VI and President Podgorny respectively.

Roosevelt summarized the proposed strategy of the western allies, beginning with the Pacific, going on to China and to the proposed Burma operation, and then turning to the strategy in Europe and the Mediterranean. The president next presented the case for Churchill's and Brooke's projected extension of operations in the Mediterranean, and then the arguments for Overlord. It quickly developed that both Britain and the United States hoped Stalin would agree with their differing strategies.

Stalin spoke briefly, giving hope to both sides as he temporized politely. "Every American and British eye and ear were fixed on the Soviet leader. Most of us were hearing and seeing him for the first time. I happened to note that Churchill did not always wait for Stalin's excellent interpreter to translate what his chief had said, but seemed to be getting the gist of Stalin's remarks."[7]

That evening Roosevelt was host at dinner for Churchill and Stalin with their staffs. The discussions continued throughout the meal. The battle lines were fixed. The Americans continued to demand Overlord, while the British wanted more operations in the Mediterranean, especially the capture of Rhodes, which should not delay Overlord "more than a month or two," as the prime minister put it. By this time Stalin had come out firmly on the American side.

During the dinner, Roosevelt suffered an acute digestive attack. Everyone was frightened that he might have been poisoned, but Dr. McIntire quickly diagnosed it as acute indigestion. The next morning FDR was himself again.

At noon there was a ceremony in which Churchill, in the name of King George, presented a sword of honor to Stalin in recognition of the valiant stand the Russians had made in defense of Stalingrad.

Following this ceremony, photographers made group pictures of everybody participating in this conference, which, if we succeed in destroying Nazi Germany will be recorded in history as comparable to the Field of the Cloth of Gold.★ There is, however, little pageantry here in this distressed area, but much suffering and squalor.

In the afternoon we had another plenary session with much controversial discussion of the date for a cross-Channel invasion, Stalin insisting on a fixed early date, Churchill asking for delay, and the President favorably inclined toward the Soviet proposal.

The meeting was conducted by the President with skill and a high order of diplomacy.

I am very favorably impressed by the Soviet's direct methods and by their plain speaking. Stalin is soft spoken and inflexible in his purpose. He appears old and worn.

During that discussion, Stalin gave an example of his bluntness by asking Churchill, "Do you believe in Overlord, or are you stalling to make us feel better?"

Churchill replied that he did believe in Overlord, but he shared Brooke's belief that the invasion might fail unless more preliminary operations whittled down German strength. He suggested that the matter be referred to the foreign ministers for advice on the political aspects.

Stalin retorted quickly and brusquely, "Why do that? We are the chiefs of government. We know what we want to do. Why turn the matter over to some subordinates to advise us?"

The heat of argument taxed the well-known skill and diplomacy of Roosevelt, who was presiding. At this same meeting, Stalin also confronted the President with an uncomfortable question. The Soviet leader asked bluntly who was going to command Overlord. Roosevelt said frankly he had not made up his mind. I was sitting next to the President and he leaned over to me and whispered, "That old Bolshevik is trying to force me to give him the name of our Supreme Commander. I just can't tell him because I have not yet made up my mind."

Stalin agreed that the appointment was the business of Roosevelt, but he added sharply that until the commander of Overlord was named he would not consider the operation was actually under way. It was evident that Stalin wanted to have that appointment announced while he was in Teheran.

★The Field of the Cloth of Gold was the site of a famous meeting in 1520 between Henry VIII of England and Francis I of France. It was noted for pageantry and splendor.

The President was absolutely honest in his reply. In my opinion he preferred to give the job to Marshall, but felt that he could not ignore the adverse reaction that the appointment would cause back in the United States. At that time I still thought he eventually would announce that Marshall would command Overlord.[8]

On 30 November, Leahy helped to force the issue and the Americans "finally succeeded in getting the British to agree to launch the cross-Channel attack on Germany in France during the month of May 1944, and to make at the same time a supporting attack on Southern France in such force as can be handled by the landing craft available in the Mediterranean at that time." Brooke expressed no reason for the British surrender to the American view, which Leahy regarded as "so logical that I cannot but believe that as professional soldiers they knew Overlord was the most sensible move to bring to an end the war with Germany in the shortest possible time."[9]

Perhaps Brooke came around when Leahy repeated Stalin's question of the previous night. As the secretary recorded in the minutes of the meeting of the CCS:

> ADMIRAL LEAHY asked Sir Alan Brooke whether he believed that the conditions laid down for Overlord would ever arise unless the Germans had collapsed beforehand.
> SIR ALAN BROOKE said that he firmly believed that they would and that he foresaw the conditions arising in 1944, provided the enemy were engaged on other fronts as well.[10]

At any rate, Overlord was on, and despite future squirming, the British never thereafter seriously challenged the concept.

Another major decision of the conference, and one which Leahy and King came to consider unnecessary, was Stalin's assurance that the USSR would enter the war against Japan once Germany had been defeated. No date was given, but it was the first time the Soviet leader had made a definite promise.

Once the decision for Overlord had been settled, Stalin agreed to mount a concurrent offensive against Germany from the east. These agreements settled the major business of the conference. It was time to celebrate, which they did at a dinner hosted by Churchill. Leahy was less impressed by the occasion than were some of the other participants.

> At eight-thirty attended a dinner of thirty-four given by Prime Minister Churchill in celebration of his 69th birthday. In agreement with a Russian custom, toasts were proposed and drunk to nearly everybody at the table, which was an exceedingly tiresome procedure. Speeches of some length were made by the President, by Churchill, and by Stalin, everything being translated by skillful translators.
> Our abiding friendship with the Bolsheviks and our common hopes for a new order in the world were stressed by the principal speakers.
> Stalin is quick in repartee and sinister in appearance.

The next day the conferees began their departure. The Joint Chiefs and the British Chiefs left in their planes for Cairo, stopping at Jerusalem en route, but Leahy remained behind at the president's request. They tidied up loose ends with Churchill and Stalin before going on to an American army camp some distance from Teheran. The next day they flew in the "Sacred Cow" to Cairo.

The British and Americans still had business to discuss. While the British still pushed for the capture of Rhodes in the eastern Mediterranean, they opposed the invasion of the Andaman Islands in support of the Burma campaign. Finally they agreed to drop both, and Roosevelt had the nasty job of informing Chiang Kai-shek that the promises made to him at Cairo would not be carried out. The reason was that every possible landing craft would be needed for Overlord and the concurrent invasion of Southern France.

Churchill had high hopes that he could persuade Turkey to enter the war on the Allied side, so he had asked President Inönü to come to Cairo. Inönü came, listened, and said no.

Finally Roosevelt put an end to speculation on who would command Overlord by naming Eisenhower to the job. Leahy was surprised, thinking right up to the last minute, in common with almost everybody else, that it would be Marshall. He was, on the other hand, relieved that the team of the Joint Chiefs of Staff would not be broken up.

On 7 December the "Sacred Cow" left Cairo, flying over the battlefield of El Alamein, where Leahy noted the wrecked tanks and machinery, the scars of the battle that had taken place fourteen months earlier. After spending the night at Tunis, the presidential party flew on to Malta, where Roosevelt presented an illuminated scroll in honor of the valiant defense of Malta for so many months. Engine trouble with the plane gave the party an opportunity for a drive through the areas that had taken the heaviest beating from Axis air attacks.

Roosevelt and his party returned to Tunis for the night before going on to Dakar the next day, flying through bad clouds that had everyone except Roosevelt exceedingly nervous. All ended well, and they soon boarded the *Iowa* which was waiting for them.

At 9:00 P.M., 9 December, the battleship got under way in company with three destroyers. Passing south of the Cape Verde Islands and Bermuda, the *Iowa* reached Chesapeake Bay on 16 December, where the party transferred to the *Potomac* for the trip to Washington.

The next morning, the yacht tied up at the Navy Yard in Washington, ending for Leahy and Roosevelt a journey of 17,442 miles by sea and air, not counting trips by automobile around Teheran and Malta.

Everyone was weary from the work, but the sea voyage had rested Roosevelt and Leahy, and their satisfaction with the decisions reached offset any letdown they might have felt at being back in the familiar work places again.

After a few days of routine work and a rather surprising feeler by Constantine Brown asking if he would accept the post of secretary of the navy in the administration of President Douglas MacArthur in 1945, Leahy spent Christmas at home, enjoying the company of his family, especially the grandchildren. He ended the year with his usual summary of world events.

> This last day of 1943 finds the world war definitely progressing in favor of the Allied nations. . . .
>
> It appears certain that the tide of war has changed in our favor and that unless we make some stupid tactical or strategic error, the Axis is certain to be defeated, although, with desperate enemies on both sides of the world, the cost to us in lives and treasure may be high.

# CHAPTER 13

# Washington Worries

As 1944 began, most of the major strategic decisions for Europe had been made. But the Pacific was another matter altogether, and much of Leahy's and Roosevelt's attention turned west past the Golden Gate to where Nimitz was conducting his campaign in the Central Pacific, where an atoll named Tarawa had become a household word.

For the first few weeks after his return from Teheran, work in Leahy's office was routine. There were the weekly meetings of the Joint Chiefs. There were the telegrams back and forth to Churchill and Stalin; there were the messages to Eisenhower in London preparing for the invasion of Normandy, still scheduled for May.

Early in January, Leahy's old friend Carl Vinson told him that he had the president's approval to introduce a bill to establish the five-star rank for two generals and two admirals. Since most of the other nations of the world had five-star ranks, it was, many leaders felt, high time that America put an end to their practice of limiting to four stars their highest military leaders.

The American Congress has always been reluctant to bestow high rank on American military officers. There were no admirals until the Civil War, and at the beginning of World War II, there were only four full admirals in the United States Navy. But during the war a situation had arisen where Eisenhower, a four-star general, might have five-star British officers under him. Of course, there was no question of authority; that had been settled by the Combined Chiefs of Staff with the approval of Churchill and Roosevelt.

But there were problems of protocol, of precedence, and other difficulties which made it desirable for the United States to have the five-star rank. According to Vinson, FDR had it in mind to give the five-star rank to Leahy and King for the navy and to Marshall and Arnold for the army. Roosevelt's first idea, Vinson continued, had been for Leahy alone to hold the rank. But when FDR had made the suggestion, Leahy had let him know that the other members of the Joint Chiefs had to be included. There the matter rested for the time, and it would take a long time for legislation to work its way through Congress.

The proposal to separate the offices of CINCUS and CNO surfaced again in January. Considerable hard feeling existed between King and Secretary Knox, whom Leahy blamed for the squabble. "This question," he wrote, "could be quickly settled by a strong Secretary of the Navy, but it is still a matter of controversy and in the hands of the President."

The hands of the president no longer had the sure, firm grasp of earlier years. He was not up to par physically. He complained that he "lacked pep." His sinus condition, for which Ross McIntire gave him daily treatments, failed to improve. At the end of March, McIntire finally got him to go to Bethesda Naval Hospital for a complete medical check. Lieutenant Commander Howard Bruenn, USNR, a cardiologist, presented the grim report. The president suffered from hypertension, failure of the left ventricle of the heart, hypertensive heart disease, and acute bronchitis. At sixty-two, Roosevelt's body was failing him. He could die at any time. With great care, his life might be extended a year or so. But how could the president of the United States in wartime follow a program of rest and limited activity? It couldn't be done.

Leahy, of course, knew nothing of the pessimistic findings of Dr. Bruenn. Ross McIntire kept them a deep secret even from the president and his family. But from that day forward, Dr. Bruenn was attached full time to the White House staff under Ross McIntire.

To make matters worse, Harry Hopkins was no longer there to take up the burden. His frail body had collapsed, and he would be in and out of Bethesda and the Mayo Clinic before finally returning to the White House in late summer. And by that time, Roosevelt was out of the habit of depending on him. Their friendship had cooled, and it was months before "Harry the Hop" was once again a member of the team.

Given Roosevelt's weakness and the departure of Hopkins, Leahy had to do his best to take up the slack. It was an impossible task. He never had the close relationship with Roosevelt Hopkins had known. Nor would he have wanted it. He looked on his job as a military and to some extent a political one, but he kept it strictly professional. "In the White House and dealing with military affairs," Averell Harriman recalled many years later, "he could have moved into almost anything that came into the White House, whether it be production matters or policy matters of almost any kind. But my impression is that he limited his activities—unless he was asked—strictly to military questions and was not looking for widening his responsibilities or widening his attitude."[1] As several of his aides have pointed out, he was no empire builder. He simply wanted to get on with the war.[2]

But the war had no letup, and the nation had to be run, even though the president remained lethargic. One day Leahy brought him an OSS report that Vice President Henry Wallace had leaked sensitive material about a meeting of the Council of Foreign Ministers in Moscow the previous October. FDR seemed mildly interested, but he didn't want to pursue the matter. It is possible, of course, that he had the incident in mind when he decided to dump Wallace when he ran for his fourth term. We can never know, for the mind of FDR, always secretive, grew more so in the last year of his life. The only two people he might have confided such a decision to were no longer there. His secretary for over a quarter of a century, Marguerite "Missy" LeHand, had suffered a stroke a year earlier and would die that summer. And Harry Hopkins would not see "the Boss" until after the convention had named Harry Truman as FDR's running mate.

With the slackening of the reins in the White House, Leahy's own activities in the first months of 1944 seem routine. He still saw the daily messages, including Ultra intercepts of Axis secret radio traffic. He brought them to the president's attention as they seemed pertinent, but Roosevelt was not much interested in details. Leahy also watched with dismay as General de Gaulle's militant supporters eclipsed the leaders Leahy believed had the real interests of France at heart. De Gaulle, who had now taken the Cross of Lorraine as his personal symbol, was too ruthless to fail.

On 26 January, Leahy dined as a guest of Vice Admiral Raymond Fénard, naval representative on the French Mission in Washington, and Mme. Fénard.

> I noted [he wrote later] that all of the French participants in this dinner were followers of General de Gaulle, and that some of them wore the Lorraine Cross. Madame Fénard related to me numerous instances of oppression and atrocities committed by officials of the Vichy government, but said nothing about the known arbitrary and cruel activities of the de Gaullists.
>
> It is apparent that propaganda has convinced Madame Fénard of the virtues of M. de Gaulle's following and the villainy of all other Frenchmen.

Leahy was by no means ready to accept the tall, vainglorious Frenchman as the natural leader of French interests. In common with most of the staff who had been with him in Vichy, he distrusted de Gaulle and his French Committee of National Liberation (FCNL). As early as the previous September, Leahy had expressed his views to friends in the State Department, and "Doc" Matthews had sent him a collection of letters and reports from Murphy and others naming chapter and verse of how de Gaulle and his followers had consistently undercut Giraud. Leahy had no particular brief for Giraud, but he was the one recognized by the British and Americans as French military leader in the Mediterranean.

For the same reason de Gaulle had been kept in the dark before Torch—because his headquarters could not keep a secret—Giraud concealed from the FCNL his invasion of Corsica in September until just before the landings. De Gaulle's response was to use the FCNL, which he now dominated, to deprive "the French Commander-in-Chief of the authority and freedom of action which both he and our own military leaders have felt was essential."[3]

Such behavior, Leahy felt, was all of a piece with what was to be expected from Charles de Gaulle and his Free French. There was no living with de Gaulle, but because of decisions made by Churchill and FDR, Leahy had to try.

Early February brought word to Washington of the successful landings in the Marshalls. An unhappy consequence was the death in action of Marine Private First Class Stephen Hopkins, youngest son of Harry.

> Dear Bill: [Hopkins wrote from the Mayo Clinic]
> I appreciate so much your kind and sympathetic note which I received in Miami.
> I would have answered it before but things have not gone as well as I had hoped and I am having another round with the Mayos.
> Stephen's short life was full of joy and happiness and I know he died bravely for his country. Naturally, I am overwhelmingly proud of him.
> I try to relax and not think of the many things that are going on in Washington because I know I can do nothing about it at this distance. I have the impression that things are going well.
>
> My warmest regards,
>
> Harry[4]

Although only a little over two months had elapsed since the Combined Chiefs had met with their leaders at Cairo, Churchill was dissatisfied with the decisions and proposed that he and the president meet in London along with the Combined Chiefs. One of the things he wanted to discuss was the American proposal that when Allied forces drove into Germany after Overlord, the Americans should cross over so they would end up in the Baltic, leaving the mercurial problems of France and Italy to the British, who could then move on, as they desired, to the Balkans.

On 26 Janaury 1944, Leahy sent the president a lengthy memorandum stressing the advantages of the cross-over as the JCS saw them.

> Although the occupation of the northern area will render our military problem more difficult initially, the long term political and military advantages to

the United States are of such importance that we should not accept the recommendation of the British Chiefs of Staff.[5]

The ostensible reason for the changeover was to make it easier to transfer American troops to the Pacific, but the real reason, it seems clear, was to saddle the British with the more difficult occupation problems.

Be that as it may, FDR was not convinced, and he accepted the British position.

At any rate, no such meeting suited the purposes of the Americans. Marshall felt that too much time was wasted in debates, and it is even possible he believed such a conference might give the British a chance to back down on Overlord again. So he had no desire to go, and King was so vehemently against the idea that Admiral Sir Percy Noble, now on the British Naval Staff in Washington, complained to Leahy of his rudeness. Leahy asked King to tone down his remarks, which he did—for a while.

That episode was mild compared to one which flared in the Pacific. It was a simple matter, and it involved territorial jurisdiction, a thing about which MacArthur was abnormally sensitive.

One of the rich prizes of MacArthur's campaign against the Bismarck Barrier was Seeadler Harbor, a magnificent anchorage in the Admiralty Islands. On one side of the harbor, Los Negros Island provided ample space for an air field, and on the other, Manus, with its more rugged terrain, was readily adaptable as a naval base. Because of its location, the harbor would be ideal as a staging base for operations against New Guinea, the Palaus, the Philippines, and Formosa. The Joint Chiefs believed that the facilities of Manus, as the complex came to be known, should be used by Nimitz's ships as well as MacArthur's. Halsey, who was under Nimitz's command, was told to get on with the job, and Nimitz, to clear up any questions of jurisdiction, proposed that the Manus complex be included in his CINCPOA area.

MacArthur was furious. The Manus area belonged to him in his Southwest Pacific Area. He looked on Nimitz's proposal as an attempt to subordinate the Southwest Pacific drive to Central Pacific operations. Furiously, he demanded the right to come to Washington to present his case.

Rather than allow MacArthur to come to Washington, Leahy decided to send Rear Admiral John Shafroth to the Pacific to find out what was going on.

"I found that MacArthur [Shafroth quoted Halsey as saying] was unwilling to have the base on Manus Island constructed except for his own naval forces and for supporting forces that might be ordered to join him. He stated that he would not stand for the proposal—that the American people would not stand for it—nor would the Australian people. MacArthur stated further that he would not stand for anything that will interfere with his march back to the Philippines."

Halsey is definitely of the opinion, formed as a result of these conferences, that General MacArthur has illusions of grandeur, and that his, MacArthur's staff officers, are afraid to oppose any of his plans, whether they believed in them or not.[6]

The argument between Halsey and MacArthur had waxed hot and heavy. Halsey told him bluntly, "If you stick to this order of yours, you'll be hampering the war effort!" MacArthur's staff gasped, and Halsey later wrote, "I imagine they never expected to hear anyone address him in those terms this side of the Judgment Throne."[7]

In the end, MacArthur won a partial victory. He was allowed to keep the Manus complex under his command, but he was directed by the Joint Chiefs to permit the navy to build and maintain the huge facilities. *All* ships of the navy were to be welcome there, whether they belonged to MacArthur or to Nimitz. So ended the controversy which Leahy characterized as "the most controversial single problem before the JCS." Looking back, it seems the most ridiculous.

Partly because of the Manus affair, but more importantly to settle Pacific strategy for the forthcoming months, the Joint Chiefs decided it was time to summon MacArthur and Nimitz to Washington for discussions and some hard decisions. As usual, MacArthur said he was too busy to come. He had had time to come when his own turf was threatened as in the Manus incident, but when the president or the Joint Chiefs wanted to talk to him, it was another matter. Instead he sent his chief of staff, Lieutenant General Richard Sutherland, a brilliant, irascible man whom few cared to cross. Nimitz, having no such idea of his own indispensability, came in person.

Working together, the Joint Chiefs and their visitors found it easy to reach agreement. MacArthur wanted to skip intermediate goals and leapfrog to Hollandia on the northern coast of New Guinea. For this, he would need the support of Nimitz's fast carriers. Nimitz objected that if his carriers, already scheduled to assist in an assault on Kavieng, had to support Hollandia as well, it would delay his Central Pacific drive until well into the typhoon season. That problem was easily settled. The Joint Chiefs cancelled the Kavieng operation. Rabaul and Kavieng would be bypassed.

Future operations were easily agreed to. Truk would be bypassed. MacArthur, with the help of Nimitz's carriers, would seize Hollandia on 15 April. Central Pacific forces under Nimitz would invade the Marianas beginning about 15 June and the Palaus on 15 September. Two months later, they would support MacArthur's invasion of Mindanao, the southernmost of the major Philippine Islands. The Joint Chiefs would decide later whether to invade Luzon in the Philippines or Formosa, but the target date for either was 15 February 1945.

On 11 March, Leahy accompanied King and Nimitz to Roosevelt's Oval Office for his approval of the projected operations. Roosevelt was not well. His face was gray, and his hands trembled so that cigarette ashes fell on his suit as he placed the long holder in his mouth. Still, he was in good spirits, and, as he often did, conducted a rambling monologue. Usually this was a conscious device to give a visitor no time to say things FDR did not wish to hear: unpopular requests or demands for decisions he was not yet ready to make. But this time, it appeared to be mere fatigue. His monologue wound down and he quickly approved the plans. Since both MacArthur and Nimitz had their marching orders, the Joint Chiefs could assume there would be no repetition of the Manus incident.

Soon after Nimitz's departure, Leahy had the pleasant experience of being reunited with some of his staff from Vichy. On 18 March he attended a reception given by Wahwee MacArthur in celebration of the return of her husband Douglas and others who had been finally repatriated from Germany. Contrary to expectations, "All said that they received sufficient food and fair treatment while detained in Baden Baden."

Leahy added that unfortunately "from their very restricted point of view, they saw no signs of an early collapse of the German people."

The next day, with the president confined to bed with a cold and a fever, Leahy had to respond to an impatient telegram from Churchill asking for a meeting of the Combined Chiefs and the president in Bermuda about 5 April. Roosevelt directed Leahy to reply that for various reasons he could not come to Bermuda at that time. Churchill answered testily that if the president could not come there was no use in having the meeting.

Churchill apparently wanted to get together with FDR so that they could present a united front to Stalin over Poland. This was no easy matter, and it would never be solved to the satisfaction of the western allies. At the Teheran conference, the Big Three had agreed that the eastern boundary of Poland would be the Curzon Line, which left Russia in possession of a considerable amount of territory that had been Polish in 1939. Poland was to be compensated with territory to the west at the expense of Germany. Now Churchill was backing away from the Curzon Line agreement.

Also in dispute was the matter of the postwar Polish government. The British had long recognized and supported a refugee government with headquarters in London, known as the Free Poles, whose status was analagous to that of the Free French. The Russians, however, had established one of their own choosing, known as the Lublin Poles. The British refused to have anything to do with the Lublin puppets.

Although the United States eventually supported the British position on the Lublin Poles, Roosevelt was anxious not to have a break with the Soviets. It seemed that one was dangerously near between Stalin and Churchill.

On 25 March, Stalin sent Roosevelt a copy of a telegram he had sent Churchill. Leahy was startled. "We had observed the bluntness of the Soviet leader several times at the Teheran conference table, but this message was the strongest and most undiplomatic document I had ever seen exchanged between two ostensibly friendly governments."[8] Later he would see even stronger ones addressed to Roosevelt.

> A dispatch received today by telegraph from Marshal Stalin indicates a definite possibility of a serious break in the cooperation between Great Britain and Soviet Russia over the Polish territorial controversy. Churchill has failed to recognize Soviet claims that a part of Poland to the "Curzon" Line is rightly Soviet territory, and Stalin refuses to have any relations with the Polish Government in exile in England.
>
> It appears to me that Stalin has very definitely stated the extent of the so-called "Polish" territory that he intends to incorporate into the Union of Soviet Republics, and that he has ample military power with which to accomplish this purpose. His message to Churchill, . . . if known to the Germans, would be highly pleasing to them.

If it wasn't Stalin, then it was de Gaulle. By the end of March, Giraud had finally seen the end of the road. He announced his intention to retire "because of the interference by the Committee of Liberation (de Gaulle) with his

WDL and members of the Joint Chiefs of Staff with Sir John Dill (far right) welcome General Henri Giraud to Washington, 28 March 1944. (Courtesy, National Archives)

military authority. There has, for a long time, been evidence of a determination on the part of de Gaulle to eliminate General Giraud."

A few days later, as Leahy was preparing to accompany the president on a journey south, came the news that Giraud had actually resigned. It was only one problem of many that interferred with the rest Roosevelt's tired body demanded he take. Persistent bronchitis encouraged FDR to accept the hospitality of Bernard Baruch at his estate, Hobcaw Barony, near Georgetown, South Carolina. Assistant Naval Aide Lieutenant William Rigdon, who accompanied the party, commented on Leahy at this stage of his service.

> My Hobcaw log, and all other logs, show that Admiral Leahy was always close to the President. He was not only the President's chief planning officer, head of the Joint Chiefs of Staff, and the highest ranking American officer on military duty . . . but he was also the President's confidant and adviser on matters other than military. FDR trusted him completely, and so did President Truman. He never was a yes man, but when he was overridden he accepted the President's decision as if it had been his own. . . .
>
> Prior to his White House days Admiral Leahy had the name in Navy circles of being extremely difficult to work for. I did not know him in those days, but if that was true, he surely mellowed as his responsibilities rose. He was one of the most thoughtful and appreciative men I have known.[9]

On 8 April, the presidential private Pullman, *Ferdinand Magellan*, was hitched to the train on the siding under the Bureau of Engraving and Printing for the trip south. The company included Leahy, Pa Watson, Ross McIntire, Lieutenant Commander George Fox (medical technician), Lieutenant (jg) Rigdon, Dr. Bruenn, and the usual crowd of Secret Service and attendants.

Leahy, who considered train travel the best way after ship of going somewhere, thoroughly enjoyed riding in the *Ferdinand Magellan*. "In these times of difficulty in obtaining any satisfactory accommodations on railroads, it is truly traveling in luxury to make a journey on the president's train."

The next day, Easter Sunday, the president's train drew up at the station in Georgetown, South Carolina.

> Upon our arrival . . . we left the train and accompanied by Barney Baruch and his daughter proceeded by motor car eight miles over indifferent country roads to Mr. Baruch's home "Hobcaw" on the Waccamaw River, where it flows into Wynyaw Bay.
>
> Mr. Baruch's estate, "Hobcaw," containing a baronial residence that is protected by some thousands of acres of untouched forest, provides a luxurious and secure place for the President's recuperative vacation from the pressure of work that is unavoidable in Washington.
>
> The temperature today is 68° F. and the quiet is almost oppressive.
>
> Mr. Baruch, who was born in South Carolina, the son of a very talented doctor of medicine, accumulated a great fortune in New York City when he was a young man and many years ago he purchased and fitted with all modern conveniences this beautiful estate "Hobcaw."

He has now passed the age of 73, but he is still a powerful influence for good in both the political and business life of America.

There were not a few people who might have disagreed with Leahy's last paragraph, but everyone would have to agree that for years he had been a powerful force, whether for good or ill, in American business and politics.

The party settled down into a routine during the stay of nearly a month in Baruch's home. In the morning, following breakfast at 8:00, Leahy would examine the night's dispatches from Washington and London, preparing replies as necessary. At noon, the president, who rose about 9:30, would go over the mail and Leahy's suggested replies before the two men lunched together at 1:00 P.M. A rest until about three or four was the order of the day. Then there would be an excursion by car or boat into the surrounding territory. Sometimes they fished, and one day Leahy accompanied Baruch's daughter Belle on an alligator hunt. He saw only two small alligators but could not get close enough to hit them. Later that day, Belle shot a five-foot specimen to carry away the honors. Dinner was at 7:30, followed by movies every night, but the president seldom attended, preferring to get to bed early.

Roosevelt had said that he wanted to sleep twelve hours every night, and for the first week or so he did just that. Certainly it was peaceful.

> The residence . . . is built on high ground twenty or thirty feet above the river and is surrounded by ancient live oak trees bearing great growths of Spanish moss. The estate includes many thousands of acres, mostly timbered. . . . Deer, wild hogs, turkey, and quail are found in the forest, and no shooting is permitted.

Visitors arrived frequently from Washington, too many in Leahy's view. Some were welcome, such as Franklin Junior, who stopped off for dinner one night. "He is," Leahy observed, "the most interesting and promising of the President's children." Another welcome visitor was Lieutenant General Mark Clark, commanding general of the Fifth Army in Italy. He told of the extraordinary difficulty of commanding or coordinating multinational forces. "In Italy the Allied armies have American, English, Canadian, New Zealand, French, Italian, and Indian troops, many of them of inferior quality compared with the Germans, and all of the different nationalities having their own ideas as to how the campaign should be conducted."

Another welcome visitation was that of Eleanor Roosevelt and their daughter Anna Boettiger. Anna, known in the family as "Sis," was a particular favorite of her father.

Less welcome was the "unnecessary number of telegraphic messages" with which Leahy had to deal each day. One, however, brought more sorrow than annoyance, telling of the death on 28 April of Secretary of the Navy Frank Knox. Leahy had never thought much of Knox as secretary but had liked him as a person.

On 30 April, MacArthur, his presidential boomlet having been shot down in the early primaries, announced that he would not be a candidate for president nor would he accept a nomination. "The President did not show much interest in the announcement, but I commented that if General MacArthur should get the nomination, he would be a very dangerous antagonist for anybody, including Roosevelt. His statement seemed to leave the Republican field open to Governor Dewey of New York."[10]

On 6 May, Leahy's sixty-ninth birthday, Roosevelt and his party left Hobcaw for Washington, FDR's health ostensibly restored. He didn't stay long in Washington, however. After naming Under Secretary James V. Forrestal as secretary of the navy, he went off for a long weekend at Shangri La [now Camp David] in the mountains of Maryland. On his return he asked Leahy to prepare plans for a transAtlantic voyage, destination unknown, and for an inspection trip by cruiser to Alaska and Pearl Harbor, thence to San Diego, Los Angeles, and San Francisco, returning to Washington about 20 August. Since this trip would extend through the time of the Democratic national convention to be held in Chicago, Leahy wondered about the political overtones. Roosevelt told him, "Bill, I just hate to run again for election. Perhaps the war will by that time have progressed to a point that will make it unnecessary for me to be a candidate."

"While I have long been sure," Leahy observed, "that the President would like to retire from his present office, this is the first time he has expressed himself to me clearly in regard to his attitude toward renomination."

The next day, Roosevelt told Leahy to forget about the transAtlantic trip but to continue to plan for the Pacific cruise.

Even as the war was approaching its climax, with Normandy less than a month away, and major moves in the Pacific not far behind, critics in the press and in Congress raised charges of "inefficiency and waste" in having separate arms of the military forces of the United States. Many savings could be realized and command authority simplified by having a single department of national defense. Following a routine meeting on 16 May, the JCS agreed to a committee to investigate the matter. Marshall and Arnold favored the notion, while King opposed it. Leahy wanted to go slow.

He insisted on the following language in the directive: "That the committee in carrying out the above directive must be designed primarily to insure the efficiency and the overall integration of the land, sea, and air forces."[11]

The four of them agreed that the Joint Chiefs of Staff should "be a permanent body responsible only to the President, and that it should advise the President on the national defense budget." As is well known, this agreement fell by the wayside in the coming years of debate on unification.

In early June, while Leahy was away from Washington, two major events took place. On 4 June, Rome finally fell, and two days later American,

British, and Canadian troops went ashore at Normandy, bringing Operation Overlord to fruition and starting western Allied forces on the road to Berlin.

It was on the eve of D-day that Leahy faced the graduating class of Cornell College in Iowa to speak on the responsibility of free peoples to resist tyranny. "Peace at any price" was wrong:

> Everybody may have peace if they are willing to pay *any* price for it.
>
> Part of this *any* price is slavery, dishonor of your women, destruction of your homes, denial of your God. I have seen all of these abominations in other parts of the world paid as the price of not resisting invasion, and I have no thought that the inhabitants of this state of my birth have any desire for peace at that price, or that they lack the fortitude that is necessary to discourage aggression by the barbarians who are now about to be driven back to their kennels, or by any other savages who may arise at some later date against our civilized Christian world.[12]

Perhaps the admiral was too optimistic about our civilized Christian world, but he meant every word of what he said. Later it became less popular to say such things, but such old-fashioned concepts caused Leahy no embarrassment. They never would.

## CHAPTER 14

# MacArthur and the Pacific

Back in Washington, Leahy had to brace himself to endure a forthcoming state visit of General de Gaulle, who had now proclaimed himself head of the provisional government of France. There were problems of security, for if the French general had his strong supporters, he also had his bitter enemies. "We were all on pins and needles," recalled Dorothy Ringquist, "thinking he was going to be shot at."[1]

Under Secretary of State Edward R. Stettinius recorded in his diary for 22 June that Leahy had not mellowed at all in regard to de Gaulle.

> Admiral Leahy went into great detail reviewing the history of our rela-
> tionship with the French committee over the past two years. He stated with
> great force that from the start they had hampered our war effort, and had caused
> us difficulty and embarrassment at every turn. The admiral placed emphasis on
> the fact that they had practically placed the former governor of Dakar in prison
> and that he had been friendly to our cause. Now, they had imprisoned Giraud.
> The admiral also stated that while French troops were useful in Italy, they were
> not fighting under the conditions laid down by the Allied military leaders. It was
> indicated that the French seemed to be doing everything possible to make
> matters difficult and that, while we were confident of winning the war in
> France, they were being of little or no help. Meanwhile, their great leader was
> "sulking" in London.[2]

Thus it was with a great deal of caution and no little interest that Leahy met de Gaulle on the afternoon of 6 July. He arrived at 4:00 by airplane and was driven to the White House, where the president and members of his cabinet met him in the reception room on the ground floor. Afterwards there was tea on the south veranda. To Leahy's surprise, he found de Gaulle "less forbidding in manner and appearance than I expected." But he continued to resent de Gaulle's arrogance, especially in proclaiming himself president, albeit of a provisional government. He disliked it in the invitation which began:

Le Général de Gaulle
Président
du Gouvernement Provisoire de la République Française
vous prie de lui faire l'honneur, etc.

The following day, the American president hosted a luncheon of forty men in honor of de Gaulle. As he could do so well, Roosevelt avoided specifics, making no political commitments, and talking in the broadest terms of the traditional friendship of the United States and France. If de Gaulle had hoped for any public statement of support for him as provisional president, he was sadly disappointed. He did, however, win a statement of acceptance of the French Committee of National Liberation as the "de facto" authority for the civil government of France.

> De Gaulle made a very good impression upon the people he met during his brief stay in our capital, including myself. I had a better opinion of him after talking with him. However, I remained unconvinced that he and his Committee of Liberation necessarily represented the form of government that the people of France wished to have after their nation's liberation from the Nazis.[3]

By the time of de Gaulle's visit, it was a foregone conclusion that FDR would run for a fourth term. Ross McIntire continued to insist, falsely, that his health was good for a man of his age. The only question was who his running mate would be. In 1940 Roosevelt had forced a reluctant party to take Secretary of Agriculture Henry A. Wallace, mystic, liberal, and visionary. The party would have rebelled in 1944, in spite of the fact that Roosevelt had said to him, "I hope it's the same team again, Henry." Actually he had no intention of supporting Wallace again and pretended that the nomination for vice president was wide open. He encouraged everyone who had any aspirations for the post, and a good many of them felt bitter resentment when his choice was finally revealed.

Roosevelt had planned his Pacific trip to pass through Chicago and then go on to the West Coast to take ship for Hawaii. That way he would be able to confer with Democratic bigwigs while the convention was going on. It is clear why he wanted to pass through Chicago. What is not so clear is why he wanted to go on to Hawaii. He said it was to meet MacArthur and Nimitz face to face, to hear their arguments on future strategy in the Pacific, and to decide between them on military grounds. Yet he declined to take the Joint Chiefs with him. In fact, he forbade them to come. King, who had been making an inspection trip in the Pacific in the weeks before the president arrived in Pearl Harbor, was in the air returning to the mainland even as the USS *Baltimore* was transporting the commander in chief to Hawaii. Only Leahy, in his role as personal chief of staff to the commander in chief and not as chairman of the Joint Chiefs, would represent the military.

MacArthur believed that the trip was politically inspired. He resented the direct orders to come to Hawaii himself and not send anyone else. Other critics have suggested that Roosevelt simply wanted to emphasize his position as commander in chief of the army and navy, showing the press and public that he was really running the war. Perhaps Roosevelt wanted a sea voyage. Since he had no need to meet Churchill at the moment, MacArthur would have to do. Whatever the reason, FDR was determined to go.

Before leaving for Hawaii, Leahy devoted a meeting of the Joint Chiefs to Pacific strategy. He felt he needed to be on top of affairs when the president met with MacArthur and Nimitz. After discussing some island invasions, he came to the question of how Japan was to be finished off. He felt that an invasion was neither necessary nor desirable.

> It appears to me probable that an invasion of Japan would be so costly in loss of life as to make it unacceptable.
>
> A large part of the Japanese Navy was already on the bottom of the sea. The same was true of Japanese merchant shipping. There was every indication that our Navy would soon have the rest of Tokyo's warships sunk or out of action. The combined Navy surface and air force action even by this time had forced Japan into a position that made her early surrender inevitable. None of us then knew the potentialities of the atomic bomb, but it was my opinion, and I urged it strongly on the Joint Chiefs, that no major land invasion of the Japanese mainland was necessary to win the war. The JCS did order the preparation of plans for an invasion, but *the invasion itself was never authorized.*[4]

Before Leahy left with the president, he was glad to welcome Harry Hopkins back from his six-month absence. Hopkins had undergone surgery at the Mayo Clinic and was even more cadaverous than ever. He was obviously out of the picture in Washington, and for some reason a coolness had developed between him and FDR. It would not be until after the Quebec conference later that year that their old relationship was restored. In any case, he was in no shape to make the trip west.

At 11:30 P.M., 13 July, the president's special train, pulling the *Ferdinand Magellan*, left Washington for Highlands, across the Hudson from Hyde Park. While Harry stayed behind to mind the store, the usual crowd was on board.

After a day in Hyde Park, the train left for Chicago. There, as the *Ferdinand Magellan* sat on a siding, various dignitaries from the convention came on board to greet the president and to try to find out what his thoughts on the vice presidential nominee were. After the train had left Chicago, FDR surprised Leahy by telling him it was Harry Truman.

Harry Truman was not even a candidate. He had promised to nominate James Byrnes, and when FDR picked him, Truman nearly refused. Only after considerable pressure did he agree and ask Byrnes to release him from the promise to nominate him. Although he graciously gave permission, all through Truman's first term Byrnes resented the man from Independence who had the job he had counted on as his own.

Leahy at that time thought that Byrnes should have had the job, but later on, seeing Byrnes at work as secretary of state, he emphatically changed his mind.

On 16 July, FDR received a telegram from Churchill urgently requesting another meeting. FDR told Leahy to answer that he could make it to Scotland in September, but not before. In fact, Roosevelt thought so well of a meeting in Scotland that he wrote Stalin a day later.

> I feel that, as things are moving so fast and so successfully, there should be a meeting in the reasonably near future between you, the Prime Minister, and me. Mr. Churchill is in hearty accord with this thought.
>
> It would be best for me to have a meeting between the 10th and 15th of September. I am now on a trip in the Far West and must be in Washington for several weeks on my return.
>
> The North of Scotland would be the most central point for me and you. You could come either by ship or by plane and I could go by ship.
>
> I hope you can let me have your thoughts. Security and secrecy can be maintained either on shore or on shipboard.[5]

As usual, Stalin replied that his duties made it absolutely impossible for him to leave the country. He agreed that a meeting was desirable. Desirable or no, half a year would go by before the Big Three met at Yalta. The September meeting would be between Churchill and Roosevelt, and it would be in Quebec.

When the train reached San Diego, Leahy had the opportunity to talk to some of his old friends he had not seen in years. He accompanied Roosevelt to a demonstration of an amphibious landing of some ten thousand men on a beach about forty miles north of San Diego. It was his first experience with a large-scale amphibious exercise, and he found it a "thrilling, informative sight." The techniques of amphibious operations had obviously come a long way since he had first experienced them in the Caribbean.

At 8:15 that evening, seated in a special communications car attached to the train, Leahy heard FDR make the formal acceptance speech of his nomination for a fourth term.

On 21 July, the presidential party boarded the cruiser *Baltimore*. As on previous occasions, the sea voyage was restful. The president occupied the captain's day cabin, while Leahy had the admiral's quarters. Although the presence of FDR aboard the *Baltimore* had been a closely guarded secret, it soon became apparent that it was secret no more. Everyone in Pearl Harbor knew the president was coming, and as the cruiser stood up the channel, spectators thronged every available space in hopes of catching a glimpse of the great man. Since the secret was known, the Presidential Flag was broken out to make it official.

Off Fort Kamehameha, as the *Baltimore* slowed to take on the pilot, Admiral Nimitz and others came on board and went to the captain's cabin where Roosevelt and Leahy awaited them. Then about 3:00 P.M., the cruiser nestled alongside Pier 22-B, "so gently that she wouldn't have crushed an eggshell." The senior officers who were waiting in gleaming white uniforms executed "Right Face!" It had been so long since they had practiced close order drill that two of them turned the wrong way, to the delight of the watching bluejackets on the ship.

Since the visit was now official, all the proper ruffles and flourishes, sideboys and other honors, had to be provided. Roosevelt received his visitors in his quarters, asking Nimitz to remain with him and Leahy as the others paid their respects. But one officer was missing. So far there was no sign of General Douglas MacArthur. It was now nearly 3:30.

MacArthur had landed at Hickam Field about an hour before the *Baltimore* had tied up, but instead of waiting with the other officers, he had gone on to General Robert Richardson's quarters at Fort Shafter to take a leisurely bath. He had been in a foul humor during the twenty-six-hour flight from Brisbane. He had paced up and down the aisles of the plane, exclaiming of "the humiliation of forcing me to leave my command to fly to Honolulu for a political picture-taking junket!" On the theory of "it takes one to know one," he apparently decided to go the president one better in showmanship.

Roosevelt was just preparing to go ashore when loud cheers and a siren from the direction of Honolulu could be heard. Soon there rolled out onto the pier motorcycles escorting what Sam Rosenman described as "the longest open car I have ever seen."[6] The car debouched the missing general, dressed in khaki trousers, a leather flying jacket, and his cap with the insignia of a field marshal in the Philippine army.

Choosing to ignore MacArthur's lack of courtesy, Roosevelt received him warmly as Leahy asked jokingly, "Douglas, why don't you wear the right kind of clothes when you come up here to see us?"

"Well, you haven't been where I came from, and it's cold up there in the sky," replied MacArthur.

There was the usual picture taking before the president and his party left the ship to go to the "cream stucco mansion," where Roosevelt was to be quartered. Nimitz returned to his quarters at Makalapa, and MacArthur went back to Fort Shafter with his host, General Richardson.

Roosevelt, Leahy, and the rest who had come on the *Baltimore* stayed in the palatial residence which had formerly belonged to the wealthy Christopher Holmes at Waikiki. During the war it had been turned from a showplace into quarters for naval aviators on leave. On this occasion, the fliers had been removed to the Pearl Harbor BOQ. For more than a week, repair gangs had been working on the residence, building ramps for the president's wheelchair, and generally sprucing it up to be fit for the commander in chief.

The next morning Roosevelt insisted on a day-long series of inspections. Nimitz and Leahy were instructed to accompany him in his car. So was MacArthur, and therein lay the problem. The command set him off again over the impropriety of the president interfering in his exercise of his own command in the Southwest Pacific. When the motorcade set out, Nimitz, MacArthur, and FDR were crowded uncomfortably in a red car belonging to the fire chief of Honolulu. Nimitz had been offered a larger black one, but had turned it down since it belonged to the madam of Honolulu's most famous brothel and would have been readily identifiable.

WDL, General R. C. Richardson, FDR, and Colonel W. Saffarans inspect the Jungle Training Center in Hawaii, 28 July 1944. (Courtesy, FDR Library)

General Douglas MacArthur, President Roosevelt, Admiral Chester W. Nimitz, and WDL discuss Pacific strategy in FDR's quarters on Waikiki, 28 July 1944. (Courtesy, FDR Library)

On the back seat, Nimitz was jammed between MacArthur and FDR, while Leahy rode comfortably in front next to the driver. Clearly he had the best of it, at least as far as comfort was concerned.

That evening, Roosevelt invited MacArthur, Nimitz, Leahy, and Halsey to dine with him. After dinner, as the party moved to the living room where huge maps and charts had been hung, Halsey excused himself. MacArthur, who had not been briefed on the subject of the conference, began to realize what he was in for.

The President began it. Pointing to Mindanao, the agreed target in the southern Philippines, he asked, "Well, Douglas, where do we go from here?"

"Leyte, Mr. President, and then Luzon!"

The issue was joined. The official navy position was that the central and northern Philippines, including Luzon, should be bypassed and the main offensive directed at Formosa, hundreds of miles farther north and hence closer to Japan. King, on his stop at Pearl Harbor, had warned Nimitz that MacArthur would attempt to divert American strategy to the south. King saw no strategic use for the Philippines that could not be better served by Formosa.

The discussion between Nimitz and MacArthur that followed was gentlemanly. As was his custom, Leahy let the two talk, each arguing his position clearly, occasionally pointing to a chart with a long bamboo pointer. MacArthur exercised his marvelous ability to organize and present material while speaking off the cuff. It was for Roosevelt, as Leahy put it, "an excellent lesson in geography, one of his favorite subjects."[7]

Nimitz had been doing a lot of thinking, and he was not at all sure that King was right in his desire to bypass Luzon. While he dutifully presented the navy's case, arguing that Formosa had a better strategic position and could be taken at less cost than Luzon, he was willing to grant the strength of MacArthur's arguments, which were based both on strategy and humanitarianism.[8]

From Luzon, MacArthur added, he could cut off all Japanese shipping from Southeast Asia, thereby depriving Japan of essential food, oil, and war materials. Even more important, the Philippines represented American honor in the Far East. If they were bypassed, thousands would be condemned to starvation, for the Japanese would take what food there was and leave the local population as well as American prisoners of war to starve. American failure in the Philippines would substantiate Japanese propaganda that Americans were unwilling to fight for their friends in the Orient. If the Philippines were bypassed, MacArthur argued, "American public opinion will condemn you, Mr. President. And it would be justified."

That was pretty strong stuff, but Roosevelt was not convinced. At one point he argued, having in mind recent reports of Japanese reinforcements in the Manila area, "But, Douglas, to take Luzon would demand heavier losses than we can stand. It seems to me we *must* bypass it."[9]

"Mr. President," MacArthur retorted, "my losses would not be heavy, any more than they have been in the past. The days of the frontal attack are over. Modern weapons are too deadly, and direct assault is no longer feasible. Only mediocre commanders still use it. Your good commanders do not turn in heavy losses."

When the discussions resumed the following morning, Leahy, away from the politically charged atmosphere of Washington, was surprised to see how smoothly the two commanders came to an understanding. He never shared the antagonism of most navy and a good many army officers toward MacArthur. He also thought highly of Nimitz.

> Both of these commanders of our available resources express certainty of success if we continue to work on the weaker points in the Japanese defenses and make no stupid mistakes. I personally am convinced that they are together the best qualified officers in our service for this tremendous task, and that they will work together in full agreement toward the common end of defeating Japan.

In *I Was There*, Leahy amplified his remarks on the conference, emphasizing how the agreed strategy would make unnecessary a physical invasion of the Japanese home islands.

The agreement on fundamental strategy to be employed in defeating Japan and the President's familiarity with the situation acquired at this conference were to be of great value in preventing an unnecessary invasion of Japan which the planning staffs of the Joint Chiefs and the War Department were advocating, regardless of the loss of life that would result from an attack on Japan's ground forces in their own country. MacArthur and Nimitz were now in agreement that the Philippines should be recovered with ground and air power then available in the western Pacific and that Japan could be forced to accept our terms of surrender by the use of sea and air power without an invasion of the Japanese homeland.[10]★

When the conference broke up at noon, Nimitz was host for luncheon at Makalapa. Right after lunch, MacArthur made his farewells and departed for Hickam Field and the flight back to Australia. As his plane became airborne, he exclaimed gleefully, "We sold it!"

While the conference was in progress, Leahy received a message from Hopkins reporting a rumor picked up by the FBI that Roosevelt was very sick and that the trip had been called off on orders of Admiral McIntire.

> I do hope this is not true and you are feeling well [Hopkins cabled]. Think it is very important that reasons other than ill health be given if future plans are curtailed. The underground to hostile interest here in relation of your health is working overtime and cannot emphasize too strongly to you how important it is that no opportunity be given them to increase their production of lies and rumors.

Leahy replied at once:

28 July 1944

From Admiral Leahy to Mr. Harry Hopkins.

> . . . Report is ridiculous. The President is in perfect condition.
>
> Yesterday he worked from 9:30 A.M. to 11:30 P.M. on what was a test of my endurance and I am pretty tough as you know.
>
> Tell FBI [Director] Hoover that this agent here should be disciplined for making a false report.
>
> McIntire says the President was never in better condition than at present.[11]

Although perhaps Leahy did not know it, conditions were not as rosy as he reported. Ross McIntire was exaggerating when he said that FDR had never

---

★The idea that an invasion of the Japanese home islands would be necessary did not die as easily as Leahy seems to suggest here. General Marshall and, to some extent, General Arnold believed that Japan had to be beaten on her own soil. The death of President Roosevelt removed from the scene a commander in chief who understood the potentialities of sea and air blockade. President Truman, with his army background, preferred to take the advice of his generals rather than that of his admirals on the matter. Marshall's belief in the necessity of invasion was one of the reasons the United States kept pressure on Russia to declare war on Japan in order to tie down the large Japanese forces in Manchuria.

been better. And MacArthur told his aides that he had been shocked by the president's appearance and that it was clear to him that the president's days were numbered.

For the next two days, as though to discredit the rumor, Roosevelt followed an inspection schedule that would have worn out a man less determined than he. He wanted to see and be seen. He visited the Jungle Training Center at Kahana and the Kanoehe Naval Air Station. In the evening after dinner, they were entertained by a native orchestra, a female vocalist who sang such Hawaiian songs as "Leilani" and "Aloha," and a hula dancer who "performed beautifully," as the admiral put it.

The next day they saw wounded men being unloaded from a hospital plane and transferred to hospitals in Hawaii. Leahy was much struck by the fact that less than thirty-six hours earlier these men had been in action on Guam. They also visited the huge naval hospital at Aiea, which engrossed Roosevelt for over an hour, as he chatted with patients in each ward.

Everyone knew that these visits were mainly political. Leahy felt satisfaction over how well they were received:

> On all our motor journeys through the streets of Honolulu and in the naval establishments, the president was greeted with enthusiastic applause by people of the different races that inhabit the island. The greater number of people seen on the streets were patently of Japanese extraction, but their expressions of enthusiasm were equal to those of the Hawaiians and the continental Americans.

After a final press conference, the president and his party went back aboard the *Baltimore* for a cruise to Alaska. Leahy saw no reason for that part of the trip. "I look forward to little of value in the remainder of our scheduled cruise on the *Baltimore*, but the entire journey has already been fully justified by our conferences with MacArthur and Nimitz in Honolulu."

As Leahy predicted, nothing of importance took place during the trip to the Aleutians and Alaska other than to familiarize the entire party with the vicissitudes of weather in that part of the world. For example, for a full day, a gale-force wind pinned the cruiser to the dock in Adak, the best efforts of tugs and her own engines failing to pull her off. A scheduled run by destroyer through the inland passage, which normally reveals spectacular scenery in that time of year was made in dense fog. The only bright spot in the trip, so far as Leahy was concerned, was his seeing firsthand the capabilities of radar in maneuvering ships in conditions of low visibility.

When the destroyer reached Bremerton, it went into a drydock so the president could make a radio address from a stable platform. His speech was poor; he had written it himself and he delivered it badly. The fatigue which worried his doctors was in full command that day. Still, Roosevelt considered the trip a success when he returned to Washington.

The decision reached at Pearl Harbor for Luzon over Formosa was in reality no decision. The Joint Chiefs still had to be sold. But they continued to argue and debate the issue. King was willing to agree to Luzon, but he wanted Formosa too, as a *quid pro quo*. If the Formosa operation was going to follow, Nimitz pointed out that it had to take place as soon after Leyte as possible in order to beat the 1945 typhoon season.[12]

Marshall opposed Formosa, and so matters stood until September, when the Joint Chiefs finally agreed that following his Mindanao campaign, MacArthur would seize Leyte in late December in order to provide a base for a further advance against Luzon—or Formosa. On that note, the Joint Chiefs went to Quebec for yet another go-around with their British opposite numbers.

A good many problems remained to be settled. China and Chiang Kai-shek presented difficulties. An American proposal to put Stilwell in command of all Chinese armies was badly received by Chiang Kai-shek and eventually rejected. Meanwhile the British and Americans split once again over delays in the Burma operation and the Joint Chiefs urged Mountbatten to occupy the Mandalay area and open the road to China "without any avoidable delay."

Then there was the ever-recurring problem of France. On 28 August someone tried to assassinate General Giraud, who was living quietly in Algiers. Even though the general had been stripped of all authority and command, he was still, apparently, a menace in the eyes of the implacable supporters of de Gaulle. In Leahy's mind, the Gaullists had done everything to expose Giraud by changing his trusted guards for their own men. And when the assassin had been captured, he had been, through a mixup, released by the police. It would probably have made no difference, for if he had not got away, he would have been "liquidated as quickly as was the assassin who killed Admiral Darlan. Dead men tell no tales."

A week later Bob Murphy dropped in to see Leahy and confirmed his suspicions that the attempted assassination had been the work of the French Committee of National Liberation, but he did not share the admiral's opinion that de Gaulle had authorized it.

Just before leaving for Quebec, Leahy took his granddaughter Louise to an invitational showing of the new motion picture *Wilson*, a distorted, idolizing portrayal of the president of World War I days. The film made even Leahy sympathetic toward the man who had "completely failed at the Peace Conference" to obtain "the lofty purposes that he had for a long time advocated and that had attracted to him a devoted following of a majority of the American people." If he spoke those sentiments to Louise, it was later, for the former president's widow was seated just behind them.

In early September, the meetings at Dumbarton Oaks, preliminary discussions for setting up the United Nations Organization, were going forward but at so slow a pace that Leahy was delighted when he heard Louise refer to them as "Dumbunny Oaks."

The day he left for Quebec, Leahy had a long talk with Hopkins, who was remaining in Washington. This would be the only meeting with Churchill that Hopkins would miss during Roosevelt's presidency. He put a good face on the matter in a letter to Churchill, explaining that he didn't have the stamina to face such a meeting. But the fact is, he hadn't been invited.

Hopkins was looking ahead toward the time when Roosevelt would no longer need him, when the war would be over. Then peacetime conditions would leave no room in the government for a man of his peculiar talents and reputation. He had no income beyond his salary. He talked to Leahy about having a civilian representative on the staff of the military government in Germany after the surrender. He would be principal advisor about economic and political activities of the Germans. He would have the rank of ambassador. Hopkins wanted that job for himself. But Leahy could only give him a sympathetic hearing. In the end, no such appointment was ever made, and Hopkins couldn't have taken it if it had been. He was too close to the end.

The Second Quebec Conference (Octagon) had been Churchill's idea. He and Roosevelt had not met since the previous December in Cairo. Matters discussed included the strategy for operations in the closing phases of the war against Japan. The Luzon–Formosa question had not been settled.

During one of the sessions, Churchill in a dramatic moment offered the British fleet for operations against Japan at an appropriate moment. Roosevelt accepted the offer, while King looked daggers. He wanted no part of the British fleet in "his" ocean. The British had different operating methods, had no experience in sustained carrier operations, and would be a logistic nightmare, for they did not have the endurance of American ships. Churchill pressed King, who answered evasively that he was preparing a paper on the subject for the Combined Chiefs. Churchill scowled.

"The offer has been made! Is it accepted?"

"It is," replied the president. That should have settled the matter, but King continued to argue until Marshall said quietly, "I don't think we should wash our linen in public."

As it turned out, the British performed magnificently in the Pacific and won nothing but praise from the American commanders they served under.

On the evening of 14 September, Canadian officers were holding a formal dinner for their American guests, Leahy, Marshall, King, and Arnold. For two days messages had been going back and forth between Quebec, Washington, and Pearl Harbor as a result of Halsey's discovery that the central Philippines seemed to be weaker than previously believed. On that basis he recommended that certain intermediate operations be canceled and that the proposed invasion of Leyte be moved up from 20 December to 20 October. Nimitz generally concurred, and so did General Sutherland, replying for

MacArthur who was at sea and observing radio silence. All of these recommendations reached the Joint Chiefs during the dinner. Marshall described the scene:

> The message from MacArthur arrived at Quebec at night, and Admiral Leahy, Admiral King, General Arnold and I were being entertained at a formal dinner by Canadian officers. It was read by the appropriate staff officers who suggested an immediate affirmative answer. The message, with their recommendations, was rushed to us and we left the table for a conference. Having the utmost confidence in General MacArthur, Admiral Nimitz, and Admiral Halsey, it was not a difficult decision to make. Within 90 minutes after the signal had been received in Quebec, General MacArthur and Admiral Nimitz had received their instructions to execute the Leyte operation on the target date 20 October, abandoning three previously approved intermediary landings. General MacArthur's acknowledgement of his new instructions reached me while en route from the dinner to my quarters in Quebec.[13]

That effectively ended the business of Octagon. On 16 September it broke up, and Roosevelt and his party left for Hyde Park. The president intended to rest for a few days before setting out on the campaign trail. While he was there FDR would play host to an oddly assorted group of personages in the kind of informal surroundings he loved.

## CHAPTER 15

# The Fleet Admiral

After only one quiet day of rest at Hyde Park, Roosevelt and Leahy began to cope with a stream of visitors. Churchill and his wife Clemmie arrived. Then Harry Hopkins showed up, bringing with him the Duke of Windsor, and the relaxation ended.

> The former King of England [Leahy admitted] made to me an unexpectedly good appearance. . . . Mr. Churchill, one of the two most powerful men of the age, bowed respectfully to the ex-king on the latter's departure. I think England is well rid of the prince-heir apparent who failed in his trust and abdicated to marry a twice divorced American woman.

During the next few days, as Churchill, Roosevelt, and Leahy were debating matters, Hopkins was unobtrusively resuming his place with them, inserting a word here, asking a question there, making a suggestion somewhere else. By the time the party returned to Washington, it is reasonable to say that Hopkins and Roosevelt, both marked for death in the months ahead, had resumed their previous close relationship. It was not the least of the accomplishments of that September.

One day, Leahy and others joined Eleanor Roosevelt for lunch. He found it a remarkable experience.

> I sat at a table with Miss [Laura] Delano, Mrs. Roosevelt, and Mr. Churchill, and listened to an hour of argument by the latter two on their general attitude toward a reorganization of the world. Mrs. Roosevelt is avowedly an uplifter

with an idea that peace can be maintained by improving the living conditions of all people of all countries. Mr. Churchill, on the contrary, said that the only hope for a durable peace is an agreement between Great Britain and the United States to prevent international war by the use of their combined force if necessary. He expressed a willingness to take Russia into the agreement if the Russians wish to join, but he does not believe that China can be anything but a trouble if it should be permitted to join. Mr. Churchill presents his case with clarity and conviction. It was an extremely interesting and instructive hour.

Talks at Hyde Park ranged from the future role of Italy in the war to "tube alloys," the curious code term Churchill used for the atomic bomb. Leahy considered the discussion of "tube alloys" rather a waste of time, for he felt the bomb would never work. When it finally did, he considered it a barbarous weapon no civilized country should ever employ.

Before Churchill left Hyde Park, he told Leahy he would like to write him from time to time in order to have an inside track on problems that might rise between him and the president. Leahy wouldn't touch the idea, believing Churchill wanted to make him a one-man lobby for British ideas.

Once back in Washington, Leahy found old and new problems. The United States finally had to come to grips with the reality that de Gaulle had won the struggle for power in France. Accordingly they recognized the Committee of National Liberation as de facto provisional government. Now as head of state, the rangy French leader believed himself in every way the equal of Roosevelt, Churchill, and Stalin. He took it as a mortal insult when he was not invited to Yalta the following February.

In China, Chiang Kai-shek got fed up with Stilwell, and the American general had to be replaced by Albert C. Wedemeyer. In the Pacific, the decision was finally made to take Luzon, as MacArthur wanted, followed by Iwo Jima, which the air force desired as a relief base for B-29s, and Okinawa, which would interdict Japanese traffic to southeast Asia as well as Formosa and which could be taken with fewer men.

The chief problem in the Pacific was that of command. MacArthur's campaign through the southwest Pacific and Nimitz's through the central Pacific had finally merged at Leyte. Therefore the area command concept would no longer work, for it was impossible politically to subordinate MacArthur to Nimitz or Nimitz to MacArthur.

> Admiral King contends that such operations should be under Naval Command and General Marshall believes they should be under Army command. In view of the fact that the forces employed will be predominantly Army, I am in agreement with General Marshall.

Many in the navy might have considered Leahy a traitor to his service for that opinion, but his job had been so long on a level far above service rivalries he was able to be objective. As a matter of fact, when he attended the

Army–Navy football game that fall as personal representative of the president, protocol required him to sit for the second half on the army side of the field!

As ever, divergences between British and American ideas of strategy kept the Joint Chiefs busy and Leahy occupied in supplying the president with ammunition to counter the blandishments of the prime minister. Even after Overlord, even after the capture of Paris, Churchill refused to accept the idea that the campaign in France was the principal Anglo–Saxon drive against Germany. In mid-October, for example, he proposed that two American divisions scheduled for reinforcement of Eisenhower in France be diverted to Italy on the grounds that British forces there had borne the brunt of the battle and were tired. Cannily the PM suggested that the British would give Eisenhower two British divisions from the Burma campaign. Since the U.S. Joint Chiefs had never agreed to the reinforcement of the Burma campaign from troops in Britain, this was no gift at all. In a memo to the president, Leahy laid it on the line.

> The action proposed by the Prime Minister would withhold from Eisenhower vitally needed fresh troops in order to commit more American forces to the high attrition of an indecisive winter campaign in northern Italy, the outcome of which will have little effect on the decisive battle in western Germany.[1]

The American Joint Chiefs throughout the war found the British, and especially the prime minister's, tendency to dissipate efforts across the globe more than a little trying.

Then there were problems of postwar adjustments. At Quebec, Secretary of the Treasury Henry Morgenthau had persuaded Churchill and Roosevelt to initial a plan to reduce Germany to the status of a rural nation. Since Germany could not support her population by agriculture alone, adoption of the Morgenthau Plan would have placed enormous burdens on the United States. The president and prime minister okayed the idea without thinking it through. Usually Hopkins intercepted and killed such ideas, but he had not been at Quebec, and Leahy, who had taken over that responsibility, was in a meeting when Morgenthau buttonholed the two leaders. Leahy, Hopkins, and others succeeded in getting FDR to scrap the idea. "You will never get your program through on Germany," Leahy told Morgenthau at lunch one day. "You know I was opposed to it at Quebec."[2]

Along the same line, Leahy was named to a committee to consider the use of Lend Lease to Britain after the German surrender. Leahy wanted no part of the problem, which he considered political and not military. It was "being handled by the Secretary of the Treasury, and . . . the Joint Chiefs of Staff should not permit themselves to become involved. . . ."

Because Leahy was by this time almost completely a presidential assistant, a post which had its political ramifications, no matter how he objected, he still got the job on the committee, working with Morgenthau and acting Secretary of State Edward R. Stettinius. After a month of talks, the committee recommended, for planning purposes only, that approximately 80 percent of the British request for $6.76 billion be approved. When the final report was typed three days later, Leahy noted that a vital paragraph, the core of the American reservation, had been omitted:

> It is understood that the recommended program does not constitute any commitment but that all schedules, both munitions and non-munitions, are subject to the changing demands of strategy as well as to supply considerations and the usual considerations of procurement and allocation.

He never did discover why that paragraph had been left out, but he had a nasty suspicion that someone was trying to extend the American commitment to Britain beyond reasonable limits.

In any case, the president approved the committee report. But the problem of Lend Lease would rise again. The law was ambiguous, and no one knew whether the president could legally authorize *any* expenditures for purposes other than that of defeating the enemy. Leahy had objected earlier:

> "Mr. President, I know almost nothing about lend-lease, and I don't want to go to jail when they begin, after the war is over, to investigate what has been done with this money."
>
> "If you go to jail," replied FDR, "I'll be going along too, and we will have good company."[3]

As it happened, no one went to jail, and Lend Lease went on to become a major cause of controversy between the United States and Russia after the defeat of Germany.

But more important than these occasional events, there was the continuing problem of FDR's tendency to act as his own State Department, and to cut Cordell Hull and others out from knowledge of affairs which had great diplomatic and political significance. Leahy had known this tendency of the president when he had been ambassador in Vichy, but he had no choice but to go along with the system. Now, however, close to the power, he deplored the tendency and believed it to be self-defeating and dangerous. After much argument, he persuaded FDR to let him establish his own direct liaison with the State Department. Roosevelt grumbled a good bit, but he went along and appointed Russian expert and linguist Charles E. Bohlen to the job.

Every morning, Chip Bohlen would come to Leahy's office to be briefed on whatever traffic from and to Stalin, Chiang Kai-shek, and Churchill had transpired during the night. This information Bohlen would pass on to senior officials in Foggy Bottom who needed to know. George Elsey, who was a Map Room watch officer and who later became a presidential assistant under Truman, believed the action in getting Chip Bohlen as liaison with State was one of Leahy's most important contributions, and one that the press never gave him credit for.[4]

While these matters were going on, the days moved inexorably toward election day. Thomas Dewey was running strong on the theme of the "tired old men," and "we can do it better." Leahy was close to the campaign as it neared its end, although he was not part of it. He simply accompanied FDR to do his duty as the president's principal military advisor. In the wonderful way of the Roosevelt administration, he had to do a lot of other things as well.

Election day that year fell on 7 November. Leahy accompanied FDR and his party on a political tour of New England. The train left Union Station in Washington at 10:30 on the evening of 3 November, with Leahy the only military officer aboard with the exception of the two navy doctors McIntire and Bruenn.

During the entire time, Leahy rode in the *Ferdinand Magellan*, working on messages received from the Map Room, cocking an eye and an ear at Roosevelt chatting affably with dignitaries who came on board to be seen with the great man and to make sure he remembered them. Fortunately there was not much Map Room traffic that required any action on the part of the president.

That evening, Roosevelt gave a major speech in the baseball park of Boston. Afterwards, as the party bosses were evaluating the campaign and the effects of the Boston speech, Leahy listened in awe.

> All the others expressed pleasure at the results of the day's work and all of them, with the possible exception of Mr. [Robert] Hannegan [Chairman of the Democratic National Committee], were assured that Massachusetts and Connecticut will give their votes to the President on Tuesday, next. I am so completely lacking in political campaigning experience as to be unable to formulate any opinion.

The next day, when the party reached Hyde Park, Leahy accompanied FDR to the house, he added:

> This, my first experience on a political campaign of any kind, has been extremely interesting and informative regarding the actual functioning of an important part of representative government as it is conducted in this year A. D. All other members of the President's party were experts of long experience, which provided me a splendid opportunity to observe methods and procedure.

As Leahy openly showed his bewilderment, FDR said to him, "Bill, you don't know a goddamned thing about politics, do you?"

Leahy grinned. "That, Mr. President, is the highest compliment you ever paid me."[5]

Election day in Hyde Park was cold and bright. At nine that evening the dining room was cleared. It had been fitted with two ticker-tape machines and a radio. Seated together at a table, Leahy and Roosevelt checked the returns as they came in.

The President did not at any time appear to have any apprehension as to the final result, and when favorable reports came from cities in northern New York State, he seemed to be sure of his re-election. A large number of relatives and personal friends were present in the house and participated in a midnight supper prepared under the direction of Mrs. Roosevelt.

Leahy stayed up checking returns and tabulating them until about 2:00 A.M. When he retired, he was unable to sleep, the result, he felt, of an injudicious cup of coffee. When FDR came up at 3:45, he evidently heard Leahy moving about for he stuck his head in the room to say: "I've been waiting four hours for that son of a bitch in New York to make up his mind and admit he's defeated. He should have known it hours ago, but he won't say anything."[6]

The next morning, after a sleepless night, Leahy flew to Washington to act as an honorary pall bearer in the funeral of Field Marshal Sir John Dill, who had died of a lingering illness. The rites were held in the National Cathedral in Washington, Bishop Angus Dunn conducting the Episcopal service. Interment followed in Arlington National Cemetery. Dill had been so universally respected by the Joint Chiefs and members of their staff that his widow and the American authorities agreed that the most suitable resting place for Sir John was in Arlington. He is the only non-American military officer to lie there amid his many American friends.

When the president returned to Washington, life went on as the war moved ahead. On 27 November, he accepted the resignation of Secretary of State Cordell Hull, who had long wanted to step down. Ed Stettinius was named in his place.

More and more of Leahy's time was taken up with things removed from war strategy. In addition to Lend Lease, he began discussing with FDR and coping with problems of tax policies, commercial aviation, and reconversion.

In mid-December, Congress finally passed the bill approving five-star rank for four naval and four army officers, and on 15 December, the president signed Leahy's commission as Fleet Admiral, making him the highest ranking officer in the United States military forces. It seemed to Leahy a "lucky landing after a half century's service in the national defense."★

★Order of seniority and date of rank:
1. Fleet Admiral William D. Leahy, USN, 15 December 1944.
2. General of the Army George C. Marshall, USA, 16 December 1944.
3. Fleet Admiral Ernest J. King, USN, 17 December 1944.
4. General of the Army Douglas MacArthur, USA, 18 December 1944.
5. Fleet Admiral Chester W. Nimitz, USN, 19 December 1944.
6. General of the Army Dwight D. Eisenhower, USA, 20 December 1944.
7. General of the Army Henry H. Arnold, USAAF, 21 December 1944.
The navy submitted only three names at that time, unable to decide between Halsey and Spruance. Forrestal left the choice up to King, who finally picked Halsey on the ground that he was the better known. Spruance was compensated by the same arrangements that were made for the five-star officers: full pay and allowances for the rest of their lives. When they finally concluded their military careers, they remained "on active duty without assignment." Halsey's

The day he became a fleet admiral, Leahy entered a brief essay in his journal, a kind of manifesto revealing his conviction that the United States should not get involved in European affairs. He called it "Atlantic Charter."

After pointing out how strategists in the press and on the radio castigated the government for supporting Tito or for not supporting him; for backing Franco in Spain or not backing him; or for failing to back "Mahatma Ghandi in his revolt against our principal ally, Great Britain," he saw a strong movement, inspired in part by the press, "to involve the United States in European politics."

> From such information as is at present available, it seems to me that the interests and future safety of America point to the necessity of this government's going on record with a public announcement that we are committed and devoted to concerted action by the Allied Nations which will act to prevent international war, but that we do not intend to sacrifice American soldiers and sailors in order to impose any government on any people, or to adjust political differences in Europe or Asia, except to act against an aggressor with the purpose of preventing an international war.

Leahy, of course, was not the only one who favored a return to isolation after the war as the best way to avoid American involvement in another one. At this stage, he did not recognize that the two super powers would fall out as the USSR pursued an expansionist policy. He would learn in the months ahead.

The remainder of the year was routine in Leahy's life. He was alarmed by the German counterattack in the Battle of the Bulge, but he felt that Eisenhower could probably handle it. Christmas he spent with his family, and he thought it was probably the last in which his grandson, aged eight, would believe in Santa Claus. Like his sister, Bobby was probably putting it over on the old man, for Santa brought more presents than grandfathers did.

To close out the year, Harry Hopkins wrote him a note which reveals a closer relationship than is generally credited between the two men.

Dec 21, 1944
Dear Bill:
    If I have seemed facetious about your promotion—this note will tell you that I am not. No one knows better than I of your devoted service to the President and your country. You deserve much from both of them.
    My warmest Christmas greeting!

Harry Hopkins[7]

---

date of rank as fleet admiral was 11 December 1945. In 1950 the army received a fifth General of the Army when Omar Bradley was promoted to that grade with the date of rank of 20 September.

Leahy began the new year with his usual summary of the strategic situation in the world. He saw the defeat of Germany and Japan as certain, but looked for a long war against Japan. "The Japanese are facing an inevitable defeat, but because of their fanatical savage resistance to the death, there is little prospect of obtaining from them an unconditional surrender within the year that lies ahead." He was undoubtedly pleased to be wrong in that prediction.

January 1945 began with preparations for Roosevelt's fourth inauguration on 20 January, which took up a good deal of time. And, as soon as it was over, it would be time to set forth again for yet another conference, this time at Yalta in the Crimea.

The British demanded that the Combined Chiefs get together for a preconference meeting at Malta. They were prepared to challenge Eisenhower's authority. Ever since the Battle of the Bulge, they had been leaking rumors that inept American generalship had nearly brought disaster and that the day had been saved only by the brilliant intervention of Field Marshal Sir Bernard Montgomery. In what the Americans felt was an egregious case of *ego elephantiasis*, Monty now demanded that Eisenhower's dual drive against Germany be halted. Instead, Bradley's primarily American push in the south would be downgraded and made to support Montgomery's campaign in the north. Montgomery sold this idea to Brooke, and at Malta, the British were prepared to give the Americans a very hard time.

Leahy was spared from accompanying the members of the JCS on the advance trip to Malta, for FDR wanted him on the crossing with him. It was a relief, for he believed that Eisenhower's plan was sound and that the British were dead wrong. In any case, the Americans were not disposed to change. In the last analysis, they had the big battalions.

In mid-January, Stalin redeemed a promise and began a winter offensive against the Germans which drove them steadily back in spite of Hitler's order not to yield a foot of ground. This news cheered an otherwise cold and gray day on which Roosevelt once again took the oath of office as President of the United States.

Inauguration day, 20 January, displayed a dull, gray sky above the freshly packed snow that had fallen the day before. In a moment of thoughtfulness, Roosevelt had arranged for Leahy's granddaughter Louise to attend the inaugural ceremonies. With her grandfather she took part in the church service held in the East Room, and then sat on the portico as Harry S. Truman and Franklin D. Roosevelt were sworn in.

Neither she nor her grandfather knew that FDR was suffering severe chest pains. After completing his address, he left on the arm of his son James. As soon as they were out of sight, FDR told James to bring him a stiff drink. Gradually the pains subsided. FDR refused to send for Dr. Bruenn. Probably if the doctor had known of the attack, Roosevelt would not have gone to Yalta.

On 22 January, at 10:30 in the evening, limousines from the White House arrived at trainside under the Bureau of Engraving and Printing, and the president and his party got aboard. In addition to the usual crowd—Pa Watson, Wilson Brown, Ross McIntire, Steve Early, and Leahy—there were some new faces. Ed Flynn, of the Democratic National Committee, was going. And so was Jimmy Byrnes. And in an unprecedented move, the president was taking his daughter Anna Boettiger on the entire trip. Eleanor Roosevelt wanted to come, but FDR turned a deaf ear to that suggestion. He could not relax with anyone but "Sis," so Anna went.

> If my observation is correct, [wrote Lieutenant (jg) Rigdon, an assistant to the Naval Attaché] no other member of his family meant so much to him in his final two years of life. I have heard Admiral McIntire say that Anna's presence "was better for the President than any medicine." She was a joy to all of us on this trip, always genial, never conscious of the special privileges she might have had as the President's daughter.[8]

Commander Bruenn was, of course, a member of the party, and there were the usual lesser lights and secret service people. Harry Hopkins was already in Europe, talking to Churchill and then trying in vain to mollify de Gaulle, who had not been invited to the Yalta Conference.

After chatting with the president, Ross McIntire, and Jimmy Byrnes until 11:30, Leahy had to turn out early the next morning when the train reached Newport News, where the cruiser *Quincy* was waiting for them. As usual FDR occupied the captain's day cabin. Leahy, however, was displaced. Anna Boettiger explained in a journal she kept on the trip.

> He [FDR] has the Capt's q'trs on starboard side of ship; explained to me he always prefers starbrd side, tho, because this is a flagship he shld be in admiral's quarters (identical) on port side. So I have Adm's qrters! Adm Leahy shld have these but they don't want a female in quarters below because there are more men there & they like to run around in underpants—so I'm told![9]

The crossing was uneventful but rough. Relays of escorts met them, and out-of-sight rescue ships stood ready to come to the assistance of the *Quincy* if need arose. Their course took them south of Bermuda and Madeira, a route giving the best promise of good weather. Movies were shown in flag country every night.

As they were making their way across the Atlantic, FDR had to deal with an unpleasant situation of his own making. When he had dumped Henry Wallace as his running mate in 1944, he had promised him a cabinet post. In January, Wallace claimed that prize, demanding to be named secretary of commerce. The problem was that FDR already had a secretary of commerce, the highly competent and irascible Jesse H. Jones. And Jones wanted to keep his job. When, on the day of the inauguration, Jones received his letter of dismissal, he was furious. He scornfully rejected the ambassadorship that FDR offered as a reward and made the whole affair public. This action made FDR look inept and made the going very difficult for Wallace in his confirmation hearings.

Leahy marveled that a man who had presided over the Senate for four years could not get a majority of his own party to vote for him. He thought FDR ought to cut his losses, and if Wallace could not be confirmed, accept that judgment of the Senate. In his opinion, FDR had better things to do than "be bothered by the personal troubles of any individual." In the end, Wallace was confirmed, but only after FDR had removed an important agency from the Commerce Department.

The next day, Leahy once again helped Roosevelt celebrate his birthday, his sixty-third, and last.

Messages flew back and forth on the desirability of Yalta as a conference site. When the *Quincy* sent a message, it had to be passed to a destroyer, which would move off over the horizon before transmitting so that the location of the *Quincy* would not be revealed to snooping U-boats. Harry Hopkins sent a message from London:

> Have had very satisfactory visit London. Leaving for Paris tomorrow. Churchill well. He says that if we had spent ten years in research, we could not have found a worse place in the world than Magneto [Yalta] but he feels that he can survive it by bringing an adequate supply of whiskey. He claims it is good for typhus and deadly on lice which thrive in those parts. Sorry to hear that Watson seasick as usual. Regards to all. Harry.[10]

As it turned out, Mike Reilly had gone ahead to inspect the facilities at Yalta and had given his approval after the Russians had done a prodigious job of restoration and American naval doctors had supervised the fumigation. Averell Harriman later told the author that he never saw an insect of any sort at Yalta.

The *Quincy* entered Grand Harbour at Valetta, Malta, on 2 February. Ten minutes after she arrived, Harry Hopkins and Ed Stettinius came on board, followed by British and American VIPs. There was a small luncheon in the president's cabin which included Churchill, his daughter Sarah Oliver, Foreign Minister Anthony Eden, Stettinius, Byrnes, Anna Boettiger, and Leahy. As usual, Churchill dominated the conversation, talking "about English problems in war time, the high purpose of the so-called Atlantic Charter, and his complete devotion to the principles enunciated in America's Declaration of Independence."

After luncheon, Roosevelt was taken on a drive around the island, which left Leahy free to preside at a meeting of the Combined Chiefs. Strategy against Germany was finally settled. Both Bradley and Montgomery would continue their campaigns, but Montgomery would get more of the available supplies. It was a clear case of the squeaking hinge getting the oil. And Montgomery was the loudest squeaker.

At 8:00 P.M., according to Leahy, he dined with Roosevelt and others in the president's cabin. This routine comment of his conceals the confusion Anna had to cope with after she had returned from sightseeing, as she noted.

> Back again to the ship where I tried frantically to find out how many people there would be for dinner. For both lunch and dinner I had to arrange for two messes—one in FDR's cabin and one in mine. Each time I made wild guesses in advance so that the mess crew could get started with the cooking—and was lucky enough to overguess by only 2 or 3.
>
> Sarah said she knew she was supposed to dine on the Orion [HMS *Orion*, a British cruiser]. So, I invited her (and Randolph Ch[urchill], son of the prime minister], who had flown in from Yugoslavia while we had tea) to come over for a drink. To my horror I found meetings going on in both cabins, so wondered where I would offer my drinks. But, finally, at 7:30 the meetings broke up; I got to Father on dinner arrangements and all was smoothed out— except that some Britishers were to be invited for dinner and Randolph was to be excluded as he annoys his father! Much embarassed I arranged to have Randy invited to eat with Tommy Thompson (the P.M.'s aide) at the mess in my cabin. But, Randy, very tactfully, had a couple of drinks with us and then explained that he and Tommy had a pressing engagement on their ship! Father had ordered cocktails for his mess at 8:15, as the P.M. had insisted he had to have his bath between the meeting and dinner. So, I told everyone including Sarah and Eden and Stettinius that they should stay in my cabin until then as I wanted Father to have a little restful time to himself—explaining that the P.M. had had a 1½ hr nap and FDR had been going strong since 9:30 without a break. To my great annoyance (and Ross's) Eden and Stettinius sneaked out at 8 o'clock while I was mixing someone a drink, and went straight to Father's cabin. And the P.M. didn't show up until almost 8:45![11]

After dinner, the party left the *Quincy* and drove to Luqa Airfield, where they boarded their planes for Yalta. The "Sacred Cow" for the president and his immediate group was a brand new C-54, containing a private sleeping cabin for FDR, and bunks which were occupied by senior officers, as well as by Hopkins and Anna. The rest of the passengers had to sit up.*

Finding that his plane wasn't scheduled to depart until about 3:30 A.M.,

---

*The plane Roosevelt used earlier in connection with the Teheran Conference had been Eisenhower's personal plane, and it, too, was sometimes called the "Sacred Cow." The one Roosevelt used to fly to and from Yalta was the first of the aircraft specifically reserved for the exclusive use of the president. After Roosevelt's death, Truman used it until it was replaced by a DC-6 which he named *Independence*. Other names have followed, but now the president's plane is known as "Air Force One." There are three identically equipped 707s in the presidential fleet; the one the president happens to fly is always "Air Force One." He usually uses one with the tail number 27000, which in the mid-70s replaced 26000, the aircraft which brought Kennedy's body back from Dallas to Washington in 1963.

FDR turned in for a good night's sleep before taking off. Leahy and the others followed suit.

The "Sacred Cow" reached Saki at 12:15 the following afternoon, and as Churchill had not yet arrived, Roosevelt chatted aboard his plane with Molotov who came to pay his respects. After Churchill got there, the two leaders inspected a guard of honor and then set off for a ninety-mile drive over curving mountain roads. Russian guards, both men and women, lined the way every few yards, standing in frozen silence as the dignitaries passed.

There was one stop en route, a brief one for the Americans, as FDR was anxious to push on, and a lengthy one for the British so that Churchill could partake of the vodka, caviar, and other delicacies amply provided by their hosts.

About 6:00 that evening the Roosevelt party reached its destination. Leahy was impressed:

> . . . we are housed in Livadia Palace, an enormous residence built by the last Czar, Nicholas II, prior to the first World War, and frequently occupied by the Royal Family before their murder by the Bolsheviks. . . .
>
> Livadia has been completely renovated during the past three weeks since its selection as headquarters for the U.S. delegation. Prior to that, the buildings were as left by the Germans in the spring of 1943; i.e., in complete disrepair; there were no furnishings [and] the grounds were in equally bad condition. Under the direction of the Soviet Security organization renovation was accomplished. Hotel staffs from Moscow were installed. All furniture and equipment, cars and chauffeurs, have been imported from Moscow and other cities or from local sanitoria and rest homes. No one coming in today can visualize fully the gigantic task the Soviets have accomplished in less than a month to accommodate this conference. The buildings naturally were not built for hotel service. The Soviets have done their best to adapt them to the needs of the large party we have brought in.

Roosevelt was given a large room on the ground floor, and Leahy had an adjoining one. King and Marshall were lodged in the Czarina's quarters, and Harry Hopkins, who was deathly ill, had another room on the ground floor. A few lucky others had private rooms, but except for the top level few, generals and colonels found themselves in dormitory type rooms and waiting in line for the few bathrooms. At first the bathroom shortage didn't seem too bad, for just outside the palace were plenty of bushes for sheltered relief. But, unfortunately, Russian guards refused to allow anyone to go into the bushes despite best gestures of explanation.

When they arrived at the Livadia Palace, they found cheerful fires blazing in every fireplace. A maître d'hôtel, with many bows from the waist, welcomed them, addressing President Roosevelt as "Your Excellency," in apparently the only English he knew. Anna wanted to serve martinis; she found the gin all right, but there was no ice to be had. Fortunately, when they sat down to dine, the vodka was plentiful and the caviar delicious. The dinner was excellent, and the party, tired from the arduous journey, was glad to turn in on completion of dinner.

The story of the negotiations and discussions of Yalta has been told many times, and another summary, even in Leahy's words, would add little to our understanding. He published in *I Was There* his account of the day-to-day proceedings.

"Bill," FDR had said, "I wish you would attend all these political meetings in order that we may have someone in whom I have full confidence who will remember everything that we have done."

The reason for Roosevelt's request was simple. With Harry Hopkins so sick that he could not participate except at the plenary sessions, Leahy was the only one who knew enough to sit by the president's side at the sessions. It seems clear that Leahy had more reservations about the Russians than FDR did. Several times the admiral protested, and FDR would answer, "I know, Bill, but it's the best I can do."

According to Admiral J. Victor Smith, who, as a commander, was one of Leahy's aides at the time of Yalta, the Russians contrasted their advances against the Germans with the recent Anglo–American reverses in December in the Battle of the Bulge. Thus, the Soviets were able to exploit their later victories to advantage in the negotiations. Also, FDR believed that on many things, he had "given my word to Stalin as a gentleman and we're going through with it."[12]

The absence of Harry Hopkins inevitably harmed the conference as far as the Americans were concerned, for not even Leahy could put objections to the president as strongly as "Harry the Hop" could. And then, again according to Smith, Chip Bohlen, FDR's interpreter, had to fill Hopkins in immediately after each session. This put an added burden on Bohlen and prevented him from closer liaison with the State Department people who were there.

The principal issues of the conference were the future government of Poland, governments of the Balkan nations, reparations, voting in the United Nations, the partition of Germany, and Russian participation in the war against Japan. Many of the agreements were paperthin, and some were so fragile that they collapsed as soon as the conferees went their separate ways.

The most urgent and most dangerous problem was Poland. The Soviets backed one group of Poles for the future rulers of that devastated country and the Anglo-Saxons backed another. Correspondence between London, Moscow, and Washington proposed solutions. Leahy called the problem, in a draft message to Stalin, "one of the most important matters facing the United Nations."[13]*

---

*The United Nations, of course, had not yet been formed. Roosevelt and Churchill often referred to the countries allied against Germany and Japan as the United Nations.

But Stalin gave no sign of yielding to correspondence, and the concessions at Yalta were not interpreted by the Russians as they were by the Americans and the British. But the Polish problem was not settled during the administrations of either President Roosevelt or President Truman, and as long as Leahy was in the service of both presidents, the Polish question, like King Charles's head, keeps turning up in his official and unofficial papers.

Another major topic of discussion was the Soviet entry into the war against Japan. On 23 January, while Leahy had been with the president crossing the Atlantic, Marshall had prepared a lengthy memorandum for the president strongly recommending a firm commitment by the Russians to enter the war in the Far East.

> Russia's entry at as early a date as possible consistent with her ability to engage in offensive operations is necessary to provide maximum assistance to our Pacific operations. The U.S. will provide maximum support possible without interfering with our main effort against Japan.

One paragraph of the memo notes the difficulty of dealing with the Russians, and it foreshadows problems to come. There is a pencil mark beside that paragraph in Leahy's copy of the document, but whether it has any significance is impossible to say.

> The working efficiency of U.S. and U.S.S.R. collaboration to date has been low, even though there appears to have been quick agreement on general principles pertaining to military problems on the highest level. This inefficiency is largely attribual [sic] to administrative delays on the part of the Russians and a reluctance on staff levels to exchange with the U.S. the information essential to the carrying out of broad decisions.[14]

Although he did not believe Russian help was necessary in the war against Japan, Leahy was generally ready to go along, especially since the president ruled in favor of Marshall's ideas.

> I personally . . . did not feel that Russian participation in the Japanese war was necessary. The Army did. Roosevelt sided with the Army. After getting the green light from their Commander-in-Chief Stalin, the Russian Chiefs of Staff gave every indication of cooperating fully and agreed to all the specific requests made of them.[15]

In the end, Leahy noted that Stalin promised to enter the war within two or three months, although he named conditions, conditions which largely came out of China's interests. It was to be FDR's job to get Chiang Kai-shek to agree to those terms.

Still, all in all, nearly everyone in the American camp was optimistic. Since American leaders have frequently been accused of "selling out to Russia at Yalta," it is noteworthy that, while FDR and Hopkins were highly optimistic about the results of the conference, Leahy had a good many reservations. He was not at all sure that the severity of the conditions to be imposed on Germany would not come back in time to haunt the victors.

> At the conclusion of this momentous conference of three nations that expect to administer in the near future a total defeat to Germany, I am deeply impressed by the unanimous and amicable agreement of the President, the Prime Minister of Great Britain, and Marshal Stalin of Russia on the action that shall be taken to destroy Germany as a military power. . . .
>
> While the German nation has in this barbarous war of conquest deserved all the punishment that can be administered, the proposed peace seems to me a frightening "sowing of dragon's teeth" that carries an appalling war of revenge at some time in the distant future.

He also foresaw many other problems, and he was gloomily not at all certain that the alliance with the Soviet Union would survive the end of the war. Certainly there had been enough clues during the conference that the USSR was determined to have her own way in eastern Europe, regardless of whatever the British and Americans felt about it. He believed that grave dangers lay ahead.

> One result of enforcing the peace terms accepted at this conference will be to make Russia the dominant power in Europe, which in itself carries a certainty of future international disagreements and prospects of another war.

Then, too, he was worried about the

> agreed fiction that France is a great nation, and its inclusion in the council of the Association with a full veto power . . . will, in my opinion, destroy the effectiveness of the United Nations Association in preventing international war.
>
> It is difficult to see how this veto power, . . . can have any other effect than to cause discord with the other small nations, disagreement among the three powerful nations, and finally cause a disintegration of the Association to Preserve Peace.

Even at that time, Leahy had few illusions about the Soviet Union and France, and those that remained didn't last long.

On the afternoon of 11 February, the American delegation departed the Livadia Palace for the drive to Sevastopol. Sharing a car with Captain Clark, Leahy's other aide, and Dr. Bruenn, Leahy immediately had to make a choice of whether to freeze or die of asphyxiation. A gasoline leak filled the interior of the car with toxic fumes. By tearing out the curtains of the open limousine, the sufferers froze but were able to breathe. Finally they reached their destination where the communication ship USS *Catoctin* was waiting for them alongside a sea wall. Throughout the conference she had served as a secure link with the outside world for the Americans. Connected by land wire to Yalta, she had handled radio communications between FDR and the Map Room, so that the Germans could not eavesdrop. Neither could the Russians, for that matter.

The *Catoctin* seemed like home to the weary travelers as they enjoyed American food after the elaborate Russian fare with endless rounds of toasts in potent Russian vodka. With a restful night behind them, the president's party was up early for the thousand-mile flight to Ismalia in Egypt. From there they went to the Great Bitter Lake, a part of the Suez Canal complex, where the *Quincy* was waiting for them.

Before returning to the United States, Roosevelt wanted to confer with certain leaders of the area, and he picked King Farouk of Egypt, Emperor Haile Selassie of Ethiopia, and King Ibn Saud of Saudi Arabia. He looked forward to those conversations, but there was a drawback. First, Roosevelt was so deathly tired from the days of the Yalta discussions that he had to make great efforts to receive his royal visitors properly. Then, Pa Watson had frightened everyone by suffering a heart attack aboard the *Catoctin*. FDR had brought him along aboard the "Sacred Cow" to the *Quincy*, but no one knew what the outcome would be. Now Dr. Bruenn had two cardiac patients to worry about.

At 11:30 on the morning of 13 February, Leahy was on the landing to receive King Farouk and a small retinue. Accompanying the king was Leahy's old friend, Pinckney Tuck, who had been his first secretary in Vichy and was now minister to Egypt. The ride out to the *Quincy* in the admiral's barge was quickly and smoothly accomplished.

Roosevelt was seated behind a 5-inch gun mount as he received the young king. A small circular table, a few Persian rugs, and some wicker chairs furnished the impromptu, open-air receiving room. Farouk, who wore the uniform of an admiral of the fleet, listened politely as FDR rambled on about future trade with Egypt. His Majesty was guest of honor at luncheon and was sent on his way bearing a framed copy of FDR's first inaugural address and the promise of a C-47 (DC-3) as a memento of the occasion.

At 3:30 Leahy escorted the king ashore and returned at 5:00 with Haile Selassie. There ensued a long private conversation between the emperor and the president, which FDR told Leahy the following morning was vague and dealt with disposition of territory recaptured from Italy.

Bright and early the next morning, Anna was sent ashore to go shopping until she was told to return. The reason: FDR was going to receive King Ibn Saud that day. As he told his daughter, "The king is a Moslem, a true believer. He has lots of wives. However, the Moslem will not permit women in his presence when he is talking to other men. Sis, when he sees such a woman, he confiscates her."[16]

As the USS *Murphy*, which had picked up the king and his retinue at Jidda, came alongside the *Quincy* she presented an amazing sight.

> The destroyer's decks, usually stripped, were covered with Oriental carpets and gold-gilded chairs were scattered about the decks. King Ibn Saud sat with great natural dignity and charm in one of the gilded chairs on the forward part of the destroyer's superstructure deck. The various other members of his party,

dressed in their flowing robes and accessories, were standing about the decks. The King's guard, with rifles, scimitars and long swords very much in evidence, were lined up—single file—along the starboard side of the destroyer's forecastle, facing us in the QUINCY. They were, no doubt, every bit as much amazed as we were at what was transpiring.[17]

Ibn Saud was an old man, crippled by arthritis, but he had great dignity. When he was helped aboard the *Quincy*, Roosevelt received him on deck just as he had the previous royal visitors. Ibn Saud admired the light, armless wheel chair in which the president had come on deck, and FDR, who had a spare aboard, gave him one. At luncheon, special dishes of lamb, rice, and grapefruit had been prepared, and the king took two helpings of everything. According to Leahy he was especially delighted with the grapefruit.

The two leaders discussed the age-old problems of Palestine, and Roosevelt tried to persuade Ibn Saud to take a sympathetic position on possible settlement of Jews in that area. The king replied "that he had no dislike for the Israelites but that they had recently treated the Arabs very badly who had been residents of Palestine for generations, and if the Israelites did not behave better he intended to throw them into the sea."[18]

> It was a wonderful privilege to be closely associated at their first meeting with two masters of political leadership, both physically crippled by age, both in a few hours acquiring a lasting friendly appreciation of each other, and both irreplaceable to their people until slow moving time shall again in their countries produce comparable leaders.

At 4:00 that afternoon, half an hour after Ibn Saud had left, the *Quincy* got underway and passed through the remainder of the Suez Canal, and the following morning, a little before 11:00, moored at a buoy in Alexandria harbor.

Although FDR hoped for a quiet, restful day, it was not to be. All kinds of high officials came on board, Secretary Stettinius in the van. About 12:30 Churchill arrived, and he and FDR were closeted together for half an hour in private conversation. At luncheon, which was to mark the last meeting of these two great leaders, Roosevelt entertained, in addition to the PM, Randolph Churchill and his sister, Sarah Oliver, Anna Boettiger, John G. Winant, American ambassador to Great Britain, Harry Hopkins, and Leahy. "It was a pleasant, social gathering in the President's cabin, and I do not recall that affairs of state intruded into the conversation."[19]

After their British guests had departed, the *Quincy* set course for Algiers. There Harry Hopkins left the ship to fly home. He disliked sea voyages, and he wanted to get back to the United States as quickly as possible for treatment. The parting of Roosevelt and Hopkins was cool, for FDR had been depending on him to write an account of Yalta and to help prepare an address to Congress. When Hopkins came to say good bye, FDR gave him a quick handshake and returned to the papers he was working on. It was a pity, for they never saw each other again.

The *Quincy's* homeward voyage was marked by sadness. Two days after they left Algiers, Pa Watson died, on 20 February, of a cerebral hemorrhage. His staff had never seen Roosevelt so shaken by the death of a close friend.

The *Quincy* reached Newport News on the evening of 27 February, where the president's special train was waiting to take the party back to Washington. Pa Watson's body was carried in a baggage car, and the next day, Leahy and others, including the president, who watched from a car, attended the burial service in Arlington National Cemetery.

It was a saddened group that returned to Washington, but there was work to be done, for the war was rushing to its conclusion. To his relief, Leahy had no large part in the preparation of the report to Congress; most of the work had been done by Sam Rosenman, who had joined the ship for the return voyage.

But even as President Roosevelt was trying to impress Congress with how splendidly he and Winnie and Uncle Joe had got along at Yalta, came disturbing news of an event, one of the first of the sort that were beginning to poison relations between the USSR and the West.

As the Red Army advanced through Poland, it overran Nazi Stalags—prisoner of war camps. In some of them were captured Americans, and soon reports began to filter out that the Russians were making no distinction in treatment between released Americans and captured Germans. On 4 March, Roosevelt hotly protested to Stalin.

The Russian leader replied that early difficulties had been cleared up.

> . . . whenever new groups of American prisoners of war are discovered steps are taken at once to help them and to evacuate them to assembly points for subsequent repatriation. According to the information available to the Soviet Government, there is now no accumulation of U.S. prisoners of war in Polish territory or in other areas liberated by the Red Army, because all of them, with the exception of individual sick men who are in hospital, have been sent to the assembly point in Odessa, where 1,200 U.S. prisoners of war have arrived so far and the arrival of the remainder is expected shortly.[20]

But Stalin refused to permit American planes to fly to points in Poland to pick up the POWs. Leahy interpreted his refusal as another example of Stalin's unwillingness to allow *any* western observers to see what was really going on in Poland.

Then there was the problem in early March of the attempt of German forces in Italy to surrender in the field. Although it was purely a military affair on a front in which the Russians were not engaged, the USSR was informed. When they demanded to have one of their own officers present at the discussions, FDR turned them down on the advice of Ambassador Harriman.

Harriman rightly believed that giving in to the Russians on that matter would only mean that they would demand more later.

That was the occasion for Stalin to explode. He accused the western allies of bad faith and that negotiations had taken place and had

> ended in an agreement with the Germans, whereby the German Commander on the Western Front, Marshal Kesselring, is to open the front to the Anglo-American troops and let them move east, while the British and Americans have promised, in exchange, to ease the armistice terms for the Germans.

Leahy drafted the reply for the president, refuting Stalin's charges point by point, and in words as close "to a rebuke as is permitted in diplomatic exchanges between states," concluded:

> Finally I would say this, it would be one of the great tragedies of history if at the very moment of the victory, now within our grasp, such distrust, such lack of faith should prejudice the entire undertaking after the colossal losses of life, material and treasure involved.
>
> Frankly I cannot avoid a feeling of bitter resentment toward your informers, whoever they are, for such vile misrepresentations of my actions or those of my trusted subordinates. [21]

Feeling he had gone far enough, Stalin let the matter drop, but as victory approached, suspicions were replacing the common purpose of earlier years, and at the next meeting of the Big Three in Potsdam, while apparently cordial relations were preserved, the three leaders were maneuvering for positions of strength in the postwar world.

It was evident that Uncle Joe was not one to give his trust when any ground for suspicion remained. And under the system by which he lived, suspicion was everywhere. FDR might have gone to Yalta with the idea that he could appeal to Uncle Joe as a friend and that the Russian leader could be influenced by friendship. But subsequent actions were quickly putting an end to any such illusions.

Just before he left for Warm Springs on 29 March FDR held a conference with Ed Stettinius, Chip Bohlen, and Under Secretary Robert Dunn over Soviet intransigence in Poland. Leahy, who attended the meeting, never expected anything else.

> The Department [of State] is very much concerned with the possible future of complications incident to what appears to be a determination of the Soviet Government to control any government that may be formed in Western Poland. At Yalta I expected that the Soviets were determined to do just that, and it does not appear likely that the messages sent today will have any beneficial effect.

When the meeting was over, Leahy accompanied Roosevelt to the south entrance of the White House where the limousine was waiting.

He was cheerful, as usual, and as he came to the door to get in his car, I remarked, "Mr. President, it's very nice that you are leaving for a vacation. It is nice for us too, because when you are away, we have much more leisure than when you are here."

Roosevelt laughed and replied, "That's all right, Bill. Have a good time while I'm gone because when I come back I'm going to unload a lot of stuff on you, and then you'll have to work very hard." That was the last time I saw Franklin Roosevelt alive.[22]

About that time Byrnes resigned as director of war mobilization, and Judge Fred Vinson took his place. In the Pacific, the Joint Chiefs finally accepted the impossibility of subordinating either Nimitz or MacArthur to the other and in preparation for the expected invasion of Japan, decided to abandon the theater command. Instead they gave all naval forces to Nimitz and all ground forces to MacArthur. Leahy felt that decision was somewhat academic, for he did not expect that the United States would have to mount an invasion of Japan.

On April 12, the fleet admiral was sitting at home, having returned from at trip to Bath, Maine, where he had watched his granddaughter Louise christen

Louise Leahy with her grandfather at the launching of the USS *Turner* (DD 834) at Bath, Maine, 8 April 1945. (Courtesy, National Archives)

the new destroyer *Turner*. Turning on the radio, he heard a flash to the effect that President Roosevelt had died that afternoon of a cerebral hemorrhage. Greatly shocked and grieved, he later recorded:

> This world tragedy deprives the nation of its leader at a time when the war to preserve civilization is approaching its end with accelerated speed, and when a vital need for competent leadership in the making and preservation of world peace is at least seriously prejudiced by the passing of Franklin Roosevelt, who was a world figure of heroic proportions. His death is also a personal bereavement to me in the loss of a devoted friend whom I have known and admired for thirty-six years, since we first worked together in the first world war.
>
> One cannot yet see how the complicated critical business of the war and the peace can be carried forward by a new president who is completely inexperienced in international affairs.
>
> The captain of the team is gone, and we are all at loose ends and confused as to who may be capable of giving sage advice and counsel to the new leader in his handling of the staggering burdens of war and peace that he must carry.

But before writing those words, he hastened to the White House to offer what help he could, to express a few words of sympathy to Mrs. Roosevelt, and to witness the swearing in of Harry S. Truman as thirty-third president of the United States.

The next morning, President Truman held a conference with his military leaders, the two secretaries, and the members of the JCS. "I remained behind for a private talk after the others departed and was impressed with the president's expressed desire and intention to follow accurately the procedure established by Mr. Roosevelt."

Leahy was not long left with the impression that the new president would be a pale carbon of FDR. He soon learned that Harry Truman had ideas and a will of his own. Those who failed to make that adjustment did not remain long as members of the Truman administration.

Leahy attended all the ceremonies in connection with the funeral and interment of Franklin Roosevelt. He was in the party that met the body at Union Station and escorted it to the White House through a crowd estimated to contain about 300,000 people, many of them weeping. "I saw one who was hysterical." There followed the impressive funeral services in the East Room of the White House, where some two hundred mourners, public officials, both foreign and American, and close friends, heard Bishop Angus Dunn read, "'I am the Resurrection and the Life,' saith the Lord. . . ."

Harry Hopkins had flown in from the Mayo Clinic. He looked like death himself.

The train bearing the president's remains arrived at Hyde Park on the morning of 15 April, and in a simple ceremony, Franklin Delano Roosevelt was buried in the Rose Garden back of the house in which he had been born.

When the brief ceremonies were ended, we all returned to our trains at the Hyde Park station and departed for Washington where we arrived at 8:20 P.M., bringing to an end a long day that was for me full of sad memories, and that also for me probably was my last visit to the home of my friend who will live in history as one of our greatest presidents. He was a great gentleman and a true friend.

Next would come the task of fully briefing the new president, a task Leahy took very seriously indeed.

CHAPTER 16

# The New President

After others had finished briefing the new president on the morning of 13 April, President Truman asked Admiral Leahy to remain behind for a minute. He told the admiral he wanted him to continue as his chief of staff. Truman described the scene:

"Are you sure you want me, Mr. President," he asked. "I always say what's on my mind."

"I want the truth," I told him, "and I want the facts at all times. I want you to stay with me and always to tell me what's on your mind. You may not always agree with my decisions, but I know you will carry them out faithfully."

With Admiral Leahy in the White House, I felt that, whether they were good or bad, all the information and communications bearing on the war would reach me promptly. Furthermore, I felt convinced that he would see that I got the facts without suppression or censorship from any source.

The admiral looked at me with a warm twinkle in his eyes.

"You have my pledge," he told me. "You can count on me."[1]

While Leahy agreed to remain, he had reservations. He had been close to Roosevelt, knew how he operated, and had considered him a friend. With Harry Truman it was all different. He had known him on Capitol Hill, but there had been only an official, not a personal, relationship. Also he had doubts about Truman's capacity to do the job. According to his son, Leahy at first considered Truman "a bush-leaguer." Later he told his aide, Commander Frank Pinney, "When I worked for Roosevelt and he asked for my opinion on some matter, I had no problems because I knew FDR would do whatever he wanted to do regardless of my views. With this fellow [Truman] when he asks for my advice and I give it, he goes right ahead and does it. I *have* to be right, and must be on top of events all the time."[2]

Such doubts were only temporary. As time went on Leahy came to appreciate the new president's habits of hard work. He realized that "there was going to be a terrific difference, but before he got through, he thought very highly of Truman. It surprised him."[3]

Harry Truman had a tremendous amount of work to do merely to acquaint himself with the major problems he had to face. As far as the war was concerned, only two people had the entire picture, Hopkins and Leahy. But Hopkins's information was not current because of his two-month stay at the Mayo Clinic. He did his best to brief the new president, but he was basically Roosevelt's man, and he was to ill to serve the new president on any permanent basis. He was, in fact, so exhausted by the funeral service in the White House that he was unable to make the trip to Hyde Park to see his great friend laid to rest.

That left Bill Leahy, chief of staff to the commander in chief. As George Elsey, who became assistant naval aide, put it:

> Truman came to office with zero background in these matters and and zero information. And hence anyone who was in a position to provide him some solid information on what had been going on was obviously going to be very, very influential. In FDR's case, he had access to all the information Leahy did and a lot more and had been in the office, and the war had been going on for some time before Leahy showed up so there was a whale of a difference in the background.

According to Elsey, Leahy's greatest service was probably his indoctrination of President Truman in the weeks immediately following the death of President Roosevelt.[4]

In contrast to the intermittent assistance Hopkins was able to give the new president, that of Leahy was constant and regular. Just as he had done with Roosevelt, he reported to the Oval Office at 9:45 each morning. He found that Truman quickly absorbed the gist of dispatches and reports. Sometimes the two men might go to the Map Room together to get details or background materials.

On 17 April, Leahy attended President Truman's first news conference. Some 350 reporters crowded into the room. The admiral was very pleased with Truman's forthright, direct, and positive answers to their questions. He liked that in a man and never had any adverse comment on Truman's greatest weakness, a tendency to shoot from the hip and answer questions on which he had not been adequately briefed.

Ever since Yalta, Leahy had become more guarded and careful in his dealings with Russia. He told Averell Harriman that he left the Crimean

conference convinced the Soviets would never allow a free government in
Poland.[5] Still, he was somewhat taken aback at an early meeting between the
president and Soviet Foreign Minister Molotov. The Russians were backing
away from one of the principal agreements reached at Yalta. Truman did not
propose to let them get away with it.

It was the problem of the make-up of the Polish government. At Yalta,
Stalin had agreed that the Lublin Poles, whom they supported, would accept
representatives of the London Free Poles, favored by the British. Now it
seemed that the London Poles would not be welcomed.

According to Averell Harriman, who had come to Washington to help
brief President Truman, the Soviets began to realize that the communist
Lublin Poles had so fragile a hold on power that they would not be able to
survive if members of the democratic Free Poles were allowed in. Or, if they
were to survive, it would require Soviet military intervention.[6]

Thus, Harriman was among the first to understand that the Soviets were
abandoning their wartime policy of cooperation. Leahy had never thought
that their alliance was more than wartime necessity, and he went along with
Harriman. He urged Truman to adopt a tougher line with the USSR. Others,
such as Stimson and Marshall, were not so sure. They wanted to do nothing to
jeopardize possible Russian entrance into the war against Japan. That argument cut no ice with Leahy. He believed that war was as good as won, and that
Russian intervention and invasion of the Japanese homeland were both unnecessary.

> Admiral Leahy, in response to a question from me, [wrote Truman in his
> memoirs] observed that he had left Yalta with the impression that the Soviet
> government had no intention of permitting a free government to operate in
> Poland and that he would have been surprised had the Russians behaved any
> differently. In his opinion, the Yalta agreement was susceptible of two inter-
> pretations. He added that he felt it was a serious matter to break with the
> Russians but that he believed we should tell them that we stood for a free and
> independent Poland.[7]

Although well aware that a serious break with the Russians might imperil
the United Nations, then being formed in San Francisco, Truman decided it
would be worse for the United States to show signs of weakness in dealing
with the Soviets.

Therefore, as Harriman put it, he decided to be firm but not offensive.
Characteristically, Truman went straight to the point. He bluntly informed
Molotov that the United States could not recognize a Polish government that
did not represent all democratic elements. When Molotov expostulated that
the United States was trying to impose its will on the Soviet Union, Truman
replied, not at all; he only wanted the USSR to live up to the agreements made
at Yalta. He said he wanted it clearly understood that the United States would

fulfill its agreements and he expected the Soviet Union to do the same. It was not a one-way street.

Molotov gasped. "I have never been talked to like that in my life."

"Carry out your agreements," snapped Truman, "and you won't get talked to like that."[8]

Although Harriman was sorry that Truman had used such rough language, Leahy was pleased. Not that Harriman cared for Molotov's feelings; the Russian was a tough old bird who could use rough language himself. Harriman felt that Truman's attitude would give Molotov an excuse to tell Stalin that Truman was abandoning Roosevelt's policy of friendship.[9]

Truman was abandoning it, but not because the new president wanted it that way. It became increasingly clear that with the end of the war, Russian and western aims would diverge. Whether the Cold War could have been averted had Roosevelt lived is dubious; certainly with Truman, it could not.

Leahy approved of Truman's attitude toward Molotov:

> The President's attitude was more than pleasing to me, and I believe it will have a beneficial effect on the Soviet attitude toward the rest of the world. They have always known that we have the power, and now they should know that we have the determination to insist upon the declared right of all people to choose their own form of government.
>
> I personally do not believe it is possible to exclude dominant Soviet influence from Poland, but that it is possible to give to the Government of Poland an external appearance of independence.

This belief, of course, turned out to be quite mistaken, for the Soviet Union had no intention of accepting in Poland any government which it considered unfriendly. Since that included any government elected by methods considered acceptable by the United States or Great Britain, it was an impossible situation. Unhappily for the Polish people the Russians were close at hand, and their will prevailed. Thus the nation, over whose territorial integrity World War II had begun, lost that same integrity at the end.

A few days later, while he was lunching with his brother Arthur at the Army–Navy Club in Washington, Leahy received a telephone call from the White House to meet with the president and the Joint Chiefs at the Pentagon at 2:00 that afternoon. When he arrived, he found everyone awaiting a telephone call from Churchill. The PM reported a German peace feeler through Sweden. Truman would have none of it. He reiterated the demand for unconditional surrender and told Leahy to send Stalin a cablegram to keep him informed. As it turned out, nothing came of this feeler, but Leahy now felt it was only a matter of a few days.

Events moved rapidly toward their close in Europe. On 30 April, Leahy noted that Mussolini had been captured and executed by partisans, and the next day his journal recorded the death of Hitler and the accession of Grand

Admiral Karl Dönitz as chief of the German state. Surrender of German forces in Italy on 2 May was followed two days later by capitulation of all German forces on the western front. Obviously these troops were trying to avoid surrender to the Russians. To avoid a Soviet charge of unilateral action, Eisenhower announced only a tactical surrender.

At the same time on the other side of the world, Mountbatten reported the capture of Rangoon, which effectively ended the Burma campaign, source of so much friction between the Allies.

Announcement of the surrender of all German forces in the west to Britain and the United States and in the east to the USSR was marred by wrangling over making the news public. The three leaders had accepted Truman's statement that formal announcement would be made at 9:00 A.M., 8 May, Washington time. The British newspapers picked up a leak and were intending to release it immediately. Churchill wanted to be freed from his promise so that the official pronouncement could come out before the newspaper stories. Leahy handled the transAtlantic telephone conversation for Truman. "In view of agreements already made," he told the PM, "my chief asks me to tell you that he cannot act without the approval of Uncle Joe."[10]

But Uncle Joe was nowhere to be found. Churchill went ahead and made the surrender announcement on the night of 7 May. When Stalin's reply arrived, just as Truman was about to speak over the radio, it was a request for further delay so the surrender documents could be further studied!

Truman went right ahead with his broadcast.

At any rate, the war in Europe was over. Reaction in Europe was of wild joy. In the United States it was more restrained. There was still the war in the Pacific to be won.

> The news reports an enthusiastic celebration in London in contrast to very little excitement here. Today marks the end of a cruel continuous attack against London, which has suffered severely for five years. Washington, far from the actual front, has not been attacked and has, therefore, no actual knowledge of the horrors of aerial warfare.

Of course, letters and messages of congratulations poured in on the White House. Leahy valued one from the former First Lady.

May 8, 1945
Dear Admiral Leahy:

My thoughts are with you today. I know that Franklin would want to clasp your hand and congratulate you for all you have done to make this victory possible.

Please accept my deepest appreciation and respect, and my affectionate good wishes.

Very sincerely yours,
Eleanor Roosevelt[11]

The end of the war in Europe did not mean the end of problems. Marshal Tito had seized Trieste for Yugoslavia as well as a part of northeastern Italy known as Venezia Giulia. This act threatened the peace in the area, but eventually the region was divided into international free zones.

Then there was the eternal problem of de Gaulle.

Churchill had once remarked that during the war the greatest cross he had to bear was the Cross of Lorraine, referring to the symbol de Gaulle had taken for himself. Admiral Smith later put it that Leahy would have agreed perfectly with that assessment. De Gaulle, he felt, seemed to have to be obnoxious in order to retain the support of the French. "He would show no gratitude whatsoever. He just simply had to be gallic!"[12]

De Gaulle was at his most "gallic" in late May when he refused to pull French forces in northern Italy back to the French border as Eisenhower had directed. Clearly de Gaulle wanted those areas to belong to France. Early in June, Leahy reported to the president that instead of obeying, the local French commander threatened to use force if American forces interfered with him.

"The French are using our guns, are they not?" asked Truman.

"Yes, sir."

"All right, we will at once stop shipping guns, ammunition, and equipment to de Gaulle."

That same day, Leahy drafted and Truman sent an unmistakable warning to de Gaulle that if he persisted in his refusal, the United States would cut off all his supplies.

> The President's plain language had the desired effect. The State Department reported shortly thereafter that de Gaulle had begun to show signs of coming to his senses. In fact, Acting Secretary of State [Joseph] Grew★ thought-that de Gaulle was likely to resign or be removed as head of the Provisional Government in France. The irascible Frenchman was so difficult to get along with that there was a possibility of this happening. Such an event would have been very pleasing to all the Allied governments.†[13]

Leahy considered de Gaulle insufferable, and he soon added contemptible to that evaluation when the French leader brought Marshal Pétain to trial on charges of treason for collaboration with the Nazis during the period of the Vichy government. In a pathetic letter, Pétain asked Leahy to come to France to testify in his behalf. Obviously Leahy could not leave his post at the president's side, but he could and did send a letter for the old marshal to use in his defense. It read, in part:

---

★Stettinius was in San Francisco at the UN meeting.

†Assistant Naval Aide George Elsey compiled a long document, "President Roosevelt's Policy toward de Gaulle," which listed many examples of de Gaulle's refusal to take orders from Eisenhower. The document concludes with Churchill's warning, "I assure you there is nothing de Gaulle will not do if he has armed forces at his disposal."[14]

During that period you did on occasions, at my request, take action that was in opposition to the desires of the Axis and favorable to the Allied cause.

In every instance when you failed to accept my recommendation to oppose the Axis powers by refusing their demands, your stated reason was that such positive action by you would result in additional oppression of your people by the invaders.

I had then, and I have now, a conviction that your principal concern was the welfare and protection of the helpless people of France. It was impossible for me to believe that you had any other concern.

However, I must, in all honesty, repeat my opinion expressed to you at the time that positive refusal to make any concession to Axis demands, while it might have brought immediately increased hardships to your people, it would, in the long view, have been advantageous to France.[15]

It would have done no good for Leahy to have gone to France to testify for Pétain. De Gaulle was determined to make a symbol of the old man. In spite of anything Leahy or anyone else could do, Pétain was convicted and sentenced to death. De Gaulle at once commuted the sentence to life imprisonment, which Pétain served on the Île d'Yeu off the Atlantic coast. He died in 1951.

Matters between the United States and the Soviet Union were not going well. There had been a brief suspension of Lend Lease shipments to both Britain and Russia, which were in Leahy's opinion illegal now that the war in Europe was over. But for political reasons they had been resumed. The Russians, ever suspicious, saw the action as yet another example of American duplicity. In San Francisco, Molotov made difficulties over voting procedures in the Security Council of the United Nations. The question of the Polish government remained as thorny as ever. Then, in what western leaders believed to be an action of sheer treachery, Soviet officials invited to a meeting, under a guarantee of safe conduct, sixteen noncommunist Polish leaders. When they proved to be stubborn in face of Russian demands, they were arrested and held incommunicado for weeks.

Harriman and Bohlen recommended that Truman send Harry Hopkins to Moscow to try to straighten out these matters. After initial reluctance, Truman agreed and Harry went, but his mission was only partially successful. He won confirmation of the Russian promise to enter the war against Japan, which Leahy thought was unnecessary. He won agreement to the American view on voting procedures in the United Nations, but he met a stonewall in the matter of the sixteen Polish leaders and other matters concerning that unfortunate nation. The only really substantive result of the Hopkins mission was agreement on the time and place of the next meeting of the Big Three in Potsdam.

About that time, Leahy appeared in an artist's rendering on the cover of the 28 May issue of *Time* magazine. The picture shows him in his winter blues, with blue cap cover, a sour expression on his face, his cold eyes staring—perhaps at a seaman before him on charges of drunk and disorderly conduct—or perhaps it was de Gaulle his eyes were pinning to the wall. Behind him, detached hands hold a sword and an olive branch, and behind the lot is a Series E War Bond in $100 denomination. The allegory is not clear, but the story, with certain inaccuracies, is highly laudatory. According to *Time*,

> Leahy swings even more weight under the new President than he did under the man who appointed him to the job. F.D.R.'s was an assertive voice. Harry Truman knows his limitations and is more apt to defer to the judgment of the old seadog who has devoted his life to naval and military affairs. At meetings of the Chiefs of Staff, Leahy is no mere observer. Among other things he is a useful moderator. Sandpaper [a reference to the Spanish play on his name *El Lija*, which was given him in Puerto Rico—it means sandpaper] is abrasive; but it also smooths.[16]

Soon after Hopkins had returned from Moscow, he and Leahy had breakfast with Truman on the South Portico of the White House. Hopkins reported on his talks with Stalin and concluded that the Soviet leader would come to Berlin and nowhere else for the forthcoming meeting in the suburb of Potsdam.

Two days later Hopkins, who was confined to his Georgetown house on doctor's orders, invited Leahy to lunch with him.

> We talked at length about possible methods of preparing information and draft decisions on many of the subjects that were expected to come up for discussion and decision [in the Potsdam Conference]. Although physically he was in low state, Harry's mind was as keen as ever and he was of great assistance in preparing an outline of Truman's statement of policy with which the President was to open the Potsdam meeting.[17]

Before leaving for Potsdam, the president and the Joint Chiefs had to work out a strategy for the last stages of the war in the Pacific. On 18 June the JCS met with the president and approved the invasion of Kyushu, the southernmost of the main Japanese islands. This was in accordance with the strong recommendation of both Marshall and King. Leahy was opposed.

The military analyst for *The New York Times*, Hanson W. Baldwin, who was a graduate of the U.S. Naval Academy, frequently interviewed Leahy, and he recalled later:

> The President apparently had been sold . . . on the necessity for an invasion of Japan. The kamikaze operations had convinced most of the military people that Japan would fight to the death and that therefore actual occupation of the islands would be necessary. But Admiral Leahy was not convinced of this. . . . He said . . . Japan was already virtually defeated, she was cut off from her supplies; with our submarines and our air power we could bomb at will, and

Japan had no recourse. We commanded the sea and the air, and this land invasion was an unnecessary thing.[18]

In addition to his belief that Japan could be defeated by air and sea blockade, Leahy opposed invasion because he thought it would be more expensive in lives. "It wasn't a matter of dollars. It might require more time—and more dollars—if we did not invade Japan. But it would cost *fewer lives*."[19] At the same time, he told Truman of "my prejudiced view" against Russia entering the war which the United States had already as good as won. But he accepted the fact that that decision had already been made at Yalta.★

President Truman, as he wrote his mother, was reluctant to go to Potsdam. Perhaps it was apprehension about meeting as an equal with Stalin and Churchill, the two towering figures of the day. He had had no experience in foreign affairs before assuming the presidency. He determined to do his best, to prepare himself by extensive reading of the briefing books provided him, and by surrounding himself with the best advisors he could find.

Harry Hopkins was too ill to join the party going to Potsdam. He had hoped to go, and his name appears on a list sent on 23 June by Leahy to Ambassador Harriman in Moscow.[21] The fact that Harry couldn't make it was probably a relief to Truman. In the mind of the new president, Hopkins was too closely connected with Roosevelt; knowing both Churchill and Stalin as he did, there was a danger he might run with the ball, ignoring the president. Truman did not intend this to happen. He intended to dominate the conference from the beginning.

Leahy was most anxious that the president be properly briefed in preparation for the forthcoming meeting, Truman's first on the international scene. He wanted, as George Elsey put it, "to make sure that every scrap of information of potiential significance was extracted from Map Room files" and made available in concise form.

> The briefing papers I prepared were used by him in reviewing matters with Truman and some of the items, such as a synopsis of the secret and unpublished agreements at Yalta were reviewed by me with Jimmy Byrnes at Leahy's direction in the sensitive weeks after Truman had decided to replace Stettinius with Byrnes, but before Stettinius was aware that he was on the way out.[22]

Shortly before leaving for Potsdam, Truman implemented his decision to replace Stettinius as secretary of state with Jimmy Byrnes. Thus it was nearly a clean sweep. As Leahy lay in his berth in the *Ferdinand Magellan* on the night of 6 July, he might well have reflected that he was the only one of the senior members of the Yalta trip who was going to Potsdam. Harriman, of course,

★Dorothy Ringquist spontaneously stated to the author that Leahy was always looking for the course of action which would be least expensive of lives. "If there was a choice of one operation against another which would take fewer lives, he would always pick the second," she said. "He had this quality of the reverence for life."[20]

WDL with President Truman and Secretary of State James F. Byrnes aboard the *Augusta* en route to the Potsdam Conference, July 1945. (Courtesy, National Archives)

would be there; as ambassador to the Soviet Union, he was essential, but no one else was in the inner circle. The Joint Chiefs would have lesser roles than before, since the war was so nearly won.

Next morning early, the train arrived at Newport News, and the presidential party boarded the cruiser *Augusta* for the Atlantic crossing. This was the same ship which had brought Franklin Roosevelt and Winston Churchill together so long ago in their first meeting at Argentia, in Newfoundland. There is a kind of cyclical fitness that the same ship brought a president of the United States to the first and to the last of the wartime summit conferences. While the earlier meeting had symbolized allied unity, this one thinly concealed the beginning of the Cold War.

Leahy felt keenly the contrast of the voyage of the *Augusta* with previous ones en route to conferences. The ships were not darkened at night, they did not zigzag, and they sent radio messages freely. The new president was an active man and inspected the ship from "truck to keelson." As a former artillery officer, he was fascinated by the guns of the main battery.

It was by no means a luxury cruise. Conferences filled most of the mornings and the afternoons as well, because Truman wanted to be completely prepared when he encountered Stalin and Churchill.

The *Augusta* reached Antwerp 15 July, and late that morning the presidential party left the ship and drove to the airfield where the "Sacred Cow" was waiting. During the three-and-a-half-hour flight they gazed down on the destruction wrought on Germany by the war. "The city of Kassel," Leahy wrote, "viewed from the air, appeared to be completely destroyed by air bombardment. I could not see a single house that was not completely wrecked."

On landing at Gatow airfield, Truman inspected a guard of honor from the "Hell on Wheels" Division; then they went on to houses prepared for the American party in Babelsberg on the south shore of Greibnitz Lake. Truman described his:

> My quarters was a three-story stucco residence at No. 2 Kaiserstrasse which had formerly been the home of the head of the German movie colony. The building, which was designated as the "Little White House," although it was painted yellow, was right on the lake and was surrounded on three sides by groves of trees and shrubbery forming a very beautiful garden that reached down to the lake. The house had been stripped of its furnishings during the war but had been refurbished by the Russians.[23]

Leahy's accommodation in the same building was "a small sleeping room and a large conference room and office."

Although the first plenary session was scheduled for 16 July, Stalin had not arrived, so Truman took advantage of the delay to have a two-hour conference with Churchill before embarking on a thirteen-mile drive through ruined Berlin. Leahy and Byrnes rode in the car with the president, while other cars followed to make up quite a motorcade.

> Every building we saw was badly damaged or completely destroyed. This one-time beautiful city, capital of a proud nation that housed four and one-quarter million inhabitants, now wrecked beyond repair, is a distressing example of the results that follow loss of moral appreciation of others and attachment to false prophets; but much more distressing than that was a long procession of old men, women, and children, presumably evicted from their homes by the Russian invaders, marching in great numbers along the country roads, carrying their remaining belongings and their small babies, probably to an unknown destination and probably without hope.
>
> In our two-hour drive we witnessed the progress of a great world tragedy and a beginning of the disintegration of a highly cultured, proud people who are racial kinsmen of the English and the Americans, but who followed false leaders to their destruction.

The next day, Stalin called on Truman at the Little White House to apologize for being late to the conference. Truman asked him to stay for lunch, but Stalin demurred. "You could if you wanted to," Truman insisted. Stalin stayed.

At the luncheon, which Leahy, Molotov, and Byrnes shared, with Chip Bohlen and V. N. Pavlov serving as translators, Truman served a bottle of California wine, which Stalin greatly admired. The president sent him several bottles as a memento of the lunch.

WDL greeting Prime Minister Winston Churchill at Potsdam, July 1945. (Courtesy, National Archives)

It would be futile to recount the story of Potsdam once again by summarizing the sessions and the decisions taken. The meetings were held in the Cecilienhof Palace in Potsdam. Leahy, as at Yalta, attended all the political and plenary sessions, but he let the leaders do the talking and make the decisions. He was there to give advice if the president wanted it.

At the first session, which began at 5:00 P.M., 17 July, Truman presided at the suggestion of Stalin. He took advantage of the opportunity to present the agenda which he had worked out on the Atlantic crossing. Specific items included the formation of a Council of Foreign Ministers, policy on Germany, policy on the liberated areas, policy toward Italy and other nations who had fought originally on the Axis side but had subsequently joined the Allies. Churchill was cautious, and Stalin wanted to add eight other items, the most important of which concerned reparations Germany was to pay.

The establishment as a permanent body of the Council of Foreign Ministers, which was intended to operate as a kind of a little Big Three, and which had been set up on an informal basis at Yalta, was confirmed. At first Truman wanted to add the foreign ministers of China and France, but in the end it was the triumvirate of Byrnes, Molotov, and Eden which was charged with setting the peace terms and with whatever else might be referred to them. Since the Big Three quickly agreed to refer any serious disagreement to the Council, those three gentlemen had a lot to do.

Hanging over the Potsdam conference, code-named in a kind of unconscious prophecy Terminal, was the outcome of the British general election, which had been held 5 July. Ballots had not yet been counted to allow those from soldiers and sailors stationed all over the world to reach the United Kingdom. On the possibility that his government might be turned out of office, Churchill had brought with him the leader of the opposition, Clement Attlee. This head of the Labour Party sat in at all plenary sessions, listening intently but saying nothing.

Truman came to the Potsdam Conference with an ace up his sleeve. He and his principal advisors knew that the atomic bomb was nearing completion. Leahy was highly dubious about the whole Manhattan Project, on which over $2 billion had been spent. In one of his less inspired statements, he predicted that it would never go off, "And I speak as an expert on explosives!" Although he had been exposed to explanations of how the bomb ought to work, his primitive Naval Academy physics was not up to grasping the concept of nuclear fission. He shared this weakness with most of the practical men of his day. The idea of unlocking the atom was too far outside the experience of anyone. Even Roosevelt had not understood when he okayed the project. He trusted Einstein, and Einstein told him it would work, so FDR gave the go-ahead.

Still, no one was absolutely sure *whether* or *how* it would work. Scientists had "split" the atom in labs, but no one had ever exploded an atom bomb. Some believed, with Leahy, that the whole thing would fizzle; others worried that the explosion might be uncontrollable and literally end the world.

On 16 July, after Stalin had left, Stimson showed Truman a cryptic message he had just received from Washington.

> Operated on this morning. Diagnosis not yet complete but results seem satisfactory and already exceed expectations. Local press release necessary as interest extends great distance. Dr. Groves pleased. He returns tomorrow. I will keep you posted.[24]

Next morning there arrived a second message, still brief, but giving more details.

Doctor has just returned most enthusiastic and confident that the little boy is as husky as his big brother. The light in his eyes discernible from here to Highhold and I could have heard his screams from here to my farm.[25]

These messages meant that the test atomic bomb had been exploded at Alamogordo and that it had been more effective than expected. Since the flash had been seen a long way away, some cover story was necessary in a "local press release." "Dr. Groves" was Major General Leslie R. Groves, commanding general of the Manhattan Project.

The second message told that the flash had been visible a distance equal to that from Washington to Stimson's home in Highhold, New York, and that it had been heard fifty miles, equivalent to the distance from Washington to the sender's farm. The bomb exploded had been the "little boy," or smaller plutonium bomb. Scientists were sure that the larger U-235 version would work.

Later in the conference, Truman casually mentioned to Stalin that the United States had developed a new explosive which they hoped would bring about an early end to the war with Japan. Stalin seemed curiously unimpressed but hoped America would make good use of it.

At the time Truman and his advisors thought Stalin's reaction meant that he knew nothing about the bomb, but it has later become obvious that Stalin knew all about it. His spies had kept him well informed.

With the success of the atomic bomb, Soviet entry into the war with Japan was no longer necessary or even desirable from an American point of view. But Leahy, Harriman, and even Marshall, believed that nothing could be done to keep them out. The Russians had interests in Manchuria, and they wanted to regain territory taken from them by the Japanese at the end of the Russo–Japanese War in 1905. Even with the bomb, Marshall was not absolutely sure that Japan could be defeated without invasion. But everyone believed that Russia would do as she pleased, and it suited her at that stage to enter the war against Japan. Stalin confirmed it a few days later when he promised that the Soviet Union would move against Japan about 15 August.

Meanwhile, without informing Stalin, since Russia was still neutral, the Americans and British spent considerable time drafting a document known as the Potsdam Proclamation calling upon Japan to surrender. Stimson, Harriman, and Leahy wanted to include a statement to the effect that the Japanese could keep their emperor, who would be subject to the orders of the supreme commander. Byrnes, however, objected, believing it would show weakness to back away from the "unconditional surrender" formula. Truman went along with his secretary of state. On 26 July, Chiang Kai-shek having approved by radio, the Potsdam Proclamation was accepted and released by Truman and Churchill. It called upon Japan to surrender to avoid complete destruction. It hinted at the atomic bomb by warning that the "might which now converges on Japan is immeasurably greater than that which . . . laid waste to the lands, the industry, and the method of life of the whole German people."

Meanwhile the day-to-day work of the conference went forward. Germany was divided into four zones, one each for Russia, Great Britain, France, and the United States. A meaningless, face-saving statement over Poland was agreed to saying that the Poles were simply assisting the Russians in taking over part of their zone.

Berlin, the prewar capital, lay far inside the Soviet Zone; the city, too, was to be under quadripartite occupation, with the Russians assuring the other three powers free access from their zones to their sectors in Berlin. *But there was nothing in writing*, as the western allies found to their sorrow in 1948 at the time of Berlin Blockade.

In the end there was no agreement over peace treaties with Italy and other countries who had fought alongside the Allies in the latter part of the war. Russia wanted to arrange with Turkey for Russo–Turkish control of the Dardanelles; Truman countered with a proposal for freedom of navigation not only in the Dardanelles but on the Danube and Don as well.

Most of the agreements, or lack of them, at Potsdam have been relegated to the historical record. But with the inability of the great powers to agree came the decision on both sides to go their own way. Nor was the relationship improved with the ouster of Conservative Party leader Winston Churchill and his replacement as prime minister by Laborite Clement Attlee. Leahy noted:

> The Soviets had indicated they did not like the British Labor Party and were not enthusiastic about Attlee, the new Prime Minister, who was expected to arrive the next day. Although he was their antagonist at almost every turn, Stalin and his top advisers appeared to have had a high personal regard for Churchill.
>
> There was a noticeable coolness in their attitude after Attlee took over. This was surprising to me, because the British Labor Party obviously was far more to the "left" than Churchill's Conservative Party. Attlee of course was not as forceful a leader as his predecessor, but he had been with Churchill at the Potsdam meetings and was completely informed on the status of most of the issues. That status seemed to be: "Referred to the Foreign Ministers for study and report."[26]

The thorniest point of discussion and disagreement at Potsdam was, as it had been at Yalta, the question of reparations. Harriman was shocked to see how the Russians had stripped German factories of machinery, leaving only bare walls. They had done this before the Potsdam meeting so that what they already had taken could not be charged to their account when reparations were formally divided up. In the end, an agreement was reached whereby the Soviets would get some of the hard goods from the western zones in return for grain from the east. Since few such grain shipments were ever made, the whole thing became academic.

During the entire conference, the longest of them all, appearances of cordiality remained, especially at the dinners, when each of the Big Three attempted to outdo the others in lavishness of food and drink. The "Battle of Music" was a comic footnote. On 19 July, Truman featured concert pianist Eugene List, who was serving as a sergeant in the army. Stalin drank to the health of the young pianist.

Two days later, Stalin was host. He had sent to Moscow for musicians, a pianist and two female violinists, "who made up in musical ability what they lacked in looks. The President and I estimated they weighed about two hundred pounds each."

Churchill and Leahy both felt that this was overdoing it. Leahy enjoyed an occasional concert, but a little went a long way. Churchill favored more martial music.

The outgoing PM got his revenge when he was host on the evening of 24 July. He had a full orchestra of the RAF to play light classics and marches, and play they did. While Truman's dinner had lasted until 1:00 A.M., and Stalin's had gone on until 1:30, Churchill made sure that his did not end until 2:00 in the morning.

Childish, perhaps, but the musical contest was a lighter moment in a conference where little was being done to guarantee stability in the postwar world.

Near the end of the conference, Stalin demanded that the historical record show that Russia had entered the war against Japan on the request of the western allies. Since Truman no longer wanted Russia in the war, he was in a dilemma, but he couldn't afford to say openly that he no longer wanted it. He temporized. Leahy explained:

> The President, in reply to Generalissimo Stalin's oral request that we ask Russia to enter the war against Japan, handed to Stalin an unsigned letter pointing out the Soviet Government's duty under the Moscow and United Nations agreements to assist in preserving world peace. The President did not ask the Soviet to join with us in the war against Japan, which I am sure Stalin will in his own interest do in any event.

When the USSR did enter the war against Japan immediately following the dropping of the first atomic bomb on Hiroshima, she proclaimed that she had gone to war in fulfillment of her promise to Britain and the United States.

On 28 July, the Japanese broadcast their response to the Potsdam Proclamation. Scholars and historians have debated exactly what Prime Minister Kantaro Suzuki meant when he announced that the Japanese would *mokusatsu* the declaration. The word could mean anything from "ignore" to "reject with contempt." Or it could mean simply, "no comment." Truman and his advisors accepted the "reject with contempt" interpretation in view of the context which stated that it was "nothing but a rehash" of previous declarations and that the Japanese government "does not find any important value in it." Truman therefore cabled Groves to be ready to drop the bomb on any of the previously approved targets no earlier than 2 August. According to Assistant Naval Aide George Elsey, Truman wanted to be away from Potsdam before the bomb was dropped.

The conference ended on the evening of 1 August, the communique papering over differences. Leahy missed the evening session because of a digestive disturbance, but the next morning he was able to eat a 6:30 breakfast and board the "Sacred Cow" for a flight to Plymouth, England. There they lunched aboard the battle cruiser *Renown*, guests of His Majesty, King George VI.

> His Majesty and I discussed the atomic bomb. The King asked me about its potentialities. I said, "I do not think it will be as effective as is expected. It sounds like a professor's dream to me!"
>
> To my surprise, I found King George well informed about the project and the possible postwar uses of atomic energy. Jestingly he said to me, "Admiral, would you like to lay a little bet on that?" I was honest when I told His Majesty that I did not have as much confidence in the new weapon as did some of the scientists and that I knew of no explosive that would develop the power claimed for the new bomb. Events shortly were to prove that in this respect I was very much in error.[27]

Following the lunch, King George returned President Truman's visit by going aboard the *Augusta*, following which the American cruiser got under way for the voyage home.

Four days out, as Truman was lunching off a stainless steel tray in the mess hall with the enlisted men, he was handed a message that the first atomic bomb had been dropped on Hiroshima. Leahy now believed that it would work, but he still underestimated it by predicting to International News Service reporter Robert Nixon "that defensive ordnance had always been developed to meet new offensive weapons and I felt that the threat of this new bomb would be met as other threats had been in the past."[28]

It was not until after the *Augusta* reached Newport News and Leahy had a chance to read in the papers of the carnage wrought by the bomb that he finally understood.

> The press this morning reports that the atomic bomb, dropped on Hiroshima day before yesterday, destroyed more than half the city and brought from the Japanese Government charges against us of cruelty and barbarism in that the attack was effective principally against non-combatants, women and children. Although Hiroshima was a naval base, it is probable that the destruction of civilian life was terrific.
>
> Some of our scientists today say that the area attacked will be uninhabitable

for many years because the bomb explosion has made the ground radioactive and destructive of animal life.

The lethal possibilities of such atomic action in the future is frightening, and while we are the first to have it in our possession, there is a certainty that it will in the future be developed by potential enemies and that it will probably be used against us.

American use of the atomic bomb made a profound impression on Leahy, and Dorothy Ringquist stated that in her opinion his health really began to fail from that day. As he told her, "Dorothy, we will regret this day. The United States will suffer, for war is not to be waged to wipe out women and children."[29]

That same afternoon, the Soviet Union announced that it had joined in the war against Japan, causing Leahy to remark sourly, "Hereafter we will be required to share both the military efforts against Japan and the rewards therefrom."

On 9 August, the second atomic bomb devastated Nagasaki, and the following day the Japanese announced by radio that they were prepared to surrender in accordance with the Potsdam Proclamation with the proviso that they could retain their emperor. Simultaneously they arranged for the offer to go through formal diplomatic channels, using the Swiss and the Swedes as intermediaries. Truman summoned Secretaries Stimson, Forrestal, and Byrnes to join him and Leahy in discussing the terms.

> Secretary Stimson had always expressed the opinion that it would be to our advantage to retain the Emperor. He urged the same point now. We needed, as he saw it, to keep the only symbol of authority which all Japanese acknowledged. Admiral Leahy also recommended that we accept the Japanese proposal if for no other reason than that we would be able to use the Emperor in effecting the surrender. Secretary Byrnes was less certain that we should accept anything short of an unconditional declaration of surrender. He argued that in the present position it should be the United States and not Japan that should state conditions. Secretary of the Navy Forrestal offered the suggestion that we might in our reply indicate willingness to accept, yet define the terms of the surrender in such a manner that the intents and purposes of the Potsdam Declaration would be clearly accomplished.[30]★

Forrestal's suggestion met with Truman's approval, and he asked Byrnes and Leahy to draft a reply along those lines. The final version accepted the idea of retaining the emperor, with the proviso: "From the moment of surrender the authority of the Emperor and the Japanese Government to rule the state

---

★There is a minor slip in terminology here. The call upon Japan to surrender was the "Potsdam Proclamation." The "Potsdam Declaration" was the communique issued by the Big Three at the end of the conference.

shall be subject to the Supreme Commander of the Allied Powers who will take such steps as he deems proper to effectuate the surrender terms."

This was precisely what Stimson and Leahy had wanted in the original draft of the Potsdam Proclamation, but which Byrnes had insisted be cut out. But it should not be supposed that Japan would have surrendered if that statement had been made before the atomic bomb was dropped. She very nearly did not *after* the two bombs had fallen. A palace revolution was barely averted.

Everyone knew that there was a possibility that the Japanese would reject the counterproposal, and Truman told Leahy and the others to continue with plans for the Kyushu invasion set for 1 November.

After considerable difficulty with the Russians, who wanted to have a veto over the name of the supreme commander, and who were rebuffed by Harriman, all the countries at war with Japan agreed to the American statement concerning the emperor. It was duly sent to Japan through the Swiss, but to prevent the Japanese government from lying to their own people, the answer was also given to the newspapers and to the radio, including short-wave stations to be broadcast across the Pacific. To make sure that the utmost pressure was on the Japanese government, a B-29 flew over Tokyo and dropped leaflets bearing a translation of Japan's offer to surrender and the American reply.

On 14 August, at 3:30 P.M. Washington time, the Map Room reported receiving a message to the effect that Japan had agreed to the surrender terms.

> This means the definite end of the world war which started in 1914, had a temporary adjournment for futher preparation 1918 to 1939, and today comes to its final end.
> I personally am oppressed by a feeling of humility and apprehension for the future—"Lest we forget."
> The next war will be for a different and a new cause, and we all hope its arrival will be long delayed by efforts of all civilized peoples to preserve peace in the world by cooperative action.

Shortly before 7:00 P.M., Truman called Leahy to come to the Oval Office for the formal announcement of the Japanese surrender. As soon as the ceremony was over, Leahy hurried to the Map Room to issue orders to the armed forces to cease military operations against Japan, except for such actions as necessary for self-defense.

When the word of the Japanese capitulation reached the country, wild celebrations broke out in every city and town. Leahy thought little of such behavior.

> A noisy celebration is going on in the city with all motor cars sounding their horns, and great crowds of shouting people milling in the streets and bringing traffic to a standstill. The radio is blaring forth news of the celebration in cities from Los Angeles to Boston, in all of which the populace seems to be celebrating the war's end with noise in crowded streets.

To me the occasion seems appropriate for thoughtful appreciation of our good fortune in having gained the victory over fanatical enemies, but the proletariat considers noise appropriate, and the greatest number of people in democracies must have their way.

The war over, Leahy felt that his personal story had been told and concluded his book, *I Was There* with the surrender of the Japanese. Yet he was to serve as chief of staff to the commander in chief for more than three additional years, some of the most critical in the history of the country.

He wrapped up his book with a long summary statement on the war and on his role as chief of staff. He touched on the new weapons, the new techniques, the new doctrines, the new strategy that had perforce been developed as the long months of conflict had continued. Of the Joint Chiefs of Staff, he felt that his three colleagues, Marshall, King, and Arnold had served with selfless devotion. On the other hand, "there were times when we seemed to be wasting too much time in talking and writing book-sized papers to say what I thought could have been expressed in a few paragraphs."

As coordinator of U.S. and, at times, Allied strategy, he possessed a unique understanding of the problems of coalition warfare. He fully realized that the United States was no longer what it had been on that dark day in early September when the Nazi juggernaut had rolled into Poland to begin the vast war just concluded. But he hated the way it had ended. While it was a triumph, it was also a tragedy. The atomic bomb had changed everything.

> Once it had been tested, President Truman faced the decision as to whether to use it. He did not like the idea, but was persuaded that it would shorten the war against Japan and save American lives. It is my opinion that the use of this barbarous weapon at Hiroshima and Nagasaki was of no material assistance in our war against Japan. The Japanese were already defeated and ready to surrender because of the effective sea blockade and the successful bombing with conventional weapons.
>
> The lethal possibilities of atomic warfare in the future are frightening. My own feeling was that in being the first to use it, we had adopted an ethical standard common to the barbarians of the Dark Ages. I was not taught to make war in that fashion, and wars cannot be won by destroying women and children. We were the first to have this weapon in our possession and the first to use it. . . . Employment of the atomic bomb in war will take us back in cruelty toward noncombatants to the days of Genghis Khan. . . .
>
> Until the United Nations, or some world organization, can guarantee—and have the power to enforce that guarantee—that the world will be spared the terrors of atomic warfare, the United States must have more and better atom bombs than any potential enemy.[31]

In many ways, Leahy belonged to an earlier age, when the phrase "officer and gentleman" was no mere cliché. When, during the war he heard of the possibility of biological warfare, he recoiled, telling FDR that it "would violate every Christian ethic I have ever heard of and all of the known laws of war." Although he abhorred the atomic bomb, and believed that Pandora's box had been opened to release not only questions but dangers for humanity, he saw no way of returning them to the box. Now the United States had to face the problems of the postwar world, the world in which the power of the atom had been unleashed.

# CHAPTER 17

# Tho' Much Is Taken . . .

On the day that General of the Army Douglas MacArthur stood on the deck of the battleship *Missouri* and sternly ordered the Japanese representatives to sign the articles of surrender, Fleet Admiral William D. Leahy was far from scenes of power, delivering a routine speech for the president. Addressing the Midwest Farmer Observance, he spoke of responsibility and of duty, especially of the civilian's duty to make "our own system of government and our own way of life . . . work better in our land than other systems work in foreign lands. Let us not fear the competition of other systems."

With the greatest war in history a thing of the past, it was time to rebuild the nation and the world. It was time to plan so that war would never again bring its destruction to man. In Leahy's mind the United States had a sacred duty of preserving the peace in spite of the dawning of the atomic age. His last years of service were dedicated to accomplishing that goal.

There were those who believed, now that the war was over, there was no longer a need for a military chief of staff to the commander in chief. Despite the fact that the military men of the United States have never failed to yield to civilian direction and have never failed to lay down their offices when their terms have expired, there remains almost a paranoid lack of trust among many liberal newspapermen and politicians that the generals and admirals they have relied on to save them from the enemy somehow become the enemy when the guns have fallen silent.

WDL being inducted as honorary chief of the Sioux Indians, September 1945. (Courtesy, National Archives)

Leahy, as the highest military officer in the United States, and as the one closest to the seat of power, was particularly suspect. None of his critics really knew what he had done; unlike MacArthur and Eisenhower, he had won no victories. He had ridden no tank, no plane, no ship into combat, and he had made no flamboyant speeches. If he appeared in the newsreels, it was in the shadow of the president. The public could understand the warrior. But could they understand the man next to the commander in chief? No matter. President Truman wanted Leahy to stay on his present job, and that settled the matter.

Although the euphoria of victory remained, it lessened every day as problems of peacetime had to be faced. The soldiers and sailors and airmen came home and had to find housing, jobs, education, to become reacquainted with wives and children, and to cope with life far removed from the army and the navy and the air force. To meet these new problems and new demands, the Truman administration had to shift emphasis and direction. Domestic problems jostled international ones from first consideration. The war was over.

Gradually the men who had served Roosevelt disappeared from the Washington scene. Their places were taken by others more compatible with the new president than with the old. On the military side, Robert Patterson replaced Henry Stimson as secretary of war. Eisenhower relieved Marshall, and Nimitz took over from King on the Joint Chiefs of Staff. Although Leahy admired King for his brilliant performance as CNO and COMINCH, he was never a close friend. And King's departure meant an end to the hated gray worsted summer working uniform he had imposed on the navy. Leahy and Nimitz refused to wear the grey, and the Navy Uniform shop in Brooklyn was directed to have always in stock several bolts of khaki tropical worsted to make their summer uniforms.

> One hot summer afternoon, [aide Commander Frank Pinney remembered], I ushered Admiral King, wearing his grey uniform and plain visored cap, into Admiral Leahy's office where he sat behind his desk in khaki shirt and pants. Looking up from under his bushy eyebrows, Admiral Leahy remarked, "Hi, Ernie, I see you're still wearing the same damned dirty dungarees." There was no reply from Admiral King.[1]

Although the war was over, Leahy still put in long hours in his office, six days a week, with an occasional visit on Sundays. Still there was some time for easing the heavy routine. He went home to lunch every day, and often he took

President Truman throws out the first ball for a game between the Washington Senators and St. Louis Browns at Griffith Stadium in Washington, September 1945. Front row, left to right: George Allen, President Truman, William Hassett, Leahy, and Charles Ross. Seated behind Leahy, smoking a cigar, is Senator Arthur W. Vandenberg of Michigan. Washington won 4 to 1. (Courtesy, FDR Library)

Dorothy Ringquist with him. He had instructed his stewards always to have a supply of sherry for her, but sometimes they forgot. "Dorothy, you'll have to drink bourbon," he'd say. "That's how I became a bourbon drinker," she recalled later.

The social life in Washington revived at the end of the war, and inevitably Leahy was invited to dinners, lunches, and cocktail parties. He accepted all the cocktail parties and seldom went. He couldn't bear to offend anyone by turning them down, but he preferred to be at home. He was a voracious reader and always had three books going at once. He delighted in the latest Perry Mason puzzle, and he loved historical novels, and he would also have a serious biography or historical study in progress as well. Now that the war was over, there was time to enjoy these things.

Still, there was not as much time as one might have thought. The president kept him busy, and the world gives no rest to those with responsibilities. The Cold War did not abate, and in Leahy's mind it never would. He feared that while Stalin might be trusted within limits, that he was not free of the pressure of hardliners in the Kremlin. Worse, when Stalin died, the Soviet Union would probably come under the sway of those who hated and feared the west.

With Averell Harriman, Leahy predicted that any remnants of the wartime alliance would soon give way to distrust, fear, bitterness, acts of isolated violence, and the constant threat of Soviet expansion in Europe and Asia.

Thus Leahy approved when Truman replaced Stettinius as secretary of state with former Associate Justice James Byrnes. Leahy felt that Stettinius had not been sufficiently forceful to stand up to the Russians, and he believed that Byrnes would bring the office the strength it needed.

The trouble was that Byrnes was determined to make his own mark on foreign affairs. In his own view, he should have been the one sitting in the Oval Office; Harry Truman was an interloper, installed because of the scheming of the men around Roosevelt. Accordingly, he intended to follow his own judgment, regardless of any instructions he might receive from Washington. The way to avoid receiving instructions was to communicate as little as possible. Averell Harriman warned him that the Council of Foreign Ministers meeting in September might collapse if Byrnes persisted in his high-handed ways. Byrnes ignored the advice, and Stalin almost recalled Molotov.

Byrnes became alarmed and put the best face on the matter by calling Leahy in Washington asking to be bailed out.

> I am satisfied, [he told Leahy over the phone] Molotov's desire to withdraw is due to other causes than the reason he gives about China and France. I suggest the President immediately wire Stalin, telling him he should communicate with Molotov and not permit the Counsel [sic] to be broken up because of the bad effect it would have on world peace.[2]

Since Truman was unavailable, Leahy took it on himself to send a telegram requesting more time. Stalin agreed, and the talks went on.

Leahy, of course, later informed Truman of his action, but there was really no need. By this time the president trusted his chief of staff completely, knowing that he would do what had to be done. If Leahy disagreed with his boss, he would tell him so, and that was the kind of associate Truman valued. He never hesitated to make his own opinions known, and he expected those around him to state theirs. The thing he could not stomach was the kind of person who pretended to agree and then did something else. Byrnes was showing signs of becoming such a person.

Leahy made clear his disagreement over the establishment of a Jewish state in Palestine. In October he showed concern in a journal entry:

> Under pressure from a Zionist organization of American Jews, the President has recently taken up with the British Government a proposal to import 100,000 Jews into Palestine, which proposal has received favorable attention by the American press and active opposition from Great Britain and the Arab world.

In a memorandum presumably to the president, Leahy felt that Truman should go further.

> The British Government should be informed that the United States does not intend to use military force in the settlement of the Palestine problem, nor does it intend to take any positive action in the matter prior to a consultation with the Arab inhabitants.
>
> Such a consultation could and should be inaugurated by the proposed Committee of Enquiry.
>
> One highly valuable result of the appointment of such a committee might be a temporary placating of partisans on both sides of the controversy in both Britain and America.[3]

He believed, as did Forrestal, that the establishment of a Jewish state would needlessly alienate the Arabs and endanger American access to the oil of the Middle East. Since there was nothing he could do about the problem, other than give his advice, he had to accept the fact that Truman was swayed by the strong Jewish vote in the United States. The state of Israel would be established, and he would have to live with it, but he didn't have to like it.

More immediately serious, as he saw it, was the influence of "communistically oriented" persons in the State Department who undermined Chiang Kai-shek and supported the insurgent Mao Tse-tung. Disagreements over the China policy would cause him to question the judgment of his former colleague on the JCS, General George Marshall.

Another problem facing the Truman administration that fall was the future of atomic energy. Most Americans wanted to keep the "secret" as an American trust. In October, Leahy worried:

> When and if the secret of the manufacture of the atomic bomb is known to foreign governments, America will be in acute danger of an attack with the new and terrible destructive weapon which we developed and used against Japan. . . .

Many uninformed people in the United States believe that its use in war can be prevented by an international control.

The admiral was, of course, right that international control would not work. In a memo for the president from the Joint Chiefs, he wrote:

> There is no present international control adequate to insure a safe disclosure [of the methods of making the bomb]. The inability of the United Nations Organization or any present international body to gain access to all nations to the extent necessary to observe or control atomic research and development must be recognized. . . .
>
> Unilateral free disclosure by the United States might be regarded as a sign of weakness by other nations and might not serve to lessen suspicion and distrust so long as censorship and secrecy exist to the present extent over large areas of the world. . . .
>
> While the Joint Chiefs of Staff consider it imperative to retain technical secrets on atomic weapons for the present, they regard it as of great military importance that further steps of a political nature should be promptly and vigorously pressed during the probably limited period of American monopoly, in an effort to prevent the exposure of the United States to a form of attack against which present defenses are inadequate.[4]

While he did not at that time foresee that Russian refusal to permit on-site inspection would make such accords useless, he did know that he did not trust them. He knew, as well as anyone else in the government, that the secrets of the production of the bomb could be kept only for a limited time. There was no secret. The physics by which the bomb worked was known to scientists all over the world. The only remaining problem was engineering technology. Only a few months after he stepped down as chief of staff, Russia exploded her first atomic weapon. Still, the United States had to try. And there were the peaceful uses of atomic energy to be considered.

But after a conference in November when Clement Attlee and Mackenzie King of Canada met with President Truman to discuss atomic problems, the conferees prepared to issue a cheerful statement, Leahy snorted:

> It is my opinion that such a statement will contain an excessive number of words, will make no positive proposals, and will accomplish little or nothing toward prohibiting the employment of atomic bombs in warfare.

Leahy thought little of the new prime minister of Great Britain, Clement Attlee, writing scathingly that he was "principally concerned with issuing a statement that will be pleasing to his constituency." He thought even less of him when Attlee embraced the idea of punishment of war criminals. "It is my opinion," the admiral wrote, "that the execution of leaders of the Axis governments is a reversion to barbarism of pre-Christian days." A year later, after the Nuremburg Tribunal had finished its work in October, with death sentences for many of the top Nazis, he wrote with some alarm:

From the little information now available, it appears that an Allied court has established a new legal principle, that the inauguration of a war of aggression is a war crime, for which the officials involved may be punished by a court appointed by the victors.

Such a principle may very probably work out to mean that a defeat in war establishes criminality and is a capital war crime.

While it is entirely possible and even probable that the Nazis are guilty of the charges for which they were convicted, and while it is practically certain that their elimination from society will improve the general average, it must be remembered that both the indictments were made and the court was appointed by those who were war enemies of the accused for four long, terrible years.

The precedent established does not appear to be in accord with American principles of jurisprudence, and its probable effect on the peace of the world seems at least doubtful.

The problem of *ex post facto* justice has not been settled even yet. Perhaps Leahy's early school teacher had a point when she said he would make a better lawyer than a sailor. His doubts are still shared by many, and the dilemma he expressed is still before the world. Nazi behavior may well have deserved death, but did the British, Russians and the United States have the authority to inflict it?

During the fall there were various rumors that Leahy might step down. He was approached about various posts outside government, and was mentioned as a possible ambassador to Spain, but in late November, the president told him that "he wishes me to remain in my present office for as long as I feel able to do so."

In politically dynamic Washington, it must have been a comfortable experience for a president to have as a close advisor and associate a man who had no political aspirations whatever.

During the fall, in view of worsening relationships with the Russians, Truman gave thought to sending Leahy "on a special mission to Moscow with the purpose of endeavoring to straighten out with Generalissimo Stalin some of the misunderstandings that now exist between our two governments."

The idea, which reminds us of Hopkins's trip the previous May, may reveal the president's growing disenchantment with Byrnes as secretary of state. Harriman was in his last days as ambassador to the Soviet Union, and Truman may have believed that he would welcome Leahy's assistance as he had that of Hopkins. But nothing ever came of the matter, and there is no other record of the idea of sending the admiral to the Soviet Union.★

★When queried by the author, no one, including Averell Harriman, Dorothy Ringquist, or any of the admiral's aides, remembered anything about such a mission. There is no further reference to it in the Leahy papers.

In addition to the Polish problem, which the United States was unable to do anything about, there was the matter of China. The Japanese surrender had brought no peace to that wartorn land. Centuries of oppression of the peasants by warlords finally led to rebellion. Western leaders looked on Chiang Kai-shek as the voice of China, her natural leader. But peasants, especially in the north, rallied to communist leader Mao Tse-tung. Chiang's resistance was weakened by the manifold corruption of his underlings. As Leahy pondered the problem, it seemed to him that Byrnes was not forthright enough in his dealings with the Russians, who by that time were openly "giving arms and assistance to the Chinese dissidents who claim to be communists." The "fratricidal war" in China, he continued, made it "practically impossible for us to assist Chiang Kai-shek in restoring order." According to the admiral, who believed that the United States should keep its promises to Chiang, he concluded:

> Three possible ways to solve this problem appear to me:
> 1. Give full and open military assistance to the National Government of China.
> 2. By diplomatic methods, force or induce England and the Soviet to give full backing to the National Government.
> 3. Provide Chiang Kai-shek with arms, transportation, and every necessary assistance, except American troops. This last method might make it possible for Chiang to get full control in some months or years.

Discussing China with Patrick Hurley, who had just resigned as ambassador in Chungking, Leahy was not surprised to hear that Hurley laid the failure of his efforts in China to "communistic leanings and actions of a number of assistants in the State Department."

President Truman immediately filled the vacancy caused by Hurley's resignation by naming General George Marshall to the post. Leahy believed Marshall was "the best possible selection," and with his ability and Truman's determination to support China, he looked for great improvement.

Then he was gradually disillusioned. State issued a paper which Truman released to the press, a disappointing document, but "the best that can be extracted from the State Department." By this time he felt that Byrnes was "not immune to the communisticly [sic] inclined advisers in his department." He was, however, pleased, when Truman expressed surprise and displeasure at Byrnes's attitude toward China. By this time, Byrnes had decided that Chiang's government could not stand alone and that he would have to take "so-called Chinese Communists into our camp."

Unfortunately for Leahy's peace of mind, Marshall also came to the view that Mao Tse-tung's people would have to be brought into the government. Leahy later told Jonathan Daniels that Marshall had "said he was going to tell

Chiang that he had to get on with the Communists or get on without help from us. He said the same thing when he got back. I thought he was wrong both times."

Daniels suggested that the communists might have taken a "historically indigestible land." Leahy replied, "Yes, I've heard that since I was an ensign and I still don't believe it."[5]

So Marshall went off to China, while Leahy continued to worry over bad advice from the Department of State. There was nothing he could do, however, especially with Byrnes as secretary of state. In his view, Byrnes had to go. As the year ended, it seemed that Leahy might get his wish.

In mid-December, Byrnes went to Moscow for a meeting of the Council of Foreign Ministers. From the first he played his cards close to his vest, making only one report to the president during the entire time, although Harriman repeatedly reminded him of the need to keep Truman informed. The one message he sent seemed to the president not like a proper report of a cabinet member to the president. Rather it was "more like one partner in a business telling the other that his business trip was progressing well and not to worry."[6]

When Byrnes returned to the United States, he asked the White House to arrange with the radio networks for a nationwide broadcast on the conference. This was too much for the impetuous Truman. He responded mildly enough, telling Byrnes to "come down today or tomorrow to report." Then there would be time enough, if advisable, for Byrnes to make his arrangements.

It was New Year's Eve when Byrnes arrived and reported aboard the yacht *Williamsburg*, where the president and his cronies, including Leahy, were awaiting the arrival of the year 1946. Accounts of what happened then are as numerous as those who told the story. According to Leahy, who believed that Byrnes had botched things, "he had made concessions to expediency that are destructive of the President's announced intention to adhere strictly to his policies that are righteous. . . . It appears now that Russia has been granted every demand that wrecked the London conference."

According to Truman's memoirs, he took the secretary aside and administered a tongue-lashing, followed by a stern letter. Byrnes took the admonishment in good grace. Leahy reported merely that the president had expressed "great displeasure" but that afterwards Byrnes "appears to have satisfied the president." Truman's great friend, John Synder, told a completely different story, to the effect that it was Leahy who took Byrnes to the woodshed. This seems highly unlikely, for Truman was never one to duck his responsibilities; he might have had Leahy administer a reprimand to someone below the cabinet level. In dealing with his principal advisors, Harry Truman could and did speak for himself.[7]

Whatever the circumstances, Byrnes accepted the rebuke, partly perhaps because he still felt he had a chance at the White House. Truman had named no vice president, and if anything happened to him, Byrnes, as secretary of state, would succeed him.★ Truman, on his part, did not ask for his resignation, for the man he had already picked to succeed him at Foggy Bottom was busy on another assignment in China. This, of course, was George Marshall. Therefore, Byrnes kept his job for the time being.

After Byrnes had left the *Williamsburg*, Leahy and the others worked on a speech for the president until the time came to celebrate "the arrival of 1946 by singing Navy songs during the first hour of the New Year."

As the new year began, it was evident that some members of the State Department were looking on Leahy as an obstruction. The story reached the public in a column of Leahy's old friend, Constantine Brown, who had once before predicted Leahy's departure from the Washington scene. After describing how the Map Room had worked, and its correlation with the State Department, the column continued:

> In the last few weeks, however, the liaison between the White House and the State Department has been less effective. The reason is said to be that some of the top policy-framers in the department dislike the chief correlator of strategy and policy—Admiral William D. Leahy, who as Chief of Staff to the Commander in Chief is also the senior officer on the Joint Chiefs of Staff. . . .
>
> When Mr. Truman became the Chief Executive, Admiral Leahy offered his resignation on the ground that the new President might wish an entirely new team. The admiral again offered his resignation after Gen. Marshall and Admiral King retired. The President, who had become intimately acquainted with the Chief of Staff in the few months he had been in the White House and learned to trust him, asked Admiral Leahy to continue his work.
>
> Lately, however, the "liberal" policy-framers in the State Department have come to consider Admiral Leahy as an "adverse influence" in the White House. He is being accused by them of advising the President to stick to the traditional policy of this country never to renege on its formal pledges regardless of how well the diplomats might be able to camouflage it.
>
> Admiral Leahy is described by the "liberals" as a man of the old school. There is no question that this description is correct. He is a fanatical believer in the Constitution of the United States and in the traditional honesty of this country toward all her pledges to other nations. He and Gen. MacArthur are of the same school. And the State Department considers them obsolete.
>
> Because his influence with the President is believed to be still strong—Mr. Truman is made of the same cloth—many official communications are being held back from Admiral Leahy, who, on specific orders from the President must put together certain reports from the State Department and correlate them with the views of the still functioning Joint Chiefs of Staff.[8]

★Before the Presidential Succession Act of 1947, the secretary of state would succeed to the presidency on the death or disability of the president when there was no vice president. That law changed the succession so that the Speaker of the House of Representatives and the President Pro Tempore of the Senate come before the cabinet members.

Leahy had better things to do than worry about what liberals in the State Department said about him. He was concerned, however, about what they might do to the country. "The American Department of State and the British Labor Government have adopted a policy of appeasment of the Soviet Government that is reminiscent of Mr. Chamberlain at Munich and dangerous to the political interests of America and England."

Of course, if the United States was going to be able to deal with Russia and China and all the other nations of the world where problems existed, it was necessary to know what was going on. The wartime OSS [Office of Strategic Services] had not been designed for peacetime, and President Truman wanted to establish something to take its place.

As early as the previous October, he had asked Leahy to work with the secretaries of war, state, and navy to work out recommendations. The three departments worked the problem over; several organizations were tried, and the problem defined. State had one view of a proper intelligence organization and the JCS another. In the end, the JCS concept prevailed, but it was diluted by the influence of the State Department and the Bureau of the Budget.[9]

The president set up a Central Intelligence Group (CIG), naming, at Leahy's recommendation, reserve Rear Admiral Sidney W. Souers to run it. Leahy, as representative of the president on the National Intelligence Authority was *ex officio* a member of the CIG. In the sophomoric humor he sometimes enjoyed, Truman celebrated the occasion with a private ceremony in the White House. He presented black hats and cloaks and wooden daggers to

WDL testifying against merger of the armed forces, 4 December 1945. (Courtesy, National Archives)

Leahy and Souers and placed a large, flowing moustache on Leahy's upper lip. He also bestowed mock commissions upon them:

To my Brethren and Fellow Dog House Denizens

By virtue of the authority vested in me as Top Dog, I require and charge that Front Admiral William D. Leahy and Rear Admiral Sidney W. Souers receive and accept vestments and appurtenances of their positions, namely as Personal Snooper and as Director of Centralized Snooping. In accepting these symbols of trust and confidence, I charge that each of you not only seek to better our foreign relations through more intensive snooping but also keep me informed constantly of the movements and actions of the other, for without such coordination there can be no order and no aura of mutual trust.
Harry S. Truman[10]

But joking aside, the deterioration of relations between the United States and the Soviet Union was no laughing matter. In late winter, Averell Harriman returned for good from Russia. He and Leahy had a long talk in which they found general agreement. Russia, they felt, while placing highest emphasis on the safety of the homeland, attached almost equal importance to the expansion of communism around the world. Harriman believed it was necessary for the United States to take a strong position in face of Soviet intransigence. Leahy agreed, but feared it would "be difficult to induce the Secretary of State to tacitly admit fault in our present appeasement attitude."

Slowly, however, the policy of containment was being born.

On 3 March, Leahy called at the British embassy to see Winston Churchill, newly arrived from rest and convalescence in Florida. Leahy found him in bed, smoking a long cigar, and scattering ashes over the sheets and the pages of the manuscript he was revising. He tossed a copy to his visitor, asking him to read it over.

"I could find no fault with his proposed address," Leahy approved.

In that speech, which Churchill was to deliver two days later in Fulton, Missouri, terminology for the cold war would be framed.

As the *Ferdinand Magellan* sped across the country, bearing Truman, Churchill, Leahy, and others, the president read the speech through. He made no comment, however, but invited his guest to play a game of low-stakes poker.

The next day, Churchill, resplendent in his scarlet academic robe from Oxford University, gripped his lapels as he looked out at the crowd in the gymnasium of Westminster College in Fulton. It was his moment of fulfillment, the first major speech since his defeat at the hands of the Labour Party the previous year. His unforgettable voice rumbled and soared. "From Stettin in the Baltic to Trieste in the Adriatic, an Iron Curtain has descended across the Continent. Behind that line lie all the capitals of the ancient states of central and eastern Europe. Warsaw, Berlin, Prague, Vienna, Budapest, Belgrade,

Bucharest, and Sofia, all these famous cities and their populations around them lie in what I might call the Soviet sphere, and are all subject, in one form or another, not only to Soviet influence but to a very high and in some cases increasing measure of control from Moscow.''

The answer, he stated, was a "fraternal association of the English speaking peoples." He did not believe that the Soviets wanted war. "What they desire is the fruits of war and the indefinite expansion of their power and doctrines. . . . From what I have seen of our Russian friends and allies during the war, I am convinced that there is nothing they admire so much as strength, and there is nothing for which they have less respect than for weakness, especially military weakness.''

Those views accorded so perfectly with Leahy's own that the speech might have been written by him if his skill in prose had equalled that of the great Englishman. The address, he felt,

> may go down in history as one of the most powerful influences in bringing about close British-American collaboration to preserve world peace. It will produce a sharply unfavorable reaction in Soviet Russia and highly unfavorable comment from the vocal communists, "fellow travelers" and "pinkies" in the United States. It was a courageous statement of Mr. Churchill's belief in the inherent righteousness and power of the English-speaking world, and it was received by his audience with marked enthusiasm.

Leahy's outspoken support of Churchill's Iron Curtain speech predictably brought unfavorable newspaper comment, some writers, trying to make fact of desire, told of his diminishing influence with the president. Others, like Marquis Childs, knew better. "There is no doubt that he has recently played an important part in persuading the President of the need to take a firmer stand toward the Soviets."[11]

Mr. Truman had to make up his mind about his attitude toward Russia later that year. It had been a period of provocation and irritating incidents. American planes flying out of European bases occasionally strayed across the Iron Curtain, and sometimes they were shot down. Sometimes they were shot down when they had not strayed across the Iron Curtain.[12]

A recurring worry that spring and summer was that European nations which had not recovered from war would embrace communism in their elections. And then there was fear that the USSR itself might decide to go to war against the United States, taking advantage of her swift dismantling of the war machine that had defeated the Axis. In March, FBI Director J. Edgar Hoover reported in a letter to Leahy that "all Soviet ships in United States ports are to be loaded immediately and clear the ports of the United States as quickly as possible."[13] Such a move created a presumption that the Soviet Union was preparing for war. Leahy quickly informed the president. But, as it happened, nothing came of the matter.

Then in May came another worry. It seemed possible that French communists might sabotage the election in June and instigate an armed uprising, which would "almost certainly result in full-scale Civil War." Plans for extrication of American forces from Paris and Marseilles were discussed in various papers. HST rejected a plan for taking a stand against possible insurgents. Instead he approved only action in defense of American lives and property, using minimum force, and taking no part in the conflict.[14]

In the year that had elapsed since the end of the war in Europe, Leahy and President Truman had become pretty well disillusioned about Soviet intentions. Nor were they alone. Many people openly urged for "preventive war" against Russia, so they might be defeated before they had produced atomic bombs. Almost no one trusted them, and this lack of trust formed the backbone of American policy.

But not everyone was so pessimistic. Some felt you could deal with the Russians and restore the friendliness that had existed under Franklin Roosevelt.

Henry Wallace, the only surviving cabinet member of Roosevelt's administration with the exception of Forrestal, embarked on a visionary crusade to relieve tensions between the United States and the Soviet Union. He was a curious mixture of the naive and sophisticated, of the mystic and the practical. After Churchill's speech in Fulton, Wallace had been shocked and made no effort to conceal it. In July he protested in a letter to Truman the recent atomic bomb tests at Bikini Atoll and urged a new approach toward the Russians. Truman made a polite answer, and there the matter rested with a general agreement among the senior advisors that, as George Elsey put it, Wallace should be indoctrinated on some of the facts of life about the Soviet Union.

Then in September, with Byrnes in Paris at a meeting of the Council of Foreign Ministers, Wallace made a speech at a Democratic rally in Madison Square Garden in New York. Before he left Washington, Wallace showed the speech to the president. As with so many other things, accounts differ about what happened. Wallace later claimed that Truman read it carefully, saying "that's right," or similar phrases as he went over it. According to Truman, he only had time to glance at it and did not take it in.

Sometime on the afternoon of 12 September, a few hours before the speech was to be delivered, Leahy told Truman that the State Department ought to take a look at it. But there was no time, for Wallace had left, and, worse, at a press conference that afternoon, Truman announced his approval of the speech.

Thus, as Wallace mounted the platform to deliver the speech that night, it seemed to have the imprimatur of the Truman administration. But his words were like a bombshell. Calling for a soft approach, he declared that the United States had to recognize that we have no more business in the *political* affairs of Eastern Europe than Russia has in the *political* affairs of Latin America, western Europe, and the United States . . . whether we like it or not the Russians will try to socialize their sphere of influence just as we try to democratize our sphere of influence. I am neither anti-British nor pro-British—neither anti-Russian nor pro-Russian. And when President Truman read these words, he said they represented the policy of his administration.

The fat was really in the fire. Truman issued a hasty "clarification" of his press conference statement, saying he had not approved the contents of the speech but only of Mr. Wallace's right to deliver it.

> Mr. Wallace is, in my opinion, [wrote Leahy] an honest "fellow traveller" with the Soviets, at least a "pink" and completely uninformed in regard to the existing international situation. His address was a definite disservice to the United States.
>
> I advised the President this morning that both Mr. Byrnes and Mr. Wallace cannot remain as members of his Cabinet unless the stated policy of the United States is radically changed.

Byrnes agreed and informed the president that there was not enough room in the cabinet for both him and Wallace. Wallace went. Averell Harriman was recalled from London where he was serving as ambassador to become secretary of commerce.

Earlier that summer Leahy had seen Harriman when he made a trip to London. The press was informed that the trip was to discuss the use of former Japanese bases in the Pacific, but according to George Elsey, "He has *no* intention of talking about business. This release about "bases" is just smoke screen to prevent "speculation" about his trip . . . These facts are from the Admiral himself!"[15]

He dined with the Churchills, finding the former PM "his old charming self in mental alertness" but depressed about the prospects of peace. He called on Foreign Secretary Ernest Bevin, and was favorably impressed by the improvement in his knowledge of the world since they had met at Potsdam. But he wondered if the British people could "be pleased with a Foreign Minister who misuses his H's." Leahy's departure was delayed by a royal command visit to the King, who was "altogether a gracious and attractive person with whom to talk on inconsequential matters."

Before coming home, he went to Paris to see the Douglas MacArthurs who had been with him in Vichy a lustrum earlier. "I was again impressed with the superlative beauty of Paris preserved since a time when France led the world in culture, power and accomplishment. That magnificence is gone, probably forever, but Paris, undamaged by the late war remains a jewelled souvenir of the greatness that was France."

WDL with President Gabriel Gonzales Videla of Chile, Fall 1946. (Courtesy, National Archives)

In the fall, Leahy made another trip, this time representing the president, for the inauguration of Gabriel Gonzales-Videla, whom he had known in Vichy, as president of Chile. The United States sent a naval squadron including the battleship *Wisconsin*, the carrier *Leyte*, and three destroyers. This impressive naval show and Leahy's friendship now renewed with Gonzales-Videla helped cement friendly relations between Chile and the United States for some time to come.

On the way back, the fleet admiral wanted to fly from Panama back home. This required that he transfer to a destroyer for the run ashore.

> He was to be transferred at sea from *Wisconsin* to the destroyer in a bo'sun's chair and, as executive officer, I had general supervision when such a high ranking officer was transferred on the high line in a bo'sun's chair. Also, it was the first time *Wisconsin*'s current crew had performed this evolution as a crew. I went back to the fantail and Admiral Leahy was looking extremely discomfited. I wondered if possibly we had done something wrong, and he said he had never ridden in one of these! . . . It was a rather rough day, but we transferred him by "high line" without incident.[16]

Safely across the rough waters, and safely through the air to Washington, Bill Leahy arrived in time for the disastrous election of 1946 which sobered the Truman administration by electing a Republican Congress. Still, there was enough spirit left for a happy trip to Key West where Leahy experienced his first dive in a submarine, a captured German U-boat. During that time, he was learning to value the friendship of the president's administrative secretary Willam D. Hassett, who went by the nickname of "Bishop" from his unobtrusive but devout faith in the Roman Catholic church. The two men fished together and on one occasion accompanied the president on a destroyer trip to Dry Tortugas to visit Fort Jefferson, where Dr. Samuel Mudd had been imprisoned for treating the wounds of John Wilkes Booth.

The year ended as it had begun for Leahy, on board the presidential yacht *Williamsburg* with toasts and music.

# CHAPTER 18

# . . . Much Abides

The new year brought a good many problems across Leahy's desk, for he was still one of the principal and closest advisors to the president. The Truman administration has often been charged with cronyism, and there is a certain amount of truth in the charge. But there were two kinds of cronies around the president: those he brought in to his administration because they were cronies, and those he made cronies as they were doing their jobs. The first group might or might not be competent, and some of the failures of the incompetent embarrassed the president considerably. There were others such as Leahy, who were superbly competent, whom Truman treated as cronies after he got to know them in their jobs. Leahy, of course, was too aloof to be a crony, but the friendship between him and the man from Missouri was real. *United States News* told its readers:

Admiral Leahy's powerful position—his office is in the White House, he sees the President daily and reporters infrequently—has been overlooked. In the last year, for example, the newspapers have contained scarcely half a dozen items about him, mostly brief and perfunctory, As one of the orginators of foreign policy in a critical period, the man, his background and ideas are of the highest importance. He does not talk about himself, and his suggestions are reserved for the President. . . .

But regardless of such circumstances as that, Admiral Leahy insists on speaking his views plainly and completely, whether the President likes it or not. In the last few months the President has liked it—very much. The decision to oppose Russia by helping Greece and Turkey is one product of the Admiral's point of view and its frequent reiteration.[1]

The decision to aid Greece and Turkey, otherwise known as the Truman Doctrine, came about because of the decline of British power after World War II. Economically exhausted, and with a Labour government more interested in domestic than foreign affairs, the British under Clement Attlee proceeded to do what Churchill had refused to consider—preside over the dissolution of the British Empire.

But before the problem of Greece and Turkey could be dealt with, on the other side of the world, General Marshall reported that he was getting nowhere in China and suggested that he be recalled. Truman wanted him home, for he intended to make him secretary of state. When he asked Leahy for advice, he was surprised to find that the fleet admiral had another choice. "In private discussions with the President of this problem I had recommended to his favorable consideration for appointment as Secretary of State the present Secretary of the Navy, James Forrestal, and General Marshall, in the order named."

Truman, however, had other plans for Forrestal and named Marshall, whose departure marked the final collapse of the administration's efforts to preserve Chiang Kai-shek and his government on the mainland of China.

On 21 February, the British embassy telephoned Secretary Marshall's office with the request for an appointment to deliver "a blue piece of paper." This curious term was diplomatic slang for an important, formal communication. Under Secretary Dean Acheson described the contents as "shockers." The British proposed to end all financial aid to Greece and Turkey and pull all their troops out of those countries in six weeks.

In both countries, the democratic governments were too weak to stand without economic help. Without such aid, both faced communist takeovers, threatened from within by their own communist citizens, and from without by the Red Army. Leahy, Marshall, Forrestal, and Acheson all agreed that something had to be done to prevent the expansion of Soviet power into the Mediterranean, and that the two friendly governments had to be propped up. But funds could be provided only by the Congress, so Truman summoned leaders of both parties to the White House. Unexpectedly, Marshall stumbled in presenting the material, but Acheson took over and made a masterly presentation, which caused Senator Vandenberg of Michigan, formerly an isolationist, but since the war a respected international statesman, to exclaim, "Mr. President, if you will say that to the Congress and the country, I will support you and I believe that most of its members will do the same."[2]

Although he believed that Greece and Turkey had to be saved, Leahy felt that there was a fundamental inconsistency in letting go of China, which "is of much more importance to America than the American states," while going all out to save Greece and Turkey. He never did accept Marshall's conclusion that there was nothing the United States could do about China.

When the Truman Doctrine was considered by the cabinet a few days later, he wanted to make sure that everyone understood all the implications of the plan. He made sure that they understood "that projection of the United States into the political problems of Europe is a direct and positive change in the political policy of the United States," and that its "purpose is to prevent Soviet domination of Europe and that the resulting destruction of what we consider democratic government in that part of the world with a future danger to our own safety."

> The President, after considering the opinion of all members of his Cabinet orally, announced a decision to ask Congress to appropriate the necessary funds, and to inform the public with full frankness as to the purpose for which the money will be used.

Leahy went on to note wryly that this was the first cabinet meeting he had attended "where a definite decision was reached and clearly announced."

When Congress approved appropriations for aid to Greece and Turkey under the Truman Doctrine, the policy of containment was established. Its necessity had been ably stated a year earlier in George F. Kennan's famous "Long Telegram" from Moscow. Kennan, who was number-two man in the embassy, stated that "at the bottom of the Kremlin's neurotic view of world affairs," was a suspicion that the west wanted to infiltrate, overthrow, and dominate Russia. The suspicion had existed since czarist days, and it would continue to exist because of the kind of people the Russians were. He went on to predict that the Kremlin would use every possible means to divide, weaken, and infiltrate the west, employing diplomacy, subversion, international organizations, propaganda, and even military means to obtain their ends. Any thought of modus vivendi, attractive as it might seem, would only serve to put western nations in positions of weakness, for as they relaxed their precautions, the Soviets would intensify their efforts, using modus vivendi, rapprochement, détente, and other accommodations as means of opportunity for deception and subversion.

Averell Harriman had copies made of this "long telegram" and distributed it throughout the government. Since he had been years in the Russian capital and claimed personal friendship with Stalin, he could scarcely be called a Russophobe. His advocacy of Kennan's views gave them widespread acceptance in government circles. Certainly Leahy agreed. The time to stop Russia, he felt, was before she got started. When Truman decided to go ahead with support of Greece and Turkey, he recorded:

> With the directness of a soldier and the vision of an experienced statesman, he has now made the issue clear.

His attitude may possibly prevent a war that has appeared inevitable between the philosophies of political freedom and political slavery. It cannot make the present position of America in the prospect of such a war any worse than it was before.

President Truman wasn't so sure that the Greeks weren't somewhat responsible for their own misfortune. And the Jews, too, for in a note scribbled on the bottom of a memo sent him by Leahy, the president wrote:

Adm. Leahy:- . . . Greeks and Jews suffer from an inferiority complex as well as a persecution complex. I've tried to help both and so far they've only given me a pain in the neck.[3]

Henry Wallace led the opposition to the Truman Doctrine, and before Congress finally approved it, Leahy's name had been kicked around on the floor of the House. He was accused of being associated with a "conspiracy to draw America into warfare on the side of reactionary Fascist elements everywhere in the world." This was a pretty sweeping statement, but Leahy didn't let it bother him. "Having for two years in Europe been maligned by Goebbel's Big League experts, attacks by amateurs from the local Bush Leagues are in comparison even complimentary."

The other major accomplishment of President Truman's first term as far as opposition to the Russians was concerned, was, of course, the Marshall Plan for European Recovery. This was one of the few important matters that Leahy had little to do with. He approved its aims, but it was outside of his field.

One matter that was very much in his field was unification of the armed forces. This had been a particular project of the president ever since the end of World War II. Leahy saw no reason for breaking up a winning combination. The Joint Chiefs system had worked well in the war, and as far as he was concerned, the system should continue.

There were many reasons in favor of unification, however, in addition to the compelling one that the president wanted it. In particular the air force wanted to be an independent arm, equal to the army and navy, and the only way this might be done was not by establishing a new service in the armed forces but by cutting down to one service with three branches. The argument that a unified department of defense would be more efficient, more cost-effective, and more capable attracted a lot of support.

From the first, Leahy felt that the proposed unification, which provided for a single commander or chief of staff under the president, threatened national security. Since he held the role most closely resembling that commander, he knew the perils. Although he was the highest ranking military officer in the United States, *he had no command function.* He spoke for the president. He firmly believed that a man with his responsibilities and with command function should not be appointed.

"It is wrong and dangerous," he wrote Sam Rosenman, "in that it effectively takes away from the President his constitutional responsibility as Commander in Chief."[4]

Still, since he knew that with the president desiring it, some form of unification was inevitable. He joined forces with Secretary Forrestal in trying to keep extremists, especially in the army and air force from crippling the navy by taking over all its functions. "The proposed 'amalgamation,'" he wrote retired Vice Admiral Thomas T. Craven, "would wreck the sea defenses in order to gain appropriation for the Army and Army Air.

"We cannot yet look with complacency upon abandoning the sea and depending on air power. That time may come in the future, but it is not yet in sight."[5]

If the army and air force could not make gains themselves, there was an effort, as many naval officers believed, to weaken the navy, especially in the Pacific, where CINCPAC was still the area commander outside of Japan. Army advocates urged that CINCPAC be separated from the fleet command. In other words, there would be two commands, CINCPAC, and CINCPACFLT. Although the document at hand does not mention it, it is easy enough to read between the lines of the navy's suspicion that the CINCPAC post might well go to an army officer.[6]

Truman, Leahy concluded, would not be satisfied unless Congress passed a law establishing a single department of defense. During 1946 and early 1947, the fleet admiral held many meetings with everyone concerned, trying to kill the idea of a single commander and trying to keep the budding air force from shooting down naval aviation and the army from killing off the Marine Corps. He persuaded the president to take a two-day cruise off the Virginia Capes aboard the new carrier *Franklin D. Roosevelt*. He felt it provided "much of interest and value to the Presdent."

Since Leahy was still the president's man, he left most of the fighting for the navy position to Forrestal. Both Leahy and Forrestal argued for a balanced concept, and near the end of 1946, Truman agreed to hold the matter over to the following year so that the forces would have ample time to work out their differences and have their say before congressional committees.

By midsummer of 1947, a unification bill was emerging from congressional committees, and on 16 July the National Security Act of 1947 was passed by both houses. It provided for three separate departments, army, navy, and air force, each with a secretary not of cabinet rank, and a single secretary of defense, who would be a member of the cabinet. As Truman envisaged the job, it seems to have been that the secretary of defense would eventually replace the chief of staff to the president; it would, on Leahy's retirement, turn the post he had held into a civilian position. It also separated

Admirals Nimitz, Leahy, and Mitscher with President Truman aboard the carrier *Franklin D. Roosevelt* off the Virginia Capes, 22 April 1946. (Courtesy, FDR Library)

the post of chairman of the Joint Chiefs of Staff from the job of chief of staff to the commander in chief. No longer would the president have direct contact with the JCS. He would deal through the civilian secretary. Thus, when Leahy stepped down in 1949, no replacement was named for his job.

President Truman named Forrestal to the post of secretary of defense, an appointment which was very pleasing to the fleet admiral.

As is well known, the first defense reorganization act was not completely effective, and a good deal of Leahy's time until he laid down the burden was spent in settling interservice squabbles.

More pleasant than umpiring interservice rivalries was a trip to Rio de Janeiro with President Truman and his family for a meeting of the Organization of American States. They flew down in the president's new plane, a DC-6, named *Independence* in honor both of the idea and of Truman's home town. The plane was a great advance over its predecessor, "The Sacred Cow," in that it had pressurization, higher speed, and more sophisticated communications equipment. It had a sofa which would make into a bed for the president and it had comfortable lounge chairs rather than airliner seats. The president's suite took up most of the after half of the plane and it was luxurious beyond anything chief executives had known earlier.

Six days of celebration, gala ceremonies, and state functions left the Truman's companions pretty well exhausted. They returned hospitality aboard the battleship *Missouri*, and at the American embassy where they were staying. They celebrated 7 September, Brazilian Independence Day, by Presidents Truman and Eurico Dutra, accompanied by Admiral Leahy in the front seat, riding in an open car to the reviewing stand, where they observed a parade of Brazilian army, naval, cavalry, engineer, and tank units, as well as a detachment of naval infantry and marines from the *Missouri*.

> Upon completion of the parade we drove through streets crowded with emotionally enthusiastic citizens who gave to President Truman such an ovation as I had never seen before, proving that his visit to Brazil was an entire success from the point of view of the people.

On the way back from Rio de Janeiro, the *Missouri*, of course, crossed the equator. Since President Truman had never crossed before on a surface ship, he had to pay his respects to His Majesty, King Neptune, Ruler of the Raging Main. When Davy Jones came on board the day before the ceremonies, he said he had heard that one of the passengers was Number One Pollywog, who ventured to call himself the President of the United States. The answer being given in the affirmative, Davy was further informed that also on board was the nation's Number One Shellback, Fleet Admiral William D. Leahy, who had paid his respects to Neptune forty-nine years earlier.

All three of the Trumans participated in the age-honored ceremonies. The president joined the others in wearing a white sailor hat turned inside out, but he balked at turning up one trouser leg and wearing his shirt backward. Margaret Truman described the ceremony in considerable detail in her biography of her father, even though she thought the proceedings rather ridiculous. "Grown men have to act like boys now and then, I suppose," she wrote in her diary.

Neptune wore the traditional long green robe and had long white whiskers. The queen, in similar costume, smoked a huge black cigar. The royal couple was greeted with six ruffles and flourishes, two more than the president rated, but with a one-gun salute. After inspecting the ship in company with Captain Robert Dennison, Their Majesties took their seats on thrones set up on the fantail. As Shellback Number One, Leahy was in the seat of honor on the left hand of Neptune. Nearby was a large dunking tank, and alongside it was a "bloodstained" operating table equipped with saws, knives, ropes, a brace and bit, and other suitable "surgical" instruments. Above the throne was the inscription, EXPECT NO JUSTICE.

Number One Shellback Leahy with Number One Pollywog Truman and Captain Robert Dennison ready for Crossing the Line ceremonies aboard the USS *Missouri*, returning from Rio de Janeiro, September 1947. (Courtesy, FDR Library)

Number One Pollywog was then summoned by the Royal Prosecutor and charged with having deeply insulted Neptune by coming south of the Line by "a despicable and unnatural means of travel, namely by air." Truman grinned and pleaded guilty, explaining that reasons of state sometimes required such action. The Royal Prosecutor, in a moment of benevolence, recommended mercy. "In recognition of the fact that you have finally delivered this large number of pollywogs for judgment before his royal court, His Majesty is disposed to exercise some leniency in your case. You are commanded to furnish each member of his royal court a card bearing your autograph, and you will further be prepared to continue and furnish a bountiful supply of Corona Corona cheroots for the shellback members of the President's mess during the remainder of this cruise and forever after."

Mrs. Truman also pleaded guilty and was given amnesty. Margaret had to bow down and lead six pollywog ensigns in singing "Anchors Aweigh."[7]

Leahy reached his office in Washington on 20 September, just in time to learn of a budding conspiracy among certain naval officers to prevent the appointment of Admiral Louis Denfeld as CNO in relief of Fleet Admiral Nimitz. Leahy had recommended Denfeld, who had been his aide when he was himself CNO. The scheme came to nothing, and in the end Denfeld relieved Nimitz in December.★

The last full year of Leahy's service was crowded with events, one crisis after another. During 1948, there was the establishment of the state of Israel, the Berlin Blockade, much interservice quarreling over the limited budget, and finally the miracle of the reelection of President Truman.

By this time, Leahy's opposition to the creation of the state of Israel was becoming an open secret. In this opposition the admiral parted company with Harry Truman. His grounds were not based on anti-Semitism, although, regretably, there was some of that in him. Of more serious concern was the apprehension he shared with Forrestal that American support of partition of Palestine and establishment of a Jewish state there would imperil America's access to Middle Eastern oil by alienating the Arabs. A JCS memo to the secretary of defense in October 1947 warned that the decision to establish a Jewish state might result in the USSR replacing the United States and Great Britain as the dominant power in the region and "would gravely prejudice access by the United States to the oil of Iran, Iraq and Saudi Arabia."[8]

On 17 January 1948, he recorded that continuing Arab resistance to the partition of Palestine as recommended by the United Nations had already "produced a dangerous condition of rioting that approaches a general civil war."

> The great dangers in the Palestine problem [he continued] are a world-wide war between Moslems and Christians or an occupation of Eastern Mediterranean countries by Soviet troops resulting eventually in American withdrawal from the oil-rich Middle East or an expulsion of the Soviets therefrom by an American–Soviet world war.
>
> At the present time I see no other way to extricate ourselves from the difficulty into which we have injected ourselves.

---

★The only documentary evidence for such a conspiracy is a brief entry in Leahy's journal for 22 September 1947. Appointment of Denfeld meant that two successive CNOs were non-aviators. Naval aviators preferred Dewitt C. Ramsey. But one can well imagine that Leahy would have spared no effort to scotch any such politicking among junior admirals in the Navy Department. To him, such action would smack of near mutiny.

From a military point of view, the position of the United States in Palestine appears very dangerous.

Later he wrote, "Russia is looking for an opportunity to get into the Middle East," and felt they might be aided by "the Communist element of Israel," and that aid "on our part to Israel would be detrimental to our tactical and strategic interest and will endanger the lives and property of US citizens."

As these views were leaked to the public, Leahy became the target of attacks from the public and the press. Walter Winchell, Drew Pearson, and other columnists scored his "militaristic" views. One story blamed him for putting the notion of universal military training in President Truman's head. Since that was one of President Truman's pet projects, and the admiral didn't particularly favor it, the story was ridiculous. But in the view of critics, the "military influence" of Leahy was particularly dangerous. The story attributed these views to a group of "prominent citizens." The "citizens" were probably named Royal, Underwood, and L. C. Smith.

Knowing that such attacks might hurt the president, Leahy offered to resign. Truman told him to forget it.

In February, Leahy accompanied Truman on a journey of inspection to Puerto Rico. It was a bittersweet experience; memories of Louise were everywhere, and the sympathy of their many friends was nearly more than he could bear. Still, he determined to come back some day when he had more time.

WDL at Puerto Rico with President Truman. Left to right: Admiral Leahy; Governor Pinero; President Truman; Interior Secretary Julius Krug; and Luis Muñoz Marín, on a terrace of the Jaqueyes Hotel, Aguas Buenas, Puerto Rico, 21 February 1948. (Courtesy, FDR Library)

The armed forces, meanwhile, were becoming more discordant than uni-fied, and Secretary Forrestal wanted to knock some heads together over the interservice bickering. Forrestal presided in person, and Leahy was rather disgusted with the conference: "All three parties to the controversy," he wrote, "fought vigorously for the interest of their own group and not for the interest of the national defense . . . ." There was not a great deal of hope, for "so far as I could see, no progress was made toward . . . working together for national defense . . . ."

On his return to Washington, Leahy prepared a memorandum for the record. Most of it is too technical for general interest, but a few of its conclusions are worth noting. The JCS agreed not to abolish the Marine Corps but to limit it to four divisions, and to allow no headquarters larger than a corps. Thus the Corps could not ever be a second land army. Each service would be allowed the research and development function to permit it to keep abreast of scientific advance. In return for being awarded primacy in strategic bombing, the air force agreed that the navy should keep its carriers. The navy, however, "would not be prohibited from attacking targets, inland or otherwise, to accomplish its mission."[9]

That nasty bit of business being over, Leahy was free to make his promised visit to Puerto Rico, which he found much changed from the days of his stewardship. The Spanish-descended aristocracy had been supplanted in power by the "lower orders" who were not careful of the sensibilities of those they had displaced. "Perhaps the same leveling process is going on through-out the world, and perhaps it is equally displeasing to the upper orders elsewhere." He did, however, thoroughly enjoy seeing friends whom he had cherished as the years had gone by.

Soon after his return to the United States, Leahy was distressed to note that President Truman recognized the state of Israel. "The President's announce-ment, made with inadequate consideration, leaves many questions un-answered." He went on for pages analyzing the disadvantages and dangers in the recognition of Israel, which he concluded was against "the interests of the United States and may drag [us] into a war between two religious groups."

But soon the problems of Israel took second place to the worst challenge to the west by the Soviet Union since the end of the war.

Berlin, lying far inside the Russian zone of Germany, was also divided among the four conquerers. The Russians had promised Britain, France, and the United States free access to Berlin through their zone, but no written agreement confirmed this understanding.

It became evident by the spring of 1948 that the three western powers and the Soviets could never agree on terms of a peace treaty with Germany. Accordingly the British, French, and Americans combined their zones into a political and economic unit, the predecessor of the Federal Republic of Ger-many. The next step was a currency reform in the western zones, to which the

Soviet Union objected when the new mark was introduced into western Berlin as well. Various harassments took place until the Russians clamped down a blockade of Berlin, a denial of access by land to the western powers which went on for eleven months.

No one in Washington had any idea of withdrawing from Berlin. To do so would be advantageous from a military point of view, Leahy felt, but it would be "very bad for those Germans who joined with us in good faith to reconstruct the economy of Western Germany." In other words, the United States should continue to keep its promises.

There followed the famous air lift, which began on a stopgap basis, but soon had to be established as a continuing operation, round the clock, day in and day out. Leahy kept in close touch with the situation; as the president's man he had to, but the running of the air lift belonged to younger men on the scene. The documents, however, bear his signature frequently, as he kept Truman informed. The Berlin Blockade was still going on when Leahy stepped down from all official responsibilities.

That fall, President Truman was engaged in the seemingly hopeless task of running for election in his own right to the presidency. No one thought he had a chance. There were too many problems, too many dangers, all of which could be blamed on the man in the White House. In addition, Strom Thurman broke with the Democratic party over states rights and formed the "Dixiecrat Party." Then Henry Wallace ran as an independent, and the two defectors took the liberal and conservative wings of the party with them. Dapper Governor Thomas E. Dewey was correcting all the mistakes he had made while he was running against Franklin Roosevelt four years earlier. All the polls predicted he would coast to an easy victory in November.

As far as Leahy's career was concerned, it made no difference to him who won, for he had told HST that he wished to step down from his job no matter how the election came out. He was seventy-three years of age, and it was time to lay down the burdens.

But, on a personal note, he cared very much who won. He admired and felt real friendship for the spunky Harry Truman who did not know the meaning of quit. But some people were trying to get the fleet admiral to quit. On the morning of 20 September, Constantine Brown broke another adverse story in the *Washington Star* to the effect that Truman's advisors were urging him to retire the admiral as an "old fashioned reactionary." Spearheading this drive was said to be Clark Clifford, a man Leahy felt to be a friend.

Bill Leahy immediately wrote the president, who was off on his "Whistle Stop" campaign, telling him of the attack and offering to resign for "any stated reason" to which "I subscribe in advance."[10]

By return mail, Leahy received a handwritten letter, characteristic in bluntness and force:

Los Angeles, Cal.
September 23, 1948
Dear Admiral:

I am writing this on the train going 90 mi. an hour. I hope you will be able to read it.

I received your letter enclosing an article by Constantine Brown. I wish I could get my hands on him and on the fellow who gave him the false information on which he based his piece.

I want you in the White House. I have the utmost confidence in you. You tell me what you think. While you and I don't see eye to eye on some things, we are always frank with each other.

Don't you pay any attention to any lying stories the gossipers write. It's part of the political farce as it's played in this country. The opposition try to hurt me by hurting my friends.

Please don't let it bother you. When I have anything to say to you, I'll say it to you.

You are my friend and I am yours come hell or high water.
Sincerely,
Harry S. Truman[11]

Clark Clifford wrote a strong letter to Constantine Brown, and the incident died away.

With such strong support from his friends, Leahy was naturally delighted with the outcome of the election "which appears to have been an astonishing surprise to everybody except Mr. Truman himself."

The next day, in one of his last sessions with the Joint Chiefs, Leahy recorded how he had had to divide the defense budget for fiscal 1950 among the three armed services, since they couldn't agree. The allocated total was $14.4 billion. He told them they would have to do with the following: army, $4.8-billion; navy, $4.6-billion; air force, $5.0-billion.

"I fear," he wrote, "that this agreement that I force upon them will be neutralized by detailed objections to be made by the services."

So much for unification.

After the election, Leahy accompanied Truman to the Little White House in Key West for relaxation. There the president urged his chief of staff to prepare his wartime journals for publication. The result, of course, was the book, *I Was There*, written with the editorial assistance of Charter Heslep. It covers the period from the time he left the governorship of Puerto Rico until the end of World War II. He must have been a sore trial to Mr. Heslep, who wanted to liven the book with anecdotes. The admiral would have none of it. "This man is always trying to get me to tell funny stories," he grumbled to Dorothy Ringquist. "And I don't want any funny stories in this book. These are the facts as they were at the time, with no embellishments."[12]

Funny stories or no, it was high time he laid down some of his burdens. In a way, time was passing him by. He was weary, and the world was changing.

WDL and Hassett after a successful fishing trip at Key West with the president, 16 November 1948. (Courtesy, FDR Library)

President Truman by his actions on unification and Palestine was indicating, however unconsciously, that Leahy was out of step. While the friendship remained, the advice was being sought more and more elsewhere. Also, his health was beginning to fail.

Right after the new year began, he entered the Naval Hospital at Bethesda for an operation to clear up a partial blockage of the kidneys. It was no easy affair; various complications ensued, and his weight dropped from 165 to 154 pounds. He became depressed, the feeling worsening by adverse reactions to penicillin.

Three days after his inauguration, which Leahy watched on television, President Truman visited the patient in his hospital room, speaking vaguely of a possible future ambassadorial appointment. A week later, the admiral flew down to Key West to recuperate, Truman and his party arriving later. It was not until 19 March that the entire party returned to Washington, and two days later, the president signed orders detaching Leahy as chief of staff to the president and instructing him to report to the secretary of the navy "for such duty as the President may direct."[13]

Four days later Truman summoned Leahy from his new office in the Navy Department Building for a surprise ceremony attended by friends and family, including most of the officers he had served with during the war. The president gave him a Gold Star in lieu of a third Distinguished Service Medal. The citation said in part:

> Eminently qualified by his experience in the fields of government and international affairs, Fleet Admiral Leahy contributed his deep wisdom and judgment to the guidance of his country. . . . His supreme loyalty to his country and his appreciation of its place in world affairs, supplemented by his fundamental concern in the welfare of humanity as a whole, transcended his already vast knowledge of military affairs to culminate in statesmanship beyond that required of any Naval officer in our history. A champion of democracy and respecter of sovereignty, defender of independence, and humanitarian in his recognition of peoples' needs and rights, the great accomplishments attained in consequence of Fleet Admiral Leahy's guidance bring to him unparalleled distinction.[14]

President Truman announced that he would not appoint anyone else to the position Leahy had held, a decision which was generally applauded by editorial writers. A piece in the *Washington Star* is typical. It concluded that after the president "had exhausted Leahy's rich store of information" he had kept the admiral on because of his companionability and . . . Mr. Truman's loyalty." It accused him, incorrectly, of blindly supporting the navy in the unification fight and of refusing to accept the atomic age with the bomb as "the absolute weapon," whatever that meant. It concluded, "We wish him long years in his retirement, though we are glad he is going."[15]

George Elsey wrote a better evaluation in some notes he prepared for an interview about the admiral. Noting that Leahy was completely unswayed by friendship or protestations, he wrote: "Sober judgment and keen penetrating mind resolved differences between Allies apparently deadlocked. I have watched him at close range since July 1942 with admiration which is now close to devotion. His greatest service since has probably been his indoctrination of Pres. Truman. . . . His greatest claim to fame—keeping J.C.S. in check."[16]

Leahy once told Elsey that when asked about him, he should, "Tell him anything so long as it's the truth."

# Death Closes All:
# But Something Ere the End

Fleet Admiral Leahy had no leisure to enjoy his retirement, for first he had to enter the Bethesda hospital for another operation, performed on 14 April. The case was more extensive than anyone suspected, and "I was seriously ill and very unhappy for ten days or two weeks."

Busy as he was in starting his new administration, President Truman found time to visit the patient, although the doctors kept almost everyone else away.

Death took no holiday that spring at Bethesda, claiming the life of Leahy's sister-in-law, Mary Niblack, in April and Secretary Forrestal in May. The admiral was curiously laconic about the death of the man with whom he had helped shape the Department of Defense, adding in pencil to the typed journal, "May 22 Secretary Forrestal died in the Bethesda Hospital, a suicide."

The last ten years of Leahy's life were a struggle to keep occupied, to find some importance in existence, now that he was no longer at the center of things. So long as Harry Truman was president, the admiral would be remembered and included in events, but when Eisenhower came to the White House, Leahy complained that he served at the pleasure of the president, who didn't give him anything to do.

Never one to neglect his family, Leahy managed to persuade the doctors to release him from the hospital in time to attend the wedding of his grand-daughter Louise to John Cusworth Walker III, in Christ Church, George-town. The fleet admiral was not entirely happy about the marriage, even

Harry Truman and party at Little White House, Key West, Florida, 6 March 1949. Front row, left to right: John Steelman; Chief Justice Fred Vinson; Truman; WDL; William Hassett. Back row, left to right: unidentified; General Landry; Admiral Robert Dennison; unidentified; Charles Ross; General Harry Vaughn; General Graham; and unidentified. (Courtesy, FDR Library)

though he found the young man "attractive," with "good manners." But he had "attracted Louise's determination to get married to him even at the expense of her final year in college. . . . Of course I appear to be entirely enthustically agreeable to the whole proposition."[1] He became more reconciled as over the years, Louise presented him with four great-granddaughters and one great-grandson.

For the rest of the year he was in and out of the hospital, and busy with work on *I Was There*. On 1 August, he gave a manuscript copy to President Truman, who had agreed to write a foreword. Actually it was written by Presidential Press Secretary Charlie Ross and by Leahy himself, but Truman's name appeared on it. For the rest of the year, he was busy with copy editor's queries, galley proofs, and page proofs.

Leahy's book tells us nothing of the events after the end of the war, and his journal adds little more once he had stepped down from active service. Thus we look in vain for illumination on the "Revolt of the Admirals" that took place in October. The revolt had its roots in the inability of the services to keep the agreements made when the National Service Act of 1947 became effective. The air force demanded seventy groups of bombers, and the army, partly out of desire to eliminate the Marine Corps, tended to vote with the air force against the navy. With Forrestal dead and Leahy on the shelf, the only strong proponents of the balanced force concept were out of the picture. Forrestal's replacement as secretary of defense, Louis Johnson, had been a large contributor to Truman's reelection campaign, and he was determined to be the undisputed boss in the Pentagon. Uninformed about and hostile to naval operations, he sided with the air force in its desire to gain complete control of military aviation, in particular of strategic bombing. Without the courtesy of informing either Secretary of the Navy John L. Sullivan or CNO Louis Denfeld, he ordered the cancellation of the super-carrier *United States*. Sullivan resigned in protest, and Denfeld's testimony before Congress cost him his job. Sullivan's replacement, Francis P. Matthews, was a Johnson man, and, while he seemed to back Denfeld for a time, he eventually gave him the axe.

Leahy intended to stay out of the fray. He knew that as president, Truman had every right to remove Denfeld, and to a reporter for the *New York Times*, he presented an appearance of neutrality, as was in keeping with his former positions as chief of staff and as chairman of the Joint Chiefs.

> Explaining that he had been "out of touch" with detailed military planning for several months, Admiral Leahy firmly declined to take sides in the current Pentagon controversy. Nor would he comment on the merit of the air power vs. sea power arguments which have been hotly debated lately.
>
> But it was apparent, despite his guarded words, that the veteran officer was horrified at the idea of active-duty military leaders engaging in a public squabble over the nation's defense strategy.
>
> "Not once during the war did the joint chiefs take a quarrel to Mr. Roosevelt. No matter how far apart we might have been at the beginning of our discussions of a problem, we always ended up by taking a unanimously-agreed decision to the Commander-in-Chief. We gave him our joint recommendations—not our differences of opinion.[2]

In a letter to classmate Joe Powell, however, Leahy let his hair down:

> The Navy is in one H___ of a situation under attack by a gang of Army and Air. There does not appear to be anything we can do about it even when the doctors let us out. Denfeld is the only one who put up a rational defense for the Navy and he is now being removed, my secretary has just told me by telephone. He will be replaced by a stooge.
>
> Things like that did not happen in our day.[3]

The "stooge" appointed was Forrest Sherman. Although Sherman proved to be one of the best and most effective CNOs, Leahy never did, from that day forward, have anything good to say about him, either in his journal or in his correspondence. Six months later, he wrote Denfeld, "Mr. Matthews apparently still has confidence in Forrest Sherman, indicating that he is an optimist."[4]

The publication of *I Was There* brought him rave statements from friends, but a cold reception from the critics, one of whom called it a "book for the record only." William "Bishop" Hassett termed it a work which would "serve faithfully the memory of a great and good war as well as the cause of history in generations to come."

At that time Leahy was in Washington, unable to "join the gang at Key West," as he wrote Hassett, "feeling like the 'wrath of God' if that is appropriate language to transmit via an Eminence."[5]

The outbreak of the Korean War caused Leahy to write gloomily on 25 June, "This may be the beginning of the collapse of the united international organization that was expected to preserve peace in the world. It has since its beginning been my opinion that it would eventually collapse."

To his surprise, President Truman asked him to sit in with him on meetings concerning the war, and invited him to Blair House for a long private chat on the situation.* It appeared to the admiral that the president "Seemed to wish to talk to somebody in whom he has confidence, or perhaps he just wanted to be polite to his one-time Chief of Staff."

The Korean War proved to the president the need for a strong navy, including carriers, and the usefulness of the Marine Corps, thus justifying Admiral Denfeld's arguments long after he had passed from the scene. It also marked the end of the trail for Louis Johnson as secretary of defense. He was replaced by General George Marshall, who once again agreed to undertake a difficult job in the service of his country. Leahy approved. "General Marshall, except for his attitude toward China, with which I have been in complete disagreement, promises much better success in the Department of Defense."

The sudden intervention of China into the Korean War came as a shock to everyone, as did the attempted assassination of President Truman by two Puerto Rican nationalist revolutionaries. This revolutionary group was headed by Abizu Campos, who had been recently released from prison. Leahy had known Campos in Puerto Rico, where he "had succeeded in killing a small number of officials in the insular government. . . . It should not be difficult to apprehend Abizu Campos in San Juan and neutralize him by a prison sentence for the remainder of his life."

In common with many naval officers, Leahy was suspicious of the fact that the Pacific, where MacArthur was fighting against the communist enemy, was being forced to take a back seat to the NATO problems which Eisenhower was facing in Europe. "I personally," he wrote later, "have no information upon which to assume that General Eisenhower can succeed in organizing an effective allied army to use against the Soviets or to succeed in preventing an invasion of Western Europe."

---

*The Trumans were living in Blair House across Pennsylvania Avenue from the White House because an inspection revealed that the executive mansion was dangerously near collapse. The needed repairs took most of Truman's second term.

By this time he had little or no use for the United Nations, feeling that most member states were unwilling to act because of their fear of Russia or their need to trade with Red China and Russia. "Little or nothing," he complained, "can be expected from the United Nations or from its membership."

There was never any room for compromise and for seeing the "other fellow's point of view" when it came to matters of the well-being of the country. When there were demonstrations in the streets to remit the death sentences of Julius and Ethel Rosenberg for espionage during the war, as far as the admiral was concerned, their guilt was clear. They had committed treason, and they deserved the severest punishment their betrayed country could mete out. It was as simple as that.

The spring included stays in Bethesda and a trip to Key West to soak up the sun. The president and others filled him in on the international situation, the establishment of the NORAD air defense system with Canada, and top secret reports on conditions from Spitzbergen to South Georgia, from Finland to Korea.

There was always Korea. As General MacArthur stopped the Chinese offensive and began to move back north, again crossing the 38th parallel, matters began to come to a head between the president and the general. MacArthur wanted to free Korea of communist presence; Truman intended to return to the status quo ante bellum. At all costs he was determined to avoid a war on the mainland of China.

Leahy had no part in the decision to relieve MacArthur, which came as a considerable shock to him, for he had known and liked the brilliant general for over fifty years, even though he had deplored his theatrical ways. He never questioned the president's authority and he felt he was not sufficiently informed to make a judgment on the question of MacArthur's relief. He wrote, somewhat mildly that the "detachment of MacArthur will stimulate aggressive political opposition by the Republican member of Congress."

MacArthur's "Old Soldiers Never Die" speech was to him of

> such a superlative quality of excellence . . . that there is no other individual . . . capable of preparing and delivering a comparable address. . . .
>
> The public enthusiasm for General MacArthur in San Francisco and in Washington was a triumph beyond anything that I have ever seen anywhere for anybody, which seems strange in view of his recent summary detachment by President Truman.
>
> If the general's popularity persists for a considerable time, it should actively effect a change in the country's international policy, and it might have a radical effect on the complexion of domestic political development.
>
> From a purely military point of view it appears that General MacArthur's attitude will be fully accepted by all qualified military authorities.

After hearing the speech, however, Leahy went to the White House to see the president, "finding him not apparently disturbed by the popular enthusiasm" for his recalcitrant general.

Still and all, MacArthur had put on a splendid performance, as Leahy wrote the general's nephew Douglas II: "I did not see Julius Caesar's return to Rome, but I am sure that in comparison it looked like a deuce of spades."[6]

Shortly after his seventy-sixth birthday, Leahy called on Truman in Blair House to express his regrets that his doctors would not let him go with the president for a cruise aboard the *Williamsburg*. While there, they discussed global strategy, and the fleet admiral pointed out the real danger of the containment policy: it gave the Russians the interior position and enabled them to attack at places and times of their own choosing, employing surrogate forces, such as the North Koreans. American forces, on the other hand, were scattered all over the world, in a manner that might prove to "be economically impracticable without wrecking our financial structure."

About this time Senator Joseph McCarthy began his attacks on the administration and on real or fancied communists in the government. His two favorite targets were Secretary of Defense George Marshall and Secretary of State Dean Acheson. Leahy snorted in disbelief that anyone could attack the patriotism of those two men. Like many others, Leahy tended to underestimate MacCarthy, writing to a friend in Wisconsin, "About a week ago I met for the first time your Senator McCarthy. He was full of his continuing attack on the Administration, particularly Acheson and Marshall. It does not appear to me that he is likely to have much success in denting these two officials as they continue to have the full support of the president."[7]

Various commentators and reporters tried to get Leahy to join the campaign against Marshall and Acheson, but he would not give them the time of day. To each he said that he had told his story in *I Was There* and had nothing more to say.[8]

The days of the Truman administration were drawing to a close. In November, while Leahy was enjoying the president's hospitality in Key West, Truman informed him and other close associates that he would not be a candidate for another term. The matter was to be kept secret until April, for he intended to announce it on the anniversary of the death of President Roosevelt.

The remainder of the year passed quickly, and Leahy noted nothing remarkable in his journal. He felt that summer that the weather was too hot for him to get actively interested in the election campaign. He believed, unlike those caught in another kind of heat, that the nation would be well served by any of the candidates of either party. When Eisenhower was elected, he wrote a cousin that he thought Eisenhower would do all right, although Taft might have been better. "Somebody will have to correct our past military mistakes."[9]

A week before Christmas, Leahy attended his final important White House function. President Truman gave a dinner in the State Dining Room for

WDL with Truman and Bill Hassett at Fort Jefferson, Dry Tortugas, March 1951. (Courtesy, FDR Library)

forty-two of his closest associates during his presidency. Leahy was guest of honor, seated at Truman's right hand. "It was a gay, informal dinner, with the best food I remember ever having in the White House.

"By next month the host and guests at this dinner will be scattered far and wide about the United States."

The inauguration of President Eisenhower really ended any vestige of Leahy's public life. He remained busy, however, expressing his opinions of Eisenhower's cabinet officers—largely negative—and of Ike's actions as president—again mostly negative. He became involved with the activities of his Naval Academy class, helping to install the Class of 1897 Memorial Bench near the statue of Tecumseh between Bancroft Hall and the academic buildings, and he kept up a wide correspondence with classmates and friends.

His eightieth birthday was celebrated by a luncheon held at the Carleton Hotel in Washington, hosted by Admiral Denfeld, with some two score guests "composed of senators and congressmen, diplomats, and officers of the navy with whom we had worked in preparation for and in operating the Second World War." Carl Vinson, the navy's greatest friend in Congress, sat on Leahy's right, and the two discussed the days when the admiral had been CNO. The main gift was a copy of the Congressional Register containing statements in praise of the fleet admiral by his friends on Capitol Hill.

After the lunch, Leahy and his aide and Dorothy Ringquist went to the home of his son in Chevy Chase, where there was a reception. Many letters of congratulation, arrived, including ones from President Truman, Nimitz, and others. The one that said the most was from the current CNO, Robert B. "Mick" Carney.

> Although I cannot be there in the flesh, I want to pay homage to one of the most distinguished officers that our Navy has produced. I well remember that, when I was a young officer, the pronouncements of Admiral Leahy had all of the validity and authority of the Sinai tablets. Captain Leahy was my idea of what the Captain of the ship should be; Chief of Naval Operations Leahy was, to me, the man whose firm and steady hand steered the ship between the political shoals that constantly beset our course at that time. From my position in the Shore Establishment Division, I was able to see many of the difficulties that confronted you, and I was also able to observe the uncompromising wisdom of your positions and decisions.[10]

Some of the glow of the birthday celebration was taken off when about a week later his grandson Robert decided to go to Princeton University rather than accept an appointment to the Naval Academy. Leahy had worked long and hard to gain the appointment which Robert had turned down, and though he respected his grandson's right to lead his own life, he was disappointed that the Leahy naval dynasty was limited to two generations.[11]

In his last years, Leahy was drawn more and more to the state of Wisconsin, especially to friends in Ashland. He made repeated trips there to give speeches, to see people, and to arrange for the bulk of his papers to be left with the State Historical Society. Interspersed with these trips were spells in the hospital. At the beginning of August 1956, came the final entry in the journal he had kept so long and so faithfully ever since the day he had graduated from the Naval Academy. The entry was routine, recording the installation of an air conditioning unit in his bedroom in the Florida Avenue house. From October to the end of the year, he was in the hospital for treatment of a fractured hip, but in February 1957, he had recovered enough to make the final trip of his life: to see his son who was commanding the Naval Station at Pearl Harbor.

The trip was made in a VIP-configured DC-6 which made a stop at Miramar en route. Dorothy Ringquist accompanied the admiral, and found the time in Pearl Harbor heavy on her hands. She had to meet a lot of people, but she always had a better time when the admiral was there, for he knew the people so well and included her in their conversations.[12]

Leahy, on the other hand, was disappointed in the stay. "I had expected a rapid improvement of my injured leg in Oahu," he wrote Admiral Dennison, "but the favorable change now promises to be very slow. At present I can get around in pleasant weather with my cane and without any distressing pain in the damaged leg."[13]

Back home, he had to go back to the hospital for treatment, but was out in time to celebrate his eighty-second birthday in the home of his granddaughter Louisita and her children. On the other hand, he could not attend the sixtieth reunion of his Naval Academy class held on 31 May at the Sheraton Park Hotel.

While Leahy had been in Pearl Harbor, Rear Admiral Richard E. Byrd, the great polar explorer, had died. Leahy had supported his expeditions with money and equipment when he had been head of BuNav and again when he was CNO, and the men kept up a friendship. Byrd's son wrote in July that the United States Board on Geographic Names had approved his father's request that a headland in Marie Byrd Land in the Antarctic be named Cape Leahy. The cape lies in position approximately 72°S., 118°W.[14]

Even though his routine was interrupted by frequent stays in Bethesda, he was still well enough that summer to put in half days at the office, and he accepted a few honorary jobs. One was chairman of the committee to restore the frigate *Constellation*. This job especially pleased him, reminding him of his first sea duty aboard the old square-rigger.

Leahy's leg continued to give him trouble. His routine became more and more circumscribed. By the spring of 1958 he was spending most of his time on the 17th floor of the Bethesda Medical Center, largely confined to a wheelchair, and suffering the indignity of shingles on his bad leg. The doctors were unable to do much, and the shingles lasted throughout the summer. Nimitz sympathized, recalling an attack of his own, and went on to talk about Eisenhower and his political affairs. "I wonder if Eisenhower regrets his having taken a second term—or even a first term. I well remember our days in the JCS—when you occasionally addressed Eisenhower—as 'Mr. President'—and how he swore he had no ambitions along those lines."[15]

By this time, Leahy was having Dorothy Ringquist answer most of his letters. People came to see him, and he read a great deal, but he had neither a radio nor a television in his suite. He received letters from all over the world, and although the world had largely forgotten him, his friends had not.

After a brief spell at home in the spring of 1959, Leahy entered Bethesda for the last time in April. By this time everyone realized that there were not many months remaining to him. In a letter to Hassett, Miss Ringquist stated that she saw little prospect of any escape from the hospital. "Although he is unable to handle any matters of business, he continues to maintain his cheerful spirit and faces his present plight with the courage of a true sailor."[16]

The end came 20 July 1959. His son was at his side as a "cerebral vascular accident" carried him off. Interment was in Arlington National Cemetery alongside his wife who had died so long ago in a foreign land. Fleet Admiral

Chester Nimitz was the only five-star officer to serve as an honorary pall-bearer, but the members of the Joint Chiefs acted as a guard of honor. Services in the National Cathedral were generally attended by all of official Washington. Harry Truman could not be present, but he sent a representative.

The military funeral, however, had one surprising variation. Bill Hassett, "Bish," in a dark blue suit, served as a pallbearer amid the shining brass and gleaming gold braid.

Former President Truman summed up in a letter to the younger Leahy.

> I was one of your father's greatest admirers. There never was a finer man or an abler public servant. I could always depend on him to tell me the truth, whether I liked it or not, a quality too seldom found in men of his position.[17]

Leahy's life exemplified that of a military officer in time of transition. He began his career under sail and ended it when the navy he loved had atomic-powered ships and had joined in the beginnings of space exploration. He had the flexibility of mind to keep up with the change, and he had the ability to undertake whatever job he was called on to do.

Extremely, perhaps excessively, formal and reserved, he was a product of his age. He wrote to inform but to keep his feelings out of what he wrote. He grew up in an era when only intimate friends called each other by their first names. In later portions of his journal, when he realized it would be read by strangers as well as members of the family, he refers to his brother Arthur as Captain Leahy, to his brother-in-law as Admiral Niblack, to his sister-in-law Mary as Mrs. Niblack, to his own son variously as Ensign Leahy, Commander Leahy, Admiral Leahy.

He was intensely loyal to his friends, to members of his class at the Naval Academy, to shipmates, and to civilians as well. Yet he was stiff and formal in his letters, except those to his most intimate friends.

His ability speaks for itself. He was the first of his class to reach flag rank and the only one to reach five-star rank. At a time when his career seemed to be over, after his retirement when he finished his tour as CNO, he embarked on new jobs that dwarfed the rest. His contribution to the stability of Puerto Rico and his work in building American defenses in the Caribbean have been neglected by historians, because his memoirs contained only a hint of those activities.

His work as ambassador to France in Vichy was controversial, and he was often criticized as being too sympathetic toward Vichy, and hence too pro-German. The canard expressed by self-appointed strategists appeared often under the inspiration of "informed opinion." The fact is that "informed opinion" didn't know what it was talking about. The man who really knew, President Franklin Roosevelt, listened to Leahy and not to his critics. Leahy's job as ambassador was to try to win the friendship of Marshal Pétain. He succeeded, when so few were willing to talk to the pathetic old man who was saddled with the thankless task of running a defeated and partially occupied country. He was simply doing the job he had been sent to do. If his critics didn't like it, their quarrel was with the man who had sent him.

His wartime role as chief of staff to the commander in chief is better known, but even there he hid his light. Where MacArthur sought publicity, Leahy shunned it. He was, as he repeatedly said, the president's man. But he had an essential quality. "I think what I admired most about the admiral," wrote Admiral Pinney, "was his almost uncanny ability to cut through all the minutiae of a complicated JSC paper and get to the heart of the matter."[18]

Admiral Roland N. Smoot, looking back over the men he had known, had another analysis:

> . . . I've tried to analyze the four five-star admirals that we've had in this Navy. I think it's the most fascinating thing in the world when you look back on it and you see that you have a man like King—a terrifically "hew to the line" hard martinet, stony steely gentleman; the grandfather and really lovable old man Nimitz—the most beloved man I've ever known; the complete and utter clown Halsey—a clown but if he said, "Let's go to hell together," you'd go to hell with him; and then the diplomat Leahy—the open-handed, effluent diplomat Leahy. Four more different men never lived and they all got to be five-star admirals, and why? What have they got in common? . . . Leadership. The ability to make men admire them one way or another.[19]

Leahy's job was similar to that of Harry Hopkins; both men knew literally everything that passed across the desk of Franklin Roosevelt. Hopkins, however, was the more controversial because of his various jobs under the New Deal, especially WPA, and his well-publicized friendship with Roosevelt. Both men were absolutely devoted to the American cause in the war, but Hopkins was better known. Leahy's formality kept matters on a business basis.

When Roosevelt died, Leahy provided a service that only he could in briefing the new president on what had to be done. He was the only one current on the situation with the Russians, for example, for what the strategy was in the closing days of the war in Europe. He was among the first to understand that the Russians were no longer acting as allies, that they had resumed their previous strategy of defeating the west, by whatever means they could employ.

He was not sure that Harry Truman was up to the job, but as he saw him in action, he changed his mind. And as he got to know the new president better, he began to expand under the hail-fellow, well-met manner in which Truman and his friends relaxed. Even after Leahy left the White House in 1949, the Trumans kept the lonely old man on their invitation list, partly out of Truman's kindness, but mostly because the president genuinely liked the old sailor.

All admirals are supposed to be "crusty," and this characteristic is expected to continue into retirement. Leahy often seemed to be crusty, formal, and distant. He had a mean eye when he faced incompetence, stupidity, or neglect of duty. But there was kindness, tenderness, and compassion. He just didn't let those qualities show so much.

An undated letter he wrote to a high school student sums it up.

> I have probably made as many errors as most of the honest Americans of my generation, but I have not committed the greatest possible error of deviation from complete devotion to the ideals of America established by our fathers and bequeathed to us.[20]

"He never did anything for his own glorification, but for country or humanity," Dorothy Ringquist concluded.

The navy was his life, and so was his country. He served both to earn the navy's cherished "Well Done."

# President Roosevelt's Instructions to Admiral Leahy for Guidance while Serving as Ambassador to France

December 20, 1940
My dear Admiral Leahy:

As Ambassador of the United States near the French Government, you will be serving the United States at a very critical time in the relations between the United States and France. I impose entire confidence in your ability and judgment to meet all situations which may arise. Nevertheless, for your general guidance I feel that I may properly outline some of the basic principles which at present govern the relations of the United States with France.

(1) Marshal Pétain occupies a unique position both in the hearts of the French people and in the Government. Under the existing Constitution his word is law and nothing can be done against his opposition unless it is accomplished without his knowledge. In his decrees he uses the royal "we" and I have gathered that he intends to rule.

Accordingly, I desire that you endeavor to cultivate as close relations with Marshal Pétain as may be possible. You should outline to him the position of the United States in the present conflict and you should stress our firm conviction that only by the defeat of the powers now controlling the destiny of Germany and Italy can the world live in liberty, peace and prosperity; that civilization cannot progress with a return to totalitarianism.

I had reason to believe that Marshal Pétain was not congnizant of all of the acts of his Vice Premier and Minister for Foreign Affairs, Monsieur Laval, in his relations with the Germans. There can be no assurance that a similar situation will not exist with the new Foreign Minister. Accordingly, you should endeavor to bring to Marshal Pétain's attention such acts done or contemplated in the name of France which you deem to be inimical to the interests of the United States.

(2) I have made it abundantly clear that the policy of this administration is to support in every way practicable those countries which are defending themselves against aggression. In harmony with this principle this Government is affording and will continue to afford to the Government of Great Britain all possible assistance short of war. You may wish from time to time to bring to the attention of Marshal Pétain and members of the Government concrete information regarding the American program to this end.

(3) I have been much perturbed by reports indicating that resources of France are being placed at the disposal of Germany in a measure beyond that positively required by the terms of the armistice agreement. I have reason to believe that aside from the selfish interests of individuals there is unrequired governmental cooperation with Germany motivated by a belief in the inevitableness of a German victory and ultimate benefit to France. I desire that you endeavor to inform yourself with relation to this question and report fully regarding it.

You should endeavor to persuade Marshal Pétain, the members of his Government, and high ranking officers in the military forces with whom you come into contact, of the conviction of this Government that a German victory would inevitably result in the dismemberment of the French Empire and the maintenance at most of France as a vassal state.

(4) I believe that the maintenance of the French Fleet free of German control is not only of prime importance to the defense of this hemisphere but is also vital to the preservation of the French Empire and the eventual restoration of French independence and autonomy.

Accordingly, from the moment we were confronted with the imminent collapse of French resistance it has been a cardinal principle of this administration to assure that the French fleet did not fall into German hands and was not used in the furtherance of German aims. I immediately informed the French Government, therefore that should that Government permit the French fleet to be surrendered to Germany the French Government would permanently lose the friendship and good will of the Government of the United States.

Since that time I have received numerous assurances from those in control of the destiny of France that the French fleet would under no circumstances be surrendered.

On June 18, 1940, Monsieur Paul Baudoin, then Minister for Foreign Affairs, assured Ambassador Biddle "in the name of the French Government in the most solemn manner that the French fleet would never be surrendered to the enemy."

On July 1, 1940, President LeBrun informed Ambassador Bullitt that France would "under no conditions deliver the fleet to Germany." On the same day Marshal Pétain assured Ambassador Bullitt that orders had been issued to every Captain of the French fleet to sink his ship rather than to permit it to fall into German hands, and Admiral Darlan told Ambassador Bullitt that he had "given absolute orders to the officers of his fleet to sink immediately any ship that the Germans should attempt to seize."

When Marshal Pétain came into power as Chief of the French State I received renewed and most solemn assurances that the French fleet would not be surrendered to Germany. Vice Premier Laval reiterated these assurances to Mr. Matthews on November 14 when he said that "the French fleet will never fall into the hands of a hostile power."

On November 16 Marshal Pétain, when the subject was again raised, told Mr. Matthews: "I have given the most solemn assurances that the French fleet, including the *Jean Bart* and the *Richelieu*, should never fall into Germany's hands. I have given these assurances to your government. I have given them to the British Government, and even to Churchill personally. I reiterate them now. They will be used to defend French territory and possessions. They will never be used against the British unless we are attacked by them." And most recently Marshal Pétain, in a conversation with the present Chargé d'Affaires ad interim, Mr. Murphy, said on December 12: "I hope your President understands that I have kept and will continue to keep the solemn promise I made that the French fleet will be scuttled before it is allowed to fall into German hands."

I feel most strongly that if the French Government after these repeated assurances were to permit the use of the French fleet in hostile operations against the British, such action would constitute a flagrant and deliberate breach of faith to the Government of the United States.

You will undoubtedly associate with high officers of the French Navy. I desire, therefore, that in your relations with such officers, as well as in your conversations with French officials, you endeavor to convince them that to permit the use of the French fleet or naval bases by Germany or to attain German aims, would most certainly forfeit the friendship and good will of the United States and result in the destruction of the French fleet to the irreparable injury of France.

(5) You will undoubtedly be approached from numerous quarters regarding food for the French people.

There is no people on earth who have done more than the American people in relieving the suffering of humanity. The hearts of the American people go out to the people of France in their distress. As you are aware we are continuing our efforts to arrange for the forwarding through the Red Cross of medical supplies and also tinned or powdered milk for children in the unoccupied regions of France. Nevertheless, the primary interest of the American people, and an interest which overshadows all else at the moment, is to see a British victory. The American people are therefore unwilling to take any measure which in the slightest degree will prejudice such a victory. Before the American people would be willing to have influence exerted upon the British Government to permit the shipment of food through the British blockade to France, it would be necessary that the American people be convinced beyond peradventure that such action would not in the slightest assist Germany.

(6) In your discussions regarding the French West Indies and French Guiana you should point out that our sole desire in that region is to maintain the status quo and to be assured that neither those possessions nor their resources will ever be used to the detriment of the United States or the American republics. To accomplish this we feel that it is essential that the naval vessels stationed in ports

of those islands or possessions be immobilized and that we have adequate guarantees that the gold which is at present stored in Martinique be not used in any manner which could conceivably benefit Germany in the present struggle.

(7) I have noticed with sympathetic interest the efforts of France to maintain its authority in its North African possessions and to improve their economic status. In your discussions you may say that your Government is prepared to assist in this regard in any appropriate way.

Very sincerely yours,

Franklin D. Roosevelt

# APPENDIX B

# Translation of Darlan's Letter to Leahy, 27 November 1942

Algiers, November 27th
To Admiral Leahy:
My dear Admiral,

I tell you here again how much I was moved when, some weeks ago you were kind enough to show me your sympathy on the occasion of my son's dangerous illness.

Since then my son nearly died, and this is why I was in Africa on November 8th. Is God's intervention to be seen in this? It is my deep belief.

The Commanding Officers of the United States Army in Africa and Mr. Murphy displayed the utmost delicacy towards me and my dear ill son. Both my wife and I feel deeply thankful to all American personalities who helped us in our sorrow.

Do you remember that, some ten months ago, as you asked me why I yielded to the Germans on some minor matters, I answered: "My only intention is to prevent them from coming to Africa, and, as I am without armament and you are very far, I am compelled to make concessions. If you had 500,000 men at Marseilles with 3,000 tanks and 3,000 planes, I doubtless could act otherwise."

If we had not promised to defend our territories against anyone who came to attack them, the Axis would have occupied North Africa long ago.

We have kept our word. As I was in Africa, I ordered a cease fire so that a ditch should not be dug to separate America and France.

Having been disavowed by Vichy, I made myself a prisoner so that the fighting of which I disapproved should not be resumed.

By that time, the Germans having breached the armistice by occupying the whole of France, and Marshal Pétain having so solemnly protested that, I thought I was entitled again to act freely. I was the more sure to be on the right track since, by confidential messages passed to me in special code by someone at the French Admiralty, I was informed that the Marshal was in the bottom of his heart of like opinion with me.

Moreover, he had often told me: "Darlan, we must always remain friends with the United States."

By adopting the line of conduct I am now following and by putting myself under the aegis of Marshal Pétain, whose place I was eventually to take and whose appointed successor I was until the day when the German was sovereign master in France, I had the certainty of rallying North Africa and French West Africa, which I certainly could not have done had I been a "dissident."

I think that when time has passed, all those difficulties between Frenchmen will be smoothed down, but for the time being, the dissidents and we must follow parallel roads, ignoring each other.

Besides, many Frenchmen were "gaullists" only from hatred of the Germans and not because they felt sympathetic to that movement's leader.

Since the day when, under German pressure, Marshal Pétain was compelled to call back M. Laval to the Cabinet and give him a title and powers which I had declined in January 1941, my personal popularity in France has considerably increased, for people understood I was not the Germans' yes-man.

In the course of purely military inspections, where there was no publicity, I have been heartily cheered by numerous onlookers.

Last April, Marshal Pétain strongly insisted upon my staying as a member of the Government. I replied to him that I preferred to retire completely.

He then declared to me: "If you go, I shall also go." I answered: "Your departure would mean disaster. I shall stay then as "dauphin" and as military chief, but I refuse to form part of a Cabinet whose ideas concerning home as well as foreign policy are not mine.

I can assure you, my dear Admiral, that the hour when the United States took action in Europe and Africa has seemed very slow to come to us Frenchmen who were under the conquerer's boot.

France is knocked down. I am just told that part of the French Fleet in Toulon has been scuttled, but fortunately the French Empire still stands, and an important part of the fleet is at Dakar and Alexandria.

By your side and with your help, we are sure that France will totally revive. If President Roosevelt and Mr. Churchill trust the team that will work with me, I am certain that we shall bring to your cause—which is ours—the totality of French subjects, especially the Mohamedans.

Being glad to work with you for the success of the Allies' cause, among whom it can be said now that the French Empire is, I address to you the expression of my best feelings.

F. Darlan.

November 29th.

President Roosevelt's generous offer concerning my son has been told to me yesterday by Mr. Murphy. It deeply moved me and I begged Mr. Murphy to convey to the President the expression of my gratitude.★

★President Roosevelt had offered Darlan the opportunity of sending his son, who was suffering from polio, to Warm Springs for treatment at the Warm Springs Foundation, at that time, the leading center in the world for treatment of the disease.

# Notes

## ABBREVIATIONS

| | |
|---|---|
| CCS | Combined Chiefs of Staff |
| FDR Library | Franklin D. Roosevelt Library, Hyde Park, New York |
| HST Library | Harry S. Truman Library, Independence, Missouri |
| *IWT* | *I Was There* |
| JCS | Joint Chiefs of Staff |
| LF/JCS/NA | Leahy File, Joint Chiefs of Staff Papers, National Archives, Record Group 218 |
| LP/LC/MD | Leahy Papers, Library of Congress, Manuscript Division |
| LP/NHC | Leahy Papers, Naval Historical Center |
| LP/SHSW | Leahy Papers, State Historical Society of Wisconsin |
| NA | National Archives |
| PPF | President's Personal File |
| PSF | President's Secretary's File |
| WDL | William D. Leahy |

## CHAPTER 1

1. Message, Roosevelt to Leahy, 15 November 1940, LP/LC/MD.
2. Note to William Harrington Leahy, in Leahy's Journal, LP/LC/MD.
3. *Ibid.*
4. Leahy Journal, 13 July 1935, LP/LC/MD. The visit to Wausau occurred on 9 July. Henceforth quotations from Leahy's journal will not be footnoted unless necessary for accurate location of material. Usually the material can be easily found by the date.
5. LP/NHC.
6. LP/NHC.

7. Thomas C. Hart, *The Reminiscences of Thomas C. Hart.* (New York: Columbia University Oral History Project, 1972), p. 44.

## CHAPTER 2

1. Gerald Eustis Thomas, *William D. Leahy and America's Imperialist Years. 1893–1917*, p. 44.
2. Letter William H. Leahy to author, 22 July 1983.
3. In addition to the diary account, Leahy gave further particulars in a letter to Shurl D. Kersham, 4 January 1946, LP/SHSW. In 1951 Ransom E. Gove, who was one of four marines on the *Boston* assigned to tend the sick, wrote Leahy a long letter describing how he had been one of those who accompanied him to the hospital ashore and later had seen him off on the voyage to New York. He also referred to several other incidents in the cruise, including two groundings, which Leahy tactfully omitted from his diary. Letter, Gove to Leahy, 29 December 1951. LP/SHSW.
4. Lash, *Eleanor and Franklin*, p. 278.
5. Davis, *FDR: The Beckoning of Destiny, 1882–1928*, p. 315.
Information from interviews with Captain Robert Adrian, USN, Retired, and with Miss Dorothy Ringquist was used in this chapter.

## CHAPTER 3

1. David F. Trask, "William Shepherd Benson," in Love, *The Chiefs of Naval Operations*, pp. 9–10.
2. Fleet Admiral William D. Leahy, "Interesting Incidents of Service in Turkish Waters by an American War Ship during a Local War." LP/NHC.
3. *Ibid.*
4. *Ibid.*
5. Letter, J. N. Mueda to WDL, 19 September 1947, LP/SHSW.
6. Letter, WDL to Harry E. Reece, 23 November 1951, LP/SHSW.
7. Letter, Harry E. Reece to WDL, 9 November 1951, LP/SHSW.
8. Letter, WDL to Harry E. Reece, 23 November 1951, LP/SHSW.
In addition, information from interviews with Rear Admiral William H. Leahy and with Miss Dorothy Ringquist was used in this chapter.

## CHAPTER 4

1. BuOrd Memo dated 25 February 1929, WDL to staff, LP/SHSW.
2. *Atlanta Constitution*, 9 January 1932.
3. King and Whitehill, *Fleet Admiral King*, p. 262.
4. "Naval Administration, Selected Documents on Navy Department Organization, 1915–1940." Quoted in King and Whitehill, p. 263.
5. Letter, Vinson to Roosevelt, 28 December 1932, PPF, Box 5901, Roosevelt Library, Hyde Park, New York.
6. These data come from various sources in the Leahy papers, especially from two speeches delivered at the Naval War College commencements on 25 May 1934 and 24 May 1935. Both in LP/SHSW.
7. Grew to Secretary of State Monthly Report, July 1933; Record Group 80, Box 1990, National Archives.
8. Letter, Sellers to WDL, 21 December 1933, LP/SHSW.
9. Halsey and Bryan, *A Sailor's Story*, p. 55.
10. Speech at the Naval Academy, 18 March 1934, LP/SHSW.
11. See footnote 6.
12. Letter, Swanson to Roosevelt, 2 November 1934, PSF, Box 28, Roosevelt Library.
13. Walter, "William Harrison Standley," in Love, ed., *The Chiefs of Naval Operations*, p. 94. An unpublished memoir by Admiral Standley which was later revised by his son and deposited with the Naval Historical Foundation (NRS 1974–37), states that Leahy went with Reeves to see President Roosevelt and at that time "Admiral Reeves used his magnetic flow of

words on the President" to win a second term as CINCUS. (p. 207). Apparently Standley lumped Leahy with Reeves in being disloyal. Letter, Dean Allard, Head, Operational Archives Branch, NHC, to author, 7 July 1982.

14. Letter, WDL to Sargent, 18 December 1934, LP/SHSW.

15. Letter, WDL to Reeves, 21 February 1935, LP/SHSW.

16. *Hearings, House Subcommittee on Naval Appropriations, 26 February 1935* (Washington, D.C.: U.S. Government Printing Office, 1935), p. 88.

## CHAPTER 5

1. Memo, President to CNO, 10 August 1936, Naval Historical Center Files, A8/ Intelligence.

2. *New York Times,* 11 November 1936.

3. *Literary Digest,* 21 November 1936, p. 21.

4. *Newsweek,* 21 November 1936, p. 12.

5. Albion, *Makers of Naval Policy,* p. 385.

6. *Complete Presidential Press Conferences of Franklin D. Roosevelt, January 8, 1937.*

7. *U.S. 75th Congress, Hearings, Subcommittee on Naval Appropriations, U.S. House of Representatives, 1st Session, January 21, 1937* (Washington, D.C.: U.S. Government Printing Office, 1937), p. 53.

8. *The Secret Diary of Harold L. Ickes,* II, p. 193.

9. Letter, WDL to Yarnell, 2 September 1937, Yarnell Papers, LC/MD.

10. Telegram, Secretary of State to Consul General, Shanghai, 5 September 1937, National Archives 793.94112/12.

11. Telegram, Commander in Chief Asiatic Fleet to CNO, 22 September 1937, National Archives 393.1115/1057.

12. Telegram, CNO to Commander in Chief Asiatic Fleet, 5 October 1937, National Archives, 793.94/10169.

13. Rosenman, *Working with Roosevelt,* p. 167.

14. Burns, *Roosevelt: The Lion and the Fox,* pp. 323–24.

## CHAPTER 6

1. Dallek, *Franklin D. Roosevelt and American Foreign Policy, 1932–1945,* p. 156.

2. *New York Times,* 18 January 1938.

3. Letter, WDL to Bloch, 2 February 1938, Bloch Papers, LC/MD.

4. *Newsweek,* 14 February 1938, p. 13.

5. Letter, WDL to Bloch, 28 April 1938, Bloch Papers, LC/MD.

6. Letter, WDL to Bloch, 13 June 1938, Bloch Papers, LC/MD.

7. "Address Admiral William D. Leahy, U.S. Navy, Chief of Naval Operations, to the Wisconsin Department of the American Legion," Ashland, Wisconsin, 14 August 1938, LP/SHSW.

8. Letter, WDL to Bloch, 30 August 1938, Bloch Papers, LC/MD.

9. Major, "William Daniel Leahy," in Love, *The Chiefs of Naval Operations,* p. 113.

10. Ickes, *Secret Diary, II, The Inside Struggle,* p. 598.

11. Leutze, *Bargaining for Supremacy,* pp. 37–40.

12. *Jane's Fighting Ships, 1939.*

13. Letter, WDL to Bloch, 17 May 1939, Bloch Papers, LC/MD.

14. *New York Herald Tribune,* 5 June 1939.

## CHAPTER 7

1. *Washington Post,* 28 May 1939.

2. William D. Leahy, "Sailor's Adventure in Politics: Puerto Rico, 1939–1940." This is a manuscript account of his stewardship in Puerto Rico. It was written in 1940, possibly during the voyage across the Atlantic to take up his new job as ambassador to France. It is far more revealing than his journal of the same period, for that document lacks the color and detail of

those he kept before 1939. It is little more than a list of activities. The "Sailor's Adventure" is a typescript of sixty pages, possibly intended for publication. The quoted passage is found on page 14. LP/SHSW. Further quotations from this document will not be noted in this chapter, while passages from the journal will be, reversing the practice followed in the rest of the book.

3. Journal, 30 August 1939. This entry partially contradicts a statement made by Forrest C. Pogue in his biography of General Marshall. Pogue describes how Leahy was pretty much at a loose end following the death of his wife and his own return from France. Marshall, according to Pogue, suggested to Roosevelt that Leahy be appointed chairman of the Joint Chiefs of Staff. FDR, whether or not he had forgotten what he had told Leahy in August 1939, said that Leahy would be a "leg man." That was a Rooseveltian term to describe almost any job given a trusted assistant. He had once characterized Harry Hopkins as a "leg man," when Hopkins was actually doing the job of assistant president. In any event, the idea that Leahy would serve in some capacity integrating strategy and representing the president did not originate with Marshall in 1942. It was there, even though incompletely formed, in Roosevelt's mind in the summer of 1939. Pogue, *George C. Marshall: Ordeal and Hope, 1939–1942*, pp. 298–300.

4. Leahy's Inaugural Address, LP/SHSW.
5. *New York Times*, 12 September 1939.
6. J. Arnaldo Meyners, "The Scrupulousness of Leahy as Governor of the Island." Naval Intelligence, Op-3204, translated by H. P. Hopper from Spanish, 28 August 1946, LP/NHC.
7. *San Juan World Journal*, 24 April 1940.
8. *Newsweek*, 17 June 1940, p. 13.
9. *New York Times*, 21 May 1940.
10. Leahy's Journal, 10 June 1940.
11. Richardson, *On the Treadmill to Pearl Harbor*, pp. 425, 435.
12. LP/LC/MD.
13. *Ibid.*

## CHAPTER 8

1. Radiogram, OpNav to Leahy, 1 December 1940, LP/NHC.
2. William D. Leahy, *I Was There*, p. 8. [Hereafter abbreviated as *IWT*.] Leahy's memoirs, which were assembled partly from the journal he kept most of his life and partly from his recollections and official papers, were prepared for publication in collaboration with Charter Heslep in 1949 and 1950. The book, after a very short introduction, begins with his summons from Puerto Rico to the post of ambassador to France. It concludes with the surrender of Japan in August 1945.
3. William L. Langer and S. Everett Gleason, *The Undeclared War, 1940–1941*, p. 78.
4. Leahy's journal, 10 October 1912, LP/LC/MD.
5. *New York Times*, 25 November 1940.
6. *The United States News*, 13 December 1940, p. 10.
7. Manuscript account in Leahy's handwriting of his trip across the Atlantic, his journey to Vichy, and his reception by Marshal Pétain. p. 8. This account differs in many respects from that given in IWT or in his journal. There are no contradictions, but the manuscript provides additional color and detail. George Elsey Papers, Harry S. Truman Library, Independence, Missouri.
8. *Ibid.*
9. *Ibid.*, pp. 5–6.
10. Jacques de Lesdain, "Les États Unis dans ce Conflit," *L'Illustration*, 4 Janvier 1941. "Pour L'Honneur du Drapeau," *L'Illustration*, 15 Mars 1941.
11. Macmillan, *The Blast of War*, p. 160.
12. Leahy, *IWT*, p. 11.
13. Letter, WDL to Roosevelt, 25 January 1941, LP/NHC.
14. Letter, WDL to Stark, 7 February 1941, LP/SHSW.
15. Murphy, *Diplomat among Warriors*, p. 93.
16. De Lesdain, "Pour L'Honneur du Drapeau."

17. Quoted from the journal. The same information appears in letters to the president and to Welles. Letter, WDL to Roosevelt, 24 February 1941; Letter, WDL to Welles, 24 February 1941, LP/NHC.

18. Letter, WDL to Welles, 4 March 1941, LP/NHC.

19. Weygand, *Recalled to Service*, p. 394.

20. Letter, WDL to Roosevelt, 19 March 1941, LP/NHC.

21. Davis and Lindley, *How War Came*, p. 195.

22. Letter, Enrique de Orbeta to WDL, 28 March 1941, LP/SHSW.

23. Letter, WDL to Roosevelt, 21 April 1941, LP/NHC.

24. Langer and Gleason, *The Undeclared War*, p. 500.

25. Letter, WDL to Welles, 19 May 1941, LP/NHC.

26. *United States News*, 30 May 1941, p. 23.

27. Letter, WDL to Roosevelt, 26 May 1941, LP/NHC.

28. Pertimax, *The Grave Diggers of France*, p. 510.

29. Letter, WDL to Welles, 30 June 1941, LP/NHC.

30. Letter, WDL to Roosevelt, 28 July 1941, LP/NHC.

31. Letter, WDL to Roosevelt, 26 August 1941, LP/NHC.

## CHAPTER 9

1. B[ert L.] W[yler], "President Roosevelt's Ear at Vichy," *Interlaken Oberlaendisches Volksblatt*, 28 August 1941, translated from the German by the Office of Naval Intelligence, LP/LC/MD.

2. Letter, WDL to Roosevelt, 26 August 1941, LP/NHC.

3. Memorandum of a conversation between H. E. Admiral William D. Leahy, United States Ambassador to France, and Myron Taylor, personal representative of the president of the United States to His Holiness Pope Pius XII, 7 September 1941, LP/SHSW.

4. Letter, WDL to Welles, 13 September 1941. LP/NHC.

5. *Ibid.*

6. Letter, WDL to Roosevelt, 15 October 1941. LP/NHC.

7. Letter, Roosevelt to WDL, 1 November 1941. LP/NHC.

8. Letter, WDL to Roosevelt, 22 November 1941. LP/NHC.

9. *New York Times*, 10 December 1941.

10. Letter, WDL to Welles, 30 December 1941. LP/NHC.

11. Letter, WDL to Roosevelt, 12 January 1942. LP/NHC.

12. Letter, WDL to Welles, 18 January 1942. LP/NHC.

13. Leahy transcribed this note in his journal, here quoted.

14. Letter, WDL to Roosevelt, 25 January 1942. LP/NHC.

15. Letter, WDL to Roosevelt, 20 February 1942. LP/NHC.

16. Letter, Roosevelt to WDL, undated, but from internal evidence written near the end of February 1942. LP/NHC. Letters written for FDR's signature usually did not have the date on the original draft, and on the final copy it was sometimes date-stamped. Occasionally there was a slip up, as in this case.

17. Letter, WDL to Welles, 15 March 1942. LP/NHC.

18. Letter, WDL to Welles, 30 March 1942. LP/NHC.

19. Sherwood, *Roosevelt and Hopkins*, p. 538.

20. Cable, Hull to WDL, 21 April 1942. LP/NHC.

21. Letter, Pétain to WDL, 21 April 1942. LP/NHC.

22. Aron, *The Vichy Regime*, p. 372.

Material from interviews with Rear Admiral William H. Leahy and with Miss Dorothy Ringquist was used in this chapter.

## CHAPTER 10

1. Pogue, *George C. Marshall: Ordeal and Hope*, pp. 299–300.

2. Interview of Dorothy Ringquist with the author, 22 April 1982.

3. Matloff and Snell, *Strategic Planning for Coalition Warfare, 1941–1942*, pp. 283–84.

4. Leahy, *IWT*, p. 111.

5. Leahy, *IWT*, pp. 112–13.

6. Harriman and Abel, *Special Envoy*, pp. 168–69.

7. Letter, WDL to Mrs. Douglas MacArthur II, 31 July 1942, LP/SHSW. The clipping from *Le Matin* is undated, but it appears with the letter.

8. Murphy, *Diplomat among Warriors*, p. 125.

9. Memo, Roosevelt to WDL, 22 September 1942, Map Room Files, Box 15, FDR Library.

10. "Reminiscences of Vice Admiral J. Victor Smith, USN," Vol. 2, p. 112. Naval Institute Oral History Program.

11. "Reminiscences of Admiral Robert Lee Dennison," p. 70. Naval Institute Oral History Program.

12. Diploma from Georgetown University to William D. Leahy, 17 October 1942, LP/NHC.

13. Murphy, *Diplomat among Warriors*, p. 140.

14. *Ibid.*

15. Sherwood, *Roosevelt and Hopkins*, p. 645. On pages 646–47, Sherwood reproduces a facsimile of the draft, with Roosevelt's corrections in his own handwriting.

16. *Ibid.*

17. Leahy, *IWT*, p. 134.

18. Leahy, *IWT*, p. 138.

19. Letter, Matthews to WDL, 10 December 1942, LP/NHC.

20. Constantine Brown, "F. D. Urged to Oust Leahy," *Washington Post*, 31 December 1942.

Background information from Leahy File, Records of the Joint Chiefs of Staff, Record Group 218, National Archives.

## CHAPTER 11

1. Interview of Dorothy Ringquist by the author, April 22, 1982.

2. Leahy, *IWT*, p. 157.

3. Deane Memo to WDL, General Marshall, Admiral King, and General Arnold, 4 May 1943, LP/NHC.

4. Bryant, *The Turn of the Tide*, p. 496.

5. Leahy, *IWT*, pp. 158–59.

6. *Ibid.*, p. 504.

7. Letter, WDL to Admiral O. G. Murfin, 4 June 1943, LP/SHSW.

8. Vigneras, *Rearming the French*, p. 56.

9. Ringquist interview, 22 April 1982.

10. Dispatch, Roosevelt to Eisenhower, 17 June 1943, Map Room, quoted in full in WDL's journal.

11. Letter, Matthews to Atherton, 25 June 1943, copy in WDL's journal.

Background information for Trident from Leahy file, Records of the Joint Chiefs of Staff, Record Group 218, National Archives.

## CHAPTER 12

1. Tully, *F. D. R., My Boss*, p. 210.

2. Draft of message, undated, WDL to President, Map Room, Box 16, FDR Library.

3. Matloff, *Strategic Planning for Coalition Warfare, 1943–1944*, p. 214.

4. Memo, WDL to President, 17 November 1943: Memorandum on Command. LF/JCS/NA, File #127.

5. "Log of the President's Trip to Africa and the Middle East, November–December. 1943," Compiled by Lieutenant (jg) William M. Rigdon, FDR's stenographer, Stephen Early Papers, FDR Library, p. 21.

6. *Ibid.*, p. 32.

7. Leahy, *IWT*, p. 204.

8. *Ibid.*, pp. 207–08.

9. *Ibid.*, p. 209.

10. Minutes of Meeting of JCS, 30 November 1943. LF/JCS/NA, File #89.

## CHAPTER 13

1. Interview of W. Averell Harriman by the author, 11 June 1979.

2. Oral History of Vice Admiral J. Victor Smith, II, p. 110.

3. Memo, H. Freeman Matthews to WDL, 1 October 1943, with enclosed telegrams, No. 1626, 21 Sept.; No. 1652, 27 Sept.; No. 1653, 27 Sept.; No. 1658, 28 Sept.; No. 1660, 29 Sept.; No. 1764, 29 Sept. LF/JCS/NA, File 113.

4. Letter, Hopkins to WDL, 24 March 1944, LP/SHSW.

5. Memo WDL to FDR, 26 January 1944, LF/JCS/NA, File 126.

6. Leahy, Memo to self, entitled "Manus Island: Oral Report by Rear Admiral Shafroth." LP/NHC.

7. James, *The Years of MacArthur, Vol. II, 1941–1945*, p. 390.

8. Leahy, *IWT*, p. 232.

9. Rigdon, *White House Sailor*, p. 100.

10. Leahy, *IWT*, p. 237.

11. Leahy, Memo for the Secretary, the Joint Chiefs of Staff, 3 May 1944, referring to JCS 749/4. Elsey Papers, Harry S. Truman Library.

12. Commencement Address at Cornell College, 5 June 1944, LP/SHSW.

## CHAPTER 14

1. Interview with Dorothy Ringquist, 22 April 1982.

2. Campbell and Herring, *The Diaries of Edward R. Stettinius, Jr., 1943–1946*, pp. 90–91. In connection with this statement, there is an interesting briefing paper "American–DeGaullist Relations: 1942–1944." On the first few pages, Leahy has marginalia which reveal clearly his impatience with both de Gaulle and with his British supporters. On page 1 of the document, where the writer refers to the "generous attitude of the British," Leahy has written in "complaisant" above the word "generous." On another page where the writer refers to de Gaulle's "pride and sensibility," Leahy had emended this to "personal ambition." The marginalia also consist of a great deal of underlining and other markings to emphasize some particularly atrocious action on the part of de Gaulle or of his followers. LF/JCS/NA, File 20.

3. Leahy, *IWT*, p. 244.

4. *Ibid.*, p. 245.

5. *Stalin's Correspondence with Churchill, Attlee, Roosevelt, and Truman, 1941–1945*, II, p. 150.

6. Rosenman, *Working with Roosevelt*, p. 456.

7. Leahy, *IWT*, p. 250.

8. Potter, *Nimitz*, pp. 317–19. There are many accounts of this meeting. I have relied most heavily on Potter and Leahy for the navy side and on MacArthur's *Reminiscences* for the army side.

9. Potter, *Nimitz*, p. 318.

10. Leahy, *IWT*, p. 251.

11. Dispatch, RED 197, Hopkins to Roosevelt, 28 July 1944; Dispatch, Leahy to Hopkins, 28 July 1944, Map Room, Box 19, FDR Library.

12. MSG, CINCPOA TO COMINCH, dtg 180437 of 18 August 1944, NCR 8754. LF/JCS/NA, File 55.

13. Pogue, *Marshall, Organizer of Victory*, pp. 453–44.

## CHAPTER 15

1. Memo, WDL to President, 24 October 1944, LF/JCS/NA, File 114.

2. Morgenthau Diary, 19 October 1944, Vol 783, FDR Library.

3. Leahy, *IWT*, p. 280.

4. Letter, Elsey to author, 24 November 1982.

5. Interview, Captain Robert N. Adrian, 21 April 1982. Dorothy Ringquist tells the same story in more toned-down language.

6. The story of Roosevelt's actions and remarks on election night varies with the teller. The account given here is a composite of Leahy's as told, with variations in the journal and in *IWT*, in Roosevelt, *Rendezvous with Destiny*, Sherwood, *Roosevelt and Hopkins*, and Hassett, *Off the Record with FDR*.

7. Letter, Hopkins to WDL 21 December 1944, LP/SHSW.

8. Rigdon, *White House Sailor*, p. 139.

9. Anna Roosevelt Halsted [Boettiger] Papers, Yalta Notes, Box 21, FDR Library.

10. Wireless, Hopkins to Roosevelt, 24 January 1945, *The Messages between Franklin D. Roosevelt and Winston S. Churchill, 1939–1945, and Related Materials*, published in microfilm, six reels, FDR Library, Reel 6.

11. Halsted, Yalta Notes, pp. 10–11.

12. Vice Admiral J. V. Smith, Oral History, II, p. 114; III, p. 127.

13. Suggested message, FDR to Stalin, 30 October 1944 (drafted by WDL), LF/JCS/NA, File 94.

14. Memo, Marshall to Roosevelt, 23 January 1945, LF/JCS/NA, File 124, pp. 1, 4.

15. Leahy, *IWT*, p. 317.

16. Bishop, *FDR's Last Year*, p. 443.

17. "Log of the President's Trip to the Crimea, January–February 1945," compiled by Lieutenant (jg) William Rigdon, USN, p. 44, FDR Library.

18. Letter, WDL to Dr. Russell D. Cole, 10 July 1956, LP/SHSW.

19. Leahy, *IWT*, p. 327.

20. Message No. 277, Stalin to Roosevelt, 5 March 1945, *Stalin's Correspondence*, pp. 194–95.

21. Message No. 286, Stalin to Roosevelt, 3 April 1945; Message No. 287, Roosevelt to Stalin, 5 April 1945, *Stalin's Correspondence*, pp. 206, 208.

22. Leahy, *IWT*, p. 342.

## CHAPTER 16

1. Truman, *Memoirs*, I, p. 18.

2. Interview with RADM William H. Leahy, 21 April 1982.

3. *Ibid.*

4. Ringquist interview. Letter, RADM Frank Pinney to author, 1 April 1982.

5. Harriman, *Special Envoy*, p. 452.

6. *Ibid.*, p. 453.

7. Truman, *Memoirs*, I, p. 78.

8. *Ibid.*, p. 82. See Harriman and Abel, *Special Envoy*, p. 453.

9. Harriman and Abel, *Special Envoy*, p. 454.

10. Transcript of telephone call from Churchill to Leahy, 10:10 A.M., 7 May 1945, LP/NHC.

11. Letter, Eleanor Roosevelt to WDL, 8 May 1945, LP/NHC.

12. Smith, Oral History, II, p. 122–23.

13. Leahy, *IWT*, pp. 373–74.

14. "President Roosevelt's Policy . . . " LF/JCS/NA, File 20.

15. Letter, WDL to Pétain, 22 June 1945, LP/NHC.

16. *Time*, 28 May 1945, p. 15.

17. Leahy, *IWT*, pp. 282–83.

18. Hanson W. Baldwin, Oral History, pp. 535–36.

19. Leahy, *IWT*, pp. 384–85.

20. Ringquist interview.

21. MSG, WDL to Harriman, 23 June 1945. LF/JCS/NA, File 61.

22. Letter, Elsey to author, 24 November 1982.

23. Truman, *Memoirs*, I, p. 339.
24. Giovannitti and Freed, *The Decision to Drop the Bomb*, p. 198.
25. *Ibid.*, p. 207.
26. Leahy, *IWT*, pp. 419–20.
27. *Ibid.*, p. 431.
28. *Ibid.*, p. 432.
29. Ringquist interview.
30. Truman *Memoirs*, I, p. 428.
31. Leahy, *IWT*, pp. 437–42, *passim*.

## CHAPTER 17

1. Letter, RADM Frank Pinney, USN (Ret) to author, 1 April 1982.
2. Memo, WDL to President, 22 September 1945, LP/JCS/NA, File 125.
3. Memo, WDL to President (?), 23 October 1945, LP/JCS/NA, File 56.
4. Memo, WDL to President, 23 October 1945, LP/JCS/NA, File 125. Same document also in PPF, Truman Library.
5. Jonathan Daniels, *The Man from Independence*, p. 317.
6. Truman, *Years of Decision*, p. 549.
7. Donovan, *Conflict and Crisis*, pp. 159–60.
8. Constantine Brown, "The Changing World," *Washington Evening Star*, 27 December 1945.
9. Troy, *Donovan and the CIA*, p. 347.
10. Margaret Truman, *Harry S. Truman*, pp. 362–63. Also in WDL's journal where "aura" is "era."
11. Marquis Childs, "The Influence of Adm. Leahy," *St. Louis Post-Dispatch*, 11 March 1946.
12. A long message from WDL to the president on 22 August 1946 discusses steps to be taken to safeguard American planes flying between Udine and Vienna and menaced by Yugoslavian fighter planes. LP/JCS/NA, File 76.
13. Letter, Hoover to WDL, 27 March 1946, LP/JCS/NA, File 71.
14. Dispatch, Handy to McNarney, 3 May 1946, LP/JCS/NA, File 18.
15. G. M. Elsey, Memo to self, dated 15 May [1946], Elsey Papers, H. S. Truman Library.
16. Oral History, Admiral Charles Duncan, USN (Ret), 1976, pp. 271–72.

## CHAPTER 18

1. "People of the Week: Elder Statesman Role of Admiral Leahy in Challenging the Russians," *The United States News*, 11 April 1947, pp. 62–64.
2. Acheson, *Present at the Creation*, p. 219.
3. Memo, WDL for JCS, The Greek Situation, 18 July 1947. Note scribbled in Truman's handwriting on WDL's copy. LP/JCS/NA, File 123.
4. Letter, WDL to Rosenman, 17 December 1945. Rosenman Papers, "Unification of the Armed Forces" file, H. S. Truman Library.
5. Letter, WDL to Craven, 15 December 1945, LP/SHSW.
6. Letter, Admiral J. H. Towers to Nimitz, undated, but forwarded to WDL on 3 January 1947. LP/JCS/NA, File 91.
7. This account is based largely on the journal; Margaret Truman, *Harry S. Truman*, pp. 377–80; and Rigdon, *White House Sailor*, pp. 236–37.
8. Memo, WDL to SecDef, 10 October 1947, The Problem of Palestine, LP/JCS/NA. File 123.
9. Leahy, Memorandum for the Record, 26 March 1948, LP/NHC.
10. Letter, WDL to Truman, 20 September 1948, PPF, H. S. Truman Library.
11. Letter, Truman to WDL, 23 September 1948, LP/LC/MD.
12. Ringquist Interview, 22 April 1982.
13. SecNav Orders 1181/1100, Pers-1B-HWP, dated 25 January 1949 and endorsements, LP/SHSW.

14. Press release dated 25 March 1949, Elsey Papers, H. S. Truman Library.
15. *Washington Star*, 24 March 1949.
16. [Notes for Gervasi article], Elsey Papers, H. S. Truman Library.

## EPILOGUE

1. Letter, WDL to Joseph W. Powell, 6 June 1949. LP/SHSW.
2. *New York Times*, 24 October 1949.
3. Letter, WDL to Powell, 28 October 1949, LP/SHSW.
4. Letter, WDL to Denfeld, 29 March 1950, LP/SHSW.
5. Letter, Hassett to WDL, 21 March 1950, LP/SHSW; Letter, WDL to Hassett, 21 March 1950, Hassett Papers, Box 8, F.D.R. Library.
6. Letter, WDL to Douglas MacArthur II, 20 April 1951, LP/SHSW.
7. Letter, WDL to John Chapple, 28 June 1951, LP/SHSW.
8. Letter, George Elsey to author, 14 April 1981.
9. Letter, WDL to Mrs. G. F. Hawley, 24 June 1952, LP/SHSW; Letter WDL to Mrs. Hawley, 29 December 1952, LP/SHSW.
10. Letter, Carney to WDL, 28 April 1955, LP/SHSW.
11. W. H. Leahy interview, 19 April 1982.
12. Ringquist interview, 22 April 1982.
13. Letter, WDL to VADM R. L. Dennison 5 March 1957, LP/SHSW.
14. Letter, Lieutenant Richard E. Byrd, Jr., to WDL, 25 July 1947, LP/SHSW.
15. Letter, Nimitz to WDL, 28 August 1958, LP/SHSW.
16. Letter, Ringquist to Hassett, 16 July 1959, Hassett Papers, Box 8, F.D.R. Library.
17. Letter, Truman to RADM W. H. Leahy, 6 August 1959, PPF, H. S. Truman Library.
18. Letter, Pinney to author, 1 April 1982.
19. VADM Roland N. Smoot, USN, Oral History, I, p. 18.
20. Letter, WDL to the Editor of "The Next Voter," Brooke School, Andover, Massachusetts. [Undated but carbon included in the correspondence of 1950]. LP/SHSW.

# Bibliography

## ABBREVIATIONS

| | |
|---|---|
| CCS | Combined Chiefs of Staff |
| FDR Library | Franklin D. Roosevelt Library, Hyde Park, New York |
| HST Library | Harry S. Truman Library, Independence, Missouri |
| *IWT* | *I Was There* |
| JCS | Joint Chiefs of Staff |
| LF/JCS/NA | Leahy File, Joint Chiefs of Staff Papers, National Archives, Record Group 218 |
| LP/LC/MD | Leahy Papers, Library of Congress, Manuscript Division |
| LP/NHC | Leahy Papers, Naval Historical Center |
| LP/SHSW | Leahy Papers, State Historical Society of Wisconsin |
| NA | National Archives |
| PPF | President's Personal File |
| PSF | President's Secretary's File |
| WDL | William D. Leahy |

In the following bibliography, only works which have made significant contributions to this study are listed. Fleet Admiral Leahy is mentioned briefly in almost every book concerning the wartime years of Presidents Roosevelt and Truman. For the most part, the writers repeat the same few stories or anecdotes.

## MANUSCRIPTS

The most important material for the life of Admiral Leahy is the manuscript journal he kept from the time of his graduation from the Naval Academy until the summer of

1956. In 1926 he recopied and revised the earlier part and had it typed, while the earlier pages were destroyed. The original and complete journal is in the State Historical Society of Wisconsin Library. There is another copy in the Manuscript Division of the Library of Congress, and microfilm copies in the Naval Historical Center in Washington and (incomplete) in the Naval Academy Library at Annapolis.

Leahy's personal and official papers are divided among the State Historical Society of Wisconsin, the Naval Historical Center, the National Archives, and the Manuscript Division of the Library of Congress. His file as Chairman of the Joint Chiefs of Staff consists of 21 boxes in the National Archives, Record Group 218.

## PAPERS

*At the Franklin D. Roosevelt Library, Hyde Park, New York*
Stephen Early Papers
Anna Roosevelt Halsted Papers
William D. Hassett Papers
Harry L. Hopkins Papers
Map Room Files
Henry W. Morgenthau Diaries
Franklin D. Roosevelt, President's Personal File [PPF]
Franklin D. Roosevelt, President's Secretary's File [PSF]

*At the Harry S. Truman Library, Independence, Missouri*
George M. Elsey Papers
Samuel I. Rosenman Papers
Harry S. Truman, President's Personal File [PPF]

*At the Library of Congress Manuscript Division*
Admiral Claude Bloch Papers
Manuscript of Harold Ickes "Secret Diary"
Admiral Harry E. Yarnell Papers

*At the National Archives*
Leahy File, Joint Chiefs of Staff Papers, Record Group 218

## ORAL HISTORIES

*At Columbia University*
Admiral Thomas C. Hart, USN

*At the U. S. Naval Academy*
Hanson W. Baldwin
Vice Admiral Bernhard Bieri, USN
Admiral Robert Lee Dennison, USN
Admiral Charles K. Duncan, USN
Rear Admiral Arthur H. McCollum, USN
Vice Admiral J. Victor Smith, USN
Vice Admiral Roland N. Smoot, USN

## INTERVIEWS

Captain Robert Adrian, USN, Retired
George M. Elsey
W. Averell Harriman
Rear Admiral William H. Leahy, USN, Retired
Dorothy Ringquist
Captain Joseph K. Taussig, Jr., USN, Retired

## MICROFILM PUBLICATIONS

*The Messages between Franklin D. Roosevelt and Winston S. Churchill, 1939–1945, and Related Materials*, six reels, Hyde Park, New York, 1977

Periodicals and individual letters as noted in the footnotes

## BOOKS

Acheson, Dean, *Present at the Creation: My Years in the State Department*. New York: W. W. Norton & Company, Inc., 1969.

Adams, Henry H., *Harry Hopkins: A Biography*. New York: G. P. Putnam's Sons, 1977.

Albion, Robert Greenhalgh, *Makers of Naval Policy, 1798–1947*. Rowena Reed, ed. Annapolis, Md.: Naval Institute Press, 1980.

Aron, Robert, in collaboration with Georgette Elgey, trans. Humphrey Hare, *The Vichy Regime: 1940–44*. New York: The Macmillan Company, 1938.

Bishop, Jim, *FDR's Last Year, April 1944–April 1945*. New York: William Morrow & Company, Inc., 1974.

Braeman, John; Robert H. Bremer; David Brody, eds., *The New Deal*, Vol. I, *The National Level*, Vol. II, *The State and Local Levels*. Columbus, Ohio: Ohio State University Press, 1975.

Bryant, Arthur, *The Turn of the Tide: A History of the War Years: Based on the Diaries of Field-Marshal Lord Alanbrooke, Chief of the Imperial General Staff*. Garden City, N.Y.: Doubleday & Company, Inc., 1957.

———, *Triumph in the West, 1943–1946: Based on the Diaries and Autobiographical Notes of Field Marshal The Viscount Alanbrooke*. London: Collins, 1959.

Buell, Thomas B., *Master of Sea Power: A Biography of Fleet Admiral Ernest J. King*. Boston: Little, Brown and Company, 1980.

———, *The Quiet Warrior: A Biography of Admiral Raymond A. Spruance*. Boston: Little, Brown and Company, 1974.

Burns, James MacGregor, *Roosevelt: The Lion and the Fox*. New York: Harcourt Brace and Company, 1956.

———, *Roosevelt: The Soldier of Freedom*. New York: Harcourt Brace Jovanovich, Inc., 1970.

Clements, Kendrick A., ed., *James F. Byrnes and the Origins of the Cold War*. Durham, N.C.: Carolina Academy Press, 1982.

Dallek, Robert, *Franklin D. Roosevelt and American Foreign Policy, 1932–1939*. New York: Oxford University Press, 1979.

Daniels, Jonathan, *The Man from Independence*. Philadelphia: J. B. Lippencott Company, 1950.

Davis, Forrest and Ernest K. Lindley, *How War Came*. New York: Simon and Schuster, 1942.

Davis, Kenneth S., *FDR: The Beckoning of Destiny, 1882–1928, A History*. New York: G. P. Putnam's Sons, 1972.

Donovan, Robert J., *Conflict and Crisis: The Presidency of Harry S. Truman, 1945–1948*. New York: W. W. Norton, Inc., 1977.

Ferrell, Robert H., ed., *Off the Record: The Private Papers of Harry S. Truman*. New York: Penguin Books, 1980.

Ford, Corey, *Donovan of OSS*. Boston: Little, Brown and Company, 1970.

Gaddis, John Lewis, *The United States and the Origins of the Cold War, 1941–1947*. New York: Columbia University Press, 1972.

Géraud, André [Pertinax], *The Gravediggers of France*. New York: Howard Fertig, 1968.

Giovannitti, Len and Fred Freed, *The Decision to Drop the Bomb*. New York: Coward-McCann, Inc., 1965.

Greenwood, John T., "The Emergence of the Postwar Strategic Air Force, 1945-1953," in *Air Power and Warfare: Proceedings of the Eighth Military History Symposium, USAF Academy, 1978*, pp. 215–44. Washington, D.C.: Office of Air History, Headquarters USAF, 1979.

Greer, Thomas H., *What Roosevelt Thought: The Social and Political Ideas of Franklin D. Roosevelt*. Lansing, Mich.: Michigan State University Press, 1958.

Grew, Joseph C., *The Turbulent Years*, 2 vols., ed. Walter Johnson and Nancy Harvison Hooker. Boston: Houghton Mifflin Company, 1952.

Halsey, Fleet Admiral William F., USN, and Lieutenant Commander J. Bryan III, USNR, *Admiral Halsey's Story*. New York: Whittlesey House, McGraw-Hill Book Company, Inc., 1947.

Hassett, William D., *Off the Record with F.D.R., 1942–1945*. London: George Allen & Unwin Ltd., 1960.

Hayes, Grace Person, *The History of the Joint Chiefs of Staff in World War II: The War against Japan*. Annapolis, Md.: Naval Institute Press, 1982.

Haynes, Richard F., *The Awesome Power: Harry S. Truman as Commander in Chief*. Baton Rouge: Louisiana State University Press, 1973.

Herzog, James H., *Closing the Open Door: American–Japanese Diplomatic Negotiations, 1936–1941*. Annapolis, Md.: Naval Institute Press, 1973.

Higgins, Trumbull, *Winston Churchill and the Second Front, 1940–1943*. New York: Oxford University Press, 1957.

Huddleston, Sisley, *France: The Tragic Years, 1939–1947: An Eyewitness Account of War, Occupation, and Liberation*. New York: The Devin-Adair Company, 1955.

Hull, Cordell, *Memoirs*. 2 vols. New York: The Macmillan Company, 1948.

Huston, Major General John W., USAF, "The Wartime Leadership of 'Hap' Arnold," in *Air Power and Warfare, Proceedings of the Eighth Military History Symposium, USAF Academy, 1978*, pp. 168–185. Washington, D.C.: Office of Air History, Headquarters USAF, 1979.

Ickes, Harold L., *The Secret Diary of Harold L. Ickes*. Vol. I, *The First Thousand Days,*

*1933–1936*, 1953. Vol. II, *The Inside Struggle*, 1954. Vol. III, *The Lowering Clouds, 1939–1941*, 1954. All: New York: Simon and Schuster.

James, D. Clayton, *The Years of MacArthur, 1941–1945*. Vol. II. Boston: Houghton Mifflin Company, 1975.

King, Ernest J., Fleet Admiral, United States Navy, and Walter Muir Whitehill, *Fleet Admiral King: A Naval Biography*. New York: W. W. Norton & Company, Inc., 1952.

Kolko, Joyce and Gabriel, *The Limits of Power: The World and United States Foreign Policy, 1945–1954*. New York: Harper & Row, 1972.

Langer, William L., *Our Vichy Gamble*, Hamden, Conn.: Archon Books, 1965.

———, and S. Everett Gleason, *The Challenge to Isolation, 1937–1940*. New York: Harper & Brothers, 1952.

———, and S. Everett Gleason, *The Undeclared War, 1940–1941*. New York: Harper & Brothers, 1953.

Lash, Joseph P., *Eleanor and Franklin: The Story of their Relationship, Based on Eleanor Roosevelt's Private Papers*. New York: W. W. Norton, 1971.

Leahy, Fleet Admiral William D., *I Was There: The Personal Story of the Chief of Staff to Presidents Roosevelt and Truman, Based on His Notes and Diaries Made at the Time*. New York: Whittlesey House, McGraw-Hill Book Company, Inc., 1950.

Leutze, James R., *A Different Kind of Victory: A Biography of Admiral Thomas C. Hart*. Annapolis, Md.: Naval Institute Press, 1981.

———, *Bargaining for Supremacy: Anglo–American Naval Collaboration, 1937–1941*. Chapel Hill: University of North Carolina Press, 1977.

Loewenheim, Francis L.; Harold D. Langley; and Manfred Jonas, eds., *Roosevelt and Churchill: Their Secret Wartime Correspondence*. New York: Saturday Review Press/ E. P. Dutton, Inc., 1975.

Love, Robert William, Jr., ed., *The Chiefs of Naval Operations*. Annapolis, Md.: Naval Institute Press, 1981.

Lukacs, John, *The Last European War, September 1939–December 1941*. Garden City, N.Y.: Anchor Press/Doubleday, 1976.

MacArthur, Douglas, *Reminisences*. New York: McGraw-Hill, 1964.

Macmillan, Harold, *The Blast of War: 1939–1945*. New York: Harper & Row, Publishers, 1967.

Marchal, Leon, *Vichy: Two Years of Deception*. New York: The Macmillan Company, 1943.

Matloff, Maurice and Edwin M. Snell, *Strategic Planning for Coalition Warfare, 1941– 1942*. Washington, D.C.: Office of the Chief of Military History, Department of the Army, 1953.

Matloff, Maurice, *Strategic Planning for Coalition Warfare, 1943–1944*. Washington, D.C.: Office of the Chief of Military History, Department of the Army, 1959.

McIntire, Vice Admiral Ross T., with George Creel, *White House Physician*. New York: G. P. Putnam's Sons, 1946.

Mee, Charles L., Jr., *Meeting at Potsdam*. New York: M. Evans & Company, Inc., 1975.

Morison, Elting, *Turmoil and Tradition: A Study of the Life and Times of Henry L. Stimson*. Cambridge: The Riverside Press, 1960.

Murphy, Robert, *Diplomat among Warriors*. Garden City, N.Y.: Doubleday & Company, Inc., 1964.

Parkinson, Roger, *A Day's March Nearer Home: The War History from Alamein to VE Day based on the War Cabinet Papers of 1942 to 1945*. New York: David McKay Company, Inc., 1974.

Pawle, Gerald, *The War and Colonel Warden*. London: George G. Harrap & Co. Ltd., 1963.

"Pertinax." See Géraud, André.

Pitz, Hugo, "U.S. Diplomatic Relations with Vichy France from 1940 to 1942." (Ph.D. dissertation). Ann Arbor, Mich.: University Microfilms, 1978.

Pogue, Forrest C., *George C. Marshall: Ordeal and Hope, 1939–1942*. New York: The Viking Press, 1966.

———, *George C. Marshall: Organizer of Victory, 1943–1945*. New York: The Viking Press, 1973.

Potter, E. B., *Nimitz*. Annapolis, Md.: Naval Institute Press, 1976.

Reynolds, David, *The Creation of the Anglo–American Alliance 1937: A Study in Competitive Co-operation*. Chapel Hill: The University of North Carolina Press, 1981.

Richardson, James O., *On the Treadmill to Pearl Harbor*. As told to Vice Admiral George C. Dyer, USN (Retired). Washington, D.C.: Navy Department, Naval History Division, 1973.

Rigdon, William M., with James Derieux, *White House Sailor*. Garden City, N.Y.: Doubleday & Company, Inc., 1962.

Roberts, W. Adolphe and Lowell Brenttano, eds., *The Book of the Navy*, Introduction by Dudley W. Knox, Garden City, N.Y.: Doubleday & Company, Inc., 1944.

Roosevelt, Elliott and James Brough, *A Rendezvous with Destiny: The Roosevelts of the White House*. New York: G. P. Putnam's Sons, 1975.

Roosevelt, Franklin D., *Complete Presidential Press Conferences of Franklin D. Roosevelt*. Hyde Park, N.Y.: F.D.R. Microfilms, 12 Vols., 1972.

Rosenman, Samuel I., *Working with Roosevelt*. New York: Harper & Brothers, 1952.

Schoenbrun, David, *Soldiers of the Night: The Story of the French Resistance*. New York: New American Library, 1980.

Sherwood, Robert E., *Roosevelt and Hopkins: An Intimate History*, Revised Edition. New York: Grosset & Dunlap, 1950.

Smith, Bradley F., *The Shadow Warriors: O.S.S. and the Origins of the C.I.A.* New York: Basic Books, Inc., 1983.

*Stalin's Correspondence with Churchill, Attlee, Roosevelt, & Truman, 1941–45*. London: Lawrence & Wishart, 1958.

Stettinius, Edward R., Jr., *The Diaries of Edward R. Stettinius, Jr., 1943–1946*, Thomas M. Campbell and George C. Herring, eds. New York: New Viewpoints, 1975.

Stoler, Mark A., *The Politics of the Second Front: American Military Planning and Diplomacy in Coalition Warfare, 1941–1943*. Westport, Conn.: Greenwood Press, 1977.

Tarpey, John F., Captain, U. S. Navy (Retired), "Uncle Carl," in *U.S. Naval Institute Proceedings*, January 1982, pp. 38–45.

Thomas, Gerald Eustis, "William D. Leahy and America's Imperial Years, 1893–

1917." (Ph.D. dissertation, Yale University). Ann Arbor, Mich.: University Microfilms, 1974.

Troy, Thomas F., *Donovan and the CIA: A History of the Establishment of the Central Intelligence Agency*. Frederick, Md.: Aletheia Books, University Publications of America, Inc., 1981.

Truman, Harry S., *Memoirs*, Vol. I, *Year of Decision*, 1955, Vol. II, *Years of Trial and Hope*, 1956. Garden City, N.Y.: Doubleday & Company, Inc.

Truman, Margaret, *Harry S. Truman*. New York: William Morrow & Company, Inc., 1973.

Tugwell, Rexford G., *The Democratic Roosevelt*. New York: Doubleday & Company, Inc., 1957.

Tully, Grace, *F. D. R. My Boss*. New York: Charles Scribner's Sons, 1949.

Vigneras, Marcel, *Rearming the French*. Washington, D.C.: Office of the Chief of Military History, Department of the Army, 1957.

Werth, Alexander, *France: 1940–1955*. New York: Henry Holt and Company, 1956.

West, Richard S., Jr., *Admirals of American Empire*. Indianapolis: Bobbs Merrill, 1948.

Weygand, General Maxime, *Recalled to Service*. Trans. E. W. Dickes. Garden City, N.Y.: Doubleday & Company, Inc., 1952.

Wheeler-Bennett, John W. and Anthony Nicholls, *The Semblance of Peace: The Political Settlement after the Second World War*. London: Macmillan, 1972.

# Index